FILMS ON ICE

Traditions in World Cinema

FILMS ON ICE

Cinemas of the Arctic

Edited by
Scott MacKenzie and Anna Westerståhl Stenport

EDINBURGH
University Press

© editorial matter and organisation Scott MacKenzie and
Anna Westerståhl Stenport, 2015
© the chapters their several authors, 2015

Edinburgh University Press Ltd
The Tun – Holyrood Road
12 (2f) Jackson's Entry
Edinburgh EH8 8PJ
www.euppublishing.com

Typeset in 10/12.5 pt Sabon by
Servis Filmsetting Ltd, Stockport, Cheshire
and printed and bound in Great Britain by
CPI Group (UK) Ltd, Croydon CR0 4YY

A CIP record for this book is available from the British
Library

ISBN 978 0 7486 9417 4 (hardback)
ISBN 978 0 7486 9418 1 (webready PDF)

CONTENTS

ILLUSTRATIONS

ACKNOWLEDGEMENTS

We are very grateful to a number of people, institutions and funding agencies for their support for and interest in this book. Immediate thanks go to *Traditions in World Cinema Series* editors Linda Badley and R. Barton Palmer, who jumped at the opportunity to give *Films on Ice* a home. Many people in Europe and North America have helped us out along the way by sharing research, offering us feedback, discussing their creative and theoretical work on the Arctic, and aiding and abetting the project in ways too numerous to mention: Nancy Abelman, Dag Avango, Henry Bacon, Ib Bondebjerg, Mads Bunch, Lisa Bloom, Marie-Hélène Cousineau, Jan Anders Diesen, Ron E. Doel, Maria Gillombardo, Birgit Granhøj, Olle Hedling, Mette Hjort, Phil Hoffman, Sabine Höhler, Caroline Forcier Holloway, Louise Hornby, Gunnar Iversen, Anne-Mette Jørgensen, Lilya Kaganovsky, Lill-Ann Körber, Mariah Larsson, Jorma Lehtola, Kari Lie, Brenda Longfellow, Susan Lord, Janine Marchessault, Gregg Mitman, Andy Nestingen, Bent Nielsen, Carl Nørrested, Bob Pahre, Eva Novrup Redvall, Peder Roberts, Otto Rosing, Petro Rossi, Judith Ryan, Mark Sandberg, Clarence 'Chip' Burton Sheffield, Jr, Larry Smith, Lars-Martin Sørensen, Ingegerd Stenport, Sverker Sörlin, Troy Storfjell, Kirsten Thisted, Sami van Ingen, Liselotte Wajstedt, Märta Westerståhl, Nina Wormbs, and Gillen d'Arcy Wood. We have also been aided by a stellar group of research assistants. We wish to thank in particular Garrett Traylor for creative and insightful contributions to the project during several years; Sara Backlund for dedicated bibliographic and film research; and Jessica Davey-Quantick for careful proofreading of the text.

Many archives and museums have been incredibly helpful and generous about granting access to their holdings and sharing research information during various research trips, including: the Arctic Institute in Copenhagen; the Arctic Studies Center of the Smithsonian National Museum of Natural History; the Danish Film Institute; the KAVI in Helsinki; the National Library of Norway; the National Library of Sweden; the National Library and Archives of Canada; the Motion Picture, Broadcasting and Recorded Sound Division of the Library of Congress; the Nordic Museum in Stockholm; the Norwegian Film Institute; the Smithsonian National Museum of the American Indian; the Svalbard Museum; the Swedish Film Institute; the Swedish Museum of Natural History; and the Royal Ontario Museum.

Essential feedback was received at numerous conferences and public appearances, including at the NordMedia Conference; Arctic Studies panels of the Society for the Advancement of Scandinavian Study Conferences; the Nordic Lights Film Festival in Minneapolis; the 'Tales from Planet Earth' Film Festival at the University of Wisconsin, Madison; and at invited talks at the University of Washington; the University of California, Los Angeles; KTH Royal Institute of Technology in Stockholm; and Queen's University, Canada.

Funding for this project has been provided by a number of sources, including: at Queen's University, the Department of Film & Media and the Graduate Program in Cultural Studies; the Fund for Scholarly Research and Creative Work and Professional Development; and the Principal's Development Fund and Senate Advisory Research Committee; The University of Illinois Research Board, European Union Center of Excellence, and School of Literatures, Cultures, and Linguistics; the Anna Lindh Fellowship in the Europe Center at Stanford University; the Barbro Osher Pro Suecia Foundation; and the Magnus Bergvall Foundation. We are grateful for an Insight grant from the Social Sciences and Humanities Research Council of Canada used in support of publication of this book.

TRADITIONS IN WORLD CINEMA

General editors: **Linda Badley and R. Barton Palmer**
Founding editor: **Steven Jay Schneider**

Traditions in World Cinema is a series of textbooks and monographs devoted to the analysis of currently popular and previously underexamined or undervalued film movements from around the globe. Also intended for general interest readers, the textbooks in this series offer undergraduate- and graduate-level film students accessible and comprehensive introductions to diverse traditions in world cinema. The monographs open up for advanced academic study more specialised groups of films, including those that require theoretically-oriented approaches. Both textbooks and monographs provide thorough examinations of the industrial, cultural, and socio-historical conditions of production and reception.

The flagship textbook for the series includes chapters by noted scholars on traditions of acknowledged importance (the French New Wave, German Expressionism), recent and emergent traditions (New Iranian, post-Cinema Novo), and those whose rightful claim to recognition has yet to be established (the Israeli persecution film, global found footage cinema). Other volumes concentrate on individual national, regional or global cinema traditions. As the introductory chapter to each volume makes clear, the films under discussion form a coherent group on the basis of substantive and relatively transparent, if not always obvious, commonalities. These commonalities may be formal, stylistic or thematic, and the groupings may, although they need not, be popularly identified as genres, cycles or movements (Japanese horror, Chinese martial arts cinema, Italian Neorealism). Indeed, in cases in which a group of films is not already commonly identified as a tradition, one purpose of the volume is to establish its claim to importance and make it visible (East Central European Magical Realist cinema, Palestinian cinema).

Textbooks and monographs include:

- An introduction that clarifies the rationale for the grouping of films under examination
- A concise history of the regional, national, or transnational cinema in question
- A summary of previous published work on the tradition
- Contextual analysis of industrial, cultural and socio-historical conditions of production and reception
- Textual analysis of specific and notable films, with clear and judicious application of relevant film theoretical approaches
- Bibliograph(ies)/filmograph(ies).

Monographs may additionally include:

- Discussion of the dynamics of cross-cultural exchange in light of current research and thinking about cultural imperialism and globalisation, as well as issues of regional/national cinema or political/aesthetic movements (such as new waves, postmodernism, or identity politics)
- Interview(s) with key filmmakers working within the tradition.

INTRODUCTION:
WHAT ARE ARCTIC CINEMAS?

Scott MacKenzie and Anna Westerståhl Stenport

With this book, we are intentionally coining a new conceptual rubric within World Cinema called 'Arctic Cinemas'. This raises the question as to why we would bring together a diverse array of films made in and about the Arctic into one discrete category. We position different forms of Arctic filmmaking not typically placed in dialogue, whose interrelations are overlooked to uncover a counter-history that reveals the complexity of Arctic visual, cultural and ideological representation. *Films on Ice* is the first book to present a range of Arctic film traditions, genres, topics and practitioners, seeking to address a great cinematic diversity of representation and production practices in the region that have so often been overlooked. Engendering a dialogue between insiders and outsiders, the book's examples are drawn from three distinct but interrelated groups: (1) films made by Arctic residents, but mostly seen in the South through film festivals, speciality TV channels, and the Internet; (2) films made outside the Arctic, typically by outsiders, and viewed mostly in the South and; (3) films made and viewed by Arctic residents through narrowcast, broadcast and alternative venues. *Films on Ice* explores, from both historical and contemporary perspectives: (a) how these three filmmaking practices interrelate with one another; (b) the stories and perceptions about the Arctic that they generate, and (c) what they teach us about the tension and mutual interdependence between local image-making and global spectatorship. *Films on Ice* challenges dominant notions of the Arctic in both popular and political culture, offering a thorough analysis of what the very concept of the Arctic has come to mean in image-making and how the term 'The Arctic' itself postulates a unifying singularity that elides the political, geographic, national, transnational and linguistic differences that define and populate the region. This approach is based on the assumption that aesthetic, cultural, political, economic and scientific interests in 'The Arctic' always have been intertwined. This introduction provides a guide for understanding the present and past of the Arctic in ways that demonstrate how moving images (cinema, television, video and digital media) have been central to the very definition of the Arctic since the end of the nineteenth century. In so doing, we identify and challenge how dominant interpretive frameworks and categories of film scholarship are reframed when interpreted from the perspective of the Arctic. *Films on Ice* ultimately seeks to alter stereotypical views of the Arctic and therefore film history itself.

CRITICAL ARCTIC STUDIES AND ARCTIC CINEMAS

Current definitions of the Arctic are based on cartography, political geography or climate zones. Cartographically, the Arctic region is generally understood as 66-plus degrees North. Geopolitically, the region is composed of the eight nation states that surround the Arctic Ocean: Canada, Denmark, Finland, Iceland, Norway, Russia, Sweden and the USA. These eight nation states are full members of the Arctic Council, alongside Permanent Participants the Arctic Athabaskan Council (AAC); the Aleut International Association (AIA); the Gwich'in Council International (GCI); the Inuit Circumpolar Council (ICC); the Russian Association of Indigenous Peoples of the North (RAIPON); and the Saami Council (SC). Climatologically, the Arctic region is defined as any location in northern latitudes where the average daily summer temperature does not exceed 10 degrees Celsius (50 degrees Fahrenheit). We are both questioning and providing an alternative view of these fixed and discrete definitions of the Arctic. The emerging field of Critical Arctic Studies is a discipline united in its interest in challenging two dominant strands of Arctic research over the last decades: (1) a policy-driven governance and geopolitical-instrumentalist approach, and (2) a natural sciences model motivated by hypothesis testing and the determining of causal relationships. Both of these research approaches elide the complexities of the region's representational and cultural history. *Films on Ice*, by deliberately juxtaposing diverse examples of Arctic filmic expression, challenges narrow national or genre traditions that have previously barred them from being considered together.

Critical Arctic Studies foregrounds the necessity of analysing cultural representations and their circulation within various public spheres. Questions of representation are key to any understanding of the Arctic in both an historical and contemporary sense, and Critical Arctic Studies offers humanists

the opportunity to engage in the debate so that cultural analysis comple-
ments those of policy, governance, geopolitics and the natural sciences (for
an example of this kind of Critical Arctic Studies approach, see Sörlin 2013;
Bravo and Sörlin 2002; Christensen et al. 2013). Engaging with cultural
representations of the Arctic is especially important in the present context,
given the popular discourses surrounding climate change that are so often disseminated through moving images. Examining Arctic cinemas from a Critical
Arctic Studies perspective therefore both reveals what has been excluded from
the study of the Arctic thus far and reframes other discourses and approaches
within a humanistic interpretive paradigm. We are thereby as interested in analysing articulations of the Arctic that homogenise as those that don't. While we
argue for a heterogenous conceptualisation of the Arctic, we would be remiss
in not exploring the historical drive towards homogeneity. As *Films on Ice*
shows, this is not an isolated or discursively remote region: it is a profound
part of a global system of representational interchange and, through moving
images, has been so for over a century.

From the Tedium and Terror of Ice to the Explorations and Ethnographies of Documentary

Frozen, inhospitable, static and sterile: techniques and tropes of mass audience
visual representation from the nineteenth century onward cemented the view
of the Arctic as an exemplar of a sublime space overwhelmed by nature and as
a point of desolation. This cultural understanding of the Arctic has been well
articulated and critiqued in scholarly works representing a wide range of disciplines and points of view. A great deal of this work, while not addressing cinematic representations of the Arctic *per se*, has nevertheless set the stage for the
works of many of our contributors in this volume (see, for example: Davidson
2005; Hill 2009: McGhee 2007; Potter 2007; Ryall et al. 2010; Scott 2007;
Jørgensen and Sörlin, 2014). Robert David, for example, examines in *The
Arctic in the British Imagination, 1818–1914* how the alien Arctic environment was technically difficult to capture in visual media: water colours froze,
photographic equipment was sensitive to cold, small canvases or sketchbooks
put limitations on rendering panoramic views, and draughtsmen were often
amateurs (or had sometimes not even visited the Arctic themselves). Not only
were techniques and media inadequate, a profound 'lack of language codes
and artistic conventions' (David 2000: 12) hampered the possibility to convey
the complexity of the Arctic landscape and its populations. Pictorial subject
matter was perceived to be limited to seascapes, ships caught in vast expanses
of ice, explorers and scientists struggling with the environment, or hunting and
trapping, with representations of Inuit and indigenous populations decreasing
from the mid-1800s onward (David 2000: 50).

A particular form of Arctic spectacle thereby emerged in the nineteenth-century European context which neglected diversity in motifs, perspective, figuration and, in most cases, colouration. In truth, the Arctic was indeed a visually varied and colourful landscape, as explorer and artist Julius von Payer (1895) attests in the essay 'An Artistic Expedition to the North Pole'. To most Western explorers, the Arctic was as visually disorienting as it was alienating. Blinding light in summer and consummate darkness in winter challenged clock (and photographic exposure) time, with optic atmospheric phenomena such as parheliae and sun mirages distorting ocular perception. Distance and perspective became thwarted, while reflections off the ice cast shadows and colourful prisms, creating a natural spectacle unknown in most other locations on earth. The unstable, varied, dynamic and shifting visual context of the Arctic experience thereby stands in stark contrast to the monochromatic and monotonous visual representations circulated through mass media, including early Arctic explorer and ethnographic films.

Developing means to render the spectacle of light, shadow and perspective inherent in the visual disorientation of the Arctic landscape was in no way the goal of early Arctic film. The emergence of cinema at the end of the nineteenth century led to the production of hundreds of *actualités* (an early prototype of the newsreel and documentary). The visual specificity of the Arctic was of no real interest to these filmmakers; they were far more focused on bringing remote and exotic parts of the world to film audiences. Early examples include Denmark's first film, the Copenhagen-shot *Traveling with Greenlandic Dogs* (*Kørsel med grønlandske hunde*, Peter Elfelt, Denmark, 1897), ostensibly set in Greenland and *actualités* such as *Klondike Gold Rush* (Edison Co., US, 1898) and *Packers on the Trail* (Edison Co., US, 1901), which are early films shot in the Yukon, detailing the trek taken by explorers on their way to the Gold Rush. The Arctic was a highly sought subject for these films; not only did the Arctic offer an exotic locale, but the trials and tribulations of getting there were already part of the popular imagination, and incorporated into the narratives.

Film cameras were brought on expeditions to the North, and the tales of endurance addressed not only the difficulties of exploration, but also the extreme testing of the technology itself. Arctic *actualités* were produced globally, including *The Voyage to the North Pole* (Robert W. Paul, UK, 1903), *From the North Cape to the North Pole* (Nordisk, Denmark, 1909) and *A Dash for the North Pole* (Charles Urban Co., UK, 1909), the last of these made from film shot in 1903–5 by Anthony Fiala from the Ziegler Polar Expedition (on the history and development of North Polar exploration film, see Diesen and Iversen 2011; Bottomore 2003; Diesen 2011). Arctic films not shot on location also used endurance as a narrative device familiar to spectators, including docudramas such as *Le ballon d'Andrée au pole nord* ('André at the North Pole', Pathé, France, 1903) and *Who Discovered the North Pole?* (Lubin Manufacturing Co., US, 1909). Polar exploration provided fodder for what Georges Sadoul calls *actualités reconstituées*, such as the perhaps unintentionally satiric and self-serving re-creation of Frederick Cook's 'discovery' of the North Pole, *The Truth About the North Pole* (Cook, US, 1912). Arctic exploration also became the stuff of magic and imagination. The most famous example is no doubt Georges Méliès's *Conquest of the Pole* (*À la conquête du pôle*, France, 1912), which instilled a fantastical, otherworldly depiction of the Arctic, complete with mystical creatures, and a tongue-in-cheek depiction of the fantasy of colonial power. These films demonstrate the diversity of approaches deployed in creating Arctic images.

In 1922, Robert Flaherty's *Nanook of the North* (US, 1922) was released and did more than any other film to codify how the Arctic was seen and imagined cinematographically well into the very last part of the twentieth century. Beyond the cinema, Nanook came to stand for the North, and the cold in particular: in Germany, 'Nanuk' was the brand name of a popular ice-cream sandwich. The film stands as the first true exemplar of documentary cinema, as argued by André Bazin (1967) and John Grierson ([1932] 2014). Of interest here is the fact that this so formative film was staged to a great degree through re-creations of Inuit cultural practices no longer in use. Nevertheless, Flaherty's film imposed a cinematographic understanding of realism onto the Arctic writ large. This points to the ways in which the Arctic has so often been reframed and reimagined for consumption for a global audience, as if the inhabitants of the Arctic, like its imposing and disorienting landscape, were visually and intellectually impenetrable without placing upon them an outside frame of reference. The Arctic had to be framed by narratives and images of the exotic other, in order to allow audiences to 'make sense' of what they were seeing. This, of course, is true of a great deal of early documentary cinema, Arctic and non-Arctic alike, but does foreground the way in which the Arctic had to be repackaged for consumption.

Shot nearly at the same time as *Nanook* but less well-known today, Leo Hansen's film about Danish-Greenlandic explorer Knud Rasmussen's crossing of the Northwest Passage (the Fifth Thule Expedition, undertaken in 1921–4 via dogsled from Northern Greenland to Western Alaska) offers a different but equally problematic representation of Inuit life and culture and its supposed loss and eradication. If, with *Nanook*, Flaherty tries to 'save' Inuit culture with his cinematic re-creations and re-imaginations of traditional Inuit practices, *With Dogsled through Alaska* (*Med hundeslæde gennem Alaska*, Denmark, 1926) showcases a quite different ethnographic practice. Rasmussen's journey was one not only of documenting, but of collecting; in contemporary parlance, he was a hoarder. This is made clear by the tens of thousands of Inuit objects appropriated and incorporated into the Danish National Museum.

Known as Denmark's first 'eskimologist', with his encyclopedic writings about Greenlandic and Alaskan Inuit culture and practices, Rasmussen set the stage for interpretations of these populations for most of the twentieth century. In *With Dogsled through Alaska*, though, Rasmussen wanted a stationary camera that captured the faces of the Arctic, thus drawing upon a long tradition in the region, including Roland Bonaparte's photographic documentation of Sámi populations in *Le Prince Roland Bonaparte en Laponie* (1884). Cameraman Hansen, on the other hand, sought to relay, with a moving camera, indigenous practices (Hansen 1953). This tension is creatively reimagined in *The Journals of Knud Rasmussen* (Zacharias Kunuk and Norman Cohn, Canada/Denmark, 2008), which retells the history of Rasmussen's Nunavut travels through the perspective of an Inuit man.

ARCTIC INTERNATIONALIST MELODRAMAS

Early feature filmmaking about the Arctic creatively appropriated aspects of polar, ethnographic and early documentary practices. In addition, it was often explicitly internationalist and generally melodramatic, including the trope of the journey over national boundaries or the outsider's experience of a foreign culture, both reflecting and transcending the production and distribution circumstances of commercial filmmaking as an emergent international enterprise. As a vehicle for Danish actress Asta Nielsen, *Eskimo Baby* (*Das Eskimobaby*, Heinz Schall, Germany, 1916) enacts a Danish colonial fantasy of a 'primitive' Greenlander being brought to urban modernity and making a fool of herself there. Based on an Icelandic play and set in Iceland, Victor Sjöström's *The Outlaw and his Wife* (*Berg-Eyvind och hans hustru*, Sweden, 1918) was filmed in northern Sweden and has subsequently come to stand as an exemplar of early 'realistic' outdoor location shooting. Sjöström's film also functions as an early instantiation of location substitution, which often played a central role in early Arctic cinemas globally. In the transition of silent film to sound, a number of popular and internationally released melodramatic films from the Nordic region and North America set in the Arctic (featuring indigenous as well as Western actors in native roles) exemplify a different mode of transnationalism in the guise of international co-productions (often recorded in different language versions for international distribution), and with actors, crew and funding from multiple national contexts. George Schnéevoigt's *Eskimo* (Denmark/Norway, 1930) is a case in point. The plot hinges partly on language and cultural acquisition: Swedish-speaking actress Mona Mårtenson plays 'Eskimo' woman Tikaluk who is taught (in Norwegian) to be civilised by a Dane stranded in Greenland (played by Norwegian Paul Richter). W. S. Van Dyke's *Eskimo* (US, 1933), set in Alaska and shot in the local Iñupiat language, is based on a novel about indigenous populations in Greenland by Dane Peter

Freuchen, who lived for many years in Thule and both acted in the film and served as MGM's consultant for it. The Leni Riefenstahl vehicle *SOS Eisberg* (Arnold Fanck, Germany/US, 1933) was funded by Universal Studios in the US and Deutsche Universal-Film in Germany (though Deutsche Universal-Film was a subsidiary of Universal Studios). Fanck's film was shot in two different versions (English and German), and filmed in Switzerland and Greenland. The latter location shoot included the active participation of local Greenlanders as well as Knud Rasmussen, who was simultaneously planning his own feature film about traditional Greenlandic customs: *The Wedding of Palo (Palos brudefærd*, Friedrich Dalsheim, Denmark, 1934).

INDIGENOUS FILM AND FOURTH CINEMA

While Flaherty's *Nanook* or Dalsheim and Rasmussen's *Palo* may be emblematic of facile conceptions of Arctic indigenous life in early film and cultural history, the 1960s and 1970s saw the rise of a large number of broadcasting and narrowcasting initiatives serving to document, relay and disperse information about and for indigenous communities all over the circumpolar North. As Elizabeth Weatherford and Emelia Seubert note: 'Since the beginning of filmmaking, Native Americans have been the subject of virtually thousands of works by both Hollywood directors and documentary producers. Not until the 1970s, with the rise of independent film and video, did native perspectives begin to be reflected' (1988: 7). Key to this development was government funding in Canada and the Nordic countries, quasi-government funding in the United States (through the Public Broadcasting Service (PBS)) and the rise of low-cost and portable filmmaking technologies. This development coincides with the rise of indigenous media self-representations around the world (see Wilson and Stewart 2008; Alia 2013), though these movements developed differently all over the circumpolar North, including for native populations of Alaska (see Fienup-Riordan 1995); Canada (see Evans 2008); Greenland (see Gant 2004; Nørrested 2011; Thisted 2013); Scandinavia and Finland (for example, Lehtola 2000; Petersen 2003; Pietikäinen 2008) and Northern Russia/USSR (Diatchkova 2008).

Jerry White argues 'in the Canadian Arctic particularly we are seeing a very radical renegotiation of the idea of public broadcasting and of the relationship among film, television, and video, a renegotiation that has produced work that is aesthetically vibrant, locally rooted, and globally relevant' (2005: 54; see also Bozak 2012: 192–4). Indigenous populations have deployed a plethora of moving image technologies to produce and circulate their own images of themselves. For both economic and aesthetic reasons Super-8, home video technologies and consumer digital technologies have been widely used, and incorporate the supposed limitations of these cameras into the aesthetic choices made by practitioners. As White continues: 'These films and videos are interesting to *look* at in a way that a lot of southern Canadian and U.S. activist video is not' (2005: 56). Arctic indigenous media, then, work outside dominant modes of image-making to engage as a form of cultural counter-programming.

The IBC (Inuit Broadcasting Corporation), based in Iqaluit, Nunavut, is an example of this local, culturally specific and resistant form of broadcasting. The IBC was formed in 1980 to counteract the pervasive images of the United States and the rest of Canada coming to Nunavut (then part of the Canadian Northwest Territories) through satellite technology (for more on IBC, see Roth 2005: 134–7). Concurrent broadcast projects arose throughout Arctic indigenous populations. NRK Sápmi, a subsidiary of the Norwegian Broadcasting Corporation (NRK) produces television programming in Sámi languages for the Sámi population. The Russian production of Chukchi and Yupik language television has the longest history, with its emergence in the Northern USSR in 1967 (Diatchkova 2008: 218).

Government organisations have also been active in this kind of alternative film production. For instance, the National Film Board of Canada's *Netsilik* film series, made between 1963 and 1965 and released in 1967, deploys a participant-based restaging, where Inuit families enact for the camera the traditions of their ancestors. The twenty-one half-hour films grant agency to the Inuit to represent the past in a way that resonates with their own understanding of their history apart from the one often placed upon them by outsider filmmakers from Flaherty onward. The NFB's Challenge for Change programme also made the participatory documentary *Labrador North* (Roger Hart, Canada, 1973), which analyses the socio-political structure of the Northern Labrador Inuit, featuring many scenes in which the inhabitants collectively debate where their society should go in the future.

In the mid-1980s, some indigenous filmmakers moved from broadcast to feature filmmaking for the first time. In the twenty-first century, examples of Arctic indigenous feature filmmaking continue to shape film history through the emergence of Fourth Cinema. Fourth Cinema develops from what Fernando Solanas and Octavio Getino call 'Third Cinema' ([1969] 2014). They position Third Cinema in contradistinction to Hollywood film (First Cinema) and European 'waves' and art cinema, including Brazilian *cinema novo* (Second Cinema), giving priority to the documentary as a form that allows for social and political analysis and transformation, calling it the main basis of revolutionary filmmaking. Whilst Third Cinema is a major movement influential around the world, it does not adequately account for indigenous or aboriginal cinema practices. In his influential short essay 'Celebrating Fourth Cinema', Barry Barclay (2003) coins a new term to examine the emergence of feature-length art cinema by indigenous peoples. Of the six examples Barclay lists as instantiations of Fourth Cinema, two are Arctic: Nils Gaup's *Pathfinder* (*Ofelaš*, Norway/Sápmi, 1987) and Zacharias Kunuk's *Atanarjuat: The Fast Runner* (Canada/Nunavut, 2001). For Barclay, these films are examples of Fourth Cinema because they are about local cultures and not implicitly or explicitly about national or international solidarity. These films also reflect the fact that Fourth Cinema becomes possible with the explosion of film festivals as a means of achieving a transnational audience, and by the way these films are subsequently purchased, if not for theatrical release, then for television broadcast and speciality TV channels (see also Columpar 2010). This is also the case for Gaup's *The Kautokeino Rebellion* (*Kautokeino-opprøret*, Norway/Sápmi, 2008), which retells a highly contested historical moment in Sámi history. It does so via a framing device of a woman's oral storytelling of the rebellion, while integrating genre characteristics recognisable from Hollywood historical epics, interspersed with captivating scenery of snow-covered mountains and migrating reindeer.

Atanarjuat was produced by Isuma, founded in 1990 in Igloolik by Kunuk and Norman Cohn. The group brought together a diverse array of filmmakers to make Inuit films. In one way, Isuma can be seen as a reversal of the colonial gaze of ethnographic cinema, with films such as *Atanarjuat* engaging in similar postcolonial and postmodern strategies to those found in Trinh T. Minh-ha's *Reassemblage* (Senegal, 1982). Isuma's reconstructions also work as antidotes to the narratives of Inuit life told by outsiders from Flaherty onwards, giving a voice to the local culture that has been silenced by others often speaking on their behalf, even for benevolent reasons. The associated collective Arnait Video Productions (AVP), founded in 1991, undertakes similar kinds of collective production from Inuit women's perspectives and brings an explicit gender focus that challenges long-standing assumptions of male normativity in the Arctic. The goals of AVP include employing women-only or women-dominated production crews, while embracing traditional forms of Inuit narration to produce works that, according to its website, will be of interest to all Canadians. For instance, Arnait's feature film *Before Tomorrow* (*Le jour avant le lendemain*, Marie-Hélène Cousineau and Madeline Ivalu, Canada, 2008), tells the story of a smallpox outbreak in Nunavik and takes a woman-centred perspective on Inuit culture, while also embodying feminist collective practice in terms of its mode of production. Co-directed by Cousineau, a Franco-Québécoise, and Ivalu, an Inuit woman, the film was made in a spirit of collectivity and solidarity, despite the lack of a shared language between Cousineau and some of the cast. In addition, Cousineau and Ivalu collaborated with indigenous film production groups in Greenland, re-enacting premodern communication routes not only of goods but also of cultural transfer, reflecting the fact that the novel upon which the film *Before Tomorrow* is based was written in Danish and is set in premodern Greenland (*Før Morgendagen*, Jørn

Riel, 1979). *Before Tomorrow* demonstrates how other modes of production can be of use in indigenous production, outside the ones mostly associated with the Arctic, namely those assumed to operate on the basis of North-South relationships or male prerogative.

Similar undertakings have developed in Sámi indigenous media production, though the outcomes of these initiatives are less well known in an international context. Support and infrastructure for facilitating Nordic indigenous film and TV production has increased during the past decade. The International Sámi Film Centre AS (ISF) opened in Norway in 2007 with ambitious plans to foster local filmmaking culture and co-produce shorts, features and documentary films. Owned by and operated in the municipality of Kautokeino/ Guovdageidnu, a location rich in Sámi cultural heritage and home to one of the first Sámi theatre ensembles, the film centre is funded by the Norwegian government with contributions from the Sámi Parliament. While the primary aim of the centre is to encourage filmmaking in the Sámi language for the Sámi population of northernmost Scandinavia, the centre also seeks to foster connections with indigenous film production globally. In addition, on its website, the centre markets itself as located in a pristine and dramatic landscape, seemingly inviting runaway productions and location shooting. Establishing the ISF reflects Europe-wide developments in promoting regional film production and film-funding centres in the interest of employment and tourism, thus it operates at least partly in a context different to the growth of Isuma in Igloolik. Sámi involvement in conceptualising and implementing ISF has been paramount, with members of the board including director Nils Gaup and members of the municipality and the Sámi Parliament.

In Russia, Chukchi producer Elena Timonina has been at the forefront of indigenous film and television production. She co-produced with Alexander Rudoy *When the Men Cry*, a film about a boy learning about reindeer herding, which was popular with both indigenous and non-indigenous audiences (Diatchkova 2008: 214). Timonina has also produced other Chuchki films, including *The Feast of Language* and *The Stone Sail* (Diatchkova 2008: 218). Other projects have also made indigenous media available in Russia. Recently, the Afbare project has worked to preserve, archive and distribute works from the Barents region, prioritising films about indigenous people and Arctic nature. As of 2006, around 1,500 television shows and films from 1964 onwards had been digitalised and made available in Rovaniemi, Finland (Afbare 2006).

Anastasia Lapsui's and Markku Lehmuskallio's feature films *A Bride of the Seventh Heaven* (*Jumalan morsian*, Finland, 2004), *Pudana Last of the Line* (*Sukunsa viimeinen*, Finland, 2010) and *Seven Songs of the Tundra* (*Seitsemän laulua tundralta*, Finland, 1999) convey indigenous experiences, practices and history of the Yamal peninsula Nenet in Northern Russia. This *oeuvre* is the first and so far only feature-length depiction of the Nenet and builds on Lapsui's biography (she is Nenet) and many connections among the local population, including as part of her work as a Nenet radio reporter. The films, slow-paced with stylised long shots of the tundra, combine legend and oral storytelling practices with historical commentary, especially about the ways in which Soviet socialism clashed with traditional nomadic life.

Since 2012, the Finnish Film Foundation has allocated funding targeted for Sámi film production, including support for the Indigenous Peoples' Film Centre in Inari. This is a regional resource centre for film and audiovisual production, operated in conjunction with the Finnish Sámi Parliament. The centre's mandate includes furthering Sámi language and culture, and providing ways for active participation by Sámi and other indigenous peoples in the Nordic and global film and media industry. Unduly overlooked in the context of major international film festivals, the Indigenous People's Film Festival 'Skábmagovat' has been operating in Inari since 1998, and has grown to become one of the Arctic region's most prominent venues for screening Indigenous feature and documentary films from the global circumpolar North. The festival programme from 2014 makes its significance explicit, artistic director Jorma Lehtola states: 'For the indigenous peoples of the Arctic, film has become an important tool both in strengthening the identity and communicating with other peoples. The circumstances of production and the resources available vary, but the field keeps expanding'. Indeed, contemporary Sámi filmmaking is robust but little-known internationally, with the exception of Nils Gaup and Tommy Wirkola, both of whom have made internationally released feature films and have also made the crossover to Hollywood productions. Paul-Anders Simma is one of the most prolific contemporary Sámi filmmakers, whose works span political documentary such as *Give Us Our Skeletons! (Antakaa meille luurankomme!*, Finland, 1999), ethnographic faux-documentary like *Legacy of the Tundra (Duoddara árbi*, Finland, 1994) and the historical comedy epic *Minister of State (Minister på villovägar*, Sweden, 1996). Twenty-first-century Sámi directors Pauliina Feodoroff, Katja Gauriloff, Johs Kalvemo, Kira Jääskeläinen, Joar Nango, Marja Bål Nango, Lars-Göran Pettersson and Liselotte Wajstedt make films for cinema and TV that range from fiction and feature-length works to mixed-genre, experimental and autobiographical documentary (see also Lehtola, forthcoming).

Indigenous film production in Greenland has grown over the past decade, with the bromance *Nuummioq* (Otto Rosing and Torben Bech, Greenland, 2009) often regarded as the first indisputably Greenland-only film, produced with local funding, and directed and cast by Greenlanders. Yet support for enhancing local film culture and building a robust film production culture has been slow, at least partially because Danish government film funding administered through the Danish Film Institute cannot be used for Greenland-only productions. This may be about to change, with a number of Greenlanders reaching outside the country with their films and promoting indigenous film culture through the Greenland Eyes Film Festival, organised by Ivalo Frank, and through filmmakers such as Pipaluk Knudsen-Ostermann.

Various film commissions in the northernmost regions of the Nordic countries take a quite different approach to filming in the Sápmi region, promoting the locations as a vast wilderness. Founded in 2005, the Swedish Lapland Film Commission celebrates the 'natural wonder' of the area as a means by which to promote location shooting; many of the films it aids and promotes are set in the Swedish far north, but others use the area for its landscape, often divorced from any cultural specificity. The Finnish Lapland Film Commission, founded in 2008, provides similar scouting services, as does the North Finnish Film Commission, whose tagline is: 'Tundra and taiga forests. Frozen harbours and the Sun that never sets. In the middle of nowhere but still close and well-connected. Northern Finland offers unique settings for unique stories' (2008). This kind of virtual cultural tourism connects film commissions around the world, but most do not celebrate the fact that, visually, they seem to be 'in the middle of nowhere'. The film commissions of northernmost Scandinavia, moreover, do not present themselves as particularly closely connected to indigenous cultures and film production, but rather come across in their web presence as conveying a conventional Southern approach to the Arctic North, namely as a blank canvas onto which imagery of a depopulated and supra-locational wondrous sublime can be conjured. This is the case also for the recent increase in international co-productions and runaway productions in Iceland, which attracts film crews because of the crisp and clean air, long light-filled summer days, relative proximity to North America, and awe-inspiring landscape. Recently called 'Hollywood of the north' (Hull 2014), Iceland, however, represents only one of many locations through the history of Arctic cinematic representation that stands in for a ubiquitous imagination of the region in popular, art, and experimental cinema.

ARCTIC ART CINEMA

Here and elsewhere (see MacKenzie and Stenport 2013) we argue for the creation of the category of 'Arctic Art Cinema', a form of cinema practice that often explicitly hovers between national and transnational cinemas (on Global Art Cinema, see Galt and Schoonover 2010; for a classic definition, see Bordwell 1979). This category allows us to cogently address some of the feature films set in the Arctic that engage with Arctic climate, locations, light and representational history (especially from the 1980s onwards), but do so in ways that narratively, aesthetically and thematically challenge established Arctic cinema conventions. Calling these works Arctic Art Cinema offers some explanatory value by raising a salient question: what does this category offer us as an interpretive frame that sheds light on the films and their representation? One reason is because there are many films about the Arctic that go against some of the normative representational tropes that we have previously identi- fied – namely the figures of the exotic other, the polar explorer, ethnographic and documentary 'voice-of-God' narration – and these films emphasise realistic settings, psychologically complex characters, and employ narrative ambiguity, faltering protagonists and the open-ended plot so central to art cinema, the European variety in particular. Here we are thinking of films like Jan Troell's *The Flight of the Eagle* (*Ingenjör Andrées luftfärd*, Sweden, 1982), Knut Erik Jensen's *Stella Polaris* (Norway, 1993), Erik Skjoldbjaerg's *Insomnia* (Norway, 1997), Stijin Coninx's *When The Light Comes* (*Licht*, Belgium/ Germany/Netherlands/Denmark, 1998), Julio Medem's *Lovers of the Arctic Circle* (*Los amantes del círculo polar*, Spain, 1998), Baltasar Kormákur's *101 Reykjavík* (Iceland, 2000), Dagur Kári's *Noi the Albino* (*Nói albínói*, Iceland, 2003), or John Akomfrah's *The Nine Muses* (UK, 2011). In these films the Arctic location contributes more than just a backdrop; it is mobilised as part of long representational, political and national histories, themselves filled with contradictions and ambiguities.

TRANSNATIONAL, WORLD, GLOBAL ARCTIC CINEMAS?

If not solely polar exploration, ethnographic, internationalist, art cinema, indigenous or Fourth cinema, are Arctic cinemas to be categorised as trans- national cinemas, world cinemas, postcolonial cinemas, or some combination thereof? Arctic cinemas necessarily challenge all of these different categorisa- tions. When, as has often been the case, the Arctic is depicted as otherworldly and at the end of the earth, it is implicitly understood as existing beyond or transcending national borders. At the same time, however, an examination of a single country's account of the Arctic usually posits the region as a subset of a national narrative, thereby marginalising it. A globally integrated understand- ing of the Arctic, taking into account its profoundly transnational character, is one that has not been rigorously explored in film studies.

Transnational film production is usually understood as amalgamating the production practices, cultural traditions, historical or contemporary events, and aesthetic movements of diverse countries (for related and complementary definitions, see Ezra and Rowden 2006: 1–12). At the same time, transnational cinemas can also be used to challenge assumptions of nationalism operative in other contexts and mobilised for ideological and political reasons. This is the context within which *Films on Ice* operates, as it seeks to challenge standard national cinema histories that have generally overlooked film pro- duction in, about, and for the Arctic region. Mette Hjort's salient typology of transnational cinemas as the 'plurality of cinematic transnationalism' is illuminating in this regard, since cinematic 'transnationalism' can productively be seen as a dynamic 'scalar concept' (2010: 13). Distinguishing between 'marked' and 'unmarked' transnationality (2010: 13), some forms of transnational cinema are more valuable for Hjort than others. The most valuable are those that demonstrate a 'resistance to globalization as cultural homogenization' (2010: 15), where a production's economic profits and potentials do not supersede aesthetics or cultural authenticity, and where there is an impetus toward solidarity and equality in production, content and distribution.

In their introduction to *Traditions in World Cinema,* Linda Badley, R. Barton Palmer and Steven Schneider foreground how most

> cinematic traditions are 'national' in the sense that they include only texts that constitute a form of difference within a larger, more diffuse and varied body of national films, and yet there are often dispensable transnational connections that foreclose any understanding of the tradition solely within the terms of its 'native culture'. (2005: 2)

Films on Ice thereby expands not only definitions of World Cinema, but also of the notion of 'cinematic traditions', the latter by including examples that are sub-national, and not representative of what is understood as a 'national' tradition. Unlike most other books in the series, ours draws upon films from a number of national and sub-national cinemas. The difference we are postulating for Arctic cinemas with regard to the category of World Cinemas is that while, say, Latin American cinema or African cinema can be understood as components of World cinema as they coalesce around various groups of nation-states, Arctic cinemas, as part of a World cinema tradition, amalgamate geographically related subsections of various nation-states.

Experimental and Expanded Arctic Cinemas

Documenting the Arctic within a realist aesthetic has no doubt been the dominant approach. This makes sense, as the desire to film the Arctic comes in no small part from the difficulty of the endeavour. Experimental and expanded cinema works have, nonetheless, been produced about the Arctic that actively challenge the dominance of the realist tradition. American experimental filmmaker Stan Brakhage's *Creation* (US, 1979) offers a vision of the Arctic at odds with most cinematic representations of it. Fragmentary and frenetic, almost devoid of life, Brakhage's image of the Arctic nevertheless engages 'a proximate inspiration for the sublime vision of a world of massive ice and scarred rock' as inspired 'by nineteenth-century American landscape painter, Frederic Edwin Church, whose works Brakhage had studied for more than a decade' (Sitney 2001: 98). Sitney argues that the structure of the film offers a skewed version of 'Genesis': 'The organization of material . . . unmistakably follows the basic Biblical scenario, although even before the division of the waters, Brakhage introduces images of vegetation, as masses of fog rise from pine covered mountains. . . . Later the water is alive with living creatures – seals – and only then do birds fly under the vault of heaven' (Sitney 2001: 100). Yet, this basic description could as easily apply to the processes of evolution. In either interpretation, however, the Arctic in Brakhage's film is seen, whether theologically or evolutionarily, as the seedbed of life – almost devoid of humans – and not, as it so often is, the place of destruction. Other experimental representations of the Arctic also offer utopian visions. For instance, *Polar Life* (Graeme Ferguson, Canada, 1967), a key example of expanded cinema, was shown at Montreal's Expo '67. The installation '. . . displayed eleven screens with two or three visible at a time as viewers sat on four revolving theatres on a large turntable' (Marchessault 2007: 34). In the 'global village', internationalist spirit of the World's Fair (titled 'Man and His World/*Terre des hommes*') *Polar Life* documents both the Arctic and Antarctic, and lives of the Inuit, Sámi and the Northern inhabitants of Alaska and Siberia. In this film, then, like many from Expo '67, it is the global similarities of the Arctic regions' human inhabitants that is shared, foregrounding the utopian and internationalist feeling of the times.

Popular (White) American Cinema: From Polar Bears to Santa Claus

In mainstream American cinema, the Arctic has been popularly conceived as a singularity, but more importantly, as a blank slate for normative Western ideological projections. As 'literally and symbolically white' and the 'site of a privileged white masculinity' (Sandhu 2010), Western and US popular culture whitewashes the Arctic as the domain of snow, polar bears, Santa Claus and explorers, to the exclusion of almost anything else. Conceptualising the region as remote or alien necessarily involves pushing the area further away from real-world ethnic, gendered or social complexity, and from lived experience, imposing a cultural distance to mirror the geographical one. One way to de-alienate the Arctic in popular cinema is, not surprisingly, to infantilise or maternalise it, and thereby to incorporate it as utterly incongruent with assumptions of heteronormative, patriarchal, white normativity. In classical Hollywood cartoons such as Chuck Jones's *Frigid Hare* (US, 1948) which, among other things, conflates the Arctic with the Antarctic, an infantilised penguin in a top hat and bow-tie (who, when sad, cries ice-cubes) lives not-so-happily alongside an Inuit hunter. Bugs Bunny plays the role of wiser, older, male, and world-savvy protector to his innocent little friend. In the Fleischer Brothers' *The Playful Polar Bears* (US, 1938), anthropomorphised mega-mammal innocence is rudely disrupted by an invasion of colonisers, with the plot focusing on a polar bear's maternal protection of her cubs. The Coca Cola polar bear filmic advertisements (1993-present) are supposedly about the bears and the need to preserve their habitat (yet they too co-mingle with penguins) while the realm of the pristine Arctic allows Coke to seem not only 'enviro'-friendly, but also, in the name of environmentalism, to reinforce normative 'family values', notwithstanding actual male polar bear behaviour that includes eating their own offspring. The educational IMAX documentary *To the Arctic* (Greg MacGillivray, US, 2012; see also *Arctic Tale* (Adam Ravetch, US, 2007)) is a prime example of a 'maternal melodrama', in which a polar bear mother must protect her cubs against both the effects of climate change (a reduced habitat in the wake of ice melt) and predatory male polar bears. The female polar bear is given narrative agency in the film through the voice-over of Meryl Streep, whereas the on-screen humans who are part of the team documenting the bears is all male. Here, then, the job of the white, male scientists is to protect the female, ventriloquised polar bear. As popular imagery of the Arctic from the outside has shifted from emphasising the terror and beauty of an unattainable sublime, it now conveys the region as endangered, volatile and in need of protection.

The figuration of masculinist, white polar heroism (often in the guise of a scientist or a military officer) has a long history in American culture (see also Bloom 1993). Superman's 'Fortress of Solitude' is only one of many examples that affirm the polar region as an appropriate location for essential masculinity. In contrast, Kathryn Bigelow's *K-19: The Widowmaker* (US, 2002), set in a 1960s nuclear submarine, pushes the boundaries of explorer masculinity in Hollywood cinema. Captain Alexei Vostrikov (Harrison Ford) embodies an über-masculine, take-no-prisoners approach to Soviet ideology, while Executive Officer Mikhail Polenin's (Liam Neeson) main concern is that of the well-being of his men, exemplifying a post-ideological, 'new male' explorer, where homosocial male bonds are more important than connections to duty and state.

Much like polar bears and die-hard explorers, Santa Claus figurations have dominated popular Arctic representations for nearly a century. In Christmas films, Santa Claus is a secular Christian capitalist, rewarding good deeds with gifts. His is an avuncular kind of Arctic masculinity; the one male representation of the Arctic, be it white or indigenous, that is safe and benevolent. As an Arctic dweller (and as of 2008, an honorary Canadian citizen), he familiarises and infantilises the Arctic through postulating an imaginary connection to a happy, primordial and uncomplicated childhood. The most widespread myth of the secular Western world's vision of childhood mirrors the infantilising and colonial vision of the Arctic world's actual inhabitants. A cornucopia of Hollywood films about Santa Claus and his merry band of elves propagate this white and benevolent view of the Arctic. An early example of this perpetually popular subgenre is *Santa Claus* (Arctic Film Co., US, 1925), filmed in part in Northern Alaska by Arctic explorer Frank E. Kleinschmidt and set in the North Pole, where Santa is seen visiting his Inuit neighbours. The holiday film, propagating an image of the Arctic where magic and timelessness rule the day, also includes recent popular hits such as *Elf* (John Favreau, US, 2003), the *Santa Clause* series (US, 1994–2006) and *Polar Express* (Robert Zemeckis, US, 2004) all of which firmly locate a tradition of Western capitalist consumerism in Arctic.

Films about Santa Claus do not simply address Christmas Eve and Fordist toy production; they also reflect the fears and formulations about the Arctic and how its natural resources are exploited. For instance, in the television film *The Night They Saved Christmas* (Jackie Cooper, US, 1984), extreme oil exploration undertaken by dynamiting the North Pole endangers Santa (Art Carney), unbeknownst to the oil executives. Santa's elves and the children of oil executives work diligently to prevent the destruction of Santa's workshop, and therefore, the North Pole. This popular example of the effects of 'big oil' on the Arctic is not limited to Hollywood productions. Indeed, with the dawning realisation of the effects of global warming and resource extraction, a plethora of films have emerged that critically address the issue.

THE ARCTIC FROM LENIN AND MONTAGE TO STALINIST SOCIALIST REALISM

Perhaps the best-known Arctic film to come out of the USSR is Dziga Vertov's *A Sixth Part of the World* (*Shestaya Chast Mira*, USSR, 1926). Based on his theory of *kinoks* ('cinema-eyes', where the primacy of what is seen through the camera is superior to what is seen by the naked eye), Vertov's film was assembled via montage. Part of the film documents indigenous peoples of the USSR. Vertov does not use documentary in the Griersonian tradition; instead he cuts together various shots of the Chukchi through the plasticity of the image to create a composite image of indigenous life in the USSR. While Vertov's film is now canonised as a central work of Soviet cinema, the Arctic was used in a wide variety of films, just as it was in Hollywood. The Lenfilm catalogue (Catalogue of Lenfilm 1991) offers one of many examples of a Soviet production studio's use of the Arctic in a wide variety of genres. For instance, Adolf Minkin and Igor Sorokhtin's *Conquerors of the Night* (*Pobediteli nochi*, USSR, 1932) is an 'essay-film' on the icebreaker Malygin going to Franz-Joseph Land in 1931. Dramatic features such as *Same Brave Spirits* (*Semero smelykh*, Sergei Gerasimov, USSR, 1936) tell the tale of plucky and intrepid explorers who brave the harsh climate above the polar circle. Children's films such as *The Two Captains* (*Dva Kapitana*, Vladimir Vengerov, USSR, 1955) recount a tale of a polar explorer lost in the Arctic and the desire of his daughter's love interest to become an Arctic pilot to find the lost expedition. Cartoons like *Three*

Friends (*Dri podrugi*, Pavel Shimdt, USSR, 1941) feature a little girl and frol-icking polar bears, and echo the same themes found in the Arctic cartoons of Disney, Warner Brothers and the Fleischer Brothers (the one key difference: the little girl wakes up, realises she was dreaming and starts to cry). What we see here is that popular Soviet cinema used the Arctic as a backdrop for adventure, propaganda, humour and romance to the same degree as Hollywood, although to a rather different ideological end.

The Bounty of the Land: Recording Resource Extraction and Climate Change

While most recent ecocritical film theory does not explicitly address Arctic cinema, this burgeoning field of scholarship brings to the foreground nature and habitat, taking humans off their pedestal and placing them on equal footing with flora and other fauna (see Gustafsson and Kääpä 2013; Rust, Monani and Cubitt 2013; Willoquet-Maricondi 2010; Bozak 2012). Such an interpretive framework is especially significant for contemporary representa-tions of the Arctic, given that dominant media renditions emphasise the ways in which climate change is directly impacting the region, from ice-melt and rising sea levels to increased resource extraction and the revelation of new territory. In contrast to a notion of environmentalism as 'a sustaining vision of the human', seeking 'to make the world safe for it', ecocritical perspectives 'focus more on dynamic systems in which any one part is always multiply con-nected, acting by virtue of these connections and always variable, so that it can be regarded as a pattern rather than simply an object' (Fuller 2005: 4). This dynamic view of the environment is especially important for understanding the vast and diverse range of documentary and activist films on climate change, resource extraction and their impact on the Arctic environment. This dynamic view also helps conceptualise the ways in which natural resources have been exploited and how these practices have been understood historically. Dating back to the eighteenth century, a perception of interminable and abundant resource availability has framed an understanding of the Arctic region. This notion extends from the colonial practice of harvesting whale blubber for oil lamps, soap and margarine to the contemporary extraction of oil, gas, and mining of rare minerals, and to the indigenous uses of the land for sustenance. Only scattered examples of recent ecocritical film theory explicitly address this Arctic dynamic. Yet resource extraction in particular has played a central role in cinema's representation of the Arctic's resources.

Depicting resource extraction in the Arctic has been central throughout film's history, spanning feature, early documentary, art cinema, and activist and local films. For instance, the recently rediscovered *The Romance of the Far Fur Country* (H. M. Wyckoff, Canada, 1920), made by the Hudson's Bay

Company, is an early example that dramatises fur trapping and the mythological role the trade played in the development of Canadian national identity. The first film to record both sound and dialogue on location – and a remote one at that – is *The Viking* (George Melford, Newfoundland, 1931), which focuses on the potential and dangers of the seal hunt (when the leader of the expedition and producer of the film Varick Frissell went out to shoot extra footage, the ship exploded, killing Frissell and twenty-seven other men). Well-known Swedish art film director Mai Zetterling's documentary *Of Seals and Men* (UK, 1980) conveys the primitivist and primordial appeal of seal hunting. The film was sponsored by the Danish Greenlandic Trade Company to counteract international public opinion against seal hunting, thus continuing a long tradition of resource extraction representation in the Arctic. Recent art films thematise the legacy of resource extraction in other ways. *Zero Kelvin* (Hans Petter Moland, Norway, 1995) is an existentialist chamber drama about a mercenary Norwegian trapper isolated on the east coast of Greenland who has utter disregard for both human life and wildlife sustainability. The Hollywood adaptation of Peter Høeg's Danish novel *Smilla's Sense of Snow* (Bille August, US, 1997) mobilises many tropes of colonialism and exploration in the service of science as it organises its plot around the thwarted discovery of a mysterious mineral mined on Greenland and its potentially disastrous consequences for the rest of the world.

The large-scale resource extraction that impacts Arctic ecosystems are often presented as clean, wondrous and beautiful technological feats that leave no real harm or trace behind, at least through the lens of 'big oil' and corporate globalisation. *Oil on Ice* (Bo Boudart and Dale Djerassi, US, 2004), for example, explores the environmental ramifications of oil extraction and the 'clean' rhetoric that surrounds potential drilling in Alaska. Oil extraction is not the only culprit in this regard: *Dreamland* (*Draumalandið*, Þorfinnur Guðnason and Andri Snær Magnason, Iceland, 2009), for instance, focuses on the intense environmental problems that emerge in the Arctic through the damming of hydroelectric projects while foregrounding how the Icelandic government brands Iceland as the home of clean and renewable energy sources.

The practices of indigenous resource extraction take on a different valence. Films such as *Eskimo Hunters* (W. Kay Norton, US, 1949) depict the sustainable practices of indigenous populations in such a way as to come across as visceral and gory, with long and bloody shots of animals, and especially seals, killed and skinned, metaphorically leaving a bright red smear across the pristine white snow. In contradistinction, historical and contemporary representations by indigenous populations living off the land – from *At the Winter Sea Ice Camp* (Quentin Brown, NFB, Canada, 1967) to *Seal Pups* (*Qulangisi*, Zacharias Kunuk, Isuma, Canada, 1995) – provide a necessary counterpoint to classical film storytelling that emphasises plot development and psychologically motivated character action by providing documentary accounts of indigenous hunting practices. Indeed, the relationship between 'man' and 'nature' in representations of resource extraction and sustainability differs greatly in those portraying indigenous peoples and those of global modernity. If indigenous representations of Inuit hunting practices show the harsh struggle between 'man' and 'nature', images documenting 'big oil' resource extraction are dominated by (white) 'man's' ability to master and conquer the natural Arctic world.

Films about Arctic resource extraction in a changing environment have also impacted policy and politics. For example, many Inuit and Sámi populations are deeply impacted by damming for hydroelectrical development and mining. Sámi opposition to building the massive Alta dam in Norway is depicted in a number of films influential within the Norwegian context (protests began in 1978 and continued until the dam was authorised in 1982). These films show, in ways quite unprecedented, the Sámi people with agency and interest in shaping not only representations of themselves as an indigenous population, but the ways in which they can challenge the Norwegian nation-state. The features *Let the River Live!* (*La elva level*, Bredo Greve, Norway, 1980) and *Land of the Dwarf Birches* (*Skierri – vaivaiskoivujen maa*, Markku Lehmuskallio, Finland, 1982) impacted local debates and help to spur a revival of Sámi indigenous cultures. These include the theatre group and community organisations in Kautokeino that proved a training ground for Sámi director Nils Gaup and his ensemble. Indigenous opposition against hydroelectric power development concurrent with the oil crisis of the early 1970s, such as the building of the James Bay hydroelectrical project in Canada, proved a lightning rod. It flooded Cree land and displaced them from their traditional land, as documented in the NFB's Challenge for Change film *Our Land is Our Life* (Boyce Richardson and Tony Ianzelo, Canada, 1974).

An increase in scientific and media reports of melting ice as a direct result of global fossil fuel consumption has led to a tectonic shift in perceptions of the polar region. Transitioning from a representation of terror and the sublime, the Arctic is now emblematic of catastrophic climate change. The documentary *Chasing Ice* (Jeff Orlowski, US, 2012) offers, through the use of digital technology, a convincing visual document of how the burning of fossil fuels erodes ice. James Balog's photography, screened around the world, emphasises the scale and perspective of the melting glaciers in Alaska, Greenland, Iceland and Montana (and, the digital 'revolution' aside, digital cameras and computer chips pose as many problems for Balog as analogue technology did for early explorers). The demands of climate and remoteness continue to dictate how the Arctic environment can be represented, even in a time of large-scale natural transformation. The ironic and self-reflexive documentary *The Expedition to the End of the World* (*Ekspeditionen til verdens ende*, Daniel Dencik,

Denmark, 2013) proclaims the expedition can reach previously unknown parts of the Greenlandic coast as a result of increased ice-melt. This ambitious work engages with the changing Arctic ecosystem in ways that tie a long history of scientific expeditions not only to nationalist pursuits, but also to representational traditions imported from elsewhere. The film is self-reflexive a tragicomedy and an existential road movie in the tradition of New German filmmakers Wim Wenders and Werner Herzog. The film also challenges dominant modes of representing climate change in the Arctic, by emphasising the subjective, the ad-hoc, and solipsistic aspects of environmental exploration and by seeking to pursue that exploration in ways that consume limited resources.

It would be misleading to argue that all contemporary Arctic documentaries engage with these issues. Some recent Arctic documentaries ignore climate change and resource extraction altogether, focusing instead on atemporal accounts of a 'year in the life' of the Arctic. This includes *Happy People: A Year in the Taiga* (Werner Herzog and Dmitry Vasyukov, Germany, 2010), a film shot in Arctic Russia by Vasyukov, but produced by Studio Babelsberg in Germany and edited by Werner Herzog, who first saw the Vasyukov footage in the United States. This film shows the changing environment of the Arctic, not through climate change, but the change of seasons, with Herzog's German romanticist, world-weary voice-over contextualising the images. In a similar vein, Jessica Oreck's *Aatsinki: The Story of Arctic Cowboys* (Finland, 2013) tells the story of a year in the life of white Arctic reindeer herders, in this case without voice-over or contextualisation, letting the inhabitants and their actions speak for themselves.

Indigenous accounts of climate change take a different tack. Isuma's *Inuit Knowledge and Climate Change* (Zacharias Kunuk, Nunavut, 2010) foregrounds local expertise that tells a complementary story of how climate change negatively affects indigenous resource extraction practices of hunting and fishing. Examining the effects of climate change and resource extraction on the Inuit of Greenland and Northern Canada, *Vanishing Point* (Stephen A. Smith and Julia Szucs, NFB, 2013) is conceived from a circumpolar and transnational perspective, while the indigenous production *People of the Feather* (Joel Heath and the Community of Sanikiluaq, Canada, 2013) connects the present state of the Arctic and the effects of climate change with the stories of the peoples who live there over seven winters. This diverse variety of films demonstrates ably the global concern about resource extraction and climate change and the plethora of approaches practitioners have adopted to address the issue.

THE COLD WAR: THE ARCTIC IN IDEOLOGICAL PERMAFROST

In the Cold War, the Arctic became a space that was used materially and ideologically to draw a line between East and West. The Arctic was seen as potentially porous, but nonetheless a solid buffer because of its expanse, frigidity and desolation. This image of the Arctic as both barrier and expanse is exemplified by such diverse works as the horror film *The Thing* (Howard Hawks and Christian Nyby, US, 1952), the political allegory *Ice Station Zebra* (John Sturges, US, 1968), and the late Cold War allegory *Orion's Belt* (*Orions Belte*, Ola Solum, Norway, 1985). All these films illustrate how the Arctic 'came to be dominated by a militarized geography' (Chaturvedi 2000: 446) and 'perceived and treated throughout the Cold War as an inanimate, passive chessboard on which geostrategic moves and countermoves were made with very little reference to ecological considerations' (Chaturvedi 2000: 454). For Hollywood at the height of the Cold War, however, the Arctic was also conceptualised as a space beyond politics and ideology, as can be seen in *Superman* (Richard Donner, US, 1978). In the film, Clark Kent travels to the Arctic to discover his heritage as a (Kryptonian) man, a heritage that places him above politics, and a force of good for all humanity. In the process, he creates an Arctic Fortress retreat, which exists in a place no one ever goes, and therefore is outside geopolitical pressures.

It was thus no coincidence that these ideological battles were cinematically conceptualised in perhaps the most remote part of the planet, as the distance and exoticism of the Arctic allowed it to become the ultimate metaphoric and mediated space to create representations of these battles, as viewers had little outside frame of reference to understand the area, the people, its environment or its history. Precisely because of its apparent vacuity, the Arctic became invested with significant power as an abstract battleground, including as a stage for missile warfare. Symbolic and material initiatives were undertaken to strengthen ideological ownership of the Arctic. For example, Canadian Inuit were moved from Northern Québec to the High Arctic in 1953–5 to create the image of Canadian sovereignty, though the Inuit had in fact left these lands hundreds of years earlier (Marcus 1988). In an act of unintentional irony, this act of creating the symbolic High Arctic 'Eskimo' for Cold War ideological reasons also included moving Flaherty's illegitimate granddaughter Martha Flaherty, with the rest of her family to Grise Fiord (Ellesmere Island), when she was five. Martha's story of relocation is told in the NFB film *Martha of the North* (*Martha qui vient du froid*, Marquise Lepage, Canada, 2008).

The intensification of the Cold War during the early 1950s brought the Arctic into focus as part of renewed colonial engagements. Greenland was critical in this endeavour, not least through the US construction of the Thule Air Base at the top of the island in the late 1950s. Tension over this neo-colonialisation is apparent in two government-sponsored Danish films about Greenland from the mid-1950s, the documentary *Where the Mountains Float* (*Hvor Bjergene Sejler*, Bjarne Henning-Jensen, 1955) and the melodramatic feature *Qivitoq: The Mountain Wanderer* (*Fjaeldgaengeren*, Erik Balling, Denmark, 1956).

These films eerily correlate with geopolitically motivated US depictions of the 1950s, from Disney's Oscar-winning feature documentaries *Men Against the Arctic* (Winston Hibler, 1955) and *White Wilderness* (James Algar, 1958) to the widely distributed United States Army Signal Corps Pictorial Service documentary TV series *The Big Picture* (1954–61). Taken together, these films represent the colonialist, nation-building final frontier, highlighting the fact that the Cold War was, in its Arctic iteration, global and endless, seemingly stretching to the ends of the earth.

Recent Hollywood films have restaged Cold War oppositions in the Arctic under the flag of environmentalism. For instance, *Big Miracle* (Ken Kwapis, US, 2012), set in 1988 in Point Barrow Alaska, addresses the plight of three stranded whales and, in doing so, conceptualises an environmental struggle through deliberate news media strategies on behalf of a Greenpeace activist (Drew Barrymore), an Iñupiat hunter (John Pingayak) and news reporter (John Krasinski), an oil executive (Ted Danson), and world leaders Ronald Reagan and Mikhail Gorbachev. In this rendition, two superpowers come together in the Arctic, not over the threat of nuclear annihilation, but to save a photogenic Arctic mammal.

GREEN SCREEN: CONTEMPORARY GEOPOLITICS AND ENVIRONMENTALISM

While *Big Miracle* postulates a nostalgic view of the emergent global environmentalist movement as the turning point in the Cold War with Soviets and Americans joining forces to save the whales, other representations of the Arctic provide the strongest example of how Cold War discourses and representational strategies live on in the post-Cold War era. As J. R. McNeill and Corinna M. Unger argue, 'Modern environmentalism . . . is, among other things, a child of the Cold War' (2010: 11). At the end of the 1970s, European anti-nuclear protests (resulting in Sweden in a 1980 phase-out of nuclear power; in Germany municipal protests against locating US nuclear warheads there) conjoined with an increased environmental awareness in the public arena. 'Fears of radiation poisoning and nuclear winter scenarios helped tilt popular culture in the direction of ecological thinking', McNeill and Unger continue, though other 'segments of the population, more committed to the vigorous prosecution of the Cold War, often viewed environmentalism with equal suspicion' (2010: 11). In contrast, in 'the Soviet Union and several of its Eastern European satellites, environmentalism eventually served as one of the few – sometimes the only – permissible form of critique of the state and the Communist Party' (2010: 12). An identifiable discursive and representational trajectory thereby links Cold War geopolitics and East-West ideological and political opposition with thermoperception of cold climates and remote Arctic regions, environmentalism, and access to resource extraction in the region, recently exemplified by Greenland lifting the ban on uranium mining and the concern this has caused in Denmark as well as in international politics. A recent Danish feature film, *The Shooter* (*Skytten*, Annette K. Olesen, 2013) exemplifies this tradition. As a remake of a 1977 eponymous Danish film by Franz Ernst and Tom Hedegaard, the contemporary version addresses the dangerous consequences of large-scale ice-melt from the Greenlandic ice sheet, while the earlier version focused on the threat of deadly contamination from a potential nuclear reactor meltdown.

The psychological horror film *The Last Winter* (Larry Fessenden, US, 2006) bases its environmental horror on a reimagining of the Cold War nuclear-winter threat, such as the one prophesised in *The War Game* (Peter Watkins, UK/BBC, 1965) and *The Day After* (Nicholas Meyer, US/ABC-TV, 1993). Set in Alaska and shot in Iceland, featuring expansive white vistas and sophisticated cinematography tailored to the stark contrast of white light against white snow, the threat of a perennial Arctic winter is deconstructed to become the threat of literal thaw prompted by climate change, turning nature back against humans and developing a vengeful agency of its own. The recent Russian film *How I Ended This Summer* (*Kak ya provyol etim letom*, Alexei Popogrebski, Russia, 2010) is set on a weather observation station in remote Chukotka in northeast Russia. A chamber play of two characters in isolation, surrounded by Cold War debris such as rusting antennas, oil barrels and, most prominently, a portable nuclear power plant (a radioisotope thermoelectric generator which works off isotopes of strontium), the film also mobilises the stark and captivatingly beautiful environment to make the legacy of the Cold War into an uncanny element of the landscape. A similar set of issues is raised in Greenlandic film artist Ivalo Frank's *Echoes* (Greenland, 2010), which juxtaposes Cold War debris in the Greenlandic landscape with the telling of personal stories by local Greenlandic populations about the implications of the American military presence in Greenland.

In what the *New York Times* and other media outlets have termed the contemporary 'Arctic Cold War', the tension lies less between state-sanctioned ideological points of view than between competing discourses of ecological environmentalism and extraction. In this sense, the New Cold War is driven by global capitalism and the desire for hegemony over resource extraction and shipping routes. Paul Arthur Birkman notes in the *New York Times* that the Arctic Council

> identified sustainable development and environmental protection as 'common Arctic issues'. But another crucial concern – maintaining the peace – was shelved in the talks that led to the council's creation. The fear then, as now, was that peace implied demilitarization. It doesn't. But if these nations are still too timid to discuss peace in the region when ten-

sions are low, how will they possibly cooperate to ease conflicts if they arise? (Birkman 2013)

Birkman's fear is that a new Cold War, in the Arctic, is imminent. These concerns are implicitly addressed in a number of recent documentary films. With the contemporary 'Cold War', films engaging a contested Arctic adopt a variety of strategies that place the 'Arctic Cold War' in relation to concerns about the environment, sovereignty, indigenous populations, global warming and transnationalism. *The Battle for the Arctic* (UK, Channel 4/Canada, 2009) examines the new Arctic Cold War and the central role that oil plays in conflicts over sovereignty, environmental policy and security. The current battle over the Arctic is not simply about resource extraction; it is also about the ideologies that justify these activities, as nation-state players attempt to keep the resources contained therein as their own, under the guise of environmentalism and sovereignty, which also highlights the irony that the release of carbon emissions from the very oil extracted from below its surface further intensifies climate change.

THE BOOK ITSELF

Films on Ice brings together work by scholars that addresses both films highly identified with the representation of the Arctic, such as *Nanook of the North*, and little-known films that nevertheless play a key role in the global and local imaginations of the Arctic. Therefore, the book is comprehensive, but it is not a historical or geographical region survey. The book is divided into four parts: 'Global Indigeneity', 'Hollywood Hegemony', 'Ethnography and the Documentary Dilemma', and 'Myths and Modes of Exploration'. Each section contains its own introduction to the chapters that follow. The individual chapters of *Films on Ice* cover all the Arctic's geographical areas, major historical developments, and film and moving image practices and approaches. A number of chapters furthermore address policies and practices of funding, producing and distributing moving images in, about, and for the Global North. Many of these works are dispersed across the globe and often unseen, stored away in archives, private collections and local collectives. Many of these largely unseen images are uncovered and discussed in *Films on Ice*. This book approaches global Arctic film from multiple theoretical perspectives, from ecocriticism to postcolonialism, historiography, indigenous studies, archival research, gender theory, critical theory, cultural studies, cultural ethnography, questions of media specificity and digital media convergence. The book is both an introduction and stepping-off point for further research into an emerging field of Critical Arctic Studies, while providing key contextual and cultural information through analytically specific case studies that will fully situate

Films on Ice as a foundational text in the field because of its breadth, depth, and scope.

BIBLIOGRAPHY

Afbare: Arctic Documentary Films (2006), http://arcticcentre.ulapland.fi/afbare/default.aspx#.U94wrUhzfyE (accessed 12 February 2014).
Alia, V. (2013), *New Media Nation: Indigenous Peoples and Global Communication*, New York: Berghahn.
Badley, L., R. B. Palmer and S. J. Schneider (eds) (2005), *Traditions in World Cinema*, Edinburgh: Edinburgh University Press.
Barclay, B. (2003),'Celebrating Fourth Cinema', *Illusions* 35: 7–11.
Bazin, A. (1967), 'Cinema and exploration', in A. Bazin, *What is Cinema?* vol. I, Berkeley: University of California Press, 154–62.
Birkman, P. A. (2013), 'Preventing an Arctic Cold War', *New York Times*, 12 March.
Bloom, L. (1993), *Gender on Ice: American Ideologies of Polar Exploration*, Minneapolis: University of Minnesota Press.
Bordwell, D. (1979), 'The art cinema as a mode of film practice', *Film Criticism*, 4.1: 56–64.
Bottomore, S. (2003). 'Polar films', in R. Abel (ed.), *Encyclopedia of Early Cinema*, New York: Routledge, 523–4.
Bozak, N. (2012), *The Cinematic Footprint: Lights, Camera, Natural Resources*, New Brunswick, NJ: Rutgers University Press.
Bravo, M. T. and S. Sörlin (eds) (2002), *Narrating the Arctic: A Cultural History of Nordic Scientific Practices*, Canton, MA: Science History Publications.
Catalogue of Lenfilm Studio Feature Films 1918–1989 (1991), St Petersburg: Lenfilm.
Christensen, M., A. Nilsson and N. Wormbs (eds) (2013), *Media and the Politics of Arctic Climate Change: When the Ice Breaks*, New York: Palgrave MacMillan.
Chaturvedi, S. (2000), 'Arctic geopolitics then and now', in M. Nuttall and T. V. Callaghan (eds), *The Arctic: Environment, People, Policy*, Amsterdam: Harwood Academic Publishers, 441–58.
Columpar, C. (2010), *Unsettling Sights: The Fourth World on Film*, Carbondale: Southern Illinois University Press.
Davidson, P. (2005), *The Idea of North*, London: Reaktion.
Diatchkova, G. (2008), 'Indigenous media as an important resource for Russia's indigenous peoples', in P. Wilson and M. Stewart (eds), *Global Indigenous Media: Cultures, Poetics, and Politics*, Durham: Duke University Press, 214–31.
Diesen, J. A. (2011), 'De Polare Ekspedsjonsfilmene', in E. Bakøy and T. Helseth (eds), *Den Andre Norske Filmhistorien*, Oslo: Universitetsforlaget.
Diesen, J. A. and G. Iversen. (2011), 'Roald Amundsen and the Documentary Canon', *Journal of Scandinavian Cinema*, 3:2, 151–7.
Evans, M. R. (2008), *Isuma: Inuit Video Art*, Montreal: McGill-Queen's University Press.
Ezra, E. and T. Rowden (eds) (2006), *Transnational Cinema: The Film Reader*, London: Routledge.
Fienup-Riordan, A. (1995), *Freeze Frame: Alaska Eskimos in the Movies*, Seattle: University of Washington Press.
Fuller, M. (2005), *Media Ecologies: Materialist Energies in Art and Technoculture*, Cambridge, MA: MIT Press.
Galt, R. and K. Schoonover (eds) (2010), *Global Art Cinema: New Theories and Histories*, Oxford: Oxford University Press.

Gant, E. (2004), 'Eskimotid: analyser af filmiske fremstillinger af eskimoer med udgang-spunkt i postkolonialistisk teori og med særlig vægtning af danske grønlandsfilm', dissertation, Aarhus, DK: Aarhus University.

Grierson, J. (2014), 'First principles of documentary', in S. MacKenzie (ed.), *Film Manifestos and Global Cinema Cultures*, Berkeley: University of California Press, 543–9.

Gustafsson, T. and P. Kääpä (eds) (2013), *Transnational Ecocinemas: Film Culture in an Era of Ecological Transformation*, London: Intellect.

Hansen, L. (1953) *I Knuds slædespor*. Copenhagen: Westermann.

Hill, J. (2009), *The White Horizon: The Arctic in the Nineteenth-Century British Imagination*, Albany: SUNY Press.

Hjort, M. (2010), 'On the plurality of cinematic transnationalism', in K. Newman and N. Durovicova (eds), *World Cinemas, Transnational Perspectives*, London: Routledge/American Film Institute Reader.

Hull, R. (2014), 'Iceland on film: a road trip around the "Hollywood of the north"', *The Guardian*, 7 March.

Jørgensen, D. and S. Sörlin (eds) (2014), *Northscapes: History, Technology, and the Making of Northern Environments*, Vancouver: University of British Columbia Press.

Lehtola, J. (2000), *Lailasta Lailaan: Tarinoita elokuvien sitkeista lappalaisista*, Inari: Puntsi.

Lehtola, J. (forthcoming), 'Saami Film', in Mats-Olov Olsson (ed.), *Barents Encyclopedia*. www.barentshistory.eu (accessed 21 May 2014).

MacKenzie, S. and A. W. Stenport. (2013), 'All that's frozen melts into air: Arctic cinemas at the end of the world', *Public: Art/Culture/Ideas* 48: 81–91.

Marchessault, J. (2007), 'Multi-screens and future cinema: the Labyrinth Project at Expo 67', in J. Marchessault and S. Lord (eds), *Fluid Screens, Expanded Cinema*, Montreal: McGill-Queen's University Press, 29–51.

Marcus, A. R. (1995), *Relocating Eden: The Image and Politics of Inuit Exile in the Canadian Arctic*, Hanover: University Press of New England.

McGhee, R. (2007), *The Last Imaginary Place: A Human History of the Arctic World*, Chicago: University of Chicago Press.

McNeill, J. R. and C. M. Unger (eds) (2010), *Environmental Histories of the Cold War*, Cambridge: Cambridge University Press.

Nørrested, C. (2011), *Grønlandsfilm: blandt eskimoer, eventyrere, kolonisatorer og etnografer. Greenland on film*, Copenhagen: North Art Magazine.

Petersen, C. (2003), 'Sámi culture and media', *Scandinavian Studies*, 75.2: 293–300.

Pietikäinen, S. (2008), '"To breathe two airs": empowering indigenous Sámi media', in P. Wilson and M. Stewart (eds), *Global Indigenous Media: Cultures, Poetics, and Politics*, Durham: Duke University Press, 197–213.

Potter, R. (2007), *Arctic Spectacles: The Frozen North in Visual Culture, 1818–1878*, Seattle: University of Washington Press.

Roth, L. (2005), *Something New in the Air: The Story of First Peoples Television Broadcasting in Canada*, Montreal: McGill-Queen's University Press.

Rust, S., S. Monani and S. Cubitt (eds) (2013), *Ecocinema Theory and Practice*, New York: Routledge.

Ryall, A, J. Schimanski, and H. H. Waerp (eds) (2010), *Arctic Discourses*, Cambridge: Cambridge Scholars Publishing.

Sandhu, S. (2010), 'Songs of migration', *Sight and Sound*, 20.2: 8.

Scott, S. (2007), 'Frozen requiem: the Golden Age of polar landscape painting', in *To the Ends of the Earth: Paintings of Polar Landscapes*, Salem: Peabody Essex Museum, 5–13.

Sitney, P. A. (2001), 'Tales of the tribes', *Chicago Review*, 47/48.4/1: 97–115.

Solanas, F. and O. Getino. (2014), 'Towards a Third Cinema: notes and experiences for the development of a cinema of liberation in the Third World', in S. MacKenzie (ed.), *Film Manifestos and Global Cinema Cultures*, Berkeley: University of California Press, 230–49.

Sörlin, S. (ed.) (2013), *Science, Geopolitics and Culture in the Polar Region: Norden Beyond Borders*, Farnham: Ashgate Publishing.

Thisted, K. (2013), 'Discourses of indigeneity. Branding Greenland in the age of self-government and climate change', in S. Sörlin (ed.), *Science, Geopolitics and Culture in the Polar Region: Norden Beyond Borders*, Farnham: Ashgate Publishing, 227–58.

Von Payer, J. (1895), 'An artistic expedition to the North Pole', *The Geographical Journal*, 5.2: 106–111.

Weatherford, E. and E. Seubert (1988), *Native Americans on Film and Video*, vol. II, New York: Museum of the American Indian/Heye Foundation.

White, J. (2005), 'Frozen but always in motion: Arctic film, video, and broadcast', *The Velvet Light Trap*, 55: 52–64.

Willoquet-Maricondi, P. (ed.) (2010), *Framing the World: Explorations in Ecocriticism and Film*, Charlottesville: University of Virginia.

Wilson, P. and M. Stewart (eds) (2008), *Global Indigenous Media: Cultures, Poetics, and Politics*, Durham: Duke University Press.

PART I

GLOBAL INDIGENEITY

PART I. GLOBAL INDIGENEITY

Scott MacKenzie and Anna Westerståhl Stenport

This first section of the book addresses global indigenous film and video-making practices in the transnational Arctic. *Films on Ice* represents the first instance that the multiple cinematic traditions from various indigenous cultures and regions of the Arctic are placed in dialogue with one another. These works encompass a wide variety of styles and genres, addressing the history of indigenous cultures, the relationship between insider and outsider representation, and indigenous filmmakers' appropriation of Global Hollywood storytelling strategies. The first chapter, Marian Bredin's '"Who Were We? And What Happened to Us?": Inuit Memory and Arctic Futures in Igloolik Isuma Film and Video' analyses the history of one of the most successful indigenous film- and video-making groups, Nunavut's Isuma. Bredin charts the emergence of this group, addressing the historical limitations on Inuit filmmaking in Canada, and considers the impact of Isuma's works on both indigenous filmmaking and global art cinema. Taking philosopher Charles Taylor's concept of the 'politics of recognition' as a starting point, Pietari Kääpä, in his chapter 'Northern Exposures and Marginal Critiques: The Politics of Sovereignty in Sámi Cinema' argues that new Sámi cinema practices in Finland eschew the image of the 'mystical' Sámi and instead address contemporary issues on land rights and the rights of indigenous people. Kääpä shows how these films function as 'sub-regional forms of political self-definition'. Ann Fienup-Riordan's 'Frozen in Film: Alaska Eskimos in the Movies' examines the history of Alaskan Eskimo representations and self-representations and also considers the ways in which Alaskan Eskimos have worked within the Hollywood system in a sporadic manner from the 1930s to the present. She then considers contemporary film and video practices employed in local Alaskan Eskimo culture. In 'Cultural Stereotypes and Negotiations in Sámi Cinema', Monica Kim Mecsei provides a history of representations of Sámi peoples in Norwegian cinema over the past century and examines recent developments in film production through the opening of the International Sámi Film Centre in Guovdageaidnu-Kautokeino. Addressing cinematography and strategies of visual storytelling, Marco Bohr in 'Cinema of Emancipation and Zacharias Kunuk's *Atanarjuat: The Fast Runner*' provides an alternative reading of Isuma's best-known film. Bohr identifies distinctive narrative techniques and cultural themes of the film, which tie it both to traditional Inuit myths and legends and to European art cinema, and concludes by highlighting the ways in which *Atanarjuat* situates local practices in a global popular culture framework. Kirsten Thisted's contribution, 'Cosmopolitan Inuit: New Perspectives on Greenlandic Film' considers contemporary acts of appropriation undertaken by Greenlandic filmmakers, as a local feature film industry has only recently emerged. In these films, Greenland is situated as part of a global network of multicultural practices and representational techniques, Thisted argues. In a similar manner, the final chapter in this section, Gunnar Iversen's 'Arctic Carnivalesque: Ethnicity, Gender and Transnationality in the Films of Tommy Wirkola' examines the way in which Wirkola, a Sámi filmmaker, ironically appropriates contemporary Hollywood films such as *The Blair Witch Project* (Daniel Myrick and Eduardo Sánchez, 1999) and *Kill Bill* (Quentin Tarantino, 2003–4) to create ironic, postmodern genres films that address questions of ethnicity and gender in contemporary Norwegian and Sámi culture.

1. 'WHO WERE WE? AND WHAT HAPPENED TO US?': INUIT MEMORY AND ARCTIC FUTURES IN IGLOOLIK ISUMA FILM AND VIDEO

Marian Bredin

INTRODUCTION

When *Atanarjuat: The Fast Runner* burst onto the international film scene in 2001 with its *Camera d'Or* win for director Zacharias Kunuk at Cannes, attention was suddenly focused on a small Inuit production company in the Canadian Eastern Arctic. Igloolik Isuma Productions, the world's first majority Inuit-owned independent film and video production company, was incorporated in 1990 and forced into bankruptcy in 2011. While to national and global audiences it may have seemed that *Atanarjuat* appeared from nowhere, the film was the cumulative result of Isuma's ten years of community-based film and video production in the Inuktitut language. The film represented a watershed for the company, marking a transition from its prior expertise in community video, television series and documentary film, to the creation of a critically successful and broadly popular full-length feature film. This chapter is an inquiry into Isuma's extensive film and video work. Focusing on specific productions, the chapter considers how Isuma's creative force reshaped dominant genres and conventions within an indigenous Arctic context. The company's unceasing commitment to Inuit language, local autonomy and indigenous cultural knowledge established a powerful mode of opposition to southern and non-Inuit media representations of indigenous peoples, while creating new visual languages and relations of production unique to the Arctic and Inuit context. During its twenty-one-year history, Isuma strategically exploited Canadian film and television policies and funding programmes to actively decolonise media production in the Arctic.

Igloolik Isuma and Theoretical Approaches to Indigenous Film

Igloolik is a hamlet of 1,500 people – 94 per cent Inuit – located on an island in the Foxe Basin, just off the Melville Peninsula in the Qikiqtani or Baffin region of Nunavut (Nunavut Planning Commission 2013). This part of the Eastern Arctic was first exposed to southern media and television in the mid-1970s when the Canadian government created a satellite infrastructure to distribute telecommunications and public and commercial broadcasting across Canada and throughout the North. Television was first introduced in larger Arctic communities to meet demands of southern administrators and resource companies. In 1975 and again in 1979, the residents of Igloolik voted against reception of satellite television in their community, because southern channels were completely devoid of Inuit and Inuktitut-language content. In the early 1980s, the federal government set aside funds to create Native Communications Societies in northern regions. This government programme helped to launch the Inuit Broadcasting Corporation (IBC). IBC opened a production centre in Igloolik in 1982, and the following year the community voted in favour of television.

The Inuit co-founders of Isuma first encountered video production during this early phase of the introduction of satellite and television technologies to the Arctic. Kunuk, a sculptor who purchased his first video camera in 1981 with income from his art, wanted to use video to record Inuit perspectives and experience (Kunuk 2006). Paul Apak Angilirq was one of the first producers at IBC and Kunuk joined him to work at the network's production centre in Igloolik in 1982. In 1985, Kunuk participated in an IBC training session in Iqaluit where the trainer was Montreal-based video artist and activist Norman Cohn. Cohn came to the Arctic in part because he had seen IBC videos created by Apak and Kunuk and identified with their narrative style and visual techniques (Evans 2008: 72). After the IBC training session, Cohn went to live in Igloolik to collaborate on community video projects. Cohn, Kunuk and Apak also worked with Pauloosie Qulitalik, a respected elder, unilingual Inuktitut speaker and head of Igloolik's Community Education Committee (Igloolik Isuma 2006a). In 1989, the team created *Qaggiq* (*Gathering Place*), their first venture into recreated fiction. By 1990 Kunuk had left IBC to work full-time on independent video and Igloolik Isuma Productions was incorporated that year with three Inuit and one non-Inuit partner: Apak, Kunuk, Qulitalik, and Cohn. Of the four founding members, Paul Apak passed away in 1998, during the production of *Atanarjuat*. Pauloosie Qulitalik passed away in 2007, after the completion of *The Journals of Knud Rasmussen* (Kunuk, Canada/Denmark, 2006). In 2011, despite more than two decades of successful film and video production, the company encountered insurmountable financial difficulties related to general economic decline in the film industry and the unique difficulties of negotiating funding for cultural production in Nunavut (*Nunatsiaq News*, 22 July 2011).

Between 1985 and 2011, Isuma produced more than forty film, video and television titles for theatrical release and distribution on Canadian and international television networks. Many more videos were created for local use on Inuit community television channels and for circulation through community video networks, art galleries and school, colleges or universities in Canada and around the world. Today, almost all of Igloolik Isuma's vast archive of Inuit-produced film and video from the 1970s to the present has been digitised and uploaded to www.isuma.tv, a comprehensive and searchable online interactive network of Inuit and indigenous multimedia.

The three feature films in the Isuma trilogy, *Atanarjuat, The Journals of Knud Rasmussen* and *Before Tomorrow* (Marie-Hélène Cousineau and Madeline Ivalu, Canada, 2008) recreate a coherent and convincing Inuit history. Careful attention to accurate details of language, social organisation, material culture, clothing, travel and hunting practices gives the films a powerful immediacy and immersive quality. While many critics have described these films as 'ethnographic' in their mode of representation, this designation risks slipping into the kind of projective essentialism that Krupat describes. Isuma films do not rely on conventions of ethnographic realism or claim to represent pure or timeless Inuit culture in its essential difference. Isuma's productions are quite consciously historical, made by contemporary filmmakers who use their cameras to recreate the past, encounter the present or imagine the future. As Avi Santo (2008: 338) suggests, Isuma film is shaped by the historical 'cross-fertilization of global and local' influences on cultural production in the Arctic.

As Ian MacRae (2012) has so cogently argued, Isuma films are produced in the 'contact zone', shaped by Inuit exposure to and negotiation of Arctic colonialism and its representational practices. The opening scenes of *The Journals of Knud Rasmussen* refer to Inuit engagement in the whaling industry in the early twentieth century, and show their mastery of European tools of representation such as syllabic writing, cartography, photography and sound recording. As MacRae (2012: 271) puts it, the film creates a 'discursive space that performs its own awareness of the politics and ethics of representation, but also of self-presentation; and we come to understand, against the received traditions of visual ethnography, that these Inuit are acting, being directed, playing their roles'. The recognition of Inuit representational agency during the experience of cultural contact documented in *Journals* avoids false dichotomies between 'subjugated nation' and 'overt oppressor', but still acknowledges the violence perpetrated by colonialism (MacRae 2012: 272). Like all of Isuma's films, *The Journals of Knud Rasmussen* provides concrete practical and visual evidence of Inuit agency in the historical processes of cultural adaption, mediation and transformation.

CREATIVE STRATEGIES: NARRATIVE, GENRE AND PERFORMANCE IN ISUMA
PRODUCTIONS

Isuma's creative strategies are grounded in Inuit collective memory and storytelling traditions. The company has been central to the formation of new indigenous film genres in part through its consistent reliance on local non-professional actors engaged in participatory performance. Aspects of visual and textual representation are closely related to Isuma's practical processes of community-based filmmaking. Isuma film and video are primarily concerned with Inuit collective memory as it was, and continues to be, sustained through the oral tradition. Examples drawn from Isuma's recreated fiction indicate an ongoing exploration of the key questions posed by Kunuk in the chapter's epigraph: 'Who were we? And what happened to us?' From 1989's Canada Council funded *Qaggiq*, to the final installment in the feature film trilogy, *Before Tomorrow*, Isuma's projects take up the traditional work of oral storytelling in visual form. Several common elements emerge from a survey of these projects. First, Inuit stories on film and video are expressions of collective memory with allegorical features; these narratives represent communal experiences and sustain patterns of intergenerational knowledge flows. Secondly, Isuma's memory work is closely tied up with Inuit life on the land and with movements through the seasons across the Igloolik region. Isuma's film and video narratives create meaning for place. A third key aspect of all of Isuma's work is the effective communication of Inuit knowledge and cultural memory through the Inuktitut language. Fourth, film and video capture the visual and performative elements of storytelling and reproduce modes of teaching Inuit children both practical skills and cultural values. Isuma's central role in the production and consumption of visual culture in Igloolik develops a heightened critical awareness of, and reflection upon, the facets of Inuit culture in the community's everyday life. Finally, while the narrative core of Isuma's historical films is grounded by memory of Inuit lives during the four millennia before Europeans' arrival, these texts also take up the story of 'what happened to us' across the rupture of colonial contact. In answer to this question, Isuma actively appropriates and resituates the ethnographic and colonial record produced by settler society. Isuma films recount the contact narrative from the Inuit point of view, permitting indigenous viewers to 'see through our own eyes what happened'.

Michael Evans (2008, 2010) argues that Isuma was actively using video to extend and transform Inuit storytelling traditions. Kunuk remarks upon the social impact of television when it finally arrived in the community in 1983 and its immediate displacement of family gatherings, visiting and storytelling: 'I thought the only way to save these stories and tell them was to put them in the box: it was time to tell these stories through TV' (Kunuk 2004: 17). The stories included the Inuit legends that his mother told at night in the family's sod house, but also the hunting stories that his father and other elders told to one another and to their children. Isuma film, video and television do not simply 'capture' these stories in video form, but recreate them in a uniquely Inuit visual style.

The characters portrayed in the *Nunavut* television series are played by actual families from Igloolik but are given fictional names. Because the series does not rely on conventions of documentary realism, these actors are not meant to represent specific historical figures or events in the Igloolik area. In the series, the fictional families attend church at the nearby Catholic mission (Episode 2: *Avaja*), build a stone house (Episode 3: *Qarmaq),* and shoot an invading polar bear at the summer hunting camp (Episode 10: *Qaisut*). These re-enacted moments represent a generalised local memory of how *Iglulingmiut* lived in the 1940s and demonstrate their self-sufficiency, ingenuity and resourcefulness. Santo (2004: 393) locates key elements of orality in the *Nunavut* series. As he argues, the stories have an additive non-linear narrative in which one event does not necessarily cause another; rather the narrative sequence works to accumulate experience. The *Nunavut* series is an allegorical narrative about the freedom and independence of Inuit life on the land prior to government programmes of forced settlement and compulsory education introduced to the Arctic in the 1950s. Wood's concept of allegory also applies to the feature film trilogy to the extent that each film plays out an allegorical narrative. *Atanarjuat* explores the disruptive forces of individual power-seeking and violation of cultural taboos within an Inuit community. *Journals* re-enacts the social and moral conflict arising from competing spiritual and religious systems. *Before Tomorrow* documents the encounter with suffering and death faced by an Inuit family which has been destroyed by the introduction of foreign disease. The feature films have more sharply defined characters and plots than the recreated fiction, but the stories they tell construct allegories of indigenous history for viewers within and beyond the Arctic and Inuit contexts.

While Isuma narratives may be allegorical, they are also concretely located in Arctic spaces and landscapes in the Igloolik area. The land plays a central role in Isuma's work (Varga 2006: 227) and recognisable local sites and landmarks are often represented. In scenes of *The Journals* as Rasmussen visits the shaman Avva's winter camp, the interconnected igloos of the Inuit 'snow palace' and the difficult journey through a blizzard from the camp back to Igloolik were carefully recreated for the film.

Inscriptions of Inuit history across Arctic places and seasons can also be seen in the recreated fiction videos. *Qaggiq* traces the seasonal meeting of Inuit in communal winter camps and related celebrations and social events, such as the marriage of a young couple cautiously negotiated between both families. Revolving around the construction of a large snow *qaggiq*, the video documents each step from initial sketch of the outline in the snow to placement of the final blocks around the vent in the roof. As the meeting place for the community, site of stories, *ajaja* songs and drum dancing, the *qaggiq* signifies the place of Inuit at home on the land during the Arctic winter. *Nunaqpa* and *Saputi* follow Igloolik Inuit to the summer caribou hunting grounds and to the riverbanks in late summer, where they build a weir to trap fish. These three videos are characterised by long steady pans of seasonal Arctic landscapes, eventually coming to rest on families or small groups as they travel, build camp or attend to the everyday tasks of a hunting culture. Long shots contrast with lengthy close-up sequences, often of feet moving through snow or across tundra grasses and lichen. Such visual techniques help capture cultural rhythms of Inuit seasonal travels in search of food and shelter (White 2005: 59). Reliance on the land and intimate knowledge of Arctic climate and resources is at the heart of Inuit cultural knowledge, not simply shaping Inuit communities but literally 'framing the possible' in the Arctic (Taylor 2011: 132). In these ways, Isuma videos create narratives that establish Arctic spaces as an integral part of Inuit lives.

Isuma productions are made almost exclusively in the Inuktitut language, a conscious choice by the filmmakers to bring film and video to Inuit audiences in their own words. While most Inuit still speak Inuktitut as their first language, its use in Isuma's historical films required more sophisticated vocabulary and the retrieval of words and grammatical constructions that have fallen into disuse. The production of *Atanarjuat* created the opportunity for actors to learn an older, richer and more colourful form of Inuktitut from the elders (Evans 2010: 57). This resulted in a revitalisation and recovery of cultural knowledge through language. Zacharias Kunuk, the first Canadian to win the *Camera d'Or* at Cannes, gave his acceptance speech in Inuktitut signifying the arrival of Inuit in the global film industry, but also focusing the international gaze on indigenous cultures and peoples within the Canadian state. The use of Inuktitut by actors and interview subjects in Isuma documentary films further prioritises the Inuit point of view and gives voice to perspectives that have been silenced in the mainstream media.

Isuma film and video also deploy a unique visual language and capture the visual elements of oral narrative. At the level of what is recorded – the visual signifiers – Isuma's recreated fiction, the *Nunavut* television series and the feature films devote much time and detail to the precise and accurate rendering of Inuit material culture and domestic life. In *Nunaqpa*, for instance, a group of men and boys skin and butcher a caribou. The meat is carefully wrapped in the caribou skin and loaded on their shoulders for the walk back to the inland camp. The sequence showing the preparation of the meat is shot in extreme close-up without dialogue or description in such a way that the skill and dexterity of the hunters is apparent. Similar sequences showing women filling the *qulliq* (soapstone lamps) and positioning the Arctic cotton wick on the very edge of the burning fat can be found in several Isuma films. These scenes can be viewed as a form of cultural preservation, recording skills and activities that are no longer a part of daily life (Evans 2008: 28). But the centrality of these everyday acts and their seamless incorporation into the story world also mimics the way Inuit children traditionally absorbed cultural knowledge by watching their elders and observing daily life. At the level of signified meaning, the images of skilful preparation of caribou meat and careful tending of the *qulliq* connect historical aspects of Inuit material survival in the Arctic to the renewed understanding of these lifeways as they are re-enacted and recorded on film and video. The stories of 'who we were' become explicitly tied to contemporary Inuit culture through the act of recording them. Evans (2008: 50) suggests that videomaking requires an active engagement with cultural memory and history such that participants reflect on aspects of their cultures more deliberately and more fully than they otherwise might. Isuma's creative strategies heighten Inuit self-awareness and critical consciousness of their past and present culture.

Finally, Isuma's visual storytelling addresses the crucial question of 'what happened to us?' by using the oral tradition to resituate the non-Inuit colonial and ethnographic record. This strategy is most apparent in *The Journals of Knud Rasmussen*, where the story's structure is built around events and photographs recorded by the Danish explorer in the *Report of the 5th Thule Expedition*. The moment of contact between Rasmussen's team and Igloolik shaman Avva and his family is not told as Rasmussen's story but as an Inuit account. Avva's autobiographical monologue is at the heart of the film, bearing witness to the beauty, integrity and complexity of Inuit spiritual lives before Christianity. While Avva's story is taken almost verbatim from the written version in Rasmussen's report, it is layered within the film's intimate portrait of Avva's family, his relationship with his daughter Apak, also a shaman, and the presence of his spirit helpers in his everyday life (MacRae 2012: 280). The film uses ethnographic and historical material from the early twentieth century to re-enact the growing tension between Inuit who 'work for the whites' and those, like Avva, who maintained their distance from the whalers, traders and missionaries. As first Apak, and then Avva and his wife Orulu, join the Christian Inuit at Igloolik, the moment of cultural rupture is encapsulated in a powerful scene at the end of the film as Avva sends his three spirit helpers, crying and wailing, away across the ice. The filmmakers have imagined Avva's sense of pain and loss within the visual narrative of film, embedding the ethnographic record within Inuit cultural memory. The intertextual strategies underpinning *The Journals of Knud Rasmussen* bring the written and photographic record to life, so that the historical facts of contact, colonisation and conversion cannot easily be divorced from the human experience of Inuit who lived through them.

The narrative patterns of Isuma films cumulate in the emergence of a distinctive genre of indigenous cinema, transforming the oral through engaging the audiovisual. In the company's recreated fiction projects, Inuit narrative inflects preconceived understandings of both documentary and drama. As a new genre, Isuma's recreated fiction is formed in the transaction between past and future, premised upon the continuous motion of Inuit culture. Columpar (2010: 168) suggests that critics tend to situate *Atanarjuat* and other Isuma productions with reference to the 'epic' or the 'ethnographic', without fully considering the extent to which the films demand a different mode of engagement altogether. Evans characterises Isuma's work as an immersion in Inuit cultural realities through the use of a unique visual language. This he describes as a non-didactic method of 'showing' more than 'telling', creating the conditions for representing Inuit culture by forcing viewers to understand the Arctic on Inuit terms, not on models or methods imposed by the Western gaze (Evans 2010: 89). Isuma's recreated fiction video and its feature films represent both the near and distant past, but imbue this history with an immediacy that is tied to local memory and participatory performance. Historical experience is recreated and interpreted by local actors engaged in the embodied expression of Inuit culture. The performance of Inuit history and culture by local participants in Isuma productions requires that traditional skills and ancient linguistic forms are rehearsed and, in effect, relived. While this cultural knowledge is captured on video, it is also revitalised in the contemporary community (Santo 2008: 329). The work of assimilating knowledge from Inuit tradition combined with the collaborative work of writers, actors, creators of material culture, directors and technical producers give Isuma film and video its unique generic attributes.

OPPOSITIONAL TACTICS IN ISUMA'S FILM PRACTICE

Isuma's relations of production originate in the collaborative and consensual aspects of Inuit culture and in the practices of community video that Cohn brought to the Arctic (Evans 2008: 46). These combined influences result in what Kunuk has referred to as the Inuit style of filmmaking: 'We work horizontally while the usual Hollywood film people work in a military style. Our entire team would talk about how to shoot a particular scene, from art directors to the sound man. We put the whole community to work' (Kunuk 2004: 17). The unique fusion of alternative video practices forged in North American urban centres during the 1970s and cooperative community relationships inherent to Inuit culture is evidence of the transcultural synergy that MacRae (2012: 267) sees as informing Isuma's work. Cohn describes this combined approach as a 'third way' of professional film production (Evans 2008: 46). Apart from subverting film's conventional industrial relations, the model of community production at Isuma also connects to economic development for Igloolik. The re-enactment of Inuit history and revitalisation of Inuit culture through film and video result in paid work for a significant number of Igloolik's residents employed as actors, script and language advisers, costume, set or artifact makers, and food suppliers (Ginsburg 2003: 828). The community as a whole has a stake in Isuma productions and their contribution to heightened cultural awareness, new social relationships and economic growth.

In its challenges to the political economy of Canadian film funding, Isuma played a major role in moving indigenous film out of the margins of the Canadian industry. When Isuma was first developing *Atanarjuat*, the film-makers realised that the film would require a much larger budget than funds available through arts grants or investments for Aboriginal programmes on Television Northern Canada (TVNC). While Isuma used a broadcast agreement with TVNC to trigger funding available for Aboriginal-language television, applications were capped at $100,000 (Seguin 2006). In 1998, Telefilm Canada had an English-language and French-language feature film fund, but no support for feature films in another language like Inuktitut. Isuma's anticipated budget for *Atanarjuat* was close to $2 million, and so the company applied to the English-language film category at Telefilm, submitting the Inuktitut and English screenplay as part of the application. Although the film had received initial development support and had already begun production, it was turned down for funding under the English-language category, prompting a vocal and very public phone, letter and e-mail campaign by Kunuk and Cohn (Seguin 2005). Isuma's response to Telefilm explicitly questioned colonial attitudes that limited indigenous-language content to a small fund designed primarily for television, arguing that the system was biased against major indigenous productions (Evans 2008: 130). Eventually the challenge was successful, Canada's National Film Board came on as a co-producer and *Atanarjuat* got sufficient funds to resume shooting in 1999.

The global success of its first feature film opened the door to a number of other groundbreaking financial strategies at Isuma. Isuma Distribution International (IDI) was first created in late 2001 after *Atanarjuat* failed to secure a Canadian distributor, but IDI continues to seek local, national and international outlets for Inuit film and video. In 2003, the company was rewarded for *Atanarjuat's* $3.7 million in box-office revenues with three years of Performance Envelope funding from Telefilm for developing new projects, including the scripts that became the next two films in the trilogy (Santo 2008: 331). *The Journals of Knud Rasmussen* was produced as a treaty co-production with Barok Film in Denmark, allowing Isuma to increase the budget substantially to $6.3 million (Baltruschat 2010: 136). Most importantly, a substantial amount of the budget for both these films was spent in Igloolik, providing income, employment and experience for local people.

As Santo (2008: 331) points out, 'global market success and recognition are vital to both the local Igloolik economy as well as to increasing Inuit cultural capital, which, in turn, allows Inuit a greater recognition within Canadian cultural politics'. Kunuk and the other filmmakers at Isuma have always stated that the first audience for their work is an Inuit audience. Inuit stories, told in the Inuktitut language, rely upon an audience that brings a 'lived understanding of the narrative event and a learned understanding of the narrated event' (Evans 2010: 102). Evans suggests that Inuit viewers recognise not only the characters, events and locations of the stories, but also the uniquely Inuit attributes of oral and visual storytelling practices. Isuma's early work also circulated among video art, community video and educational audiences, viewers for whom interpretation of recreated fiction and historical re-enactment resonated with their prior interest in ethnographic cinema, postcolonial aesthetics, alternative and indigenous media, or performative documentary. With the global success of *Atanarjuat*, Isuma's work also became available to a larger popular audience who were less aware of Inuit history in the Arctic. While Krupat possibly over-states the potential size of the conventional audience, he perceptively argues that Isuma filmmakers reach out to cross-over viewers, encouraging them to appre-ciate the film by 'translating it into their habitual interpretative comfort zones' (Krupat 2007: 610) and by providing online resources and companion books about Inuit culture that promote a more knowledgeable response. Santo (2008: 327) suggests that Isuma's global marketing strategies risk reducing 'complex cultural and political practices into easily recognizable global commodities that conform to stereotypical assumptions about Aboriginal "authenticity" already familiar to global consumers'. While the global popular audience may rely on the codes and conventions of dominant cinematic forms to appreciate Isuma's feature films, the distinction between Inuit, 'postcolonial' and popular audiences are not as fixed as they might seem at first glance. As a filmmaker, Kunuk grew up watching movies in Igloolik in the 1960s and the community had been exposed to satellite television for nearly fifteen years when *Atanarjuat* was being made. Inuit audiences might also respond to and appreciate the codes and conventions of popular cinema, while still experiencing the film as a genuine expression of their lived experience and history. Further, the global audience may connect to Isuma films not solely as consumers, but also at the level of affect and empathy. Writing about *The Journals of Knud Rasmussen*, Norman Cohn suggests that the universal audience for the film moves toward social change through the encounter with 'real time' emotion:

> As agents in our own lives, and spectators of others, we recognize authentic meaning only in emotions experienced in 'real time'; that is, not the fake and fractured time of conventional filmmaking but the three-dimensional time of real life. Bringing the heightened awareness of real time to dramatic storytelling enables empathic identification between character and witness at a level of meaning where social action becomes

possible. Made for Inuit *The Journals of Knud Rasmussen* brings Avva's story forward with dignity and generosity; while for the universal audience *The Journals* also brings video art forward where emotion is a vehicle of time travel whose destination is social change. (Cohn 2008: 160)

Cohn positions the popular audience as potential witnesses to the lived experience of cultural contact and colonialism, not as passive consumers but as active agents. This seems a more nuanced understanding of how both Inuit and non-Inuit viewers may respond to films that transform dominant discourses about indigenous peoples through the kind of relived drama and recreated fiction that Isuma has invented. In this way Isuma film moves both Inuit and non-Inuit audiences toward decolonisation. The body of Isuma's work since 1989 links mode of cultural authority to political autonomy and social justice for Inuit in the Canadian Arctic.

BIBLIOGRAPHY

Apak, P. and Wachowich, N. (2002), 'Interview with Paul Apak Angilirq', in P. A. Angilirq, Z. Kunuk, H. Paniaq, P. Qulitalik, N. Cohn and B. Saladin d'Anglure (eds), *Atanarjuat: The Fast Runner: Inspired by a Traditional Inuit Legend of Igloolik*, Toronto: Coach House Books and Isuma Publishing, 13–15.

Baltruschat, D. (2010), 'Co-producing First Nations' narratives: *The Journals of Knud Rasmussen*', in S. Baldur Hafsteinsson and M. Bredin (eds), *Indigenous Screen Cultures in Canada*, Winnipeg: University of Manitoba Press, 127–42.

Bessire, L. (2003), 'Talking back to primitivism: divided audiences, collective desires', *American Anthropologist*, 105(4), 832–7.

Brody, H. (2004), '*Atanarjuat The Fast Runner*', in G. Robinson (ed.), *Isuma: Inuit Studies Reader: An Inuit Anthology*, Montreal: Isuma Publishing, 10–17.

Cohn, N. (2008), 'When your work speaks for itself, don't interrupt', in G. Robinson (ed.), *The Journals of Knud Rasmussen: A Sense of Memory and High-definition Inuit Storytelling*. Montreal: Isuma Publishing, 159–60.

Columpar, C. (2010), *Unsettling Sights: The Fourth World on Film*, Carbondale: Southern Illinois University Press.

Evans, M. R. (2008), *Isuma: Inuit Video Art*, Montreal: McGill-Queen's University Press.

Evans, M. R. (2010), *The Fast Runner: Filming the Legend of Atanarjuat*, Lincoln, NE: University of Nebraska Press.

Gaul, A. (2012), 'Northern restoration' [electronic version], *Ryerson Review of Journalism* (accessed 15 May 2013). http://rrj.ca/m18433/

Ginsburg, F. (2003), 'Atanarjuat off screen. from "media reservations" to the world stage', *American Anthropologist*, 105(4), 827–31.

Hearne, J. (2006), 'Telling and retelling in the "ink of light": documentary cinema, oral narratives, and indigenous identities', *Screen* 47(3), 307–26.

Huhndorf, S. (2003), '*Atanarjuat, The Fast Runner*: culture, history, and politics in Inuit media', *American Anthropologist*, 105 (4), 822–6.

Igloolik Isuma Productions (2006a), 'Our people' (accessed 15 May 2013). http://www.isuma.tv/en/isuma-productions/our-people.

Igloolik Isuma Productions (2006b), 'The Journals of Knud Rasmussen, press kit' [electronic version] (accessed 15 May 2013). http://www.isuma.tv/sites/default/themes/isuma_prod3/files/Press_kit_JKR.pdf.
Igloolik Isuma Productions (2007), 'Atanarjuat: the legend on the land' (accessed 15 May 2013). http://www.isuma.tv/en/atanarjuat/the-legend-on-the-land.
Jasen, S. (2013), 'The archive and reenactment: performing knowledge in the making of The Journals of Knud Rasmussen', Velvet Light Trap, 71, 3–14.
Kunuk, Z. (2006), 'The art of Inuit storytelling' (accessed 15 May 2013). http://www.isuma.tv/art-inuit-story-telling.
Kunuk, Z. (2002), 'I first heard the story of Atanarjuat from my mother', in P. A. Angilirq, Z. Kunuk, H. Paniaq, P. Qulitalik, N. Cohn & B. Saladin d'Anglure (eds), Atanarjuat: the Fast Runner: Inspired by a Traditional Inuit Legend of Igloolik, Toronto: Coach House Books and Isuma Publishing, 13–15.
Kunuk, Z. (2004), 'The public art of Inuit storytelling', in D. Kessler, G. Robinson and J. Kunnuk (eds), Isuma: Teacher's Resource Guide, Montreal: Isuma Publishing, 16–18.
MacRae, J. (2012), 'Siqqitiq (crossing over): paradoxes of conversion in The Journals of Knud Rasmussen', Journal of Canadian Studies, 46(2), 263–97.
Maracle, L. (2008), 'Mapping our way through history: reflections on Knud Rasmussen's journals', in G. Robinson (ed.), The Journals of Knud Rasmussen: A Sense of Memory and High-definition Inuit Storytelling, Montreal: Isuma Publishing, 17–22.
Marubbio, M. E. and Buffalohead, E. L. (2013), 'Introduction: talking back, moving forward', in M. E. Marubbio and E. L. Buffalohead (ed.), Native Americans on Film: Conversations, Teaching, Theory, Lexington, KY: University Press of Kentucky.
Nunavut Planning Commission (2013), Igloolik (accessed 15 May 2013). http://nunavut.ca/en/communities/baffin/igloolik.
Rader, D. (2011), Engaged Resistance: American Indian Art, Literature, and Film from Alcatraz to the NMAI, Austin: University of Texas Press.
Raheja, M. (2007), 'Reading Nanook's smile: visual sovereignty, indigenous revisions of ethnography, and Atanarjuat (The Fast Runner)', American Quarterly, 59 (4), 1159–85.
Said, S. F. (2006), 'Everyday white', Sight & Sound, 16(9), 36–9.
Santo, A. (2004), 'Nunavut: Inuit television and cultural citizenship', International Journal of Cultural Studies, 7(4), 379.
Santo, A. (2008), 'Act locally, sell globally: Inuit media and the global cultural economy', Continuum: Journal of Media & Cultural Studies, 22(3), 327–40.
Seguin, D. (2005), 'Freeze frame', Canadian Business, 78(17), 42–6.
Siebert, M. (2006), 'Atanarjuat and the ideological work of contemporary Indigenous filmmaking', Public Culture, 18(3), 531–50.
Singer, B. R. (2001), Wiping the War Paint off the Lens: Native American Film and Video, Minneapolis: University of Minnesota Press.
Soukup, K. (2006), 'Report: travelling through layers: Inuit artists appropriate new technologies', Canadian Journal of Communication, 31(1), 239–46.
Taylor, T. (2011), 'Zacharias Kunuk: man standing' [electronic version], Canadian Art (accessed 15 May 2013). http://www.canadianart.ca/features/2011/11/10/zacharias_kunuk/
Varga, D. (2006), 'Atanarjuat: the Fast Runner', in J. White (ed.), The Cinema of Canada, London, New York: Wallflower, 225–34.
White, J. (2005), 'Frozen but always in motion: Arctic film, video, and broadcast', The Velvet Light Trap, 55(1), 52–64.

2. NORTHERN EXPOSURES AND MARGINAL CRITIQUES: THE POLITICS OF SOVEREIGNTY IN SÁMI CINEMA

Pietari Kääpä

In 2012, the Finnish Film Foundation (FFF) established a funding initiative devoted to developing Sámi film production, a move marking a significant development acknowledging the marginal status of Sámi cinema within the Nordic countries. While the fund is part of the FFF's focus on developing marginal film production practices and themes, and thus not a long-term charity case, its introduction is indicative of a range of key considerations. First, Sámi cinema has received increased attention in the Nordic countries in the 2000s as both a filmmaking practice and a topic of representation. Reflecting the geoculturally contested status of the Sámi land (the Sápmi), covering northernmost Norway, Sweden, Finland and Russia (the Sámi population is estimated at 164,000 globally, of whom 133,000 are residents in Sápmi), the Sámi have been infrequently represented by their dominant 'host' populations in the past. The majority of these depictions emerge from Finland and Norway (see Chapter 4 in this collection, by Monica Kim Mecsei, for more on Norwegian film production). Finnish producers have depicted the Sámi as villains or mystical forces of nature in films such as *The Curse of the Witch* (*Noidan kirot*, Teuvo Puro, 1927) and *The White Reindeer* (*Valkoinen Peura*, Erik Blomberg, 1952), respectively. In both these cases, the focus is on conceptualising Lapland as an untamed territory especially threatening to the young women whose gendered otherness acts as a suitable cause by which to establish white masculine dominance over the region as the men have to act as heroes containing the threat posed by Sámi mysticism. In contrast to this long history of exotic depictions of the 'mythical' Sámi, contemporary documentary and fiction films by Sámi directors such as Katja Gauriloff and Paul-Anders Simma, among others, focus on indigenous rights and the complexities of coexistence within nation-state structures. This attention is of a qualified nature, however, as both the films and their directors are considered as distinct 'others' in relation to the dominant national cultures. This attitude positions the Sámi in a problematic role characterised by alterity and difference, a position that the very act of evoking one's historical and sovereign identity reinforces.

These contradictions are reflected at all levels of Sámi film culture. Thematically, the politics of contemporary Sámi cinema evokes transitory identities and contrasting lifestyles. Aesthetically and narratively, Sámi films combine observational and activist filmmaking practices with the type of explicit political messages that pertain to postcolonial cinema. In this, they maintain a conflicted status: their themes take issue with historical injustice and the importance of cultural and political Sámi sovereignty, but as film productions, they largely rely on the funding and distribution mechanisms of the host state, despite their small budgets and digital form. To unpack some of these dynamics of sovereignty and dependence, I explore a range of Sámi productions, emphasising the ways in which they propose sub-regional forms of political self-definition, while challenging the fundamental principles supporting nation-state sovereignty and regional homogeneity.

To explore the implications of these films in a wider transnational context, I compare contemporary Sámi production in Finland with the Inuit film *Atanarjuat* (Zacharias Kunuk, Canada, 2000). The comparative approach makes sense as both the Inuit and the Sámi productions take part in what Charles Taylor has referred to as 'politics of recognition' (Taylor 2011), which involves a transcultural notion of subalternity concerning the constant striving of minority populations to claim cultural and political sovereignty from dominant populations while acknowledging the constitutive role they continue to play even in the self-determinacy of the minority. As we will see, the politics of 'giving and withholding recognition' (Taylor 2011: 36) adopted by the democratic states of these Nordic countries structures much of the production infrastructure and thematic scope of Sámi cinema produced in Finland. But simultaneously, a politics of diversity necessitates that the Sámi are able to enunciate their own perspectives, though the scope and effectiveness of these strategies remain topics of debate.

The 'Smallness' of Sámi Film Production

Scholarship on the cinema of the Sámi is limited, at least in English (in Finnish, see Lehtola 2000). Work in ethnography and anthropology explores, in passing, cinematic representations of the Sámi. The studies often raise valid points about the cultural politics of Sámi sovereignty (Ragazzi 2008; Seurujärvi-Kari,

Halinen and Pulkkinen 2011) but cinema is only a very minor aspect of these works. Discussions of the Norwegian filmmaker Nils Gaup, and especially of internationally distributed historical epics such as *Pathfinder* (*Ofelaš*, Norway, 1987) and *The Kautokeino Rebellion* (*Kautokeino-opprøret*, Norway, 2008), have generated considerable discussion around Sámi culture and politics, with interpretations positioning them as important contributions to Norwegian cinema (Iversen 2005) or as Scandinavian, politically engaged genre productions (Nestingen 2008). These perspectives demonstrate that Gaup's films are not only 'Sámi films', but have also been incorporated into various 'canons'. Domestically, they are seen as both minority and heritage cinema, with the latter especially playing a forceful role in their incorporation into a multicultural constitution of Norwegian cinema. Despite recognition of the Sámi cause, this continues the sense of othering that has seen the Sámi caricatured as shamans, *enfants sauvages*, villains or damsels in distress throughout the history of Nordic film culture. Internationally, these films are considered as art cinema, despite adhering to the conventions of the historical epic. While the 'indigenous mode' of Gaup's films and those produced by directors from dominant populations, such as the Finnish examples listed above, play along with established narrative and thematic patterns, the adoption of such conventions becomes an effective strategy to attain a wide audience for Sámi film. This is a real Catch-22 situation that structures most of the contemporary forms of Sámi production. It also provides a rationale for seeing Sámi cinema as representative of the position of minority cinema in the global North.

Indigenous cinema of Paul-Anders Simma

The films of the Sámi Paul-Anders Simma illustrate these considerations in the Finnish context. Simma has been an active producer of Sámi cinema since 1991, with films that range from documentaries to feature-length productions. The films involve a variety of different approaches to the politics of recognition, combining more light-hearted comedies and activist documentaries with chronicles of Sámi sovereignty. Films such as *Let's Dance* (1991), *Lecacy of the Tundra* (*Duoddara árbi*, 1994), *Minister of State* (*Minister på villovägar*, 1997), *Give Us Our Skeletons!* (*Antakaa meille luurankomme!*, 1998) and *The Tale About Arctic Love* (*Iskko-Máhte máinnas*, 2000) take place in different parts of the Sápmi and illustrate the dynamics between Sámi sovereignty and the national constellations that underlie them. The funding and distribution structures of these films are distinctly smaller than those of Gaup, for example. Whereas *The Kautokeino Rebellion* was a significant undertaking, costing up to €6 million, Simma's most expensive production, *Minister of State*, cost around €1 million (13,200,000 markkas). His documentaries and short films have had significantly lower budgets.

Figure 2.1   Veikko Feodoroff, spokesman for the Skolt Sámi, *Cry into the Wind* (2007).

The short film *Let's Dance* is a case in point: not only was it Simma's first film but its very smallness provides a viable alternative perspective to the conventional exoticism of large-scale Sámi film or non-Sámi productions. The initial sense of difference emerges in its name, which is based on language and cultural customs often considered alien to Sámi culture. As if to show that such expectations are in themselves an imposed construct, the film tells a typical coming-of-age story, following the protagonist Lassi's attempts to meet up with the cashier of the local shop at the community dance. Lassi's shy and reserved demeanour is that of a teenage boy rather than a protagonist marked as Sámi. In fact, were it not for certain iconographic markers it would be difficult to identify the film as a Sámi production. The signifiers that place the events in the Sápmi concern the depiction of the dilapidated Northern communities and the comprehensive changes the traditional society is under- going. Initial scenes take on a darkly comic tone as we see the father of the family trying to hang himself in the barn. The act is a failure but is clearly not the first of its kind – numerous broken ropes hang from the rafters. The Sámi community is portrayed in a distinctly unmythical light, with reindeer herding and shamanism replaced by (comparatively) modern shops and bars. The drinking and dancing is entirely in line with conventional cinematic depictions of small-town banality. Lassi and his tobacco consumption are the only things that stand out. By divesting Sámi everyday life of its exotic connotations, the film emphasises the universal nature of teenage life, no matter where one's community is located.

In contrast to this distinctly grounded take, the short fable *The Tale of Arctic Love* combines deconstructive realism with romantic shenanigans and surreal forms of mysticism. Iisko-Matti is in love with the local village chief's daughter and takes her for a ride on a snowmobile, which is due to be repaired in his shop. Attending the funeral of her aunt, he is given the task of transport-ing the dead woman's corpse on the snowmobile to her resting place. As he is well aware of the mystical spirit world of the Northern regions that may lead to confrontations with the unknown, he is understandably hesitant. As predicted, the dead woman does wake up mid-journey, and she chases him up a tree. The next day he is found in the tree, but instead of suffering scorn and ridicule he is viewed in positive terms for his ability to withstand the horrors. He is even given 100,000 markkas to buy the snowmobile and is allowed to ask for the daughter's hand in marriage.

While the inclusion of mysticism in the story relates to mythical portrayals of the Sámi, its role is more complicated than simple exoticism. Instead of being an element of othering, the mystical angle works alongside the film's depiction of the contemporary complexities of the Sápmi. The visual language of the film is arguably more like 'traditional' representations of the Sámi than the more everyday world of *Let's Dance*, given how the film uses conventions of ethnography and even the horror film. But the elaborate collage of visual idioms appropriately mirrors the geocultural space of the Sápmi. Rather than being defined by simplistic binaries and oppositional politics, this space is conceptualised as a complex multidirectional area of overlapping cultural constellations and power relations. Nowhere is this more evident than in the use of language, as the protagonist is considered an outsider by most, even the dominant Sámi. To illustrate this, Iisko-Matti largely communicates in

Figure 2.2   Veikko Feodoroff takes his cause to the Finnish Parliament, *Cry into the Wind* (2007).

Finnish, in contrast to the other Sámi and the Swedish businessman whose snowmobile he borrows. The relationship between the individuals is certainly based on simplified stereotypes (affluent Swedish, down-to-earth Sámi, and so on), but this is in line with Simma's politics of caricatured irony. The Sápmi is thus a space that exists along multiple modes of contestation and geopolitical appropriation. Simma's film captures this multitude of modes from the perspective of Sámi agency.

This depiction is especially relevant to Simma's use of an autoethnographic approach – that is, to represent one's own cultural heritage to complement or counter various other representational paradigms – to reconsidering Sámi history. Traditions contrast with the ways in which snowmobiles, cars, mainstream entertainment and migration challenge the traditional lifestyles around which the communities are still organised. These oppositions are largely based on binary distinctions where modern conveniences evoke ephemerality and transience and contrast with the grounding force of traditional customs and communality. But the ways in which these contradictions are conveyed rely on an ironic critical distance that resists the more simplistic, oppositional politics that often emerge in nostalgic evocations harking back to utopian times. Through this, the film establishes Simma's autoethnographic stance as a deconstructive approach, one that aims to facilitate a reappraisal of cinematic representations of the Sámi.

Visual Sovereignty and Sámi cinema

Simma's early films are highly suggestive in their often-simultaneous utilisation and deconstruction of traditional Sámi iconography. In this respect, his approach has much in common with the Isuma collective's Inuit epic *Atanarjuat*, a tale of rivalry set in the Igloolik at the dawn of the first century. The Inuit film combines in-depth depictions of Inuit lifestyles with an emphasis on mysticism and the central role that shamanism and spirituality hold for Inuit culture. The film culminates in an unusual reversal. As the end credits roll, Kunuk shows the Inuit actors in their contemporary everyday life, wearing jeans and listening to headphones, partly challenging the traditional modes through which the Inuit are othered in the context of Canadian cinema (see Bohr, Chapter 5 in this volume). Simma's juxtaposition of contemporary Sámi traditions and the language politics of the Sápmi mobilise strategies which form a transcultural and transnational correlation between Arctic minority film cultures. Taken together, these films demonstrate a mode of 'visual sovereignty' (Raheja 2007). This mode is concerned with an approach that confronts the spectator with the history of caricaturing and assumptions involved in representations of the other whilst also centralising the involvement and complicity of Inuit and Sámi in these power structures.

MINISTER OF STATE AND POLITICS OF RECOGNITION

Simma's feature film *Minister of State* illustrates similarities between Sámi and Inuit visual sovereignty, especially as they relate to the film's respective politics of recognition. The initial set-up of *Minister of State* brings to mind some of Nils Gaup's work as we see shots of the fells underscored by a *joik* (a traditional form of Sámi music). Soon we cut to a car and an older man telling a story about fire-breathing monsters to a child clad in Sámi clothes – all somewhat typical visual and narrative material for a Sámi film. A flashback takes us to World War II and we see two soldiers wandering around the Sápmi, stealing food and dodging the Germans who are operating throughout Lapland. As the soldiers blow up a bridge, one of them is wounded and taken to a local village where he is able to convince locals that he is in fact a minister of the Finnish government.

The use of the *joik* as a narrative device engages the film's politics. The song presents Sagojoga as a place in between three countries 'where people do not pay tax or recognise borders'. As in *Legacy of the Tundra*, language plays a key role in cultural affiliation in the Sápmi. Here, the inhabitants of the village demonstrate shifting notions of national allegiance by using diverse languages to address different people, providing an even more complex depiction of the ways in which language politics relate to relations of dominance and subversion than that seen in *Atanarjuat*. Culture too is malleable as villagers negotiate their allegiance according to circumstances, for example, by taking out a bottle of vodka once they hear the Russians are on the way. The villagers are a mixed bunch of Norwegians, Swedes, Russians, Finns and Sámi, and they all have dubious motives for exploiting their liminal status between nations, except for the Sámi, with whom the soldier protagonist finds a mutual sense of affinity. While the film plays up the comedy value of the diversity of the Sápmi, there is a clear political mission to this. The reference is not only to the Sámi's lack of inherent allegiance to national identities, but also to the ways they have had to negotiate such identities historically. Self-referential humour, director Simma states,

> has been a way of survival for minorities. Us Sami have feared that others consider us as primitive people and that we do not have the same worth as them. The development of both politics and culture has allowed these perceptions to progress. The Sami have such a strong identity that they can withstand this type of irony and comedy. (Simma 1997)

The focus on the Sápmi allows the film to challenge the ways in which indigenous minorities are incorporated into the structures of dominant national cinema narratives. Yet, the film is also a production financed by several official Nordic sources and advertised as a Sámi film in some instances, and a specifically 'national Sámi' text in others. Appropriating such artifacts as a tool of multicultural politics can validate the construction of the dominant national self, film scholar Monika Siebert suggests in relation to *Atanarjuat*. According to her, authorities turn:

> to symbols of local indigeneity to assert their national distinctiveness. Respect for difference becomes the dominant logic of social and cultural relations. But this new historical period (and its) multiculturalism effectively demands that American Indians put their indigeneity on display. While it prohibits Euro-Americans from playing Indian . . . it requires that the Indians themselves play Indian to help legitimate the multiculturalist democracies they cannot help but inhabit. (Siebert 2006: 532)

Siebert's argument suggests the difficulties faced by indigenous cinema in working alongside dominant film cultures. *Atanarjuat* potentially avoids some of these difficulties by setting the majority of its narrative in a pre-colonial past. While evoking the contemporary moment, the emphasis on the past can also be interpreted as ignorance of the ongoing injustice perpetrated on Inuit communities and cultures. *Minister of State* works in a similar way, with most of the narrative focusing on historical events within an establishing frame of the present. It has much in common with *The Kautokeino Rebellion* in terms of adapting the conventions of the historical epic, which arguably works in relation to the 'dominant culture's representations of the indigenous which consequently incorporates the colonizer's idiom' (Siebert 2006: 537). While such a mode allows the indigenous a comparatively wider means of expressing their identity, they have to do this within the parameters provided by the colonisers, thereby effectively reinforcing a marginalisation of their rhetorical and ideological modes of self-representation. *Minister of State* exemplifies Siebert's notion of rhetorical sovereignty as operating 'only within the horizon of multiculturalism and its politics of recognition' (Siebert 2006: 541). Simma's film does not contain representational twists that shatter narrative othering, which is part of *Atanarjuat*'s climactic revelation of performing indigenosity. Indeed, in comparison to the politics of recognition in Simma's earlier short films, *Minister of State* ultimately amounts to what Siebert has criticised as 'the need to perform cultural difference in order to gain recognition in ways that precipitates official incorporation into the state and its capitalist economy' (Siebert 2006: 548).

DOCUMENTARY POLITICS AND VISUAL SOVEREIGNTY

Offset against such soft multiculturalist takes on Sámi politics, Simma's documentary *Give Us Our Skeletons!* is pronounced in its politics of sovereignty.

Before Gaup produced his epic take on the Kautokeino uprising of the Sámi against the Norwegian authorities in 1852, Simma's documentary focused on the racist attitudes and prejudice directed at the Sámi in a wider European context. The initial set-up of the film is a recreation of the Rebellion and the injustice meted out to the Sámi. The recreation is done in the form of animation showing the trial and subsequent beheading of the two leaders of the rebellion, as if to refuse the conventions of historicising Sámi difference – it is the rudimentary qualities of the animation that provide an exemplary case of visual sovereignty, a notion based entirely on its heightened difference to conventionalised norms.

The film is less interested in autoethnography than in producing an explicitly politicised realignment of historical narration. Accompanied by a driving and militant score, *Give Us Our Skeletons!* traces the history of eugenics and the division of the Sápmi along the hegemonic states of the Nordic countries. The main story follows Niila Somby, one of the great-grandchildren of the rebellion leaders, as he works to reclaim the skull of his ancestor from a laboratory in Oslo where it has been used in research to prove the impurity of the Sámi people. Intercutting between the Nazi eugenics programme and the activities of the hegemonic populations governing in the Sápmi, the film uncovers a history of shameful propaganda and oppression. Countering attacks on Sámi heritage and genetic composition, the film chronicles the efforts to retrieve the skull and focuses on the cultural and political work revealing this ignored history within Nordic countries.

This sort of participant documentary has much to offer Sámi cinema in that its politics of recognition foregrounds how any national project is necessarily premised on suppression of difference. But as with the other explicitly politicised takes on Sámi sovereignty, the reliance on the politics of otherness continues the perpetration of Sámi marginalisation as a cinema of the other. Establishing a politics of recognition tends to be problematic for historical narratives. Any assertion of sovereignty and difference becomes, instead, a part of the coopting of indigenous economic structures. Sámi come to participate in the dominant state's political structure, contributing to the 'enactment of a national cinematic project that embodies the nation as a federation of linguistically and culturally distinctive societies' (Siebert 2006: 547). But Simma's film complicates Siebert's criticism by providing agency to the Sámi, since it largely refuses the schematic narrative trajectories critiqued above. This is not at all a surprise considering Simma's history of providing alternative angles on the conventions of Sámi self-representation. Considering the powerful constitutive space in which these ideas must ultimately be vocalised, can it ultimately stand apart from the conventions of historiography?

The organising logic of multiculturalist politics suggests that only by demystifying the impression of a primal and more natural people can cultural sovereignty be envisioned. Perhaps the clearest case for illustrating successful negotiation of these positions comes forth in Simma's *The Legacy of the Tundra*. The documentary negotiates boundaries between the traditional iconography and contemporary existence of the Sámi. It shows us in realistic terms how the Sámi consciously use iconography as a form of cultural capital. In preparing for the 1994 Winter Olympics in Norway, a group of Sámi practise reindeer sleigh riding in their traditional cultural costumes. Meanwhile, the focus of the film is on the everyday lives of the protagonists, including relationships and communal activities. By showing us the ways in which their everyday lives differ from such exoticised iconography, the film employs a dual level of signification similar to *Atanarjuat*'s concluding performative dimension. Similarly, by showing the group performing at the Olympics, *The Legacy of The Tundra* emphasises that performances of traditional cultures may be necessary for retaining a sense of cultural self. But simultaneously, such conscious performances leave room for self-reflexive politics that maintain a critical understanding of the limiting connotations of such performances.

SELF-REFLEXIVE AUTOBIOGRAPHY AS RHETORICAL SOVEREIGNTY

Visual sovereignty is a dynamic way of conceptualising the multiple means indigenous film producers use to challenge established norms of domination. While films by non-Sámi directors such as Hannu Hyvönen take up the Sámi cause via land ethics and resource politics in *Last Joik in Samiland* (*Viimeinen joika Saamenmaalla*, 2009), Sámi directors such as Katja Gauriloff continue the politics of recognition engaged by Simma in films such as *Cry into the Wind* (*Huuto tuuleen*, 2007). Gauriloff's work comprises an intriguing and particularly dynamic companion piece to that of Simma since it is almost entirely devoid of the traditional imagery one associates with the Sámi. Most references to traditional customs are minimised as the film instead chronicles the everyday tasks of a local councillor and teenagers who find the geographical isolation restrictive. The focus is on the lives of 'ordinary' Sámi outside the realm of explicit politicising, yet politicisation is an unavoidable facet when discussing questions of one's ethnic identity.

For Gauriloff too, ethnicity and the representation of one's culture are key concerns. Yet by focusing on ordinary offices or backrooms, the politics are not so much about the travails of otherness, but about geographical marginalisation and the bureaucratic fallacies of the Finnish state. Gauriloff states that she has encountered criticism from the community for depicting it too negatively, but it is precisely this aspiration to show individuals not only as Sámi but also as individuals that matters to her (Gauriloff 2012). Tellingly, such a lack of the exotic is reflected in the production and distribution history of Simma's small-scale productions and Gauriloff's *Cry into the Wind*, which was produced on a very low budget.

> When we did *Cry into the Wind*, the Finnish Film Institute did not want to fund it as they had apparently done a Sami project a few years back. It was not for AVEK (The Centre for the Promotion of the Audiovisual Arts), even though they did give some script writing assistance. It was a risk for us to embark on the production without funds but National Geographic gave us a grant which we used to shoot the film. I think the topic was not interesting or sexy enough for FFF or AVEK. (Gauriloff 2012)

Gauriloff's statement illustrates the infrastructure limitations for Sámi film production in Finland. While it is important to try to garner domestic production support, often producers must seek funding from sources that support projects predicated on a sense of cultural difference or diversity – as arguably National Geographic did in this case. When funding is allocated to minority cinema, one must investigate the rationale carefully. Notions of 'permissive tolerance' can often be detected in policy decisions, exemplified by Finland's Ministry for Education and Culture establishing a programme in 2012 designed for the revitalisation of Sámi language:

> In 2010, The Education and Culture Ministry of Finland assessed the need to bring more attention to make the status of the Sami more equal within the Finnish state. The information shows that the number of Sami has risen to 10,000, but people speaking the language have decreased. According to the Constitution, it is the right of indigenous minorities to uphold and develop their native language. Consequently it is the role of the state to facilitate this especially as the role of the language is minor and faces the problem of migration away from the Sápmi. (Opetus- ja Kulttuuriministeriö 2012)

The statement is revealing in its 'handout politics' practised by the institutions of dominant nations, but also in emphasising the importance of indigenous rights. In this conundrum, the Sámi are granted a special status as a threatened species of sorts. It is also clear that their cultural expression and activity require support from 'above' to facilitate ongoing development. How are we to approach such cultural support from a critical perspective while acknowledging its important function for cultural production? Is this yet another case of the problematic politics of recognition, a part of the multiculturalist project of assimilation, concerning a clear 'allowance' of minorities to express themselves in their own language? In practice, it would not be difficult to consider the funds a part of contemporary Finland's consolidation of liberal credentials, yet such funding and policy are necessary to increase the visibility of Sámi productions. Without these, it would be very difficult to consolidate any film production in Northern Finland.

Elina Kivihalme, the commissioner in charge of the establishment of the Finnish Film Foundation Sámi fund, makes it clear that this is a one-off funding initiative, not any sort of permanent mechanism, and yet that it is vitally important that the Culture and Education Ministry improve the Sámi industry:

> This is about development money as well as infrastructure for local production companies to boost their activities. The Sami have a training centre for vocational education in media production but when they come to Helsinki they need to compete with everyone else. (Kivihalme 2013)

She is also highly aware of the contentious nature of such funds, which link to the more problematic aspects of the politics of recognition. According to her, the oral tradition in particular poses clear difficulties as the traditional, often cyclic, modes of storytelling are difficult to transcribe into competitive scripts. Yet, this level of difference makes the films interesting and relevant as part of the multicultural mosaic, while also categorising them as too different to be able to compete with other productions on an equal scale. Kivihalme emphasises that outside this specially funded project, Sámi producers do not occupy a special status in attaining funding but have to offer quality projects that meet the FFF standards. For her, the notion of 'positive discrimination' remains a substantial concern and any types of Sámi funds are considered earmarked funds that may be given to other groups in other years, possibly to increase the representation of children or youth in Finnish cinema. There are no easy answers to these institutional and infrastructural problems, since these are forms of politics that indicate a system of inequality and a history of problematic exploitative relationships. The films attempt to address these problems by evoking the very same history that enforces the dynamics of inequality.

CONCLUSION

Considering the interminable balancing act of Sámi cinema as both a minority practice and one that seeks to avoid such reductive labels, it is not surprising that discussion of it seems to go in circles. As the scope moves from the local communities to the level of nations, from a sense of universal indigeneity to a more transnational understanding of the Sápmi, it is clear that these are complexities that Sámi cinema shares with other minor cinemas, confronted as they are by the inclusivist strategies of their multicultural democracies as well as the inevitable othering of sovereignty. On one hand, we have a range of different exposures of the Sámi lifestyle, with some of them utilising Sámi images explicitly for more hegemonic politics, and some for more egalitarian goals. What these have in common is the notion of appropriation as cultural or political capital to emphasise the liberal credentials of the speaker in question. On the other hand, they foreground the marginal critiques often produced by the Sámi themselves. Yet, these do not remain problem-free as they have to use exoticised imagery or antagonistic politics to make themselves understandable in the wider context in which they operate.

These two rhetorical positions are indicative of the wider politics of contestation in producing indigenous cinema. Certainly, from the perspective of the indigenous people, more resources and increased recognition are certainly beneficial. And realistically, the only way to achieve this is to adopt some of the conventions of the dominant cultural sphere, mirroring Gayatri Chakravorty Spivak's strategic essentialism (Spivak 1988). This indicates an approach that seeks to play out the key constituents of Sámi identity when they are necessary, but also with the sort of critical distance that enables reflexivity and a sense of critical rethinking. In some ways, the politics of many of the films discussed acts as the type of rewriting of national narratives that another well-known theorist of the postcolonial, Homi Bhabha (1994), uncovers in many works by immigrant writers. The difference here is that the Sámi do not so much unravel dominant national narratives as pose, at the very least, parallel narratives, or even fundamental objections to most of the practices pertaining to such narratives.

The Sámi cinema production infrastructure in Finland both supports and challenges rhetorical sovereignty, a fact which filters into the exhibition of these films. Venues such as the 'indigenous cinema' festivals Skábmagovat and the Arctic Film Festival devote their catalogues to this impression of otherness. Put simply, when many of these films are screened in such egalitarian venues, they are shown as Sámi or indigenous films, a label that creates normative assumptions about content and their expected level of participation in festival discussion. Yet such festivals would not exist without recourse to both strategic essentialism and a chance of rewriting historical narratives, supported as they are by funds from cultural authorities such as the Ministry of Education and Culture in Finland. In a somewhat similar way, when the 2012 Sámi film funds were announced by FFF, many of the usual suspects received funding, including Simma and Gauriloff, for projects focusing on representing Sámi politics. Through this, it seems as if Sámi cinema, at least in Finland, has been able to gain increased support and presence, but infrastructurally, many of the restrictions, not least on the level of its official state perception, remain.

BIBLIOGRAPHY

Bhabha, H. (1994), *The Location of Culture*, London: Routledge.
Iversen, G. (2005), 'Learning from genre: genre cycles in modern Norwegian cinema', in Andrew Nestingen and Trevor Elkington (eds), *Transnational Cinema in a Global North*, Detroit: Wayne State University Press, 261–78.
Opetus- ja Kulttuuriministeriö (2012), 'Toimenpideohjelma Saamen kielen elvyttämiseksi', http://www.minedu.fi/export/sites/default/OPM/Julkaisut/2012/liitteet/tr07.pdf?lang=en (accessed 20 May 2013).
Nestingen, A. (2008), *Criminal Scandinavia: Fiction, Film and Social Change*, Seattle: University of Washington Press.
Ragazzi, R. (2008), 'Toward pedagogical awareness: teaching cine-ethnography', *Visual Anthropology Review*, vol. 23, issue 1, 1–15.
Raheja, M. (2007), 'Reading Nanook's smile: visual sovereignty, indigenous revisions of ethnography, and *Atanarjuat (The Fast Runner)*', *American Quarterly*, 59: 4, December 2007, 1159–85.
Seurujärvi-Kari, I. P. Halinen and R. Pulkkinen (eds) (2011), *Saamelaistutkimus tänään*, Helsinki: SKS.
Siebert, M. (2006), '*Atanarjuat* and the ideological work of contemporary indigenous filmmaking', *Public Culture*, 18: 3, 2006, 531–50.
Simma, P. A. (1997), 'Sagojogan ministeri', *Kaleva*, 8 March 1997.
Spivak, G. C. (1988), 'Subaltern studies: deconstructing historiography', in Ranajit Guha and Gayatri Chakravorty Spivak (eds), *Selected Subaltern Studies*, Oxford: Oxford University Press, 2–25.
Taylor, C. (2011), 'Politics of recognition', in Charles Taylor (ed.), *Multiculturalism*, Princeton: Princeton University Press, 25–73.

INTERVIEWS CONDUCTED BY THE AUTHOR

Katja Gauriloff (Helsinki, 19 March 2012).
Elina Kivihalme (Helsinki, 20 February 2013).

3. FROZEN IN FILM: ALASKA ESKIMOS IN THE MOVIES

Ann Fienup-Riordan

THE ESKIMO IMAGE IN TWENTIETH-CENTURY CINEMA

In 1995 I published a book entitled *Freeze Frame: Alaska Eskimos in the Movies*. By that time, I had already worked as a cultural anthropologist for more than twenty years among Yup'ik people in southwest Alaska. I was motivated by a keen interest in the evolution of the Eskimo stereotype, which failed in so many ways to fit the people I had come to know. Eskimos, I had learned as a child, were happy smiling folk, living peacefully in igloos in small, nuclear family groups including noble hunter, wife and child. Their environment was harsh and unforgiving, requiring constant efforts to survive. My Yup'ik friends, in contrast, lived in a rich environment where food was abundant every season of the year. Moreover, they had a complicated and rich history. In winter they gathered in large settlements made up of homes of sod, not snow, for women and small children, as well as one or more *qasgit* (semi-subterranean communal men's houses) where up to thirty men and boys over the age of five worked, ate and slept together. Far from peaceful, they engaged in bloody bow-and-arrow wars of revenge and retaliation into the early 1800s, until epidemic diseases left their traditional regional groups diminished in size and strength.

The Eskimo stereotype, in fact, originated in the Canadian Arctic, familiar to Euro-Americans a century before the first non-Natives ever set foot in Alaska. When I began work in southwest Alaska in 1974, Yup'ik people and their history and traditions were poorly understood by non-Natives. Small wonder the gap between image and reality was so large. Fired by this misfit,

I conceived the idea of a book on the Eskimo image with chapters covering children's stories, fiction, scholarly and exploration literature, and the movies. I started with this last chapter, and *Freeze Frame* was the result. For the book's cover, the designer chose a photo of Iñupiaq actor Ray Mala, Alaska's first and still most prolific Hollywood star, rubbing noses with his smiling co-star, demonstrating the famous 'Eskimo kiss'. An Athabascan friend once confided to me how offended he was by this cover photograph but that, when he read my book, he loved it. A sobering compliment indeed.

I used the term 'Eskimo' throughout *Freeze Frame*'s discussions of stereotyping, and I would do the same today. As I explained then, the name 'Esquimau' (Eskimo) was first used in Europe in the early seventeenth century and was long considered to have derived from the Algonquin word *esquimew* (eater of raw meat). Eskimo is now thought to come from the Montagnais word translating as 'those who speak the language of a foreign land' or 'those who wait a long time [at seal butchering holes]' (Mailhot 1978, in Collignon 2006: 5). Beginning with land claims and indigenous rights movements generally in the 1960s and 1970s, the term Eskimo came under attack. In 1977, participants of the first Inuit Circumpolar Conference (including representatives of Alaska, Canada and Greenland) voted to replace Eskimo with Inuit (singular Inuk), which Canada did in 1978.

Inuit is, however, a regional name for residents of the Canadian North and does not fit well in Alaska, which is the homeland for Iñupiaq, Siberian Yupik, Central Yup'ik, Cup'ik, Cup'ig, Alutiiq and Sugpiaq peoples. During the 1970s struggle over land claims in Alaska, these disparate groups often referred to themselves jointly as Eskimo, with bumper stickers and posters proclaiming 'Eskimo power' and 'I'm an Eskimo and proud of it'. Over the years, use of the term Eskimo has declined in favor of regional self-designations such as Yup'ik, Iñupiaq, and Alutiiq (all translating as 'real or genuine people'). Yet Alaska Native men and women still use the term Eskimo not only among themselves but also as part of their self-representation without the pejorative connotations the term has acquired in Canada and Greenland. Following a sobering experience in 2010 with funders who were convinced that the term Eskimo had no place in the postmodern world, I was on the alert for the 'E' word. During a trip to the village of Emmonak in January 2012, Yup'ik friends invited me to eat Eskimo ice cream and to come with them to watch Eskimo dancing. Travelling back to Anchorage, I met a young Yup'ik friend with new, round wire-rim glasses who asked me who I thought he looked like. His answer: Eskimo Harry Potter!

ESKIMOS IN HOLLYWOOD

Freeze Frame took a look at the development of the Eskimo image through nearly a century of film, from the pioneering documentaries of missionaries and Arctic explorers to Eskimo Pie commercials in the 1990s. Some of these works were serious attempts to depict a culture; others were unabashed entertainment, featuring papier-maché igloos and zebra-skin parkas. Even filmmakers who sought authenticity were likely to build igloos in villages that had never seen one and to hire non-Native actors to portray the Alaska Native principals.

A first principle of *Freeze Frame* was the marked contrast between the depiction of American Indians and Eskimos in the movies. The early days of film showcased hundreds of Indians in a negative light, most often opposed to civilisation. In contrast the few Eskimos in early films revealed the foundations of civilisation. Robert Flaherty's groundbreaking film *Nanook of the North* (USA, 1922) solidified the popular impression of Eskimos and set the precedent for dozens of movies to follow. Arguably the most famous Eskimo movie ever made, this faked documentary was judged realistic by millions of viewers. In fact, *Nanook* was staged to present a pure past in which guns, phonographs and the diseases that plagued Canadian Inuit in the early 1900s were equally nonexistent. For Nanook, the noble savage, the harsh environment was his enemy. While contrived in many respects, Flaherty's film was innovative in the story it told about Nanook and his wife as real people, not faceless Others. A romantic primitivist, Flaherty emphasised Nanook's similarity to us, not his difference. All other Eskimos in the movies refer back to his enduring image.

During the years Flaherty was filming in the Canadian North, a young man named Ray Wise was growing up in northwest Alaska. What Nanook became for the Canadian North, Ray Wise (later known as Ray Mala) became for Alaska Eskimos in the movies. His story is worth telling. Born in 1906 of an Iñupiaq mother and Jewish gold miner in Candle, Alaska, Ray was raised traditionally by his grandmother speaking the Iñupiaq language. Following his father's return to the Lower Forty-Eight and his mother's death, and in the wake of the influenza epidemic of 1918–19 that decimated his extended family, Ray walked 100 miles to Nome to find work. The early 1920s saw filmmakers beginning to penetrate the Alaska North, and Ray's manual dexterity combined with a hardy constitution landed him a job with Captain Kleinschmidt, who used him as a cameraman while filming on Wrangel Island. Pathé cameraman Merle LeVoy remembered the young man, helping him land a job as an assistant cameraman at Fox Studios in Hollywood. While working for Fox, Ray wrote a film script called *Modern Eskimos*. Though never produced, this script represents the first attempt by anyone, Native or non-Native, to depict contemporary Iñupiaq people on film.

After a year in Hollywood, Ray returned to Alaska with Ewing Scott in 1926 to film *Igloo* (USA, 1932), which, like *Nanook*, pitted primitive man against a harsh, unforgiving environment. Ray acted the part of the noble hunter, Chee-ak. The film depicted a pure past complete with igloos and exotic

61

customs, including both infanticide and senilicide (found nowhere in Alaska). Arctic explorer Vilhajalmur Stefansson (author of *The Friendly Arctic*) roundly criticised these liberties, in contrast to film-industry advertising that *Igloo* presented 'real life'. In fact, *Igloo* presented the stereotypic Eskimo without regional specificity. Like *Nanook*, the film was viewed by thousands, while Stefansson's scholarly rebuttal reached relatively few readers. *Igloo*'s goal was entertainment, not ethnographic accuracy. Following the release of *Igloo* in 1932, the Universal Studios press machine dubbed Ray the 'Eskimo Clark Gable'. To this day, he is Alaska's only truly homegrown Native Hollywood star.

While *Igloo* marked Ray Wise's debut, his place in history is defined by his role as leading man in the 1933 Metro-Goldwyn-Mayer film *Eskimo*. Directed by W. S. Van Dyke in the great tradition of expeditionary movies, *Eskimo* was the first full-length major studio picture ever shot in Alaska. Like *Atunarjuat: The Fast Runner* (Zacharias Kunuk, Canada, 2001) seventy years later, *Eskimo* was remarkable in that it was filmed in the Iñupiaq language using English subtitles. Based on the novel *Storfanger (Eskimo*, 1927; trans. 1931) by Danish explorer Peter Freuchen, the story was – once again – about the Canadian North. Freuchen came to Alaska for the filming, working on the set building igloos and helping to create the Eskimo image Van Dyke required.

The storyline of *Eskimo* pitted the pure primitive – the hunter Mala – against corrupt civilisation, in the form of a duplicitous whaling captain (played to perfection by Freuchen himself). Ironically, Ray was originally rejected for the role because of his 'impure' pedigree in favour of the Iñupiaq hunter Robert Mayo of Wales, Alaska. As filming got under way, Mayo resented the non-Native camera crew's attentions toward his wife and returned with his family to Wales unannounced. Van Dyke wired MGM, and Ray was on the next boat north.

During the ten months Van Dyke filmed in Alaska, the Teller reindeer station was transformed into Camp Hollywood, complete with caviar and a four-star chef. Altogether, forty-two crew members, as well as three Asian actresses (called 'Oriental' in the 1930s) playing the parts of Mala's sweethearts and wives, joined local Iñupiat in a project that would cost $1.5 million (a huge budget at that time). The loss of Mayo was not Van Dyke's only gaffe. Seeking primitive Eskimos, swathed in furs and eating blubber, he paid them too well. Many left midway through the shoot as their earnings provided them ample means to satisfy their finite needs, in contrast to their non-Native guests whose wants seemed infinite in comparison to what they viewed as limited means.

Eskimo opened in New York in 1933, with Ray in attendance but the Asian actresses safely hidden under wraps. Advertisements invoked its authenticity, and the film won the first Academy Award for directing. Audiences empathised with the struggle of the mighty hunter and were fascinated by the film's exotic customs, including wife-sharing. Like *Nanook, Eskimo* was an instant classic, pitting the pure, noble Eskimo against corrupt civilisation. In fact, Mala's natural nobility was presented as superior to civilisation. Clothed in the apparent realism of documentary, with Mala and other Iñupiaq actors speaking their language, *Eskimo* was a powerful representation of the North not to be matched for decades.

Following the release of *Eskimo*, Ray Wise became a matinee idol, changing his name to Ray Mala. Over the next decade he acted in a series of South Seas movies, playing the part of the quintessential Native. After 1940, he returned to work as a cameraman, gaining the respect of his co-workers and actors alike for his fine eye and steady hand. In 1951, he re-entered the film industry with the Cold War movie *Red Snow* (Boris L. Petrof, USA, 1952) a story about the Alaska Territorial Guard (ATG) fighting invading Soviets. The Eskimo image remained alive and well in *Red Snow*, complete with nose-rubbing and the ATG living in igloos. Ray Mala died in 1952 aged forty-four. He remains Alaska's most prolific film star, Iñupiaq or otherwise.

ALASKA MOVIEMAKING IN THE TWENTY-FIRST CENTURY

One of the twentieth century's last films shot in Alaska was Steven Seagal's *On Deadly Ground* (USA, 1994). This grade-B movie employed a handful of Yup'ik men and women alongside the ubiquitous Asian actresses still deemed necessary to play the part of sultry Eskimo maidens, while filmed at an Eskimo village Seagal had constructed at the foot of Worthington Glacier near Valdez (300 miles south of the Arctic Circle). Exceptional filmmaking did take place in Alaska during the 1970s and 1980s, however. Lenny Kamerling and Sarah Elder produced a series of brilliant documentaries, most notably *Drums of Winter* (*Uksuum Cauyai*, USA, 1989), which won nine international awards and was added to the National Film Registry in 2006. The oil boom of the 1980s also helped fund important local programming, such as the dozens of films produced collaboratively by the Yup'ik and non-Yup'ik employees at Bethel's KYUK-TV. The combined work of Kamerling and Elder and KYUK-TV provided the hopeful ending to my *Freeze Frame* narrative.

I put down my pen in 1994. The question here is, have things changed in the twenty years since I wrote *Freeze Frame* or have they remained the same? The short answer: a little of both. The past two decades have seen a media revolution. The celluloid copy of *Eskimo* that I viewed in 1990 was shredded by Alaska Pictures Inc. the next year when they walked away from renting reels of film and turned to video. Public telecommunications across Alaska have also been transformed. Practically every Yup'ik person I know has a cell phone, with ringtones ranging from goose calls to singing grandchildren. Yup'ik and Iñupiaq people are taking their own pictures and making their own movies of local events, sharing them widely on Facebook and YouTube. Google 'Yup'ik', for example, and you get a wealth of moving images, including

'Yupik Elders' (a humorous look at elder women on a visit to Washington, DC) and the surprise YouTube Christmas hit, 'Hallelujah' (www.youtube. com/watch?v=LyviyF-N23A).The Internet has also exposed Alaska viewers to the rich movie imagery of the Canadian North, including the work of Isuma.

What of recent local production in Alaska? While KYUK-TV remains an active station, the decline in oil revenue as well as cuts in federal and state funding beginning in the 1990s have limited its ability to continue to produce the documentaries that were its trademark in the 1980s. The television side of KYUK took the brunt, giving up its local signal in 1995 to rebroadcast Alaska One, a signal from the Fairbanks public television station, KUAC-TV. Also in 1995 the station chose to operate ARCS-TV, the statewide satellite television service. Its goal was to preserve the station's television production facilities, and KYUK continues to document local Yup'ik history and culture, though at a much slower pace than previously (McBride 1997). What it does produce, however, continues to be outstanding (see, for example, Mike Martz's short video *The Way We Genuinely Live* (*Yuungnaqpiallerput*, USA, 2007]).

Over the past decade, Alaska has actively pursued moviemakers like never before. In 2008, the state of Alaska passed a film incentive programme allowing eligible movies and television shows that spend at least $100,000 in Alaska to be reimbursed for up to a third of their budgets. The two biggest productions to take advantage of this scheme were *Big Miracle* (Ken Kwapis, USA, 2012), which tells the story of the rescue of three gray whales caught in the ice off the coast of Barrow, and *The Frozen Ground* (Scott Walker, USA, 2013), a thriller based on the arrest of Alaska serial killer Robert Hansen in 1980s Anchorage. Reimbursements covered by the incentive programme include star and crew salaries, transportation, set construction and wardrobe, editing, and other production costs, food and hotels. These are among the most generous public subsidies in the nation, and movie industry officials affirm they are a huge draw. Along with the subsidy, film professionals note the need for infrastructure, such as a studio and sound stage for indoor shoots in Alaska, if the state really intends to attract the film industry. These incentives brought millions of dollars in revenue to Alaska's small businesses and created hundreds of new jobs for a few years (Hopkins 2013).

Since 2011, however, the Alaska film industry has experienced a lull. Dreams are not dead of transforming Alaska into 'Hollywood North' (a nickname currently held by Vancouver, Canada, a city that has built up its film infrastructure and pulls in over a billion dollars a year), though the industry spent much of 2012 and 2013 in hibernation. No new feature films are in production, and no new projects involve Alaska Natives. Of the projects approved by the state for an Alaska film subsidy, nine are reality TV shows, including *Coast Guard Alaska, Yukon Men,* and *Swamp People,* among others, following on the heels of *Sarah Palin's Alaska* (TLC, 2010). Indeed, among the many interesting developments in moviemaking in Alaska was the entry of an Alaska Native corporation, NANA Development Corporation. It invested 'several million' in 2010 to purchase a 33 percent ownership of Evergreen Films, a high-tech Alaska production house with studios in Anchorage and Hollywood. Helvi Sandvik, president of NANA Development, noted that this is an exciting new field for the corporation and shareholders alike (Barbar 2010). With NANA's backing, Evergreen Films has talked to Anchorage officials about a possible public-private partnership to build needed infrastructure, including a sound stage. Not content to act in movies, Alaska Natives have entered the production process.

BIG MIRACLE

Among the handful of big-budget films made in Alaska in the past two decades, the most noteworthy – and the only one to involve Alaska's First People – was *Big Miracle*. Not as groundbreaking as *Eskimo*, *Big Miracle* stands out as the first major feature film made in Alaska to give a serious look at Alaska Natives in the late twentieth century. As Anchorage reporter Richard Mauer (2012a) aptly noted, once Iñupiaq whaler Roy Ahmaogak decided to report three gray whales trapped in the ice near Barrow rather than leave them to their fate, it was probably inevitable that their story wind up in Hollywood. Twenty-three years later it did.

Originally titled *Whales on Ice*, then *Everybody Loves Whales*, Universal Pictures' *Big Miracle* is not only the first major movie in decades filmed entirely in Alaska but also the first high-profile production subsidised by the state's film incentive programme (without which the film's production would probably have gone to Canada). As history shows, stories about Alaska and Alaska Natives have long attracted filmmakers and moviegoers, but the vast majority have been filmed outside Alaska. Recent thrillers *30 Days of Night* (David Slade, USA, 2007) and *The Fourth Kind* (Olatunde Osunsanmi, USA, 2009) were set in Barrow and Nome but filmed in New Zealand and Bulgaria, respectively. More than issues of authenticity, the economic benefits of filming in Alaska drive the state's efforts to entice filmmakers north. Waving a reel at a 2010 meeting of Anchorage businesses, Carolyne Robinson, owner of the Anchorage-based film company Sproketheads LLC, told her audience, 'Think of this can of movie film as a barrel of oil. We can build a new kind of pipeline'. Film industry professionals in Alaska remain hopeful that more movies – and money – will come down that pipeline soon (Barbar 2010).

Big Miracle is based on Tom Rose's *Freeing the Whales: How the Media Created the World's Biggest Non-Event* (1989), and it is a fictionalised retelling of the 1988 gray whale rescue near Barrow that received huge international attention at the time. The film is a feel-good PG-rated family movie, with stock Alaska characters – wise Iñupiaq hunters, environmentalist, and greedy oil man – balancing its sentimental side with a sizable dose of cynicism and humour.

Filming *Big Miracle* spanned sixty days and more than twenty locations in Alaska – most of them in Anchorage – in fall 2010. Alaskans enjoyed both the process and the finished product because of local people and places featured in the film, including the Hotel Captain Cook and the iconic Anchorage eatery, 'Mexico in Alaska'. The film also included our former KTUU reporter Megan Baldino, as well as a cameo clip of the 1980s-era, big-hair Sarah Palin as a KTUU-Channel 2 aspiring sportscaster. Kid actor Ahmaogak Sweeney of Anchorage had a major role as the son of a Barrow whaling captain, and Ted Danson's character, J. W. McGraw, was inspired by real-life oil company executive Bill Allen (now in federal prison for taking bribes).

The leading Iñupiaq role was landed by Cup'ik dance leader and educator John Pingayak of Chevak. John played the Iñupiaq elder whaling captain, Malialuk or Malik for short, who sees the public relations value in aiding, rather than eating, the three whales. John moved to Anchorage for filming, and he described a positive experience there. His biggest challenge was learning his Iñupiaq lines, which he did with the help of an Iñupiaq coach and fellow cast members. John also enjoyed the whales, which were puppets made by Australians and controlled from a box, set up in an area filled with man-made ice near the Anchorage port, where a mini-Barrow had sprung up next to the boat harbour: 'They really looked real coming up and going underwater' (Lincoln 2011).

Along with John's character Malik, *Big Miracle* showed the unlikely range of people involved in the 1988 whale rescue who all found themselves on the same side, including Greenpeace, Veco's Bill Allen and the oil giant Arco, Ted Stevens, the Soviets, the US military, a chainsaw distributor, a couple of Minnesota ice fishermen, and most important, a brigade of Iñupiaq whalers who normally hunted whales for subsistence. How this working relationship was forged is the heart of the film. Certainly everyone had their own agenda. Greenpeace activist Rachael (played by Drew Barrymore) blackmails politicians to help the cause, or else she'll go public and accuse the Reagan administration of not caring. Adam (John Krasinski) is the local TV reporter in Barrow who breaks the story, then uses his ensuing fame to land a job at the networks. Ted Danson plays an oil-industry tycoon who offers boats and helicopters to the operation free of charge because, as he says, money can't buy that kind of PR. As presidential aide, Vinessa Shaw advises the government to get involved because Reagan's second term is coming to an end and a successful whale rescue, with the whole world watching, could do wonders for George Bush's presidential aspirations. Even the Soviets join in, using their icebreaker in the final scenes, as the Cold War isn't really going their way (Mauer 2012b).

The Iñupiaq hunters, too, have something to gain: increased respect and understanding for their way of life. As public interest in the whales mounts, the Barrow whaling captains meet to decide what to do. Originally considering killing the animals for food (though bowheads, not grays, are their normal targets), Malik points out the merits of working to save them by cutting breathing holes using ice picks, and eventually chain saws. Following his suggestion, the men put the teamwork of hunting whales into saving them, cutting a line of some fifty breathing holes extended two miles toward an ice ridge and open water beyond. These actions showed the world not only the compassionate but the resourceful side of Iñupiaq people. *Big Miracle* premiered in Washington, DC, in January 2012, and was out on DVD and Blu-ray in June of the same year. Although critically well received, it was not a box-office success. Costing around $30 million to produce, the film made only $25 million worldwide. By comparison, *The Grey* (Joe Carnahan, US, 2011), a wolf-attack movie set in Alaska but filmed in Canada, hit theatres at about the same time and made more than $30 million domestically (Hopkins 2012a).

Although *Big Miracle* was not a commercial success, Alaskans remained big fans. At the Anchorage opening, Yup'ik actor John Chase of Bethel agreed with John Pingayak that it was good to see Alaska Natives on the big screen (Hopkins 2012b). Other Alaskans also commented. Rebecca Noblin, Director of the Alaska Center for Biodiversity, applauded the film's treatment of Iñupiaq efforts to join the modern world while remaining true to their traditions. She noted the empathy that united the Iñupiat, scientists, oil-industry folks and environmentalists: 'If we can all come together to save a couple of gray whales, surely we have it in us to tackle bigger problems'. Oil company spokesman Curtis Smith agreed. As a high-school student in Soldotna in 1988, he remembered the event as breaking news: 'The story of two whales being freed from the Arctic ice gave me a new appreciation for Alaska's special place in the world . . . Real-life problems are solved when everyone pitches in and that's certainly true in Alaska . . . Sometimes, that means asking for help. Loudly'. Smith added that while promoters gave Drew Barrymore top billing, Alaskans, especially Ahmaogak Sweeney, stole the show (*Anchorage Daily News* 2012).

Director Ken Kwapis said it was a challenging shoot, with cold weather, three large robotic whales that did not always work, and a large ensemble cast, including people who had not been in a movie before. Producer Michael Sugar noted the filmmakers' low expectations coming into Alaska, given the lack of experience among Alaskans working with movie crews. In the end, though, they were happy with how it worked out: 'We were so embraced' (Cockerham 2012). I saw the film on the big screen with eighty-two-year-old Lizzie Chimiugak, who had made the gut parkas for Steven Seagal and who had never been to a movie theatre. Like Sugar, my expectations had been low but I found myself smiling and chuckling throughout. Lizzie did too, commenting in Yup'ik as we left the theatre, 'I'm glad I saw this movie before I died'.

THE POWER OF VOICE: ALASKA NATIVES MAKING MOVIES

With the release of *Big Miracle*, we see one dream of Ray Mala's coming true: a filmic presentation of contemporary Iñupiaq life, not as a stand-alone drama but in its global connectedness and complexity. What is more, in an increasing number of locally made films, Alaska Natives are taking charge. Although Alaska can boast nothing as vibrant and prolific as Isuma in the Canadian North, it can boast a growing number of films produced, directed and acted in by Alaska's First People.

Many of the men and women making films in Alaska today saw their first movies in local village community halls when they were young. Theresa John, a Yup'ik scholar and dancer from Nelson Island, recalled how the bell rang for two reasons in her hometown: church and the movies. Watching Westerns as a child, she always identified with the cowboys, not the Indians. Much of traditional Yup'ik culture was suppressed by the local Catholic Church when she was born in 1956. Her father, Paul John, tells the story of how dancing was revived in her village in the 1960s. The nearby community of Tununak had invited their neighbours to their community hall, where they surprised them with the showing of a movie. Returning home, the people of Nightmute were downcast. How could they repay such an extravagant gift? One elder spoke, reminding them of their dance tradition, which they revived as a return gift.

In 2005 media specialist Steve Alvarez of the Alaska Native Heritage Center in Anchorage founded the Indigenous World Film Festival as a showcase both for films Alaska Natives are making today and for films made by indigenous people worldwide. Alvarez was inspired when he attended a film festival at the newly opened National Museum of the American Indian and thought, 'Wow, this is kind of cool, I think we can do this here. I thought the first year, maybe we'd have seventy-five or eighty people come, but before I knew it we had 1,200 people' (Judd 2009). Held annually in Anchorage since 2005, the festival's goal is not only to give voice to indigenous filmmakers but also to inform non-Natives so they can better understand their Native neighbours. It features films directed or produced by indigenous people, with indigenous talent or an indigenous theme. All films have something to do with Native people: Alaska Natives, Canadians, Lower Forty-Eight Native Americans, New Zealanders and Australians. Over the years, the festival has provided a perfect venue for a variety of small, independent Alaska productions, including the world premiere of *Growing up Native in Alaska* (2009), produced by Alaska filmmakers Jonathan Stanton and Alvarez and based on a book of the same name by Anchorage author A. J. McClanahan. Another local production was *Finding*

Their Own Dance: Reawakening the Alaska Alutiiq Arts (Ellen Van't Hof, USA, 2009), a film describing how Russian and American ownership of Alaska took different approaches to repressing Alutiiq culture on Kodiak Island.

The festival first screened two recent remarkable films celebrating the growing number of Native pilots in southwest Alaska. The first, *Yuut Yaqungviat* (USA, 2009), was a 26-minute movie by Jacqueline Cleveland of Quinhagak documenting the Bethel flight school of the same name. The 27-minute documentary *Unraveling the Wind* (USA, 2009) explores the same theme. The film was directed by Deborah Schildt, who was drafted into the project by three Wasilla-based women who had become fascinated by stories of Native Bush pilots, including Alice Alstrom-Henderson, whose family has been a pioneering force in Alaska aviation ever since twin brothers Frank and William Alstrom took to the air in the 1920s. The Alstrom brothers flew out of the lower Yukon village of Alakanuk, where a second and third generation have become Yup'ik pilots (Judd 2009).

The festival highlight in 2009 was *On the Ice* (*Sikumi*, USA, 2009), a Sundance award-winning dramatic short by Andrew Okpeaha Maclean of Barrow. The film features an Iñupiaq cast and has continued to rake in world-wide attention and major awards, including the Crystal Bear Award for best debut film at the 2011 Berlin International Film Festival. Another 2009 local production by Barrow resident Rachel Naninaaq Edwardson was *History of the Iñupiat: The Voice of Our Spirit*. This 50-minute film was funded and produced by the North Slope Borough School District. It foregrounds the effects of English-only policies of Bureau of Indian Affairs (BIA) schools after 1914, pushing the Iñupiat in the direction of assimilation. The film's target audience is contemporary young people, showing them the strength and beauty of their language and culture. At the same time, the film provides historical context and raises questions to stimulate young Native leaders, asking whether a truly Iñupiaq educational system is possible without the use of the Iñupiaq language (rarely spoken in northwest Alaska by those under the age of forty). Yes, today the Iñupiat enjoy increasing local control, but, the film queries: 'are we exercising political control over a system that perpetuates education in terms of white, urban culture?' The film resonated with many Alaska Native viewers at the festival, who recalled being prohibited from speaking their own language.

Along with language loss and issues of local control, Alaska Natives contend with a host of serious social problems today. In 2011, Matt Gilbert of Arctic Village published an opinion piece aimed at suicidal youth in the Bethel newspaper, *The Tundra Drums*, titled 'Make your own Native Hollywood in the village'. In his letter, Gilbert contrasts the Hollywood movies Alaska Native youth see on TV and in theatres, depicting the life or look they 'should have', with the reality of contemporary village life. Hollywood is fake, he says. He admonishes them to do what Rachel Edwardson does:

Make movies in your village and make Natives cool . . . Your Yup'ik, Inupiaq, and Athabascan ancestors left you lands that are yours, and that is something no other indigenous teen on this planet has, and you want to shoot yourself? . . .

Build a fancy two-story house, get Internet, make movies, become a correspondent journalist for Alaska Newspapers in your village . . . take photographs and send them out . . . record your elders' oral stories and find grants or do it for free like I did. (Gilbert 2011)

One recent independent film seems to be doing exactly what Gilbert advises. In 2011, Bristol Bay Native Corporation (BBNC) produced the wonderful *Day in Our Bay: Voices and Views from Bristol Bay*. BBNC invited its shareholders to share their voices, views and values through personal videos showing people, places and cultural practices most important to them. All footage was shot with individual iPhones on one day, 15 October 2011. Sixty-two entries were submitted from as far south as Chignik Lake, west to Togiak, and east to Kokhanok as shareholders of all ages took part in this innovative competition. Bristol Creative Service and Affinity Films, Inc. subsequently reviewed more than 100 hours of video, compiling the entries into a short film that not only provides a unique opportunity for Yup'ik people to make their voices heard but for non-Natives like me to listen to what they have to say. As BBNC president and CEO Jason Metrokin noted: 'We are a region that is facing the potential of monumental change, so it's never been more important for Alaskans and people worldwide to get a better understanding of who we are'.

Twenty years after I wrote my book *Freeze Frame*, Alaska is in the news and on the forefront of change – global warming, mining development, shipping through an ice-free Arctic – in ways unimaginable two decades ago. Yes, some of the same Eskimo stereotypes remain. This is all the more reason to take notice of and be thankful for the increasing number of talented Alaska Native men and women who are taking cameras in hand, willing and able to share their important and unique stories.

BIBLIOGRAPHY

Anchorage Daily News (2012), 'Trio of Alaskans offer their thoughts on "Big Miracle"', *Anchorage Daily News*, 30 January, A10.
Barbar, V. (2010), 'NANA invests in entertainment', *The Tundra Drums* (Bethel, AK), 23 September, 14.
Cockerham, S. (2012), 'Movie, filmed entirely in Alaska, makes a splash in DC', *Anchorage Daily New*, 26 January, A1, A10.
Collignon, B. (2006), *Knowing Places: The Inuinnait, Landscape, and the Environment*, Circumpolar Research Series No. 10, Canada: Canadian Circumpolar Institute (CCI) Press.

Fienup-Riordan, A. (1995), *Freeze Frame: Alaska Eskimos in the Movies*, Seattle: University of Washington Press.

Freuchen, P. (1931), *Eskimo*, New York: Grossett and Dunlap.

Gilbert, M. (2011), 'Make your own Native Hollywood in the village', *The Tundra Drums* (Bethel, AK), 11 July, 4.

Hopkins, K. (2012a), '"Big Miracle" hits the Anchorage DVD stores', *Anchorage Daily News*, 20 June, A1, A14.

Hopkins, K. (2012b), 'Whale of a tale.' *Anchorage Daily News*, 30 January, A1, A10.

Hopkins, K. (2013), 'Filmmakers press pause on Alaska movie productions', *Anchorage Daily News*, 10 April, A1, A12.

Judd, T. (2009), 'Art teaches life lessons in indigenous films', *The Tundra Drums* (Bethel, AK), 15 January, 7.

Lincoln, G. (2011), 'Cup'ik actor featured in "Everybody Loves Whales"', *The Delta Discovery* (Bethel, AK), 2 March, 3.

Mailhot, J. (1978), 'L'etymologie de "Esquimau" revue et corrigee', *Etudes/Inuit/Studies* 2(2): 59–69.

Mauer, R. (2012a), '1988 Barrow whale rescue: the real story', *Anchorage Daily News*, 3 February, A1, A6–7.

Mauer, R. (2012b), 'Big Miracle', *Anchorage Daily News*, 3 February, P1, P5.

McBride, R. (1997), 'Lack of support is killing KYUK', *The Tundra Drums* (Bethel, AK), 31 July, 4, 6.

McClanahan, A. J. (2000), *Growing Up Native in Alaska*, Anchorage: CIRI Foundation.

Rose, T. (1989), *Freeing the Whales: How the Media Created the World's Biggest Non-Event*, New York: Carol Publishing.

Stefansson, V. (1922), *The Friendly Arctic: The Story of Five Years in Polar Regions*, New York: Greenwood Press.

4. CULTURAL STEREOTYPES AND NEGOTIATIONS IN SÁMI CINEMA

Monica Kim Mecsei

During the past decades, representations of Sámi culture in cinema in Norway have changed from emphasising the perspective of an outsider to emphasising that of an insider. This transition is related to a process of cultural revitalisation, which, as in a postcolonial framework, positions Sámi cinema practice, production and funding as a negotiating field for establishing a collective identity. This political, cultural and scholarly revitalisation has gained increasing prominence since the late 1950s, and has contributed to nuancing views on the Sámi as a diverse minority culture in the context of a long history of colonialism and assimilation policies. Portrayals exoticising and othering Sámis as savages or noble savages living in some distant, nature-bound past have historically homogenised the Sámi and disregarded them as active participants in larger national historic narratives or as part of a national majority population. Similar assumptions held sway in Sámi cultural studies until the 1960s (Hansen and Olsen 2004; Olsen 2010), as well as in most conventional studies of film representations (for example, Christophersen 1994; Wright 1998). This chapter addresses Sámi cinema history, a series of Sámi film case studies from 1987 to the present, and the role and function of the recently opened International Sámi Film Centre with the goal of foregrounding films that have a distinct connection with Sámi cultures in Sápmi and contribute to the (re) shaping of a collective understanding of cultural stereotypes in this context (for related chapters on Sámi cinema in this volume, see Kääpä on Finland, Chapter 2, and Dahlquist on Sweden, Chapter 21).

SÁMI FILM HISTORY

Visual representations of the Sámi can be traced back to the sixteenth century. The map *Carta Marina* (1539) and the explanatory and illustrated companion *Historia de gentibus septentrionalibus* (*History of the Nordic People*, 1555) by Swedish clergyman Olaus Magnus, and the illustrated book *Lapponia* (1673) by German Johannes Schefferus show a distinct Arctic landscape and people living in and by nature. These representations were widely disseminated, often as fanciful and false copies, to a European audience ignorant of Nordic cultures, and they have become stereotypes by repeatedly showing a traditional way of living associated with mountain highlands, hunting and gathering, reindeer herding and nomadism (Høydalsnes 2003). Constituting a body of repeated visual characteristics, this place on the periphery of the Nordic countries and Russia has become invested with figurations of exotic animals and uncivilised people, Sámi tents (*lávvo*) and turf huts (*goahti),* colourful traditional costumes (*gákti*), and Sámi skiers in distinct snow-covered landscapes (*dalve duoddarat*). Such images of people living in the High North could be referred to as a Sámi iconography constructed by outsiders to signify sáminess in general (Høydalsnes 2003).

The earliest account of a Sámi film character is in the 1917 fiction film *Young Hearts* (*Unge hjerter*, 1917) by Norwegian film pioneer Peter Lykke-Seest (Christensen 2013). The film has been lost, yet must be understood as a sign of an awareness of Sámi culture as a source for film stories. Extant early film representations of Sámi culture include *Growth of the Soil* (*Markens grøde*, Gunnar Sommerfeldt, 1921), *People of the Highlands* (*Viddenes folk*, Ragnar Westfelt, 1928) and *Laila* (George Schnéevoigt, 1929). These feature films are productions with little or no Sámi influence. All of the films were made in Norway with support from Norwegian production companies, with Danish and Swedish directors. *Laila*, which was made in three versions, is based on the work of the Norwegian linguist and author Jens Andreas Friis (1821–96), known as an influential 'lappologist' engaged in the study of Sámi culture. His popular novel *Laila* (Friis 1881) was originally published under the title *Fra Finnmarken. Skildringer* (*From Finnmark: Descriptions*) and was reprinted several times up until World War II. All three films are regarded as examples of the rural, national, romantic films that dominated the 1920s in Norway, many of them based on canonical literary works.

The Sámi character Os-Anders in *Growth of the Soil* embodies many stereotypical characteristics of the Sámi. He is depicted as dark, short, nomadic and eerie. Although he is a supporting character appearing just a few times, his impact on the story is decisive and largely negative; he is representative of the other, demonic and barbaric, in contrast to the Norwegian settler Isak Sellanrå. On the other hand, *People of the Highlands* and *Laila* are more inclined to represent the Sámis as noble savages. Predominantly positive, this portrayal allows for some character complexity. Still, Sámi culture is shown to have a strong relation to nature. The films of the 1920s represent Sámi culture as ambivalent, varying from demonising to romanticising representations. This is in accordance with the dominant attitude towards Sámi culture in the inter-war period. As such, representations of Sámi culture are regarded as relational and subordinate in the individual film stories, as well as in scholarly studies (Skarðhamar 2008; Iversen 2011; Christensen 2013).

A later comedy, *Operation Sea Spray* (*Operasjon sjøsprøyt*, Knut Bohwim, 1964) about life in the Royal Norwegian Navy, also underpins the Sámi's close relation to nature. The Sámi girl Aina and her family come from 'the mountains', live in a *lávvo* and herd reindeer. Aina works in a souvenir shop, an occupation that is not uncommon in reality. From a postcolonial perspective, however, a diverse culture is reduced to simple symbols that are taken for granted in the narrative. The film also furthers a stereotyped notion of sámi-ness, combined with cultural commodification, which reinforces the imperial and touristic gaze. Representing Sámi people as savages, or most often as noble savages, has made their supposedly wild and romantic nature an exotic part of imagined Sámi identity. In this way stereotypical representation creates an order for the audience and maps boundaries of centre and periphery, as well as legitimate and acceptable behaviour (Dyer 2002; Shohat and Stam 2003, 2004).

A gradual turn from this colonial view towards an empathic representation is found in *Last of the Nomads* (*Same Jakki*, Per Høst, 1957), *Same Ællin* (Titus Vibe-Müller, 1971), *Ante* (Arvid Skauge, 1977) – based on the children's television series *Ante* (Arvid Skauge, 1975) – and *Let the River Live!* (*La elva leve!*, Bredo Greve, 1980). These films have a documentary style. Høst's and Vibe-Müller's films echo the tradition of documentary film pioneer Robert J. Flaherty's *Nanook of the North* (1922), by using staging and dramaturgic suspense. *Same Jakki* and *Same Ællin* portray traditional reindeer herding culture and the threat of modern society. Greve's film depicts the intense activism against the development of a controversial hydropower project, the so-called 'Alta action', in the 1970s. The story itself is fictional, although original newsreels and interviews with authentic participants are woven into the film.

These films raised awareness and addressed both traditional Sámi heritage and modernity. They recognised that traditional Sámi culture was subject to previous assimilation policies and that local knowledge and judgement were ineffective in influencing state regulations, especially regarding rights to land and water. Popular among the public, these films gained broad media coverage though the narratives were told from an outsider perspective within a paternalist and primitivist discourse. At the same time, they contributed to changing the cultural stigma of being a Sámi (Christensen 2013). Social movements calling for recognition of Sámi peoples as a minority with distinct cultural practices and indigenous rights began to gather strength from the 1960s. After the uprising against the Alta hydropower project in 1981, these gained steam. By then, the rights of minorities and national recognition of the state's responsibility for historical injustices had begun to be publicly addressed, as represented also by international polices and global ethnopolitical struggles (Ginsberg 2003). The Sámi Parliament in Finland was established in 1973, in Norway in 1993 and in Sweden in 1993. In 1990 Norway ratified the UN's International Labour Organisation (ILO) Convention 169 about the rights of indigenous and tribal peoples.

CASE STUDIES: CONTINUITY AND CHANGE IN SELF-REPRESENTATIONAL FILM STORIES

Sámi feature films produced after 1987 represent Sámi culture from a local point of view, recontextualising and renegotiating cultural stereotypes. Films like *Pathfinder* (*Ofelaš*, Nils Gaup, 1987), *Minister of State* (*Minister på villovägar*, Paul-Anders Simma, 1997), *Bázo* (Lars Göran Pettersson, 2003) and *The Kautokeino Rebellion* (*Kautokeino-opprøret*, Nils Gaup, 2008) all address the complexity of cultural hybridity and difference within. These feature film representations can be understood as inside stories because of their strong relation to the Arctic border areas where Norway, Sweden and Finland meet, an area often regarded as the heart of Sápmi, since these areas have managed to maintain cultural distinctiveness despite assimilation policies. Self-representational sáminess is produced by several factors: Sámi setting and shooting location, Sámi actors and language, visual identity markers like Sámi costumes, reindeer and snow, and the geographical distinctiveness of northern Sápmi's fjords, coastal and mountain areas. The different representations are not necessarily exclusive, but appear sometimes parallel, sometimes intersecting and sometimes conflicting (Holander 2014). Sámi iconography and Sámi cinema participate in a negotiating field where cultural identity markers seem different, depending on the historical and geographical starting point. Long-term assimilation policies, visual and cultural stereotyping and ongoing revitalising processes contribute to future imaginaries by negotiating the complexities of tradition and modernity.

On 30 September 1987, the first Sámi feature film had its premiere in Norwegian cinema theatres. *Pathfinder*, by Sámi debut director and screenwriter Gaup, represents a significant contribution to the Sámi cultural revitalisation process. Regionally, *Pathfinder* can be related to the cultural and ethnopolitical awakening among active artists and musicians at that time, as well as to international activism and recognition of indigenous peoples (Christensen 2013; Ginsberg 2003). As a genre director Gaup successfully appropriated the American Western genre to a so-called 'Northern'. Thus, *Pathfinder* represents an important contribution to the enhancement of a small national as well as a small minority cinema culture and indigenous cinema culture (DuBois 2000; Iversen 2005; Ginsberg 2003). *Pathfinder* gained Sámi, national and international recognition and represented Norway in an Academy Award nomination for best foreign film. It is regarded as a turning point in Sámi film history, and the impact of this film is said to have shaped the discourse of a collective Sámi identity. *Pathfinder* and *The Kautokeino Rebellion* have become visual textbooks and major examples of Sámi culture in national and international indigenous filmmaking. Both films have contributed to raising awareness of a minority within the Nordic nation-states and increasing cultural pride within Sámi communities.

Pathfinder and *The Kautokeino Rebellion* deal with the past in different ways and are reconstructions of Sámi cultural heritage moulded to bolster Sámi cultural pride. *Pathfinder* is based on a Sámi-Nordic-Russian travel story – the *Pathfinder* myth – about armed strangers, *tsjudes*, who intrude on other people's territory. The evil *tsjudes* need a pathfinder to ambush the peaceful community. The pathfinder, however, manages to save the community by slyly leading the intruders to a steep cliff where they fall into the abyss (Drannikova and Larsen 2007). *The Kautokeino Rebellion* is based on a historical event from 1852, where a group of Sámi reindeer herders rebelled against the local authorities in the small Sámi village Guovdageaidnu/ Kautokeino, Finnmark County, the northernmost county in Norway. Several people on both sides were killed, and as a result, some of the rebels were imprisoned and later decapitated. The event has been neglected, however, by the Norwegian authorities, and has also been suppressed by the Sámi community. The film story is told from the viewpoint of Elen Aslaksdatter Skum and the members of her Sámi group (*siida*). The sáminess that is brought about in both films can be related to at least two historical narratives: first, the repetitions of Sámi iconography which disturb the colonial images, and second, self-representation and cultural revitalisation.

In many ways, the Sámi iconography familiar from outsiders' representations is repeated in Gaup's films. Like previous imperial practices of visual representations, *Pathfinder* and *The Kautokeino Rebellion* emphasise a traditional and homogeneous Sámi reindeer-herding culture, with its related symbols and closeness to nature. For example, the introduction of the Sámi protagonist Aigin in *Pathfinder* places him in a beautiful snow-covered landscape. He is dressed in light-coloured fur-wear and his cheeks are rosy. He is a skilled skier and comes towards us in a stunning panoramic shot of a snow-covered landscape. From behind his skis, a single steady trace is left in the powdery snow. This Sámi hero is immersed in the nature surrounding him. He functions as a natural part of a greater whole. *The Kautokeino Rebellion* similarly uses

Figure 4.1   Sámi cinema: Nils Gaup's *Pathfinder* (*Ofelaš/Veiviseren*, 1987).

reindeer as a visual leitmotif to indicate the social and emotional well-being of Elen's reindeer and her *siida* (Christensen 2013). When there is peace and harmony, the reindeer are calm and at ease. When Elen and her fellow accomplices are imprisoned or threatened, the reindeer are anxious. These strategies align the Sámi people with the land and nature, a gesture germane to outsiders' visual representations.

Despite the use of Sámi iconography, Gaup's film productions are undoubtedly also Sámi. They operate on an assumption of authenticity mobilised by evoking mythology and history central to Sámi culture. The *Pathfinder* myth is accentuated as particularly Sámi, while its transnationality is downplayed. On the other hand, *The Kautokeino Rebellion* is based on a historical event that works as a metaphor for suppression. Gaup's Sámi background, the use of Sámi actors and language, and the shooting locations in Finnmark and Troms are all important signs for communicating Sámi authenticity. Gaup's repetition of Sámi iconography might be understood as a challenge to stereotypical colonial images of othering by transferring such images into a discourse of authentic self-representation that is able to encourage pride and self-esteem. Reindeer, mountain highlands, *lávvo*s or wearing a *gákti* or *beaska* are part of the traditional reindeer-herding Sámi culture in inner Finnmark. In *Pathfinder* and *The Kautokeino Rebellion*, these symbols are infused with positivity. Gaup's use of Sámi iconography is, in fact, a way of demarcating cultural difference. Hence, both *Pathfinder* and *The Kautokeino Rebellion* are understood as presenting an inside voice from a minority. The Sámi activism that fought for recognition, self-representation and cultural revitalisation has indeed grown out of inner Finnmark. Gaup's Sámi films arguably recontextualise cultural stereotypes from a negative and simplistic understanding to one that is a self-empowering and revitalising force.

From this perspective, the films emphasise indigenous culture as a continuing, unbroken tradition and insist on its place in modern society. *Pathfinder* presents the origin of a community and how it is kept together and survives despite threats. The story proves that this Sámi community can overcome problems and devastating intruders and has thus passed the test of viability. *The Kautokeino Rebellion* expressly addresses the colonial past and retells history from insiders' perspectives. The film makes an attempt to come to terms with the past in order to move on. By representing a distinct group identity and a long-lived homogeneous culture, with roots going back to the beginning of time, Gaup constructs a bridge between the past and the present. This gives the impression of cultural continuity and a sense of validity and genuineness. However, re-using Sámi iconography might create a division between 'real' and 'spurious' culture. The backdrop of complex assimilation and postwar experiences, a widespread land area and cultural diversity within is not prominent in Gaup's feature films.

NEGOTIATING CULTURAL DIVERSITY AND HYBRIDITY WITHIN: *MINISTER OF STATE* AND *BÁZO*

Pathfinder and *The Kautokeino Rebellion* largely represent cultural unity and connect the past to the present, thereby perhaps ironically aligning with Norwegian state policies, museum exhibitions and a tourist industry based on ideas about Sámi culture as homogeneous, as well as separate and distinct from Norwegian culture (Olsen 2010).

In contrast, *Minister of State* and *Bázo* offer counter-images that are explicit ruptures of Sámi iconography, not just distortions. Local history and local encounters in these films differ greatly from Gaup's films by addressing cultural hybridity to deconstruct ideas of ethnic or national homogeneity. *Minister of State*, by Sámi director Paul-Anders Simma, reveals a multicultural community through a burlesque and coarse comedy that mocks the notion of homogeneity. The story takes place in the last months of World War II in a small remote Sámi village, Sagojokk. German troops are ravaging the territory. One day a deserting soldier enters the village and is wrongfully taken for a minister from the Finnish Government. The domineering village merchant, Antti Neia, is suspicious, but the village people are easily fooled by the fake minister, who promises a road straight to the capital and a landowner reform act that will give them their own piece of land – at the expense of Neia.

Sagojokk is located in the north of Finland, bordering Sweden and Norway. The village inhabitants are a mixture of Kvens, Sámis, Finns, Swedes and Norwegians. These identities are presented as interchangeable and pragmatic in the film, especially in encounters with outsiders and the nation-state regulations. For instance, when German troops and tanks are about to cross the river and enter the village, Neia, a Kven patriot, shouts: 'You know what to do! Get at it – God damn it!' The village people run about and switch all traces of Finnish identity for Swedish identity markers. They change the large flag, put up a border post, switch a photo of the Finnish president for the Swedish king, and even replace a bottle of Finnish vodka with a mug of milk. The village merchant shouts at the German soldiers that they are Swedish and hence neutral, before continuing to sing the Swedish national anthem and waving small Swedish flags. These scenes point to the insignificant, even absurd, meaning of the nation-states' borders in Sápmi.

The multicultural community and the unstable identities in *Minister of State* recognise cultural diversity and cultural hybridity in the northern border areas of Sápmi. The majority of the Sámi population do not have an evident connection to the images that have been, and still are, put forward as traditional Sámi culture or territory. *Minister of State* shuns (ethnic, national or cultural) identity markers as fixed or essentialised. The film's deliberate blurring of allegiances is accentuated by the chaotic war situation and the representation of Sagojokk as a place in a state of constant change. The inhabitants' cultural identity is relational and can be switched from Finnish to Swedish and back again in a few minutes. Their multilingual practice is effortless. In this film, cultural identities are constructed and not represented as stable or as having a long and continuous tradition.

The road movie *Bázo*, by the Swedish, Kautokeino-based director Pettersson, portrays contemporary Sápmi with a critical eye. The notion of sáminess and Sámi peoples living as in a prehistorical past is recontextualised by applying

Figure 4.2   *Bázo*, a contemporary Sámi road movie (2003).

a social-realistic context, and by repeating distorted postcard images of northern identity. *Bázo* is a journey through the border areas of Sweden, Norway and Finland. The main character, Emil, lives with his father on a small remote farm in the forests of northern Sweden. People call him *Bázo*, a Sámi expression for 'fool'. One day they get a message that Emil's brother has died. Emil is then obliged to search for the belongings of his dead brother.

Bázo depicts an unglamorous society far from the mythical and historical past of *Pathfinder* and *The Kautokeino Rebellion*. For instance, reindeer and nature are part of a production culture where economic gain seems to be a predominant goal. There are no ecological or religious motifs related to the reindeer – they do not stand out as a symbol of the Sámi culture per se. *Bázo* also problematises the fact that the county hospital cannot perform advanced medical operations, that the school has failed in its basic language education, that families cannot support their children (so that giving one child away to a stranger seems like a fair solution), and that locals support illegal border trade and maintain law and order with their own militia. The counter-images in *Bázo* are critical of how the border area is treated by the welfare state and how the Sámi community seems to create its own mafia, with depictions of crime, poverty and the failure of the nation-states' institutions creating a cool distance to the beautiful landscape.

The cinematic imagery in *Bázo* does display, however, vast and beautiful panoramic landscape settings. But it cannot be said to produce strong national-romantic, or nature-romantic, imagery like, for instance, the Norwegian rural films in the 1920s. The northern landscape is a vast place with barren plains. None of the characters encounters Mother Nature with ease or shows specific surviving aptitude for living in and by the wilderness. None shows skills in skiing, hunting or tracking. Emil does not travel on foot, on cross-country skis or by reindeer sleigh. He travels by modern means: cars, buses, a tractor and a garbage van.

In addition, the film style produces a distance between man and nature. Landscape views are displayed with intersecting roads or from vehicle windows with vertical and horizontal lines. The roads cut through the landscape and prevent the impression of pristine wilderness. To enter the beautiful landscape, Emil needs to stop the car, open the door and get out. The window views are shot from a higher angle than shoulder height and point slightly downwards – or lower than shoulder height. What we see are truncated images: parts of the road, parts of the forest or parts of the majestic landscape. Thus the images in *Bázo* do not seamlessly match images from landscape paintings, photographs from touristic brochures, or American road movies. Instead, they offer a nuancing and negotiating view of Sámi identity.

The case studies above can be regarded as insider stories from northern Sápmi. Gaup's films represent the beginning of an imagined, united Sámi nation, while Simma and Pettersson explicitly renegotiate the notion of cultural unity and stereotyped representation, and therefore construct a representation of cultural diversity within. Film policy directed at Sámi filmmakers, and the support for Sámi cinema since the 1980s, can be explained by this acknowledgment of self-representation and cultural revitalisation.

Sámi Film Policy: Telling Their Own Stories

Sámi cinema is part of a national and regional film policy that aims to strengthen, preserve and protect a minority culture, thus providing diversity and counteracting previous representations of otherness. Government interference is grounded in democratic rights that intend minority voices to be heard in a larger society. But such policies also apply to small nations, small cinemas and minority groups, as well as indigenous peoples. They are deeply grounded in Norway and in the Nordic countries. The basic idea is that culture is a social good for all, regardless of social and economic background. Such policies are decentralising and aim to strengthen regional and local differences, as well as rights of self-determination. In addition, a small nation like Norway wants to prevent economic leakage and to counteract unwanted influence from international and multinational cultural industries. Protecting cultural specificity, like national languages, and self-representation are then two sides of the same coin. Thus, small cinemas form part of policy supporting minority cultures (Hjort and Petrie 2007).

Opened in 2007, the International Sámi Film Centre (ISF) is located at Guovdageaidnu/Kautokeino in inner Finnmark. ISF aims to establish a transnational field for Sámi filmmakers and provide opportunities for producing insider stories from Sápmi. Funding and production support for Sámi filmmaking continue to be drawn from diverse sources. Since the early 1980s, the regional North Norwegian Film Centre (NNFS) has been obliged to produce a minimum of one Sámi film per year, continuing to support projects and activities that strengthen North Norwegian film. Other institutions include the regional film centre in mid-Norway; the National Film Institutes; Sámi parliaments in Norway, Sweden and Finland; regional counties and local municipalities; and transnational Nordic and pan-European film funds. In its first years, ISF has focused on raising basic film development competence, such as scriptwriting and technical skills, and locating external support. In the period 2009–12, its film activities have resulted in twenty-eight film projects: documentaries, short films and television productions. ISF has also spearheaded a global network for indigenous film that promotes indigenous voices in the global media circuit, especially for film festivals and indigenous conferences. The activities initiated by ISF help carve out a field where self-representational Sámi narratives can serve as vital tools for mediating decolonising cultural experiences. As such, ISF carries a valuable symbolic significance for Sámi cinema and can be understood as a principal supplier of what is regarded as Sámi film.

Despite the fact that ISF's engagement makes a strong contribution to the establishment of a minority film culture within Northern national and transnational territories, its policies are controversial. ISF practises an instrumental film policy, where language revitalisation is the main goal. All film projects must be in the Sámi languages. These languages are on UNESCO's list of endangered languages. At a national and institutional level, the language requirement can be understood as aiming to revitalise and encourage Sámi culture. However, ISF's language policy can also be understood as a gatekeeper. Because the Sámi majority are non-Sámi speakers due to assimilation policies, some very important cultural counter-narratives can be dismissed through such restrictions. Specifically, the language requirement creates spatial and temporal borders within Sápmi. This is especially evident between the region encompassing fjord, coastal and southern areas, which were the most assimilated, and inner Finnmark, which maintained more cultural distinctiveness. Several documentaries, like *Suddenly Sámi* (*Min mors hemmelighet*, Ellen A. Lundby, 2008) and *The Family Portrait* (*Familiebildet*, Yvonne Thomassen, 2012), feature stories that thematise a rejected Sámi cultural identity. They also tend to show how these narratives are intertwined with assimilation policies, postwar experiences and the significance of local belonging (Holander 2014). One recurring theme is how the Sámi language has been rejected as a sign of cultural identity due to internalised assimilation processes, as well as a sign of how at least two generations have lost their language. From a regional standpoint, ISF's policy could thus be understood as a marginalisation of Sámi cultures that continues a 'reversed' assimilation policy.

Sámi cinema and ISF's policy deal with the forging of cultural heritage and with facing the challenge to communicate cultural diversity. Stressing the Sámi languages as paramount for script development and production support is a way of delimiting a cultural difference. It has a long tradition in ethnographic studies from the nineteenth century – for instance those of Lappologist Friis – as well as in assimilation policies that stressed the use of Norwegian language. In addition, the EU's minority policy and national film policy point at language as a significant cultural identity marker. Sámi film before 1987 tended not to emphasise language specifically as a way of marking a cultural difference. *Pathfinder, Minister of State, Bázo* and *The Kautokeino Rebellion* all establish the Sámi language as a point of cultural difference. In this way ISF buttresses previous self-representing feature films, as well as Sámi cultural studies and international and national policies. However, communicating the complexities of cultural diversity, hybrid identities and local histories in lived experiences is challenging in a transnational media culture. As a result, these films may struggle to find a common ground. Still, ensuring increased possibilities for Sámi film production might potentially be a step in the right direction to ensure diversity in the imagination of collective identities.

BIBLIOGRAPHY

Christophersen, B. S. (1994), 'Sosialitetens pris. Om framstillinger av samer og fanter i norske spillefilmer fra mellomkrigstiden', Masters thesis at Department of Media and Communication, University of Oslo.
Christensen, C. (2013), *Religion som samisk identitesmarkør. Fire studier av film*, PhD dissertation, University of Tromsø.
Drannikova, N. and R. Larsen (2007), 'Tsjuder i norsk og russisk folklore', in N. Drannikova and R. Larsen (eds), *I tsjudenes fotspor. Tsjuder i historiske kilder, predannier og sagn i Nord-Norge og Arkhangelsk oblast*, Tromsø: Arktisk Forlag, 15–33.
DuBois, T. A. (2000), 'Folklore, boundaries and audience in *The Pathfinder*', in J. Pentikäinen (ed.), *Sami Folkloristics*, Åbo: Nordic Network of Folklore, 255–74.
Dyer, R. [1993] (2002), *The Matter of Images. Essays on Representations*, 2nd edn, London: Routledge.
Ginsberg, F. (2003), 'Screen memories and entangled technologies: resignifying indigenous lives', in E. Shohat and R. Stam (eds), *Multiculturalism, Postcoloniality, and Transnational Media*, New Brunswick, NJ: Rutgers University Press, 77–98.
Hansen, L. I. and Bjørnar Olsen (2004), 'Introduksjon' and 'Skiftende syn på samenes opprinnelse', in L. I. Hansen and B. Olsen, *Samenes historie fram til 1750*, Oslo: Cappelen Akademisk forlag, 9–17, 18–51.
Hjort, M. and D. Petrie (2007), 'Introduction', in M. Hjort and D. Petrie (eds), *The Cinema of Small Nations*, Edinburgh: Edinburgh University Press, 1–19.
Holander, S. (2014), '"Faces like landscapes": postcolonial documentary autobiography in Northern Scandinavia', *Interventions. International Journal of Postcolonial Studies*.
Høydalsnes, E. (2003), *Møte mellom tid og sted. Bilder av Nord-Norge*, Oslo: Forlaget Bonytt.
Iversen, G. (2005) 'Learning from genre. Genre cycles in modern Norwegian cinema', in A. Nestingen and T. G. Elkington (eds), *Transnational Cinema in a Global North. Nordic Cinema and Television*, Detroit: Wayne State University Press, 261–77.
Iversen, G. (2011), *Norsk filmhistorie. Spillefilmen 1911–2011*, Oslo: Universitetsforlaget.
Olsen, K. (2010), *Identities, Ethnicities and Borderzones. Examples from Finnmark, Northern Norway*, Stamsund: Orkana Akademisk.
Shohat, E. and R. Stam (eds) (2003), *Multiculturalism, Postcoloniality, and Transnational Media*, New Brunswick, NJ: Rutgers University Press.
Shohat, E. and R. Stam [1994] (2004), *Unthinking Eurocentrism. Multiculturalism and the Media*, London: Routledge.
Skarðhamar, A. K. (2008), 'Changes in film representations of Sami culture and identity', *Nordlit*, 23, 293–303.
Wright, R. (1998), *The Invisible Wall. Jews and other Ethnic Outsiders in Swedish Film*, Carbondale: Southern Illinois University Press.

5. CINEMA OF EMANCIPATION AND ZACHARIAS KUNUK'S *ATANARJUAT: THE FAST RUNNER*

Marco Bohr

INTRODUCTION

Set in Igloolik in Canada's Eastern Arctic over 1,000 years ago and performed in the Inuit language Inuktitut, *Atanarjuat: The Fast Runner* (ᐊᑕᓈᕐᔪᐊᑦ, Canada/Nunavut, 2001), directed by Zacharias Kunuk, is widely celebrated as a landmark in Indigenous film production in North America and elsewhere. The film was produced by Igloolik Isuma Productions, the first independent Inuit production company which was co-founded by Kunuk, Paul Apak Angilirq and the cinematographer of the film and one of the few non-Inuit crew members Norman Cohn. With a running time of nearly three hours and featuring mainly non-professional actors shot with digital video technology on location in the surroundings of Igloolik, *Atanarjuat* constitutes a visually arresting depiction of Inuit traditions, oral history and Arctic peoples and environments. The film opened to critical acclaim at the Cannes film festival in 2001.

Despite its visual and cinematic appeal, most discussions on *Atanarjuat* focus on elements 'outside' of the film such as the Inuit stake in climate change, the reception of the film on the global festival circuit, or the prolonged process of obtaining funding for the film. Ironically, in most of these discussions, the film itself, its intricate plot, its visual methodologies, and its representation of the Arctic have not received the attention that it deserves. This chapter aims to shift the discourse on *Atanarjuat* towards an analysis that seeks to deconstruct and interpret the meaning of the film as a visually complex and politically loaded cultural text.

Following Peter Wollen's call to study film as a 'system of signs', this chapter will place a particular emphasis on visual devices which help to support the plot and which create new meanings that must be analysed in more detail (1970). Beyond looking at the plot and the interrelatedness between the main characters in the film, the chapter considers the reappropriation of Inuit representations in a postcolonial context, the application of magical realism as a reference to Inuit folklore as well as the representation of the Arctic which is visually and contextually anchored by references to space and time. As the film consistently breaks with cinematic conventions, the chapter considers how *Atanarjuat* constitutes a 'cinema of emancipation' that speaks about Inuit concerns from within.

THE CINEMATIC RUNNER

Based on a traditional Inuit legend, orally passed down from one generation to another over the centuries, the plot hinges on a feud between two family clans, with Atanarjuat – entangled in a complex web of love, jealousy, betrayal and revenge – at the centre. Induced by a shaman's curse, the conflict escalates as Atanarjuat and Oki, his antagonist, become interested in the same woman called Atvat. Following an assault, naked Atanarjuat escapes in a daring run across the ice of the Arctic on his bare feet. The plot's emphasis on (thwarted) conflict resolution is complemented by elements of shamanism, mysticism and Inuit folklore.

Figure 5.1   *Atanarjuat: The Fast Runner*: the chase.

Atanarjuat's run across the Arctic constitutes a major element in the film. Inasmuch as it is the cornerstone of the Inuit legend, it also functions as an important scene, laden with symbolism, in the cinematic representation of the story. The film scholar Lúcia Nagib aligns this important scene towards the middle of the film with avant-garde cinema in which the physical representation of running functions as a metaphor for the advancement of the cinematic medium. Nagib writes: 'Running and cinema intersect at key moments in film history' (2011: 19). More specifically, Nagib relates the extended representation of running to visually and symbolically similar scenes in François Truffaut's *The 400 Blows* (France, 1959), Glauber Rocha's *Black God, White Devil* (Brazil, 1964) and Idrissa Ouedraogo's *Yaaba* (Burkina Faso, 1989). Like *Atanarjuat*, which is widely celebrated as the first Inuit feature film, Nagib argues that at the birth of the French *nouvelle vague*, at the height of Brazil's *cinema novo*, and the emergence of an independent Western African cinema, cinematic runners are 'conquering hostile, harsh, even extreme environments' (Nagib 2011: 19). The physical advancement of the runner functions as a metaphor for the advancement of an independent and autonomous cinematic movement. Nagib continues:

> In all cases, however, their protracted act of running takes the upper hand over the diegesis and imposes its own narrative, one related to recognising, experiencing, demarcating and taking possession of a territory, and, in so doing, defining a people and its culture. (Nagib 2011: 19)

The historical and geographical order of Nagib's comparison is important in this context. She traces an avant-garde aesthetic from France, Brazil and West Africa to the land of the First Nations in Canada. This trajectory clearly points to the democratisation of the cinematic apparatus in parallel to the discourses of postcolonialism and globalisation. *Atanarjuat* is part of a global emergence of Indigenous film production or what the Maori filmmaker Barry Barclay has usefully referred to as 'Fourth Cinema' (Hearne 2012: 18–21). The term 'Fourth Cinema' distinguishes itself from 'First Cinema', or films produced in industrial studios such as Hollywood, 'Second Cinema', or European art films centred on the individual expression of the auteur director, and 'Third Cinema', a politically revolutionary cinema predominantly from African, Asian, and Latin American countries.

In the case of *Atanarjuat*, the daringness of the run and the metaphorical advancement of 'Fourth Cinema' is further emphasised by the sheer physicality of running barefoot on ice. If the run itself is a metaphor for avant-garde cinema, then Atanarjuat's struggle across the ice – his feet bleeding and his naked body slipping into ice-cold puddles of water – is equally metaphorical for the difficulties of filmmaking in such an environment. In that regard, the increased availability and decreased cost of digital technology in the new millennium makes film production more accessible, more mobile and therefore also more independent. Apart from the reduced cost of producing a film with digital video (as opposed to 35mm analogue film), the technology also allows Kunuk and his team to work in extreme climate conditions, far away from the usual logistical and technical support of bigger film productions. Instead of having to get analogue film negatives developed, the digital film 'stock' can be processed, accessed and even edited on location. Partially as a result of the increased accessibility of film via digital technology, the camera reaches places beyond the edge of the perceived centres of cinematic production. Atanarjuat's action of running across the ice is thus deeply symbolic as it signifies the advancement of the cinematic apparatus into territories hitherto not reached by a truly independent as well as indigenous cinema.

Cinematically Fixing an Oral Tradition

Even before filming for *Atanarjuat* began, Kunuk and his crew faced a dilemma: a legend which slightly changes and shifts as it is passed down from one generation to another is to be represented in a medium which is static and unchangeable. Interpretations of the film might vary depending on which cultural, social or historical context it is viewed in, yet the plot and cinematic conventions remain contained within the film itself. The filmmakers thus had to contend with the notion of translation on two important levels. In the first instance, the legend had to be translated from Inuktitut to English in order to make the cinematic text legibly to an international and globalised audience. In addition, *Atanarjuat* was also translated into the international language of art cinema: a complex semiotic code analysed and interpreted by a select yet equally diverse audience across the world. *Atanarjuat* thus represents a clear case in which a local and historically specific microcosm is not only represented in the medium of cinema, but also, it is transformed into a transnational aesthetic removed from the original context of the film itself.

Atanarjuat addresses this culturally complex notion of translation as the film self-referentially begins with the following line narrated by the strange shaman from the north: 'I can only sing this song to someone who understands it'. From the very start, the film introduces the notion of communicating across cultures. On a micro-level the shaman is concerned that his song is not understood in the community that he visits. Yet on a macro-level, this element in the film, too, is deeply symbolic for Kunuk's position as cultural agent, communicating Inuit oral history to a globalised cinema audience. Within a discourse of indigenous cultural production, this opening line introduces an outside element – that the film is eventually viewed, analysed and perhaps even misunderstood outside of the Inuit context.

In the first instance the phrase 'I can only sing this song to someone who understands it' ironically references the non-Inuit audience's inability to understand the language spoken in the film. The fact that *Atanarjuat* was subtitled into English led to the comical if also tragic consequence that it was listed as a foreign language film in Canadian branches of Blockbuster Video stores in 2001. *Atanarjuat* thus also fits into a larger cultural context specific to Canada in which *Québécois* cinema is usually treated as foreign language film in an industry dominated by the English language. The bias towards English as *lingua franca* is further promoted through the cinematic centres Vancouver and Toronto where Hollywood film productions are frequently outsourced as a result of tax incentives and lower production costs. Yet apart from referring to the notion of literal translation, the phrase uttered at the beginning of *Atanarjuat* also refers to the traditions of Inuit oral history which are, in this instance, retold via the medium film. 'I can only sing this song . . .' thus establishes an important parallel to the very form with which the legend is communicated. Here, 'singing' functions as a powerful metaphor for narrative cinema.

As *Atanarjuat* represents a defining moment in Indigenous culture in Canada, it is important to emphasise that the first Inuit feature film production specifically focuses on oral traditions. The legend of Atanarjuat was recorded by Captain George Lyon as part of the British expedition to explore the Northwest Passage in 1821–3. Indeed, Kunuk and his team utilised Lyon's sketches of Indigenous clothing as an important visual source for the film (Knopf 2008: 319). *Atanarjuat* thus reclaims an integral part of its culture which was historically recorded – and therefore ideologically also occupied – by European colonisers. Kunuk and his team thus consciously reappropriate an aspect of Inuit tradition historically represented by those outside the Inuit context. Here, the film creates an intriguing back-and-forth between a form of representation which was initially produced by the coloniser and which is now, through films such as *Atanarjuat*, reappropriated by the colonised. This reappropriation does not ignore the notion of colonialism, nor does the film aestheticise or exoticise its own culture akin to the cultural process Edward Said has called Orientalism (2006). Rather, in the context of a geographically, politically and economically marginalised community in Canada, the act of filmmaking becomes an act of reclaiming aspects of indigenous culture. In her analysis of *Atanarjuat*, Indigenous film scholar Michelle Raheja writes that 'sovereignty is a creative act of self-representation' (Raheja 2007: 1161). For Arnold Krupat, modes of indigenous cultural production 'counter the repressive hegemony of the European metropolis by presenting and representing the world in ways that have challenged colonial representations' (2007: 606) Yet art as physical and collectable object can, and also has been, an active force in the very process of colonisation. To 'own' a piece of the world is to collect its art and cultural artifacts. *Atanarjuat* may be an art form widely consumed on the international film festival circuit, yet also, it is an intangible form of media, and it communicates about that culture from within. If 'media has been complicit in the processes of colonization and assimilation', Shari Huhndorf argues, 'in the contemporary Arctic it thus also constitutes a means of refiguring Inuit histories, culture, and identity in ways that support Native campaigns for self-determination.' (2003: 825). For Kerstin Knopf,

> The autonomous presentation of Inuit culture from an inside perspective helps to de-exoticize the filmed material and its cultural context. In consequence, the film belongs to a decolonized film discourse that consciously merges Indigenous and Western cultures. (Knopf 2008: 347)

By mixing 'Western' forms of representation and technology with Indigenous culture, the very fixity and indexicality of film appears to contradict the ongoing cultural process of an oral tradition characterised by fluidity and change. In that sense, the legend told and retold over the centuries is never entirely the same as it reflects aspects and variations of the culture as it evolves. The representation of the legend in a film inadvertently halts this process – a fact that in itself could have caused controversy when *Atanarjuat* was first shown in the very community in which it was produced. Despite the director's initial concerns over cinematically fixing an oral legend – and slightly altering this very legend as I will explain later – the film was warmly welcomed by the community that helped to produce it.[1]

Shifting Binaries

From love to hate and from jealousy to revenge, the legend of Atanarjuat incorporates a diverse range of human emotions. Yet as Raheja points out, like most Native American oral stories, there are no absolute binaries between good and evil (Raheja 2007: 1172). The 'hero' Atanarjuat, for example, has obvious character flaws as he foolishly falls for another woman called Puja. Conversely, even after his brother is killed by Oki and his gang, Atanarjuat describes Oki as not an essentially bad person, but as suffering from an evil curse. In other words, evil is not inherent to the human subject, but rather in the realm of mysticism. The ambiguity between human nature and mysticism also functions as an important metaphor for the cinematic representation of real and imagined elements within the legend. Atanarjuat and others thus periodically experience flashbacks or spiritual illusions. The film also challenges the boundaries between those parts of the legend anchored in the actions of the subject, and those parts anchored in what the subjects imagine.

Figure 5.2 *Atanarjuat: The Fast Runner*: magical realism.

To highlight this ambiguity, Kunuk applies the cinematic device of 'magical realism' in at least two key scenes. Next to an actual representation of an Arctic rabbit, the film briefly depicts a much larger rabbit, too big too be real, fading into obscurity on the surface of the snow. The fade alludes to the notion that the smaller rabbit remaining has been sent by the spirits to eliminate Oki's vengefulness. Another scene towards the end of the film shows the return of the shaman from the north, finally chased away by the elders who recognised the destructive effect the curse had on their community. Like the giant white rabbit, the shaman simply fades into obscurity. These shifts from a cinematic representation of the real to the imagined stand in contrast to American and European cinematic traditions and have the inevitable effect of obscuring the plot. Apart from the narrative of the legend, this break from cinematic traditions also occurs with regard to the sensual experience of the film. Comparably long takes, a running time of nearly three hours, the use of a handheld camera to assume the subjective viewpoint of the protagonists, even the slight pixilation of the film on screen consistently challenge the viewer to give up preconceptions about the cinematic experience. In that regard, the Canadian literary critic Peter Dickinson writes that the repetition of long takes functions 'as the visual equivalent of oral pauses in storytelling, in that they force the listener/viewer to acknowledge his/her participation in the performative event of the film's elaboration, to reflect on the very act of looking, or else to look away' (Dickinson 2007: 101).

With the subliminal backdrop of the Arctic, the film addresses its differences to American or European cinema most prominently on a visual level. For large segments the plot of the film thus unfolds on a blank canvas of ice and snow. The Arctic condition is cinematically emphasised by setting the exposure of the camera primarily to the subjects of the plot and not to the landscape they are situated in. The Arctic glare emitting on the surface of the screen, further emphasised by a slight over-exposure of the snow, has the dramatic visual effect of suspending the subjects from their surroundings. The suspension of the subject within the cinematic representation of the Arctic can be read as an important metaphor for how the film is physically and psychologically consumed by the viewer of the film. The viewer too must suspend his assumptions and preconceptions about cinema as a visual experience in order to properly engage with the legend of Atanarjuat.

At the same time, however, the film also grounds its protagonists in two important ways: in time and space. In the first instance, the film places great emphasis on representing the separation between generations, and within this chronology of family relations, seasonal changes as a reference to the passing of time. In the winter the men wear thick clothing and distinctive looking snow goggles (*ilgaak* or *iggaak*) to protect their eyes during the hunt. With the arrival of spring, the ice in the bay begins to melt and becomes thinner while the hunt gradually shifts onto land. With the arrival of summer, birds return to the hamlet and wildflowers begin to bloom as various camera shots indicate. Yet references to the change of season are also less direct as the protagonists diet becomes more varied and less reliant on walrus meat during the summer. Reminiscing about old hunting experiences, such as when Atanarjuat and his brother once brazenly hunted on thin ice, is an important narrative method that allows the protagonists to reflect on these changes in time.

In the second instance, the film grounds the protagonists' experience in relation to very distinct spaces. Some of the most important developments in the film (the arrival of the shaman, Atanarjuat's fight with Oki, Puja's expulsion from Atanarjuat's family, and so on) take place within the confines of either an *iglu* or a *tupiq* (a traditional Inuit tent made of seal or caribou skin, primarily used in the summer). With reference to both time *and* space, the film consistently emphasises physical actions necessary for survival in the Arctic and captured in close-up shots: the preparation of food with an *ulu* knife, the burning of oil from a seal in a crescent-shaped cup of carved soapstone called *kudlik* or *qullic*, and the touching scene in which a baby is passed into the distinctively large hood of the woman's parka *amauti* that allows mothers to carry a baby on their back. The realism in these scenes, often carefully paced and depicted with great attention to detail, is further underscored by light sources that appear to be exclusively natural: long shadows are created by the low winter sun while the fire in a tent creates a warm glow on the bodies and faces of those depicted by the camera. In contrast to the magical realism applied to emphasise the mysticism in the legend, these overtly realistic depictions of traditional Inuit cultures create the effect of quasi-documentary film. This suspension of cinematic orthodoxies and the radical diffusion of the separation between fiction and documentary, as Rob Stone has argued, are one of the prime characteristics in *avant-garde* cinema (Stone 2006: 66). Just as much of the separation between day and night is obscured by the omnipresent sun in the Arctic summer, on the surface the film appears to be neither distinctly fictional nor realistic.

An important element in the film, and a further method of breaking down the dialectic between fiction and documentary, are small moments in which the actors appear to look or glance into the camera. These moments are perhaps promoted by a cast which largely worked on the set as amateur actors. The film not only represents Igloolik, but is also facilitated through members of this very community. As opposed to the invisible camera institutionalised by both 'First Cinema' and the visual methodology of fly-on-the-wall documentary filmmaking, these glances into the camera disrupt and even subvert the cinematic experience. In his analysis of *Atanarjuat*, Dickinson writes that 'the actors make no attempt to disguise their awareness of the apparatus of the camera; often they look directly into it, returning our gaze with a bright smile, a sidelong wink, or a defiant stare' (Dickinson 2007: 102). Similar to an argument advanced by Knopf (2008: 345), Dickinson writes that the film thus 'foreground[s] a resistance to and returning of the ethnographic gaze, making visible the very processes and mechanisms of representation and non-representation that . . . other films seek to elide' (Dickinson 2007: 13).

Kunuk's techniques appear to align with Bertolt Brecht's well-known theatrical technique called the 'estrangement effect' (*Verfremdungseffekt*), by which actors address or physically engage an audience for the purpose of making the audience consciously critical. To achieve this effect, 'the actor has to discard whatever means he has learnt of getting the audience to identify itself with the characters which he plays' (Brecht 1964: 193). The actor thus must appear on stage in a 'double role', as a fictional character *and* as an actor playing that character (1964: 194). The brief instances in *Atanarjuat* when the actors look into the camera thus have two very important effects on the viewer: first, they disrupt the realist conventions of cinematic representation, and secondly, they prevent the viewer from passively identifying with the subjects represented in the film. In other words, by alluding to the fact that the actors are acting, the viewer is asked to actively engage with the film's subject and the representation of the subject. The effect equally debunks any mythical conceptions of cultural isolation in the Indigenous community as somehow optically innocent of and towards the camera. In opposition to this, the glances into the camera clearly situate the subject in relation to, not in isolation from, the cinematic apparatus.

GENDERED DIMENSIONS

The shifting of dominant binaries between narrative cinema and documentary film, as well as the dissolution between the cinematic representation of a real and an imagined space, functions as an important leitmotif introduced at the very beginning with the arrival of the shaman from the north, who is a stranger, an outsider, setting foot inside a small community. Not only does the shaman allude to the binary between the individual and the group, he also establishes a powerful framework of two cultures colliding. Importantly, the arrival of the stranger also brings disequilibrium to the community – the balance of power and social order shifts into chaos. The strange and unsettling effects of the shaman thus function as a metaphor for the fate of the Inuit community in the historical context of European colonisation and the expansion of the British Empire to the most remote Native Canadian communities.

With the shaman metaphorically alluding to the difficulties faced by Indigenous communities vis à vis the arrival of European settlers, the film actively promotes comparisons to Native Canadian cultures in today's context. In particular, the film repeatedly addresses a gendered dimension in both the destruction and the reconstruction from within the community. The shaman from the north brings a curse to Igloolik, yet it is the people within the community who eventually turn on each other. In this context, the women in the film are depicted lacking agency and authority as they succumb to the will of other men. The right to marry Atuat, for instance, is settled through a fight which has been set up by the male elders. As one of the main female figures in the film, Atuat is thus subjected to a patriarchal system of power handed down from one generation to another. Later in the film a rape scene in which Atuat is attacked by Oki and his gang brutally exemplifies the imbalance of power between the genders. The rape scene in particular can be seen as a reference to the high rate of domestic violence and family abuse in the Inuit communities today. As Natalie Loukacheva has pointed out, despite its small population, Nunavut has the highest crime rate in Canada particularly as a result of high levels of domestic violence (Loukacheva 2007: 100).

Although *Atanarjuat* depicts women under the traditional rules of a patriarchal system, in certain instances the film also highlights women as empowered and highly influential forces within the community. In that regard, the violence against Atanarjuat and his brother are, in fact, instigated by Puja's transgressions and her apparent desire to provoke tension amongst the clans. Yet apart from Puja, the influence of women can mostly be observed as moderators seeking to bring peace and harmony to the community as a whole. Absolutely crucial in this context is the divergence between the legend of Atanarjuat as oral history and the legend as represented in the film (Kern 2009: 45). In the former, Atanarjuat finally kills Oki and the violence thus continues to the bitter end. Yet in the latter, the film diverges from the 'original' legend: in a dramatic fight scene set in an *iglu*, Atanarjuat purposefully smashes a baton not onto but next to Oki's head into the ice as he demands 'The killing stops here!'. Shamed and humiliated, Oki is denounced in front of the community as the necklace signifying his position as leader is taken away from him. The curse of the shaman is finally expelled.

In a dramatic and touching monologue at the very end of the film, the matriarch Panikpak concludes that the only way for the community to come together is for her own grandchildren Oki and Puja, as well as their co-conspirators, to leave the group forever. Panikpak's intervention highlights the notion of reconciliation as an important Inuit concept that stands in contrast to the Euro-American justice system which foregrounds the punishment of a crime. In other words, rather than exercising revenge to the bitter end, the community does not so much punish Oki and Puja in the judicial sense of the word, but rather, they seek to literally distance themselves from those most badly affected by the curse. In this context, the film clearly alludes to the effectiveness of traditional Inuit methods of social control and dispute resolution.

A two-minute postscript directly addresses contemporary Inuit cultures to signal that retelling the legend of Atanarjuat fulfills a social purpose not only for those who participated in it, but also on whose behalf the film is speaking.

Figure 5.3   *Atanarjuat: The Fast Runner*: postscript.

As the end credits are rolling, various 'making-of' scenes unfold in slow motion to highlight production methods. One shot shows how the epic running scene was filmed by using a sled pulled across the ice. Another shot shows Oki's character in a rockabilly leather jacket listening to music on his headphones. These short shots situate the production process back into the community. They also show the lack of visual trickery and gadgets usually associated with feature film production.

By metaphorically breaking through the Fourth Wall, Kunuk inverts the apparatuses of cinematic production into a spectacle in its own right. Apart from fulfilling an important social function in the context of Inuit cultural production, the postscript philosophically aligns itself with Jacques Rancière's theory about the 'emancipated spectator', which involves 'linking what one knows with what one does not know; being at once a performer deploying her skills and a spectator observing what these skills might produce in a new context among other spectators' (2009: 22). The postscript in *Atanarjuat* precisely alludes to the blurring between performer and spectator – two roles that are otherwise diametrically opposed in Hollywood cinema. This emancipation of the spectator who recognises her own role in the cycle of the cinematic experience functions as a powerful symbol for the optical experience of cinema, but also as a symbol for the emancipation of a community actively engaged in the process of narration and translation.

Conclusion

Rather than solely viewing *Atanarjuat* as a representation of ancient Inuit traditions or contemporary social issues, the film lends itself to be seen as a hybrid cultural product. In doing so, to borrow from Homi Bhabha, the film allows us to 'elude the politics of polarity' or a strict division between one cultural context and another. In the first instance, the filmmakers achieve the notion of a hybrid product in cinematic terms: by meshing aspects of narrative cinema with documentary, as well as magic realism and a reference to metacinema towards the end of the film. Here, the filmmakers thus consciously evade rigid definitions of Euro-American cinematic production. The film appears to blend and mesh different cinematic methodologies that suit the notion of a fluid oral tradition as well as the incorporation of mysticism and shamanism. The film thus constitutes an important epistemological break in the way that the Inuit context is represented: rather than being recorded or depicted by a cultural outsider, the film actively engages with its own traditions and histories by speaking for the Inuit community from within. Ultimately, the cinematic representation of Atanarjuat is as a tale about agency and empowerment as well as forgiveness and reconciliation.

NOTE

1. Kunuk's concerns about how the film would be perceived in the Inuit community were expressed at a Kodak Lecture at Ryerson University, Toronto on 29 November 2002. The film was so popular in Igloolik that it had to be shown several times a day over a three-day period in the local community centre. Kunuk also stressed that the final cut of the film was approved by elders in the community.

BIBLIOGRAPHY

Brecht, B. (1964), *Brecht on Theatre* (ed. and trans. John Willett), New York: Hill and Wang.
Dickinson, P. (2007), *Screening Gender, Framing Genre: Canadian Literature into Film*, London: University of Toronto Press.
Evans, M. R. (2010), *The Fast Runner: Filming the Legend of Atanarjuat*, Lincoln, NE: University of Nebraska Press.
Hearne, J. (2012), *Smoke Signals: Native Cinema Rising*, London: University of Nebraska Press.
Huhndorf, S. (2003), 'Atanarjuat, The Fast Runner: culture, history, and politics in Inuit media', *American Anthropologist*, 105: 4, 822–6.
Kern, A. (2009), 'Atanarjuat/The Fast Runner'. In *Encyclopedia of American Indian Literature*, New York: Infobase Publishing.
Knopf, K. (2008), *Decolonizing the Lens of Power: Indigenous Films in North America*, Amsterdam: Rodopi.
Krupat, A. (2007), 'Atanarjuat, the Fast Runner and its audiences', *Critical Inquiry*, 33: 3, 606–31.
Loukacheva, N. (2007), *The Arctic Promise: Legal and Political Autonomy of Greenland and Nunavut*, Toronto: University of Toronto Press.
Meeuf, R. (2007), 'Critical localism, ethical cosmopolitanism and Atanarjuat', *Third Text*, 21: 6, 733–44.
Nagib, L. (2011), *World Cinema and the Ethics of Realism*, London: Continuum.
Raheja, M. (2007), 'Reading Nanook's smile: visual sovereignty, indigenous revisions of ethnography, and Atanarjuat (The Fast Runner)', *American Quarterly*, 59: 4, 1159–86.
Rancière, J. (2009), *The Emancipated Spectator*, London: Verso.
Said, E. [1978] (2006), *Orientalism*, London: Penguin.
Stone, R. (2006), 'Mother lands, sister nations: the epic, poetic, propaganda films of Cuba and the Basque Country', in Dennison, S. and S. H. Lim (eds), *Remapping World Cinema: Identity, Culture and Politics in Film*, London: Wallflower Press.
Wollen, P. [1969] (1970), *Signs and Meaning in the Cinema*, London: Thames and Hudson.

6. COSMOPOLITAN INUIT: NEW PERSPECTIVES ON GREENLANDIC FILM

Kirsten Thisted

Greenland National Museum, April 2006. Frank Sinatra's classic 'New York New York' is flowing out of the speakers: 'I want to wake up in a city that never sleeps ... These little town blues are melting away ... I want to be a part of it ... I'll make a brand new start of it ...' The song is the soundtrack to the video installation *Nuuk York Nuuk York,* produced by the organisation Inuit Youth International[1] in connection with the project *Rethinking Nordic Colonialism.*[2] With the help of visual collages, trick photography and carefully chosen localities, Nuuk is resurrected in the video as Nuuk York. The old colonial harbour with its vilified 1970s apartment buildings is transformed: behind the apartment buildings towers a city of skyscrapers that looks unmistakably like Manhattan. Through this new, pulsating city rush busy urban people, who in clothing and aura are reminiscent of Japanese businessmen, goal-oriented and serious, dressed in expensive three-piece suits, with smart glasses, watches and cell phones. The video concludes with a meeting in the sky-top penthouse of an international hotel, somewhat reminiscent of Nuuk's Hotel Hans Egede, but where the usual view of the fjord is exchanged for skyscrapers, maintaining the Nuuk York vision. This is the entire plot of the film, but nonetheless *Nuuk York* was the highpoint of the exhibition and what everyone was talking about. By making the lyrics of 'New York New York' their own, the young people expressed their vision of the Nuuk of the future. Yet a digitally connected modern life is a reality that young people are already living: a life markedly differentiated from the customary pictures of Greenland as an almost untouched natural state. Eighty-four per cent of the population of Greenland live in cities today, one quarter of them in the capital city Nuuk, and only a few have personal experience of hunting, trapping or fishing.

By playing on their physical resemblance to the Japanese, the young people assumed the identity that the 1970s generation renounced with the category 'indigenous people' and its attendant romantic conceptions of a 'truer' humanity (cf. Inuit = people), unspoilt by alienating Western civilisation. Even if the Japanese are not white Westerners, they have conquered modernity, associated with high technology, economy and materialism. In *Nuuk York*, identification with a (global) late modern identity is not misapplied in a Greenlandic context as the concluding meeting is conducted in effortless Greenlandic. Here the picture of 'the Japanese' is dismantled to the advantage of young, competent Greenlanders, who master the big city and find themselves at the top of it – not at the bottom, as is so often the case in documentaries and TV or radio reports. Depicting the constant checking of time on wristwatches, the artwork rebukes an ingrained stereotype of the Greenlander, supposedly by definition living in harmony with nature, as a stranger to abstract, linear time – a stereotype that in a less kind version depicts the Greenlander as unsuited for a steady job.

Youth Writes Back was the title of the workshop that produced the video, and the intention was naturally that the youth should take part in the show-down with the postcolonial, which was the object of the conference. However, the youth were born under Greenlandic home rule (introduced in 1979), and the clash with the Danes was their parents' cause. They were uninterested in the role of victim (and, with it, a position as loser) into which the subject of postcolonialism could place them; if the video wrote back, then it was rather to the parents, who in their time contributed to locking Greenland and the Greenlanders in a narrative that the next generation does not find appropriate. *Nuuk York* thus signals an interest in opening Greenland to new stories and possibilities for identification, and lots of examples could be provided to show that those kinds of dreams are not only dreamt in Nuuk (Thisted: 2013a). The Arctic is in motion – not only the much talked about melting glaciers, but society as a whole. By 2012, the phrase 'Nuuk York' had become common-place in Greenland to describe the building boom that is well on its way to giving Nuuk an actual skyline.

Greenlanders are actively engaged in formulating a cosmopolitan and urban modernity that reflects a range of globalisation processes. Recent film production in Greenland helps exemplify these trends and portrays distinctive representational paradigms of Arctic popular culture. Greenland's first two films, *Nuummioq* (*The Man From Nuuk*, Otto Rosing and Torben Bech, Greenland, 2009) and *Hinnarik Sinnattunilu* (*Henrik's Dream*, Angajo Lennert-Sandreen, Greenland, 2009), will be examined here to show how the films navigate relative to both the outside world and home audiences' expectations of representations of Greenland as locality. At the same time,

Danish Greenland films constitute a considerable framework of reference and background conditions for the new Greenlandic film.

Films by Danish (and international) directors have been made in Greenland, including films with the participation of Greenlanders as actors and film-makers, since the inception of cinema (Thisted 2013b; Norrested 2011; Gant 2004). Well-known Danish Greenland films often seek to either commemorate an already nostalgic notion of indigenous hunter-fishing cultures, which is the case in *Palo's Wedding* (*Palo's Brudefaerd,* Friedrich Dalsheim, Denmark, 1934), *SOS Eisberg* (Arnold Fanck, USA/Germany, 1933), *Qivitoq* (Erik Balling, Denmark, 1956, and *Heart of Light* (*Qaamarngup Uummataa/ Lysets Hjerte,* Jacob Grønlykke, Denmark, 1998), or use Greenland to present materialism and rootlessness as downsides of Danish welfare state modernity, as represented by *Tukuma* (Palle Kjærulff-Schmidt, Denmark, 1984). What film constitutes as 'Greenlandic' has been contested during the past few years. Mike Magidson's *Le Voyage D'Inuk* (Ce la Vie Films/Docside, 2010), for example, was labelled as Greenlandic in the Greenlandic media on the basis of it being filmed in Greenland, with a Greenlandic subject and with contributing Greenlandic actors, even if the production company and director were foreign.

To Be – and Remain – from Nuuk

Nuummioq was marketed as the first feature film produced in Greenland, but several productions actually preceded it. These include *Takorluukkat Sisamat* (*Four Visions,* Albert Nuka, 1985) and *Tikeq, Qiterleq, Mikileraq, Eqeqqoq* (*Index Finger, Long Man, Ring Finger, Little Finger*, Ujarneq Fleischer, 2008), and Inuk Silis Høeg's popular shorts *Eskimo Weekend* (2002), and *Good Night* (*Sinilluarit,* 1999). *Nuummioq* is in genre a kind of bromance about three friends, Greenlanders and cousins Malik (Lars Rosing), Michael (Angunnguaq Larsen), and Dane Carsten (Morten Rose). 'Nuummioq' means 'one who lives in Nuuk', and the title conveys attachment to place, family and friends. In Greenland, too, the multicultural big city elicits discussion around being 'home' or 'foreign', which characterises the debate on the national level. All the Greenlanders in the film constantly shift between Danish and Greenlandic, just as English is naturally present, partly through the soundtrack by the Greenlandic singer and songwriter Nive Nielsen, partly because of Michael's idea of exporting ice from the inland ice. A central scene in the film involves making an English-language commercial for the project. The Nuuk depicted in *Nuummioq* is cosmopolitan and multicultural in a sense that goes far beyond the fact that one can, as the film also demonstrates, eat Thai food and buy palm trees there. This 'inclusive differentiation', which can contain differences rather than exclude them, is a hallmark of contemporary 'second modernity', in Ulrich Bech's terminology, contrasting with first modernity's

exclusive differentiation: 'frozen, separate worlds and identities that dominated the first modernity of separate nationally organized societies . . .' (2006:
6). In *Nuummioq*, city and wilderness are depicted as two landscapes that
mutually supplement each other in modern life – just as the city's taverns are no
longer a metaphor for lost souls, but a place where one goes out to have fun –
or a place to get dead drunk when one finds out that one has incurable cancer.
Short-circuiting ingrained cultural preconceptions, the films shows city life to
be an integrated part of the modern world in Greenland. Indeed Malik, the
most Danish looking and most Danish speaking of the cousins, has the deepest
emotional connection to Greenlandic nature, and masters classic Greenlandic
virtues such as hunting and fishing, while Michael, who both looks and sounds
more 'Greenlandic', is completely hopeless at these. This idea may be inspired
by *Eskimo Weekend* where a similar short-circuiting of prior expectations surrounding the connection between appearance, culture and nationality is used.
The subject is important in a Greenlandic context because under colonialism
Greenlanders were brought up on a race-based conception that 'crossbreeds'
constituted some kind of natural bridge builders between the primitive and
the civilised. The attitude towards these crossbreeds was ambivalent from
the Danish side because the 'unmixed' hunters were considered the 'real'
Greenlanders (Thomsen 1998), while the crossbreeds came a little too near to
the Danes' own culture and therefore were discredited as rootless and split.

Figure 6.1 A still used for a promotional poster for the 'bromance' *Nuummioq* ('The
Man from Nuuk', 2009). Photograph by Andreas Rydbacken.

Thus *Nuummioq* becomes, in the same way as the *Nuuk York* video, a reckoning with the discourse of earlier generations. The film can be seen as a counterpoint to what is often called modern Greenland's first feature film, Danish-funded and Denmark produced *Qaamarngup Uummataa/Lysets Hjerte*, which largely repeats stereotypes of modern Greenlanders as victims of modernity, plagued by alcoholism and drug use. Reversing the title of Joseph Conrad's famous *Heart of Darkness*, a central text in postcolonial theory, *Heart of Light* figures the journey toward the pre-colonial as a journey from dark to light, stressed by the film's images that move from the *mørketid* (time of darkness) of the big city towards radiant sunshine over the snow-covered mountains out in the great wilderness. *Nummioq*'s insistence on foregrounding city life constitutes a marked contrast with this earlier filmmaking tradition.

GREENLANDIC DYNAMITE

While the reception of *Nuummioq* at various international film festivals was positive, economically it was a fiasco: it did not receive international cinema distribution, even in Denmark. *Hinnarik Sinnattunilu* handles the expectations of what a Greenlandic film should be about in a completely different and radical way. While *Nuummioq* had a budget of about $1 million, *Hinnarik Sinnattunilu* was produced for barely 200,000 kr. (approximately $36,000). Quite unpretentious, it is aimed at local young people rather than international film festivals. In this film, we are never further from the city than the mountain right behind the Nuuk airport. Dressed in a black curly wig and a white wool beanie, the lead character Hinnarik (Angajo Lennert-Sandgreen) shares character traits with both Sacha Baron Cohen's *Borat* figure, and teenage cult film character *Napoleon Dynamite* (Jared Hess, USA, 2004). An awkward teenager (like Mr Dynamite) dissatisfied with his real life, Hinnarik spends most of his time in a dream world and, like Borat, wants to advance himself internationally. He attempts with cosmopolitan enthusiasm to teach himself English, German, French, Japanese, Chinese and 'African'. Though nonsensical, Hinnarik's character and the film's plot combine traditional Greenlandic myths and storytelling with strategies of recent US independent film stories that have been globally successful. The film runs on two tracks. In the first, we encounter situations marked by miracles and fantasy the way Hinnarik himself experiences them: he catches an enormous fish, masters karate, skis like a wizard, and implicitly impersonates a central figure in Greenlandic oral storytelling, the young and bullied orphan Kaassassuk, who, though feeble, gained superhuman strength through magic to beat his oppressors (this mythical figure has also become an emblem for Greenlandic opposition to Denmark). In the second, we see these situations from the outside, where the miracles perhaps have a more

Figure 6.2   A Greenlandic Napoleon Dynamite? *Hinnarik Sinnattunilu* ('Henrik's Dream', 2009).

logical explanation. Regardless of the reason, Hinnarik comes to believe a little more in himself (at least partly because of the romantic subplot of the film, where he gets the pretty girl at the end) and that may be the film's miracle. Elements from Greenlandic oral tradition and Christianity are blended in the film's symbolic world, together with accounts of people's communication with the supernatural from global popular culture. Hinnarik's *Star Wars* poster replaces the Christian-motif pictures of many Greenlandic homes, and it is in front of this image that Hinnarik prays. Solemnity is removed from religion and 'cultural heritage', while respect for the practice of worship is preserved. A parallel scene, balancing between seriousness and comedy, involves a figure from the other side haranguing Hinnarik about using his newly found strength properly. This figure occupies a space that can represent everything from the Christian God to 'The Force', regardless of whether it refers to Greenlandic, Inuit or Hollywood traditions.

Hinnarik Sinnattunilu becomes a symbol of globalisation in Greenland in other ways also. The film ended up in court, simply because it had been stolen and copied up and down the coast, even before it was finished. While popular in Greenland, it is doubtful whether *Hinnarik Sinnattunilu* would hold its own on the international market, where people would not discern all the whimsical elements and irony which result from the Greenlandic localisation, given that the film was produced with the Greenlandic public foremost in mind. This is evident from the soundtrack of the film, where no effort was made to infuse the film with 'Greenlandic' sound, even if Greenlandic music is included. The music is used primarily to support Hinnarik's moods and the character of his grandiose fantasies, and it features a range of styles from Kletchmer to classical. With a less ambitious objective, *Hinnarik Sinnattunilu* is freer to give a global scope to the Greenlandic, without inversely being obliged to brand the local to make it palatable for export.

As exemplified by *Nuuk York, Nuummioq* and *Hinnarik Sinnattunilu*, globalisation makes possible a rapid phasing out of the relationship with Denmark as the only or necessarily central one for contemporary Greenlandic (popular) culture. Yet, examined against the background of Greenland's history of colonisation, decolonisation and nation-building, it is not so surprising that Greenlandic narratives continue to focus on the place-bound and local, and reconfigure such traditions for the contemporary moment. Tumit Productions, for example, has already released its next film: *Qaqqat alanngui* (*The Shadows in the Mountains*), a horror movie, which has its basis in the Greenlandic *qivittoq* stories, modernised with inspiration from other *zombies* and a global cult phenomenon like *The Blair Witch Project* (Pedersen 2008).

Through world media, Greenland is maintained in the image of a remote place, characterised by a sublime landscape and populated by indigenous Inuit who still live according to the traditions of an ancient hunting culture, as exemplified by the BBC's documentary *Human Planet: Arctic – Life in the Deep Freeze* (2011), in which nature and culture are seen as a amalgamated whole, both of them under threat from global warming, and where even the bustling town Ilulissat in Disco Bay, one of the centres of Greenland's fishing industry, is made to look 'traditional'. A similar strategy is employed in *Silent Snow* (Jan van den Berg and Pipaluk Knudsen-Ostermann, Netherlands, 2011), while *Village at the End of the World* (Sarah Gavron and David Katznelson, UK, 2012) demonstrates how there is Internet access even in the most remote settlements. These days Greenlanders take part in all sorts of transnational networks, through official channels and as individuals. So in Greenland globalisation is not just something that happens 'out there' in the abstract, in the media, or in economics. Greenlandic biographies are definitely 'global' in the sense that almost every Greenlander counts a non-Inuit among her or his closest relatives, and many Greenlanders live outside Greenland. People spread their lives over separate worlds, crossing the borders of nations, continents, languages, ethnicities, race, and so on, and thus it is people's individual lives, their personal biographies, that have become globalised. Recent film production in Greenland exemplifies this change.

NOTES

1. Started in Nuuk in 2001, see http://old.nanoq.gl/imageblob/showimage.aspx? objno=47017.
2. See http://www.rethinking-nordic-colonialism.org/ (last accessed 15 March 2012); see also Thisted 2011.

BIBLIOGRAPHY

Beck, U. (2006), *The Cosmopolitan Vision*, trans. Ciaran Cronin (original title: *Der kosmopolitische Blick oder: Krieg ist Frieden*, 2004), Cambridge, Malden: Polity Press.

Gant, E. (2004), 'Eskimotid: analyser af filmiske fremstillinger af eskimoer med udgangspunkt i postkolonialistisk teori og med særlig vægtning af danske grønlandsfilm', dissertation. Aarhus University.

Nørrested, C. (2011), *Grønlandsfilm. Blandt eskimoer, eventyrere, kolonisatorer og etnografer / Greenland on Film: Amongst Eskimos, Adventurers, Colonisers, and Ethnographers*, Copenhagen: North.

Pedersen, B. K. (2008), 'Young Greenlanders in the Urban Space of Nuuk', *Études/Inuit!Studies* 32.1: 91–106.

Thisted, K. (2013a), 'Discourses of indigeneity. Branding Greenland in the age of self-government and climate change', in, S. Sörlin (ed.), *Science, Geopolitics and Culture in the Polar Region – Norden beyond Borders*, Farnham: Ashgate, 227–58.

Thisted, K. (2013b), 'Grønlændere på film', in: S. Frank and M. Ümit Necef (eds), *Indvandreren i dansk film og litteratur*. Hellerup: Spring, 75–104.

Thomsen, H. (1998) 'Ægte grønlændere og nye grønlændere – Om forskellige opfattelser af grønlandskhed', *Den Jyske Historiker*, 81, 21–56.

7. ARCTIC CARNIVALESQUE: ETHNICITY, GENDER AND TRANSNATIONALITY IN THE FILMS OF TOMMY WIRKOLA

Gunnar Iversen

In the last ten years, a new wave of northern Norwegian comedies have been parodying conventional images of the Arctic region. These comedies are lowbrow and carnivalesque, a cinematic continuation of a raunchy, specifically northern Norwegian oral comedy tradition. However, the parodic treatment of the Far North is entirely new to Norwegian feature film. More than ever before, these films question ethnic, gender and national identities associated with the global North. Most of the films also engage transnationally with Hollywood genre movies.

These films use genre elements associated with American movies, though these aesthetic elements are also used in movies from other countries. The use of these genre elements are new in a Norwegian context, and are most often used specifically to parody Norwegians and Norwegian culture. However, the use of elements from specific, popular American films or associated with American cinema more generally not only parodies Norwegian culture, but also the original American movies. Thus, the carnivalesque laughter in these movies is directed at both American and Norwegian culture.

At the centre of this new wave of northern Norwegian comedies is the young filmmaker Tommy Wirkola. He was born in the small northern town Alta in 1979 and is of Finnish Sámi descent. After studying media at Finnmark University College, the northernmost university college in the world, and film at Lillehammer University College, Wirkola completed a Bachelor degree in film and media at Bond University in Australia. Returning to Alta, his hometown, Wirkola produced, co-wrote and directed the feature *Kill Buljo: The Movie*

(Norway, 2007). A low-budget Sámi parody of Quentin Tarantino's *Kill Bill* (2003–4), the film became a success in Norway, and launched his film career.

Tommy Wirkola's best-known Norwegian feature is *Dead Snow* (*Død snø*, Norway, 2009), a Nazi zombie film that also engages in a dialogue with American genre cinema. In 2010, Wirkola made *Kurt Josef Wagle and the Legend of the Fjord Witch* (*Kurt Josef Wagle og legenden om fjordheksa*, Norway, 2010), a parody of *The Blair Witch Project* (Daniel Myrick and Eduardo Sánchez, USA, 1999) set in the Far North of Norway. This movie also parodies the conventional images of northern masculinity and art cinema, where men are strong, taciturn and virile, like a force of nature, especially through a parody of the immensely popular documentary *Cool and Crazy* (*Heftig og begeistret*, Knut Erik Jensen, Norway, 2001).

In 2013, Wirkola's first Hollywood feature premiered, *Hansel and Gretel: Witch Hunters*, and the same year he began filming a sequel to *Dead Snow* that continues where the first film left off. Nazi zombies this time meet zombies from the Soviet Red Army, placing some Norwegian youngsters in a tight squeeze.

In this chapter, I will discuss how Wirkola's Norwegian feature films problematise the ethnic, gender and national identities associated with northern Norway. I will place these films in the context of a new wave of northern Norwegian lowbrow comedies enabled by new structures of state film support that challenge traditional images of the Arctic.

FILM PRODUCTION IN NORWAY AFTER 2001

The new wave of northern Norwegian comedies have been possible because of recent changes in film policy and the government support system for feature films. In 2001, the Norwegian Ministry for Cultural Affairs created a new institution to distribute production support. Norsk Filmfond (Norwegian Film Fund) replaced a number of smaller independent organisations, and was itself replaced by a reorganised Norsk filminstitutt (Norwegian Film Institute) in 2007. Since 2007, the film institute has distributed all production support for short films, documentaries and feature films in Norway.

Production support was principally intended to fund films with artistic aspirations, although support was not limited exclusively to art cinema. However, since 2001, more funding has gone to popular cinema, especially through the so-called '50/50 Scheme' modelled on the Danish system that was added in 2001 and strengthened in 2007 (Bondebjerg 2005: 121–2). The 50/50 Scheme provides automatic advance support to features for which producers have independently raised at least 50 percent of the budget.

These changes aimed to provide the national film production sector with more freedom, to counterbalance elitist tendencies, make producers more accountable, and simply get more feature films for the government's money. The policy resulted in an immediate boost of output. In 2003 nearly twenty feature films were made in Norway, and in 2011 the number of features released reached more than thirty.

Since the 50/50 Scheme was implemented, both established big production companies and small new companies have utilised this opportunity. A new type of independent cinema has emerged in Norway: commercial, low-budget productions working in formulaic genres like horror and comedy. Tommy Wirkola's films have all been made via the 50/50 Scheme and they combine comedy and horror to parody both Norwegian and American cinema.

New Images of the Global North

The year 2003 is important in the development of a new wave of northern Norwegian comedies. This year two feature films premiered that engaged with transnational genre elements and created new images of the global North. In different ways, these two films suggested how film directors from the Arctic could redefine their region through filmic images and stories.

The Norwegian-Swedish-Danish *Bázo* (Lars Göran Pettersson, 2003) is a Sámi road movie about a man everybody regards as a *bázo*, a Sámi word for idiot or fool. When Emil's brother dies under mysterious circumstances, he travels to find out what happened to his brother and to pick up his brother's things. On the road he meets different people, becomes responsible for his brother's unknown son Kevin, and finally gets his revenge on some gangsters who may or may not have killed his brother.

Bázo uses elements from film noir and crime films as well as comedy to create a different image of the global North. Where traditional representations of the northern Norwegian landscape emphasise the spectacular, sublime aspects of the rugged terrain, the film insistently presents the landscape as bleak and boring. Social ills emanate from the white, non-Sámi community, as a white Finnish councilman is responsible for shady deals that get both Emil and his dead brother into trouble. The film also criticises the 'touristisation' of Sámi culture in a scene in which Emil takes his brother's son Kevin to SantaPark, which is on the Arctic Circle in Rovaniemi in Finland. The boy has been begging to go to the park, but when a group of American tourists mistake him and his colourful Sámi clothes for part of the attraction and start photographing him, the boy, overwhelmed, runs to the bathroom and throws up.

Bázo uses elements from genre cinema to create new and unconventional images of the Arctic region, but even more important to Tommy Wirkola's movies was *Burnt Negro* (*Svidd neger*, Erik Smith-Meyer, 2003). This is a wild and lowbrow comedy about life and love in northern Norway. Two families live in a remote coastal area, on either side of a mountain, but discover each other by accident. After a fire they have to live together. Both families are extremely dysfunctional, and the film engages in a grotesque critique of ethnicity and gender. At the centre of the story is Ante, a black boy who was discovered in a box on the beach as an infant. He regards himself as a Sea Sámi, speaks the Sámi language, and even wears traditional clothing. These he gets from the Sámi Nilas, who does not want to be Sámi, but wears biker clothes with a confederate flag over his heart. The film parodically juxtaposes Ante, who is treated as black although he sees himself as Sámi, and Nilas, who is treated as Sámi although he identifies with the American South. Ante discovers his 'true' identity when he finds a Jackson 5 vinyl record on the beach.

Burnt Negro is a grotesque comedy about identity, which uses images from American horror films as a critical vocabulary to make fun of northern Norwegians and traditional images of life close to nature. The father in one family drinks Jack Daniels bourbon all the time, is extremely violent and vulgar, and wears a dress. He has murdered his wife many years ago, and the dress connects his psychopathology with gender deviance, a common device of horror cinema (Clover 1992). The movie questions the masculinity of all the male characters, and they all seem to be gathered from a mythic American South, provocatively linking the Global North with the American South via a shared 'redneck' culture (Iversen 2009).

In different ways *Bázo* and *Burnt Negro* question traditional images of northern Norway. Both use American movies and popular culture as a way to create carnivalesque and non-traditional images that upend ethnicity, gender and nationality. Both movies were produced in the Far North, and especially *Burnt Negro* showed Tommy Wirkola a way to continue the critique of traditional images of northern Norway.

KILL BULJO AND THE ARCTIC CARNIVALESQUE

One of the most interesting of these new Arctic carnivalesque comedies is Tommy Wirkola's *Kill Buljo*. In this movie, four white Norwegians crash the engagement party of the young Sámi Jompa, and kill everyone, except Jompa himself. Jompa is wounded, but wakes up after a period in a coma, and takes a bloody revenge. He kills the four Norwegians who massacred the guests at his engagement party, and the white Norwegian man behind it all: Buljo himself.

In recent years, several movies have been produced in Norway that question the conventional image of Norway as a homogeneous, egalitarian nation-state with no colonial background. The best known, *The Kautokeino Rebellion* (*Kautokeino-opprøret*, Norway, 2008) by Sámi director Nils Gaup, uses the Sámi revolt of 1852 as a way to revise historical accounts of the Sámi

Figure 7.1   A scene in *Kill Buljo* parodies Norwegian art cinema by copying a famous scene from Knut Erik Jensen's *Burnt by Frost* from 1997.

Figure 7.2   Stig Frode Henriksen as the Sámi Jompa in *Kill Buljo*; Tommy Wirkola's parody of Tarantino's *Kill Bill*.

population. History and the attitude of white Norwegians towards the indigenous Sámi population lies at the heart of *Kill Buljo* too, but Wirkola's movie is all about Kautokeino today. Gaup's movie is a conventional historical drama that places the Sámi population as victims of the white Norwegians; *Kill Buljo*

Figure 7.3   Male rape inspired by John Boorman's *Deliverance* in Tommy Wirkola's *Kill Buljo*.

refuses to see the Sámi population only as victims or as limited to the past, and creates a violent fantasy about revenge.

Like *Bázo*, the film criticises the touristisation of Sámi culture and pits Sámis against malevolent white Scandinavians. We discover that Jompa's family and friends were killed because Jompa has accidentally seen the Norwegian Buljo creating fake rock carvings in order to create a big tourist centre in Kautokeino. By killing Jompa and his family, Buljo intends to replace a traditional way of living with modern tourism.

Another way the movie thematises antagonism between white Norwegians and the Sámi is through the character Sid, played by Wirkola himself, a white Norwegian police officer who leads the investigation of the Sámi massacre. Sid immediately puts the blame on Jompa, and tries in every way to frame Jompa for the killings. Only after the intervention of a white female police officer who has been kidnapped by Buljo's men will Sid acknowledge the fact that Buljo is behind it all. Until this happens, he is constantly saying bad things about the Sámi population.

Kill Buljo restages an iconic moment of Norwegian history in a parodic way, by linking the police officer Sid and his attitude towards the Sámi people to the demonstrations in Alta in the years 1979–81, one of the most famous cases of civil disobedience in modern Norwegian history. In a flashback we learn that Sid was on the side of the official Norwegian government as a police officer, and tried to remove demonstrators who wanted to prevent the construction of a large dam and power plant that would change the traditional

Sámi way of living. Needing to pee, Sid goes on his own down to a small river, where he is humiliated and raped by two Sámi men, in an overt reference to *Deliverance* (John Boorman, USA, 1972) – once again linking Sámi men to American rednecks in a curious conflation of Global North and American South.

As in many other films in the new wave of northern Norwegian comedies, the film uses references to American genre movies to make fun of American as well as Norwegian culture. *Kill Buljo* has a particularly complex relationship to American movie culture. Often these references lampoon the original film, like a scene in which Jompa makes a hole in a wall with a chainsaw, sticks his head through the door, and shouts 'Here's Jompa', with a reference to *The Shining* (Stanley Kubrick, USA, 1980). One of the female villains is named Lara Kofta, a combination of the name Lara Croft and *kofte*, the Norwegian word for a traditional Sámi collar (or *gákti*). Additionally, in a flashback in which Jompa recalls his background as a fisherman, Jompa mimics the iconic scene from *Titantic* (James Cameron, USA, 1997) in which Leonardo DiCaprio holds Kate Winslet over the water at the bow of the ship. In *Kill Buljo*, Jompa loses his grip on his girl, and she is caught in the propeller and killed. In the same scene, Wirkola also parodies the 'official' high-culture art films of northern Norway, by recreating an infamous scene in Knut Erik Jensen's *Burnt by Frost* (*Brent av frost*, Norway, 1997), in which a man and a woman make love in a boat on a bed of codfish. In *Kill Buljo*, Jompa cannot stop complaining about the smell of the fish. In this way, the numerous references in the film are used to burlesque both Norwegian high culture and American genre movies.

Kill Buljo and other recent movies from northern Norway create a deliberately trashy and anti-romantic image of indigenous people. In *Kill Buljo* Jompa himself is an idiotic producer of moonshine who accomplishes his revenge mostly by accident. The film makes fun of Sámi like Jompa as well as white Norwegians, and Wirkola is careful not to victimise Jompa in a romantic way.

Not only does *Kill Buljo* attack high culture, white Norwegians, American movie culture and the Norwegian police, it also attacks the myth of white Northern Norwegian men's hypermasculinity. Masculinity is the butt of the joke, in a quite literal sense, with the depiction of a number of male rape scenes, as well as constant jokes about men and bodily functions. All of Wirkola's movies can be seen as Norwegian examples of vulgar trash and exploitation movies, but, unlike many exploitation films, the film treats women much better than men. Though they do not escape being made fun of, they are not put down in the same vulgar and excessive way as men are, nor are they put on bodily display. In *Kill Bujlo*, white women and Sámi men are pitted against official Norwegian culture.

DEAD SNOW AND THE BURDEN OF HISTORY

Tommy Wirkola's best-known and most popular film is *Dead Snow*, defined on the DVD cover as a 'Nazi-zombie-horror-splatter-comedy'. In this movie, eight medical students go on Easter vacation to a hut in a remote mountain area in northern Norway. They joke about horror movies, but are soon in a horror movie themselves, being surrounded and killed off one by one by Nazi zombies.

Where *Kill Buljo* parodies the Alta protests, *Dead Snow* takes on the even more sacred national memory of the Nazi occupation of Norway during World War II, and, in particular, the Nazi's 'scorched earth' policy in northern Norway. The film tells a story of how evil Nazis terrorised the local community in this remote area during the war, and stole all their belongings when the soldiers understood that they would lose the war. Enraged, the Norwegians take revenge, kill a number of soldiers, and chase the evil Colonel Herzog and his men into the mountains, where they are destined to die in the cold snow. As in *Kill Buljo,* Wirkola uses history in *Dead Snow* as a way to create a wild story of revenge. In the movie's backstory, the northerners are not only victims, but also avengers. However, this is once more turned around in the movie's present. The young medical students, mostly from the south or west coast of Norway, are killed by the Nazi zombies. The Nazis kill them not only out of blood lust, but also because the youngsters discover and take the old loot from the Nazis.

Dead Snow uses American horror movies, like the two *Evil Dead* films (Sam Raimi, USA, 1981, 1987), to create a carnivalesque and grotesque comment on the way World War II has become a special part of the identity of northern Norway. Instead of creating serious occupation dramas or art cinema about victimisation or the burden of History, as other Norwegian filmmakers have done, Wirkola makes a wild horror parody out of one of the most important historical events in modern Norwegian history. American movies are used throughout the movie in this subversive game with conventional images of war and history, from the prologue where the film's only star actor is killed off after just two minutes, before the credits, in a reference to *Psycho* (Alfred Hitchcock, USA, 1960), to the end of the film and the uncertain destiny of the Final Boy, a comment on numerous modern horror movies with Final Girls (Clover 1992).

Dead Snow can also be seen as a grotesque inversion of one of the most popular and beloved Norwegian occupation dramas. In Oscar-nominated *Nine Lives* (Arne Skouen, Norway, 1957), the wounded resistance fighter Jan Baalsrud manages to run away from German soldiers and miraculously survives thanks to the local community in northern Norway that hides and cares for him (Iversen 2012). In *Dead Snow*, on the other hand, the locals are represented by an old man who is quickly killed off. Only one of the Norwegian youngsters survives, ironically the one medical student who early on faints at the sight of blood.

PARODYING HIGH CULTURE AND MASCULINITY

The single movie that has come to define northern Norwegian identity in recent years is the documentary *Cool and Crazy* (2001) by Knut Erik Jensen. The movie profiles the Berlevåg Male Choir in a tiny fishing village near the North Cape. More than 600,000 Norwegians saw the movie and it became one of the biggest box-office successes in the history of Norwegian cinema. Everybody praised Jensen's movie, which became a national event, earning the Berlevåg Choir something of a cult status (Iversen 2006). *Cool and Crazy* is a documentary about the dignity of ordinary lives lived under extreme circumstances, and it depicts a disappearing world and way of life. Jensen's documentary shows that when changes in the international fishing industry turn a thriving fishing village into a shadow of its former self, not much is left. However, what is left, and what probably made the movie into such a big national success, is its warm nostalgia for simpler times, for an older and simpler masculinity and male comradeship, for nature and 'Norwegians in the middle of nowhere'.

Jensen's documentary celebrates the uniqueness of the northern Norwegian, and especially the masculinity of the northern Norwegian man. Tommy Wirkola starts his movie *Kurt Josef Wagle and the Legend of the Fjord Witch* with two scenes that explicitly make fun of Jensen's movie and the type of male subjectivity portrayed in *Cool and Crazy*. Wirkola takes two of the most famous scenes in Jensen's movie, and turns them around, parodying both official culture and masculinity.

The most famous scene in Jensen's film is an interview with the old singer Trygg Lund when he is in his bathtub at home. The scene paints a loving portrait of an old and charming man, and he talks about his relationships with women and sings a song by Elvis. Wirkola's film portrays the village idiot Rock in the same way, in the bathtub. He is trying to keep afloat, talks rubbish, and when he tries to keep his breath under water he can only stay under for a few seconds. The similarity between the scenes is striking, and Wirkola makes fun of not only Jensen's film but also of the person Trygg. The name Rock has some of the same connotations as Trygg, which means 'solid' or 'safe'. In Jensen's movie, the old man is the rock of society and a representative of a disappearing culture, but in Wirkola's movie he is just a complete idiot. The next scene also explicitly refers to *Cool and Crazy*, another famous scene of an old fisherman at sea, praising simple life and fishing. Again Wirkola makes fun of Jensen's popular choir members and their nostalgic masculinity.

Figure 7.4 In *Kurt Josef Wagle and the Legend of the Fjord Witch,* Tommy Wirkola parodies the popular documentary *Cool and Crazy* by Knut Erik Jensen, and at the same time he makes fun of Northern masculinity.

Kurt Josef Wagle and the Legend of the Fjord Witch is mostly a parody of the American horror movie *The Blair Witch Project,* but Wirkola starts his movie by making fun of the official version of northern Norwegian masculinity. The movie itself is all about a motley crew of weird characters searching for the son of Kurt Josef Wagle, who they suspect has been taken by a local 'fjord witch'. Strange things do happen on their journey, but the son is soon found in the arms of his gay lover. Wirkola's movie is a vulgar parody of both American genre cinema and Norwegian official cultural versions of the masculinity of the Arctic region. All aspects of traditional masculinity are made fun of in a carnivalesque critique of the images of old masculinity in the far north of Norway, and through this wild trashy parody, he also criticises the appropriation of this image of the North by Norwegian national culture. As in *Kill Buljo* and *Dead Snow,* people from southern Norway are ridiculed, and their images of the Arctic region are equally made fun of in a symbolic destruction of authority and official culture.

ARCTIC CARNIVALESQUE AND HUMOUR AS REBELLION

Mikhail Bakhtin looked favourably on the vulgar laughter of the carnival, seeing it as an act of riotous subversion, and modern social theorists of laughter and ridicule like Michael Billig have noted the rhetorical nature of laughter

(Bakhtin 1984; Billig 2005). Rebellious humour that mocks serious conventions uses ridicule as a weapon, and is rooted in social processes.

Tommy Wirkola's movies may at first glance look like simple examples of the most vulgar northern Norwegian blemish humour, preoccupied with bodily functions. However, at the same time, his movies engage in a social critique of dominant Norwegian culture – not only through the content of the movies and the depictions of life in the Arctic region, but also through the production of the movies. Wirkola is not interested in making high movie art, but rather loves to make fun of established film production culture in Norway, exploiting the new possibilities in the 50/50 Scheme.

In his films, Wirkola mocks conventional images of northern Norway. He questions the ways that historical events have been used to create a specific northern Norwegian identity by making fun of this process of creating a social identity. In *Kill Buljo* it is the civil disobedience of the Alta hydropower development, while in *Dead Snow* it is the special formative experiences of German occupation and the scorched earth policy of World War II that is used as material for parody. Here sombre remembrance of the war is turned into a wild zombie comedy.

Humour is not a simple phenomenon, and it always has contradictory elements. The same is true in the case of Wirkola's movies, and especially the transnationality of his usage of genre elements and specifically the relationship to American genre cinema. Sometimes references to American movies are used to question and make fun of Norway, and sometimes Sámi or northern Norwegian elements make fun of American movies. Wirkola's movies, as well as other northern Norwegian comedies like *Bázo* and *Burnt Negro*, use American genre movies, especially horror and comedies, as a critical vocabulary to create a symbolic destruction of official culture and authority, represented by art cinema from the north and southern Norwegian images of the Far North. In his movies, Tommy Wirkola makes fun of all the sacred cows of official northern Norwegian culture. Kicking from below, through wild, grotesque and trashy humour, Wirkola parodies conventional images of northern Norway. Humour, ridicule, and parody are used to question northern Norwegian identity as well as the ethnic, gender and national identities associated with the global North.

BIBLIOGRAPHY

Bakhtin, M. (1984), *Rabelais and His World*, Bloomington: Indiana University Press.
Billig, M. (2005), *Laughter and Ridicule: Towards a Social Critique of Humour*, London: Sage Publications.
Bondebjerg, I. (2005), 'The Danish way: Danish film culture in a European and global perspective', in A. Nestingen and T. G. Elkington (eds), *Transnational Cinema in a Global North*, Detroit: Wayne State University Press, 111–39.

Clover, C. (1992), *Men, Women and Chain Saws: Gender in the Modern Horror Film*, London: The British Film Institute.

Iversen, G. (2006), 'The Old Wave: material history in *Cool and Crazy* and the new Norwegian documentary', in C. C. Thomson (ed.), *Northern Constellations: New Readings in Nordic Cinema*, London: Norvik Press, 175–88.

Iversen, G. (2009), '"Texas Norway" – mythic space in recent Norwegian crime films', in R. Moine et al. (eds), *Policiers et criminels: un genre populaire européen sur grand et petit écrans*, Paris: L'Harmattan, 35–43.

Iversen, G. (2012), 'From trauma to heroism: cultural memory and remembrance in Norwegian occupation dramas, 1946–2009', *Journal of Scandinavian Cinema*, vol. 2, no. 3, 237–48.

PART II

HOLLYWOOD HEGEMONY

PART II. HOLLYWOOD HEGEMONY

Scott MacKenzie and Anna Westerståhl Stenport

From the earliest days of cinema, the Arctic has played a central part in American and Hollywood cinematic imaginaries. Its oft-cited remoteness and exotic locale additionally exemplify Hollywood's long tradition of location substitution. However, as the chapters in this section demonstrate, the Arctic in Hollywood cinema mobilises diverse cultural, political, gendered, historical and aesthetic perspectives. For instance, Hollywood cinemas have used the environments and populations of the Arctic to make claims about capitalism, communism and proto-fascism. And even in the supposedly unknown Arctic, similar conventions of heteronormativity and patriarchy obtain, in this case replete with figurations of heroic and rugged explorers or noble indigenous hunters. In the chapter 'Fact and Fiction in "Northerns" and "Early Arctic Films"', Russell A. Potter situates burgeoning American feature film production as a continuum of pre-cinematic practices that presented the unknown Arctic, and its populations, through staged and recognisably fictional sets and exhibition modes. As these practices developed into narrative Hollywood silent cinema, the malleability of the Arctic region continued to be made evident through location substitution. Addressing location substitution in the comedies of Sennett, Keaton and Chaplin in the 1920s, Mark Sandberg, in his chapter 'California's Yukon as Comic Space', examines the ways in which Hollywood was able to build a simulacrum of the entire world on its backlots. In the case of the Arctic in particular, Sandberg delineates the claims for authenticity made by these films and the publicity machines that surrounded them, despite their artificiality. In '"See the Crashing Masses of White Death . . .": Greenland,

Germany, and the Sublime in the "*Bergfilm*" *SOS Eisberg*', Lill-Ann Körber traces the history of this Hollywood-Germany co-production, considers it in relation to the rugged, purity-of-nature *Bergfilm* ('mountain film') genre and examines its proto-Nazi leanings. She also analyses Fanck's perhaps spurious claims about the authenticity of his representation of the Arctic, which were used as promotional material for the film. In her chapter 'The Threat of the Thaw: The Cold War on the Screen', Anna Westerståhl Stenport examines how the Arctic was figured as a porous sheet of ice separating the East and West blocs during the Cold War and held a privileged position in Hollywood filmmaking from the 1950s to the 1980s. Ranging from early alien invasion films and national epics to political thrillers, Stenport analyses a wide swath of cinematic forms not previously analysed in tension with one another to show how these are put to environmental and ideological uses. Björn Norðfjörð also addresses location substitution in his contribution 'Hollywood Does Iceland: Authenticity, Genericity and the Picturesque'. Norðfjörð considers how the landscape of Iceland is configured as beautiful, sublime and fantastical. At the same time, he shows how they become generic background fodder for Hollywood cinema, precisely because of their seemingly otherworldly characteristics. Identifying how appropriations of Hollywood horror films engage the notion of an Arctic sublime, Sabine Henlin-Strømme examines how contemporary Norwegian horror films are mobilised partly to subvert gender and ethnicity hierarchies predominant in the Heroic Exploration narratives of Norway. Her chapter 'White on White: Twenty-First-Century Norwegian Horror Films Negotiate Masculinist Arctic Imaginaries' highlights how dominant historical narratives of the Arctic can begin to be renegotiated through forms of popular global culture.

8. FACT AND FICTION IN 'NORTHERNS' AND EARLY 'ARCTIC' FILMS

Russell A. Potter

From the very earliest days of the cinema, the screen depicted a curious blend of the everyday – the Lumières' factory workers and breakfasting babies – and the exotic, such as the Edison films of the Sioux Ghost Dance or Professor Welton's boxing cats. As it did throughout the era of what Tom Gunning has aptly dubbed the 'cinema of attraction' (Gunning 1986), the camera remained stationary for both kinds of subjects, and yet, as the appetite of audiences for exotic scenes and peoples continued to grow, by stages – at first sated and then whetted for more – the possibility of taking the camera itself to a display of exotic peoples offered one ready way to satisfy them. The exhibitions of various ethnic 'villages' at World's Fairs, a staple of such exhibitions since the 1870s, offered one relatively inexpensive means to do so, and in fact we find that both Edison and the American Mutoscope and Biograph Company brought cameras to the 1901 Pan-American Exposition in Buffalo, NY partly for that purpose. Thus, the very earliest footage of Inuit people ever made was taken at that fair's 'Esquimaux Village', with three Edison shorts preserved as paper prints at the Library of Congress our first evidence of the Arctic fascination. They were classed as 'actualities', of course, but since the icebergs were made of plaster and the dogsleds set on wheels, they might well be considered more fictional than factual.

Therein lies a central problem of early Arctic films: their audiences, schooled by earlier visual entertainments, 'knew' only a few things about the 'Frozen North': of course they had seen snow, fur-clad Eskimos (Inuit), and igloos but as far as they knew the same region contained totem poles,

French-Canadian trappers, old prospectors and any number of saloons. If presented as 'actualities' – an early name for films made from footage actually or purportedly shot at the actual place or event – they were willing to take the word of the intertitles as to what was happening, but when presented with narratives, they preferred strong good and bad characters, dramatic plot twists and a melodramatic conclusion. There was always a blur between the two forms, as no one knew enough about the 'actual' Arctic to be able to assess the veracity of a film, and so audiences judged it mainly by how well it conformed to their existing assumptions, which themselves were derived from previous exhibitions and pre-cinematic entertainments. Through panoramas, dioramas and lantern shows, as well as at World's Fairs and expositions, the public was already 'familiar' with igloos, polar bears and lost explorers, visual tropes which were fodder for early filmmakers (Potter 2007). Many films from this era have 'mixed' authenticities: actual Inuit in a staged setting, or staged Inuit in an actual northern landscape, or either one as background for a thrilling chase by dogsled across the frozen wastes of 'Alaska' which was, in all probability, shot in the mountains of California. For the purposes of this chapter, I will exclude actual known footage of polar expeditions, but include all 'Northern' melodramas and narrative film *set* in the Arctic, whether real or feigned (Bottomore 2003).

EARLIEST ARCTIC FICTIONS

By these criteria, the earliest two Arctic 'fiction' films appeared in 1906. The first, *Isbjørnjagt* ('Polar Bear Hunt'), was directed by Viggo Larsen for Nordisk, and proved to be an immensely popular film (Petterson 2011: 191). In making it, Larsen benefitted from the cooperation of the German pioneer of zoological gardens, Karl Hagenbeck, who had exhibited Arctic animals alongside Inuit people at his Hamburg zoo as far back as 1880, and whose *Eismeer-Panorama* ('Sea of Ice Panorama') of 1896 featured a full-scale living diorama of Arctic fauna, including both polar bears and seals (the latter of which were protected from their natural predators by a deep trench) (Ames 2008: 154). Hagenbeck was more than willing to sacrifice a couple of his older polar bears as the objects of this fictionalised hunt, the staging of which, much like his Tierpark, involved using naturalistic scenery to depict the hunt in a 'realistic' manner, complete with the actual killing of the animals at its conclusion. *Isbjørnjagt* was thus essentially a safari film, and although it is no longer extant, Larsen likely used similar montage and narrative techniques as he did in *Løvenjagten* ('Lion Hunting'), which does survive and has been analysed at length by historian Eric Ames (Ames 2008: 201–6). A lithographic poster is known which depicts what may be several scenes from the film: two bears approach an icebound ship; a hunter, dressed in a strange, almost Bedouin-type costume and accompanied by two Eskimos, is seen shooting an upright bear; the bear is seen dead on the ice, and later being dragged on a sledge. It was doubtless, as Ames remarks of the lion hunt film, in essence a 'simulated safari', complete with preparations, stalking, the kill, and the aftermath. Despite the protests of animal advocates in Copenhagen, the film, like its predecessor, was released and seems to have done well in European cinemas; the structure of the hunt and the natural climax of the kill gave filmgoers a readily graspable, dramatic, and brief storyline (the film was released in the US by the Miles Brothers in 1907, under the title *Polar Bear Hunt*).

The second fictional Arctic film of 1906 was Pathé's *In the Polar Regions*, also a lost film, but described thus in their catalogue:

> A party of Arctic explorers have their ship blocked in the ice, and we see them passing their time by hunting bears and whales. One day one of them, crossing a bridge of ice, which crumbles under his feet, is precipitated down a crevice, from which he is with great difficulty rescued by means of ropes. Despite all their efforts they ultimately succumb for want of food, and the last, while attempting to revive his companions with brandy, is himself overcome. We see his dream in an aurora borealis, and then the snow, falling gradually, covers him and his companions.

The film, in other words, was staged as a series of spectacles or set-pieces, each of which could be managed with a small interior set, and advanced the narrative one notch. Like earlier lantern shows of Arctic expeditions, it was more a sequence of dramatic scenes than a dramatic narrative film in the modern sense. The same sort of thing can be seen even in later films, such as Georges Méliès's *Conquest of the Pole* (France, 1912) which, in almost exactly the same manner as in his 1902 film *Trip to the Moon*, is constructed from a series of elaborate set-pieces, each one of which 'stages' one stage in the planning and execution of the voyage. It seems no coincidence that this was among Méliès's last films; long before its release, audiences had come to demand a narrative – and a camera – that moved in more ways than merely from scene to scene.

Gunning himself identifies 1906 as the beginning of the shift between the cinema of attraction and narrative film, referring to the change as a 'synthesis of attractions and narrative' (Gunning 1986: 68). In this period, the use of intercuts, the blending of formerly independent film types such as an exterior race or chase, with interior scenes meant to follow or take place simultaneously, expanded considerably, from a feature such as *In the Polar Regions*, which ran to around 450 feet, to a full 1,000-foot reel of film, a length which allowed for, and even required, a more complex narrative. There could still be set-pieces, and short actualities at times shared a 'split reel' with a mid-length narrative feature, but the stakes had been raised, and audiences began to expect that a 'movie' would be more than merely a series of animated vignettes.

When it came to Arctic subjects, this was not an easy task, as illustrated by the failure of an early attempt at a northern drama by no less a light than Edwin S. Porter, 1909's *A Cry from the Wilderness* (Edison). The film's convoluted plot centred around the rivalry for the daughter of an Eskimo 'chief' between a white trader and a young 'Esquimau'. It was littered with chase scenes (including one with a horse!), cliffside struggles and desperate murders (at one point the Esquimau beats a policeman to death with his own club). The film elicited unusually strong negative notices, with the reviewer from *Moving Picture World* offering a stinging indictment:

> This picture was evidently made by the Edison company in the wilds of Canada during the Winter, and some of the scenes possess weird beauty that is not to be denied, but the story is so vaguely constructed and acted, and the photography so obscure, taken in snow scenes with the different characters impossible to recognise, that there might as well be no plot or story so far as the spectator is concerned. We see an Esquimau village and a fight with a white trader; a vacant house in the wilderness; a murderous assault on the trader by an Esquimau; another man on horseback pursuing this Esquimau; this man killed by the Esquimau; another Esquimau rescuing the first wounded man, and the Esquimau murderer pursued by other Esquimaus, and disappearing over a precipice, and finally the marriage of the trader to an Esquimau girl. If anybody can piece together a story out of such material he can do more than the writer of this review. To make matters worse, the picture is full of inconsistencies in detail, such as white underclothes on an Esquimau baby, people freely using their bare hands in the bitter cold that is supposed to prevail, a man on horseback in the Esquimau country and a helpless, wounded man being dragged on a sled over rough country without being fastened to the sled and without any attempt to protect him from the cold. (*MPW*, 3 April 1909: 397)

There are two issues here, which are closely related – the first is narrative coherence, which was also a problem with many early fiction films, whatever their setting, and the second is perceived authenticity. The public might know little about the actual daily lives of Eskimos, but they knew that snow was cold, that dogsleds rather than horses were used in the North, and that Eskimo children probably did not wear underwear. Similar complaints were made around this time about other films, with many objecting (for example) to the visible telephone wires and poles in Vitagraph's Eastern-filmed Westerns, but Arctic fiction films posed a special problem: not only did they demand, sooner or later, real snow, but they needed some kind of simple yet compelling narrative, one that could unfold and conclude in the magical ten minutes of a one-reel film. Even the foundational storyline of the genre was uncertain: was it to be the life-struggle of doomed explorers like those of *In the Polar Regions*, the vexed interaction of white people with 'savage' Eskimos, as in *A Cry From the Wilderness*, or a 'Northern' version of the 'Western' melodramas which were rapidly coming to dominate the cinema in this era? The answer, as we will shortly see, is 'all of the above'.[1]

The Human Element: Selig Polyscope's Early Northerns

All that was missing from this kind of fictional film was to enlarge the element of *human* drama, with some kind of broader narrative arc. The initial impetus for this came in the wake of the Peary/Cook controversy over who had discovered the North Pole in 1909, when the Arctic suddenly became, as it were, a hot topic, with more than a dozen fictional films with polar themes released between March 1909 and December 1911.[2] Most of these films were, in their narrative content, fairly conventional melodramas, using the 'Frozen North' as their setting for dramatic effect and topicality, but a few went further, adding depictions of Inuit life, and including actual Inuit as cast members. Some of the earliest were produced by the Selig Polyscope company, an organisation which was not only increasingly committed to shooting films on location, but also had unparalleled access to a considerable variety of animals in its resident menagerie, animals that could be shipped almost anywhere the company might need them for use in such films (Erish 2012: 23).

The first three, Selig's *In the Frozen North*, *In the Great Northwest*, and *The Long Trail* (all 1909–10), were apparently filmed partly at Mount San Jacinto near Banning, California, and partly at Truckee in the Sierra Nevada mountains. Both locations had the advantage of being close enough to Selig's nascent California operations that his actors and film crews could be dispatched there relatively quickly by rail, spend a few days shooting, and return with a marketable 'snow picture'. Truckee proved to be the better choice in many ways: it offered mountain scenery in abundance, and was accessible via both road and rail from Sacramento, a little over 100 miles away. By 1920, writing in *The Romance of Motion Pictures*, Lee Royal could fairly state that 'Truckee, California, has become a regular little winter film capital by itself. It is at this point where most of our famous Alaskan or North woods snow scenes are taken (Royal 1920: 56).

Yet back in November of 1909, when the Selig company started filming at Mount San Jacinto, the 'North Woods' film was not yet established as a genre, and there was no set formula for producing one; the company hit on Truckee as a back-up location when, on returning to Mount San Jacinto for re-shoots, they found the road closed by snow. Conditions proved to be so ideal at Truckee that they stayed into January 1910, shooting additional footage that would eventually comprise three films. The first, *In The Frozen North*, set in the Alaskan gold rush, apparently centred on a woman who had unknowingly remarried after being falsely told that her first husband had died; it soon appears that the first is a scoundrel and the second a good man. The action concludes on an upbeat note, as an obliging old gambler shoots husband number one, freeing the 'widow' to live happily ever after with number two. *In the Great Northwest* was set in northern Canada, where French-Canadian fur trappers – to judge from the characters' names (Jules, Pierre, Jon and 'Julie, the Factor's Daughter') – but little is known of the specifics of the plot; the same is true of *The Long Trail*, described in the trades simply as 'a strong drama of the far North'. This last film is chiefly notable for being one of the 200-odd films directed by early Selig stalwart Francis Boggs before his untimely death at the hands of a deranged employee. Curiously, although some film historians have suggested that these films depicted scenes relating to Peary and Cook's polar claims, none of them seems to have actually taken this up as its subject (Zwick 2006).

This new genre of film – known variously as 'Northerns', 'North Woods pictures', or 'snow pictures' – proved popular with audiences, and Selig and other studios soon churned out dozens of them. Most are known only by their titles and a brief synopsis; between 1910 and 1913 Vitagraph brought out *A Klondike Steal*, *In the Arctic Night*, and *Pierre of the North*; Solax had *Out of the Arctic* and *Frozen on Love's Trail*; Edison offered *Under Northern Skies*; Independent had *Hearts of the Northland*, *Justice in the Far North*, and *In the Northern Woods*. As the titles suggest, these films were generally quite formulaic, featuring barmaids with hearts of gold, bad guys with black (fur) hats, and chisel-chinned Mounties to chase them down with dogsleds and bring them to justice. Some of the synopses seem to indicate that Eskimo or Indian figures were present, but as Lee Royal noted a few years later, Japanese-American actors were most commonly employed in these roles.

FINDING REAL ESKIMOS

Such substitutions, of course, were to be stock-in-trade in films for decades, but one studio, Selig Polyscope, was particularly committed to finding subject and locations that would be – or at least *seem to be* – more 'authentic'. And, thanks to a fortuitous series of events in 1910, they acquired the services of a troupe of Labradorian Inuit, including some of the very group that had been filmed by Edison in 1901 in Buffalo. Indeed, this group – led by Esther Eneutseak and her husband John C. Smith – had been appearing in World's Fairs since 1893, and by the time Selig hired them they were veterans of many such shows, as well as of a European tour which included Paris and Madrid. In 1909, they had been the hit of the Midway – known then as the 'Pay Streak' – at the Alaska-Yukon-Pacific Exposition in Seattle, where Esther's sixteen-year-old daughter, Nancy Columbia, had won the fair's beauty contest. After the A-Y-P, they joined up with 'Caribou' Bill Cooper, an Alaskan musher whose booth had been next to theirs on the Pay Streak, and headed to the Appalachian Exposition in Knoxville, Tennessee.

At Knoxville, the amusement area was known as the 'Midway Jungle' and featured not only Caribou Bill and the Inuit troupe, but Ferare's Snake Den, Hannihan's Goat and Monkey Circus, Big Otto's 'trained wild animals', and Zack Mulhall's Wild West Show, which at the time included future cowboy star Tom Mix. Mix had already appeared in a number of Selig one-reelers and had been asked by the head office to round up some 'natives' to appear in a series of historical subjects planned for filming that winter near Jacksonville, Florida (Jenson 2005: 43). Perhaps to Selig's surprise, Mix did not hire Indians from the Wild West shows in which he worked, but instead hired the Inuit troupe, who appeared in a number of shorts made that season – *The Seminole's Sacrifice*, *The Witch of the Everglades*, and possibly others – in the role of Seminole Indians.

THE WAY OF THE ESKIMO

During the shooting of these Florida films, Selig's scenario writer, William V. Mong, had a falling-out with the director, Otis Turner. Convinced he could make an impression on the boss and direct his own films, Mong wrote to Selig to propose he bring the Inuit troupe north to make some Arctic-themed films, and Selig apparently agreed. After arriving in Chicago, the group was sent north by train to Escanaba, Michigan, to make two films (again simultaneously), for one of which – *The Way of the Eskimo* – Nancy Columbia herself received credit for the scenario. This film was in fact the very first 'Northern' drama to feature a nearly all-Inuit cast and writer – ninety years before Zacharias Kunuk's *Atanarjuat: The Fast Runner* made that claim.

The Way of the Eskimo is a lost film, but thanks to the researches of Kenn Harper and myself, we have some remarkable documentation of its production, including newspaper coverage by the Escanaba paper and photos taken on the set; the original scenario and a number of trade flyers survive in the Selig papers at the Margaret Herrick Library. When the cast and crew arrived

Figure 8.1   Panoramic view of the filming of *The Way of the Eskimo* (1911). Photo courtesy of Kenn Harper.

in March 1911, they set about enlisting the interest and assistance of Escanaba residents, who were invited to watch the filming, although Mong had to partially retract the invitation when some of them started wandering into the frame. At some point, a decision had been made to shoot material for a second film which, like *Isbjørnjagt*, would feature the hunting and killing of a polar bear. Selig's agents delivered the bear, said to be named 'Bruno', and he was housed at a local tannery, Schram's Hide House.

Fortunately for the filmmakers, the ice on the lake was still robust, though the production was at first interrupted by rain showers, which flooded low-lying areas of ice and raised concern that it might break up prematurely. Finally, on 16 March, conditions improved, and with the aid of local residents, a small village of igloos was built, and props and costumes brought out onto the ice by local teamsters. Apparently, some residents believed that the film was about Cook's or Peary's claims on the North Pole, though we now know that this was not the subject of either film. *The Way of the Eskimo* told the tale of an Eskimo maiden (played by Nancy Columbia) who encounters a trapper (played by Mong); their brief romance ends when the girl is summoned back to her village to be re-baptised into the tribe with seal oil, concluding with an Eskimo ceremony of bidding goodbye to the sun.

The second film shot at Escanaba was *Lost in the Arctic,* which in its title and theme seems designed as a companion-piece to *Lost in the Jungle,* one of the Jacksonville films from the previous winter and a vehicle for Selig stalwart Kathlyn Williams. The scenario does not appear to have survived, but by accounts in advertisements and newspaper reviews, we know that the plot involved two explorers, one played again by Mong, and one by John C. Smith, Esther Eneutseak's husband and the troupe's manager. In a stereotype sadly to be repeated in many subsequent portrayals of Inuit culture, Nancy played an 'orphan girl' who was deliberately set adrift because she was too sick to contribute to the tribe. Nancy is then found and rescued by the first explorer (Mong), who in turn is saved by the second explorer (Smith), who had been sent to search for him. The highlight of this film, however, was not these rescues but the hunting and killing of a polar bear, for which purpose the unfortunate 'Bruno' was brought forth onto the ice. Aputik, the senior member of the troupe and the only one with actual experience hunting in the Arctic, threw his spear at the bear, while, as a precaution, two local hunters fired shots simultaneously from outside the frame. According to local press accounts, the precaution was needless, as Aputik's spear was found to have pierced the bear's heart. Afterwards, there was a polar-bear meat banquet at the local saloon, and Mr Schram – who had some claim on the remains in return for having earlier housed the bear – sold glass jars of 'polar bear oil', which he claimed could cure baldness!

These two Selig features enjoyed a robust market in the United States and abroad; Selig not only advertised the authenticity of the Eskimos in the film, but claimed that it had actually been shot in Labrador. The release flyer for *The Way of the Eskimo* showed Nancy and the 'trapper' walking happily forth from the igloo village, while two fur-clad natives exchange an 'Eskimo kiss'; the flyer for *Lost in the Arctic* shows a lone sledge and two dogs with an American flag, which certainly evoked the Peary/Cook dispute, even if the film's plot did not. We are fortunate in having a photograph, made using a special 'panoramic' camera, which shows a scene in progress with two Eskimos struggling before a sled; the wide frame takes in the fur-clad camera-man. It is a rare image in that, unlike the still and other photos on the Selig release flyers, it depicts an actual scene as it was being shot, and is thus among the earliest photographs of its kind.

The Way of the Eskimo was a full reel in length; in fact, the footage was a little over the 1,000-foot limit and had to be trimmed.[3] *Lost in the Arctic*, however, fell a little bit short, and so was included in a 'split reel' with a brief news feature, *Noted Men*. Neither film survives, but the association between Esther Eneutseak and John Smith's troupe and the motion picture industry was to prove a continuing one; they later appeared in at least three other feature films of the multi-reel era, as well as in newsreels. After Escanaba, they only once again appeared at one large public exposition – ironically, this was at 'Nordland', a Hagenbeck-managed show in Berlin – and moved a few years later to Santa Monica, California, perhaps in part to be near the film studios rapidly being established in the area. They established a small 'Eskimo Village' attraction on the Santa Monica Pier, acquired several new Inuit members, and staged an elaborate 'Eskimo Wedding' at this attraction in 1915, which was included in an early Pathé newreel.

FILMING GOD'S COUNTRY

The Santa Monica Eskimo Village, alas, was destroyed in a fire on Christmas night in 1915, having existed as a venue for less than a year. And yet, because they were up in the Santa Monica Mountains working on a film, the members of Esther and John Smith's troupe survived, along with most of their furs and dogs. This film, *God's Country and the Woman*, was one of the early multi-reel feature films in the 'Northern' genre; directed by Rollin S. Sturgeon for Vitagraph, it introduced Nell Shipman, who was to star in, and later direct, a number of similar dramas. It was based on a novel by James Oliver Curwood, whose north-country potboilers were the most popular source for such films. The film is lost, but according to press accounts, Nancy appeared in it, as did her mother Esther; Esther appears in one surviving still, but in a non-Eskimo role, so it is not clear whether other members of the troupe appeared as Eskimos. The completed film, which ran to a then-remarkable eight reels, was marketed by Vitagraph as a 'blue ribbon' prestige feature, and in at least one case, a cinema in Los Angeles was festooned with a wagon-load of furs to promote it.

Figure 8.2   The 'Petite Theatre' in Los Angeles decorated for the premiere of *God's Country and the Woman* (1916). Image courtesy of Suzanne O'Connell.

God's Country and the Woman was filmed at Big Bear Lake in the San Bernadino Mountains, a spot which has played host to dozens of Hollywood features from that day to the present; early publicity for the film came from news stories that the film's cast and crew had been trapped there by heavy snow. Several articles in the trades made fun of their predicament, saying they had been reduced to eating the strings off a fiddle, but the story and subsequent news of the party's 'rescue' made good free copy. It is also worth noting that, after this film, Nell Shipman went on to make her own partnership with James Oliver Curwood, and produced and directed a sequel, *Back to God's Country* (1919). This film, which was recently rediscovered, also had Eskimo characters in several scenes, but since it was shot primarily in Idaho and Alberta, the Inuit group was not available, and Asian-American actors depicted them instead. In *Back to God's Country*, despite the substitution, the native roles are portrayed with sympathy, but also with stereotypes; a group of Eskimo women are brought on board a whaling ship as 'guests', and we see one crewman attempt to seduce a woman with Fels-Naptha soap (which she eats with relish), another with gramophone music, scenes which in strange ways prefigure both Nanook's gramophone scene and Peter Freuchen's rapacious whaling captain in 1933's *Eskimo*.

REALISM THAT IS REAL IN ALL CASES

In 1917, Nancy and Esther's group were involved with the Dorothy Dalton vehicle *The Flame of the Yukon*, an Ince film which promised 'a miniature village of thirty Eskimos' as well as 'Real Husky Dogs'. They likely worked on a number of other films around this time, including Selig's most successful 'Northern', 1915's *The Spoilers*, a rollicking gold-rush epic, but in nearly all these cases, they were, essentially, extras; while a village of 'real' Eskimos might add a modicum of realism, it was costly when compared with other scene-setters. The multi-reel era proved to be problematic for producers of the 'Northern' genre; creating the perception of authenticity remained expensive, and perhaps ultimately peripheral to the melodramas that had the greatest audience appeal. In 1917, the silent star Anita Stewart spoke with some trepidation about her upcoming role for Vitagraph – the film was *Baree, Son of Kazan*, a dog-driven Curwood 'Northern' – she seemed to believe that she would actually have to travel to Canada or Greenland (this may of course have been a publicity stunt). Of the studio, she remarked that 'they are seeking realism that is real in all cases, and it is the desire of Vitagraph to get some good snow pictures and Eskimo village scenes' (*Seattle Daily Times*, 5 August 1917: 30) The studio ended up casting Nell Shipman, flush with her success in *God's Country*, in the role instead, but in any case the movie – a sort of proto-Rin-Tin-Tin story of a faithful dog who rescues his mistress – was widely panned by reviewers.

LATER INFLUENCE OF THE 'NORTHERNS'

The 'Northern', as a major genre, faded after the late 1910s, though a few of its classics, including both *The Spoilers* and *God's Country and the Woman* were remade more than once in the decades that followed. One indication of the popularity of this genre, as well as a sign of its decline, was the number of 'Northern' spoofs in the early 1920s (see Chapter 9 in this volume). The best-known of these is, of course, Charlie Chaplin's *The Gold Rush* (1925), a film which has retained its comic power long after the 'snow pictures' it satirised have fallen from public knowledge and memory, but there were many others, two of them appearing the same year (1922) as *Nanook of the North*: Slim Summerville's lost *The Eskimo*, and Buster Keaton's delightful *The Frozen North*, which survives. Keaton is in fine form in *The Frozen North*: he arrives in the Arctic via an icebound subway escalator, attempts to rob a saloon using a cardboard cutout of a bandit, and engages in an ice-fishing contest with a burly 'Eskimo' that resonates with the seal-fishing tug-of-war in *Nanook*; his use of two guitars found in an igloo as snowshoes is both comic and – for guitarists, at least – heartbreaking.

The Northern melodramas, and the satires of them that followed, were a major ingredient in Hollywood's construction of the idea of the 'North', and along with early 'Eskimo' and hunting films, framed the Arctic for decades to come. Ray Mala in 1933's *Eskimo* brought melodrama and realism together briefly, but in later features such as *The Savage Innocents* (1960) – where 'Inuk' Anthony Quinn nearly abandons his infant child *and* his mother (Anna May Wong in one or her later and sadder performances) – they quickly diverged. In comedies such as Abbott and Costello's *Lost in Alaska* (1952), igloos and totem poles mingled freely, and the public imagination was more or less where it had been nearly half a century earlier. These films from the first two decades of the twentieth century offer striking documentation of how these filmic stereotypes of the North were established, as well as of the rise and fall of the 'Northern' – a genre that, before its fall, rivalled the Western as a source of surefire box-office gold.

NOTES

1. I would like to mention here Ann Fienup-Riordan's *Freeze Frame: Alaska Eskimos in the Movies* (Seattle and London: University of Washington Press, 2003).
2. In roughly chronological order these were: *A Cry from the Wilderness* (Edison, 1909); *The North Pole Craze* (Phoenix, 1909); *Who Discovered the North Pole?* (Lubin, 1909); *Little Willie's Trip to the North Pole* (Nordisk, 1909); *In the Frozen*

North (Selig, 1910); *In the Great Northwest* (Selig, 1910); *The Long Trail* (Selig, 1910); *Johnny's Pictures of the Polar Regions* (Pathé, 1910); *Out of the Arctic* (Solax, 1910); *A Klondike Steal, or The Stolen Claim* (Vitagraph, 1911); *The Way of the Eskimo* (Selig, 1911); *Lost in the Arctic* (Selig, 1911); and *In the Arctic Night* (Vitagraph, 1911).

3. Margaret Herrick Library, 14-f.418 *The Way of the Eskimo*, William V. Mong; 1911 (General Film Co., 1911) folder contains cutting continuities, list of titles.

9. CALIFORNIA'S YUKON AS COMIC SPACE

Mark Sandberg

This chapter concerns the 'snow line' of silent comedy in 1920s Hollywood cinema: the line that separates the use of natural snow from its artificial substitutes. At stake is a literal question of climate control, one that resonates not only with Hollywood's developing compromises between studio production and location shooting in the 1920s, but also with more general cultural trends towards the domination of weather through technology. Climate control was actually a wide-ranging American project of the first decades of the twentieth century; the Hollywood case simply plays out the film technology version thereof. This essay turns to comic variations of the Hollywood 'snow picture' in order to show their overt treatment of a conceptual issue more deeply buried in the snowdrifts of the usual dramas of the Frozen North, namely that there were limits to Hollywood's dual fantasy of geographic access and climatological control. And it all comes down to melting snow.

The prerequisite genre for these comedies was known variously in the 1910s and 1920s as the 'snow picture', the Yukon film, the Mountie film, or even the 'pure white drama', as one unnamed journalist put it when describing the genre target of Buster Keaton's parody *The Frozen North* in 1922 (Chamberlain n.d.). That group included films by William S. Hart and others, films that were essentially Westerns transposed for the sake of narrative variation to the setting of the Far North. The four comic films chosen here, however, were later inversions of the Yukon film at the point in the mid-1920s when the northern formula had become cliché. As one reviewer of *The Frozen North* put it, this was a film that 'will reinvigorate all those who have suffered from the "Northern" picture' ('First runs' 1923: 818). In addition to the Keaton film, this analysis deals with three others: two are closely related films made by Mack Sennett with cross-eyed comic actor Ben Turpin (*Homemade Movies* from 1922 and *Yukon Jake* from 1924); the third and best known is Charlie Chaplin's *The Gold Rush* from 1925. With the exception of *Homemade Movies*, all of these were filmed in Truckee, California, in the Northern Sierra Nevada mountains, which were also a favourite destination for location shooting when making snow films in the 1910s and 1920s. For that reason, one might well call the Lake Tahoe area 'California's Yukon', adding one more imaginary referent to the famous Paramount Studios location map, which identifies the area as a stand-in for Switzerland, the French Alps and Siberia. This map, which has circulated widely on the Internet in recent years, seems to originate with Paramount location scout Fred Harris in the late 1920s, and is attested as early as 1930 in a newspaper report that confirms seeing the map hanging on Harris's office wall, elaborating that as a location scout he 'has the unique position of making distant places come to him, for it is his duty to find duplicates of every spot on earth within easy traveling distance of the studios' ('Paramount "Location Map"' 1930: A2).

The ease of substitution promised by such a map – California's supposedly 'universal geography'– was a lure for attracting film production to the Los Angeles area. Nearby practical stand-in locations could save money and effort while making possible a greater range of narrative material. Similarities were often visually superficial, of course, and not always as convincing as touted; alert viewers could sometimes find points of resistance in the details of flora and fauna that peeked through the fictional setting, eluding the control of filmmakers and set dressers alike. Of course, location verisimilitude may not have been equally important to all filmmakers and audiences, some of whom operated with more of an attitude of 'place promiscuity', as I have called it in another context (Sandberg 2014: 42). For all but the place purists, there was something irresistible about the geographic variety within reach of Southern California: one could find surf, desert, farmland, winding rivers, mountains – and also snow. But since snow can be fickle in California, it makes an especially interesting example of nature's potential non-cooperation with Hollywood's confident ambitions of total climate control.

The filmmaking 'snow line' in the 1920s bisected a continuum that would look something like this: at one logical end of the spectrum would be the expeditionary logic of location shooting that one finds in *Nanook of the North* from 1922, shot in Hudson's Bay, or fiction films like Norman Dawn's *Lure of the Yukon* and *Justice of the Far North* from 1924–5, which were shot in an area north of Fairbanks in Alaska. It would be wrong to identify expeditionary location shooting automatically as the 'authentic' end of the spectrum, of course, since the act of filming or photographing already imposes a system

Figure 9.1   Paramount Studios location map.

of visual representation on a landscape (Geller 2004: 7–8). For the purposes of this essay, however, expeditionary Alaskan or Yukon films (both ethnographic and fictional) can at the very least function as a placeholder for the idea of 'maximum travel' and a high degree of visual correspondence between actual and intended locations. At the opposite far end of the spectrum would be studio snow such as one could find on Chaplin's set for *The Gold Rush*, with its bragged-about 200 tons of plaster, 285 tons of salt, and 100 barrels of flour ('Mimicry' 1925: 20), and the 'simulated snow of mica and cornflakes' that he arranged to have blown about by airplane engines to create the effects of the blizzard scenes (Manson n.d.: 13). At what I am calling the 'snow line' in the middle of this imagined spectrum, one finds the compromise solution of shooting on location at Lake Tahoe, as Buster Keaton did at Donner Lake for *The Frozen North*. Snow itself was an amusing subject for comedy since it allowed for new variations on familiar warm-climate gags and created different physical properties to explore in the colder setting, but slapstick's metafictional tendencies also led 'California Yukon' comedies to exploit the conceptual contradictions posed by the snow line's demarcation of the artificial from the natural. To put this in spatial terms, one might say that these comedies were interested in the expeditionary side of the snow line only insofar as it could be spoofed, and that their most productive tensions lay in the back-and-forth between studio snow in Los Angeles and 'California snow' in Lake Tahoe. The comedies are located at the more artificial end of the spectrum because unlike the dramas, they had no real incentive to undertake expeditions in search of visual correspondence; their project was instead precisely to mine for comic potential the place discrepancies that can be found at the heart of this more intermediate location shooting practice and the fabrication of studio snow.

Most of the 'sincere' Yukon films produced by Hollywood studios in the 1910s and 1920s took short cuts with location shooting. A 1920 film, *Out of the Snows*, pursued a typical bifurcated production strategy of mixing location and studio shooting, as touted in this trade-press publicity:

> When you see Zena Keefe in this scene of a Selznick picture, you'll probably hope that she doesn't contract a cold or something even more serious. But have no fear – the picture above tells the tale . . . of the painted snow-covered peaks; the fans blowing an electric gale, and pounds of artificial snow. The exteriors actually were photographed in the frozen North. Not so the cabin scenes. Which goes to prove . . . you never can tell! ('You never can tell' 1921: 41)

It was not just the sense of mixed media that would provoke comment, however: for those in the know, a place substitution done at a compromise location could set off waves of audience derision. In a 1924 *Los Angeles Times* interview with Norman Dawn, called 'Real vs Cinema Alaska', Dawn describes from experience actual Alaskan audience reactions to snow scenes shot in 'California's Yukon':

> The Alaskans are most friendly and helpful to picture makers who come up there; but they don't like the poor imitation Alaskan pictures at all. To go to a picture theater when a pseudo-Alaskan picture, made in California, is being shown is to see and hear an uproar of laughter and good-natured razzing, such as these old sourdoughs can surely give. (Kingsley 1924)

The interviewer also mentions that 'Mr Dawn declared that riding on a dog sled in Alaska isn't the simple stunt it is riding behind some movie dogs in Truckee', and 'Norman Dawn believes in realism, so when he wanted to make an Alaskan picture, he didn't depend on the salt peter snow and the made-to-order wind-machine storms, but took his company up into Alaska during the wintertime'.

By the early 1920s, there was in other words already an established idea among purists that despite its 'real snow', the status of the Truckee location was closer to a movie set than to wild nature, and further that much of the snow one would see in any film about the Frozen North was anything but

Figure 9.2   Advertisement for *Out of the Snows* (Ralph Ince, 1920). From the collections of the Margaret Herrick Library.

frozen. This was a perception ripe for comedy when Mack Sennett made his metafilmic *Homemade Movies* with Ben Turpin in 1922, which essentially lampoons Hollywood's precarious game of climate control. *Homemade Movies* depicts the travails of inept amateur filmmakers trying and failing to make a snow comedy in the midst of a Los Angeles summer. Here is how the unpublished archival synopsis states it: 'We show them engaged in making their picture. The amateurs blindly encounter the difficulties of making a forty below zero picture in Southern California with the thermometer at one hundred and ten in the shade' (Sennett n.d.: 1).

Many gags from this film (unfortunately not extant) seem to have depended on combinations of hot and cold, or rather, the filmmaking crew of the amateur film not being able to prevent the actual Los Angeles heat from penetrating the 'frosty' scenic façade. In the archival materials for the film, one can find a surprisingly extensive list of 126 alternative main film titles considered for the film, with many of the suggestions circling around this amusing juxtaposition of extreme hot and cold: *A Tropical Frost*; *Warm Hearts and Cold Feet*; *Ice and Lemons*; *Sunburned Icicles*; and *Snowballs and Hot Work* are just a few examples. It is not hard to see why some of these titles were rejected (sunburned icicles?), but the access to the brainstorming process is almost more interesting than the final title choice because we see the writers attempting to exploit the central paradox of Hollywood snow films, namely the jamming together of climate extremes that underlies the actual production process there.

A running gag in the scenario notes was the idea that amateurs can't quite keep the Southern California landscape at bay, whose constant pressure on the illusion is apparent in these suggested gags:

> We now show the same street being changed to a snow scene. (NOTE: THIS IS TO BE DONE WITH SALT.) Trucks of salt coming in, general scattering of salt on roofs, etc. Do gag of palm tree tied up. This comes down, exposes that it is really in Southern California. Do bear gag, fixing them up to look like polar bears ([Scenario 1922]: 3; original capitals).

The plot of the eventual film seems to have turned out differently, but it is clear from the publicity photographs that the main comic point of the film was to show a filmmaking process full of climatological paradoxes. In one film still, one can see the bendy fake icicles being brought onto the set by a crew member dressed for the heat. In another, Ben Turpin and his sweetheart are positioned in front of 'Black Dan's Dance Hall' and are framed by the film crew with their parasols and fans. One might say that the running joke of Sennett's metafilm is that while it is diegetically cold, it is enunciatively hot, which layering mimics the kind of deconstructive production still that often circulated in the trade press and fan magazines, showing the studio tricks behind the scenes (as shown

1285 X

Figure 9.3   Film still from Mack Sennett's *Homemade Movies* (1922). From the collections of the Margaret Herrick Library.

in Figure 9.2, for example). A hand-coloured picture postcard from the film includes a caption made for exactly that kind of discourse ('"Faking" a snow scene in tropical California'), except that in this case the depiction of the set actually comes from the film itself, whose behind-the-scenes logic the scenario makes clear. The fundamental disparity between filmic illusion and filmmaking practice that results when one tries to make a snow film in Los Angeles is the film's main source of comedy.

Homemade Movies parodied the idea of studio snow, but in the same year, Buster Keaton made a Truckee film that examined the paradoxes of proximity inherent in place substitutions like the exchange of Tahoe for the Yukon. The opening sequence of the film, which shows Keaton inexplicably emerging from a subway stop in a snowy field, is often cited as one of Keaton's most surrealistic images, with its bizarre public-transportation interface between civilisation and the wild. There is in fact something surrealistic about the way the city and the Yukon are forced together, but then, there is more than a hint of surreality in any location substitution. When one realises that Keaton's film was shot up near Truckee, where film crews from Los Angeles could in effect

"Faking" a snow scene in tropical California, with Ben Turpin
at the Mack Sennett Studios, Edendale.

Figure 9.4   Postcard made from a film still from *Homemade Movies* (1922). From
the collections of the Margaret Herrick Library.

'commute' to the snow instead of making a full expedition to the Far North,
the idea of the Yukon being available at the end of the subway actually seems
to be a fairly good allegory for the kind of film work carried out in intermediate
locations.

The Truckee comedies all contain jokes about an unexpectedly domesticated
Arctic. *The Frozen North* is most often described as a send-up of the William
S. Hart Yukon films or as an investigation of the comic properties of snow. It
also pursues a running line of gags about analogues of civilisation in the Arctic,
however, including a scene from the inside of an igloo featuring a 'carpet'
cleaner and cozy furniture. The laughs come from the improbable but matter-
of-fact conflation of domesticity and snow, but the scene also serves up a nice
allegory for proximate location, which could be defined as a place having both
the look of the wild and hidden qualities of modern convenience for the cast
and crew.

The best allegorical comic representation of the convenience of the Truckee
location can be found in Ben Turpin's *Yukon Jake* from 1924. Many of the
rejected scenario ideas from *Homemade Movies* two years before show up in
this follow-up 'snow picture', which instead of revealing the palm trees behind
the studio snow, as the earlier metafilm had done, was actually shot on location in Truckee like *The Frozen North*. The first half of the film, though, is
a Western comedy with Ben Turpin as the cross-eyed sheriff, appropriately
named 'Cyclone Bill'. When the villain 'Yukon Jake' comes to town from out
of the North and steals the mayor's daughter, the scene shifts abruptly to the
Arctic (and location shooting in Truckee) for the rest of the film. The stand-out
visual gag is the scene in which Turpin pursues the villain by walking across a

Figure 9.5   Frame enlargement from Buster Keaton's *The Frozen North* (1922).

split screen. The two halves of the scene are marked 'North of 54' and 'South of 54', using a fairly arbitrary latitude line. (The unpublished scenario for the film was provisionally entitled 'North of 57'; the actual latitude line for the southern border of the Yukon lies at 60 degrees exactly, and the Canadian border is the forty-ninth parallel.) When the switch from the palm trees on the right of the line to the blizzard on the left is accomplished with a single step, however, the film lays bare the strange logic of convenience inherent in proximate location substitutions. Sennett's split screen evokes the same conflation as Keaton's impossible interface between the subway station and Donner Lake: a comic proximity.

Chaplin's *The Gold Rush* from 1925 is familiar to many, but perhaps not for its costly experimentation with the snow line. The original plans included extensive filming up in the Sugar Bowl ski resort area of Lake Tahoe at a replica mining village constructed for the film at the foot of the Palisades peaks. The famous dramatic opening scene depicting miners crossing the Chilkoot Pass is one of the few scenes that remains in the finished film from the Tahoe location shooting, which was abandoned after a short stay. Although some accounts of the failed location shoot blame the cold, sickness in the

Figure 9.6   Exposing the 'seam' between hot and cold in *Yukon Jake* (1924). Frame enlargement.

crew, or the complications of Chaplin's secret affair with the film's actress Lita Grey, publicist Edward Manson's memoir reveals that the central problem was instead that the snow cover kept melting out from under them in the warm late April sun. Capturing the impressive scene of the string of miners trudging up the peak was a matter of luck, since after an impatient wait for the crew, a foot of late spring snow allowed them to hurry up and film it in one day. The entire enterprise was one long battle with the snow line; Manson writes, 'The snow was melting fast and with the crowd milling about, mud and slush was taking the place of snow', and at the end of the day's shoot, the crew made its way back through the 'freshet streams that were now almost rushing rivers' (Manson n.d.: 7, 8). The next day, the on-location set was scuttled and burned, and the cast and crew returned to Los Angeles to complete the picture with more compliant snow made of salt, plaster, flour, mica and cornflakes. During that summer back in Los Angeles, David Robinson notes, 'A small-scale mountain range was built. Its "snow" – capped peaks, glistening in the sun, were visible miles off, and brought hundreds of curious sightseers for a closer view' (Robinson 1985: 345). The advantages of this strategy were clear to a science journalist of the time, who concludes his discussion of the technical tricks of the film's production by stating, 'In fact, practically the entire picture was taken within the four walls of the studio, and thus the necessity of waiting for favorable weather was eliminated' (Schallert 1925).

This was a common solution at the time; another film from 1921, *Neeka of the Northlands* (also known as *The Girl from God's Country*), ran into similar problems with melting snow when filming in King's Canyon, California, prompting this comment in *Pictures and the Picturegoer*:

> The Frozen North is a treacherous ally, as perilous as it is fascinating, and it is small wonder that many producers prefer the imitation to the real thing and content themselves with snow storms safely manufactured in the studio, and with quickly congealing paraffin poured on the water to simulate a freeze-up. (E.R.T. 1924: 17)

Even if studio snow could sometimes appear artificial and unconvincing, this writer continues, '. . . they have not the disadvantage of holding up production for a couple of weeks while the weather makes up its mind what to do . . .'

Figure 9.7   Artificial snow in the studio set for *The Gold Rush* (1925). Frame enlargement. From the collections of the Margaret Herrick Library.

The impatient frustration with uncooperative weather (and the melting snow in particular) conveyed by these accounts reveals how the unpredictability of the California snow line undermined fantasies of technological control in the studio filmmaking system: the studios clearly often met their match in natural snow. The retreat to the studios only increased the sense of climate control, which might be said to have reached its logical climax in the elaborate Arctic pageant that Sid Grauman staged as a theatrical prologue to the premiere of *The Gold Rush* at his Egyptian Theater in Los Angeles. According to various newspaper sources, this 100-person spectacle included a painted Klondike panorama, dancing Eskimos, furs, seals, frost-sprites, a balloon dance, a dance hall, and simulated ice skating, complete with enough artificial snowfall on stage during the first couple of months of performance that it would have covered seven blocks of Hollywood Boulevard with four inches of the stuff, according to one article ('Heavy fall' 1925: 20). Using the usual metrics of authenticity, the article goes on to say, 'Old "sourdoughs" who made the pilgrimage to Alaska have congratulated Grauman on the effect produced, declaring they thought at first real snow was used'.

Well, it takes a lot to fool an 'old sourdough', at least in the journalistic film discourse of the time. They often show up there as the ultimate spectator-arbiters of authentic Northern locations, and are usually depicted as deeply sceptical of films made in 'California's Yukon', as shown earlier in this essay (Kingsley 1924). They are here used to show that Grauman's Arctic extravaganza had passed the authenticity text, a perhaps unnecessary touch since Sid Grauman himself had travelled to the Yukon during the Gold Rush and had been on location with Chaplin, perhaps to help authenticate the filming process (Manson n.d.: 4). Discursive supports aside, there was another added sensory trick installed in Grauman's theatre especially for this film, one with much wider implications:

> In planning for his presentation of 'The Gold Rush,' Charlie Chaplin's comedy-drama of Alaska, Grauman called in refrigerating experts. After the experts had seen Grauman's scintillating spectacle of the prologue, with its frosty mountains and icy cliffs, they arranged for gusts of cold air to accompany the snow flurries off the shimmering crystal to make the stage picture of the North even more realistic. ('Cold wind' 1925: 15)

The deeper logic in this offhand comment is that these 'refrigeration experts' were actually at work across the country that summer of 1925 installing the first dependably functional air-conditioning systems in several key picture palaces, like the Rivoli in New York, which reportedly almost tripled its attendance in June 1925 owing to the suddenly pleasant summer viewing conditions ('Cooling' 1925: 1). Editorials in *Motion Picture News* trumpeted to fellow exhibitors the mastering of the climate, eliminating the need to shut down the movie houses in the summer: 'Now there will be no summer slump', as one exhibitor put it, because 'Modern engineering has made possible the manufacture of ideal weather under scientific conditions' ('Ice plants' 1925: 178).

The range of studio practices on the domestic side of the snow line are all wrapped up in much broader quintessentially modern discourses about the mastery of geographical and climatological difference, one that manifests itself as much in location proxemics as it does in the cultural history of air conditioning. As Marsha E. Ackermann puts it in her definitive work on the subject, 'A man or woman's encounter with air-conditioning was embedded in ideology even before it was experienced physiologically. It *felt* modern' (Ackermann 2002: 45). She goes on to detail how the rise of effective air-conditioning systems in the 1920s and 1930s radically transformed everything from shopping and leisure to the settlement patterns of the American Southwest. The technological control of excess heat came much later in human history than the modulation of cold, which has long been mitigated through other traditional heating methods (GilFillan 1920: 396), and air conditioning seemed to promise the final missing piece of modern climate control – an ideal of 'comfort' that could insulate mankind from a climate's natural extremes (Ackermann 2002: 49).

For reasons that should be clear in our current day, when global climate change profoundly undermines that quintessentially modern fantasy of technological mastery, when melting snow and ice are no longer only a California problem, and indeed when air conditioning and other 'comfort' technologies have been shown to be part of the problem, the lessons of early Hollywood filmmaking along the snow line seem even more resonant. The 'domestication' of filmic location and the simulation of snow and ice, all in the pursuit of more efficient film production, are perhaps less harmless pursuits than first imagined. It was left to Arctic comedies to expose contradictions that in our day turn out not to be funny after all.

Bibliography

Ackermann, M. E. (2002), *Cool Comfort: America's Romance with Air-Conditioning*, Washington, DC: Smithsonian Institution Press.
Chamberlain, A. (n.d.), Scrapbook #45, Margaret Herrick Library, unsourced 1922 newspaper review of Buster Keaton's *The Frozen North*.
'Cold wind is real in "Gold Rush"', *Los Angeles Times*, 5 July 1925.
'Cooling the theatre', *Motion Picture News*, 20 June 1925.
E.R.T. (1924), 'Snow kings and queens', *Pictures and the Picturegoer*, January 1924.
'First runs on Broadway', *Exhibitor's Trade Review*, 17 March 1923.
Geller, P. (2004), *Northern Exposures: Photographing and Filming the Canadian North, 1920–45*, Vancouver: UBC Press.

GilFillan, S. C. (1920), 'The Coldward Course of Progress', *Political Science Quarterly* 35:3, 393–410.

'Heavy fall of snow does not halt "Gold Rush"', *Los Angeles Times*, 13 September 1925.

'Ice plants boost summer attendance', *Motion Picture News*, 11 July 1925.

Kingsley, Grace (1924), 'Real vs Cinema Alaska', *Los Angeles Times*, 13 July 1924.

Manson, Edward (n.d.), 'That Mexican Affair', Margaret Herrick Library, unpublished manuscript.

'Mimicry in "Gold Rush" came high', *Los Angeles Times*, 19 July 1925.

'Paramount "Location Map" plays odd trick on world', *The Washington Post*, 2 March 1930.

Robinson, D. (1985), *Chaplin, His Life and Art*, New York: Da Capo Press.

Sandberg, M. B. (2014), 'Location, "location,": on the plausibility of place substitution', in J. Bean, L. Horak and A. Kapse (eds), *Silent Cinema and the Politics of Space*, Bloomington, IN: Indiana University Press, 23–46.

Scenario for *Snow Picture* (1922), Mack Sennett Collection, Margaret Herrick Library.

Schallert, E. (1925), 'Trick photography in The Gold Rush', *Science and Invention*, December 1925.

Sennett, M. (n.d.), synopsis for 'Homemade Movies', Mack Sennett collection, Margaret Herrick Library.

'Suggestions for main title Turpin Snow picture' (title list), Mack Sennett collection, Margaret Herrrick Library.

'You never can tell!', *Motion Picture Magazine*, April 1921, full-page advertisement.

10. 'SEE THE CRASHING MASSES OF WHITE DEATH . . .': GREENLAND, GERMANY AND THE SUBLIME IN THE 'BERGFILM' SOS EISBERG

Lill-Ann Körber

Why transfer a film to an iceberg when every ascent of an iceberg is more dangerous than any conquest of the most difficult Alpine peaks?' (Fanck 1933: 9; trans. by the author)

A FILM EXPEDITION TO GREENLAND AND THE THIRD REICH

Arnold Fanck (1889–1974), director of *SOS Eisberg*, raises this question at the beginning of his book about the so-called 'Greenland expedition of the Universal film *SOS Eisberg*', which was published in 1933, the year of the film's release. This is just one of a number of publications about the shooting of the film, which took place in Western Greenland in 1932 (for other accounts, see Riefenstahl 1933; Sorge 1933; and Udet 1935). The shoot is often referred to as a 'film expedition' and, consistent with this view, the cast are described as 'expedition participants' in Fanck's book (Fanck 1933: 5f). This analogy between the shooting of a film and a polar expedition is one remarkable feature of this – in Fanck's words – 'first major film about Greenland that it was possible to shoot in this unexpectedly beautiful country' (Fanck 1933: 7). The set-up of the undertaking mimics the Arctic expeditions and their filmic representations, which were familiar to the public at beginning of the twentieth century. *SOS Eisberg* could even be read as a feature film adaptation of the silent scientific documentary *Die deutsche Expedition vom Jahre 1929 auf dem grönländischen Inlandeis*, a film set in the context of a scientific expedition to Greenland led by meteorologist and polar scientist Alfred Wegener (1880–1930), who died on a subsequent expedition to Greenland in 1930 (cf. Müller 2011b: 309–30). A scientist himself, Fanck was deeply interested in intersections between science and aesthetics in film, and used explicit references to the Wegener expeditions that would have been immediately understood by the contemporary German cinema audience. These references can be found both in the choice of cinematic devices, such as the use of cartography to show the expedition's geographic destination in Greenland, and on the narrative level. The film tells the story of an expedition to Greenland to find a certain Professor Lorenz, who – driven by his desire to be the first (white) man ever to reach and traverse the Karajak Glacier – left a previous scientific expedition and became lost in the perpetual ice. We follow the luckless, adventurous, hazardous search for Lorenz carried out by his colleagues. Out of the party, only Lorenz and his wife Hella (Leni Riefenstahl) survive, rescued from an iceberg by pilot Ernst Udet and a carefully choreographed fleet of eighty kayaks. The other participants of the fictional expedition fall prey to a polar bear, succumb to Arctic hysteria, or drown when attempting to reach the mainland by swimming across the polar sea.

The German/US co-production *SOS Eisberg* was one of Arnold Fanck's last successful *Bergfilme* ('mountain films') and was also one of the last successful examples of this German genre in general. Christian Rapp chose not to include an in-depth reading of *SOS Eisberg* in his book *Höhenrausch* ('High-altitude Euphoria'), a study of the German *Bergfilm* (Rapp 1997). In the following essay, I would like to explore the question of if – and in which sense – the spectacular Greenlandic icebergs of *SOS Eisberg* function in ways similar to the Alpine mountains that figure prominently in the *Bergfilme* of Fanck and other directors. A reading of *SOS Eisberg* within the framework of the German *Bergfilm* genre of the 1920s and 1930s allows an understanding of the link between representations of the Arctic and political, as well as media-related issues relevant in Germany at the time, namely the unfolding of a fascist ideology and aesthetics.

The shooting and release of *SOS Eisberg* coincides with the National Socialists' seizure of power in 1933. Most of the shooting took place in the summer of 1932, close to the settlement of Uummannaq in northwestern Greenland. The transition from the democracy of the Weimar Republic to the dictatorship of National Socialist Germany can be said to have started with the transfer of governmental power to the NSDAP and its allies on 30 January 1933. Additional footage was shot in the Swiss Alps in the spring and summer of 1933, before the film was released and had its premiere on 30 August 1933 in Berlin. As one of the consequences of this course of history, co-scriptwriter Friedrich Wolf, a member of the German Communist Party, was omitted from the credits.

The question is whether *SOS Eisberg*, along with other Fanck films, exhibits features of a pre-National Socialist aesthetic. Siegfried Kracauer was the first to explore the foreshadowing of a proto-fascist aesthetic in Weimarer Republik film in his seminal study *From Caligari to Hitler* (1947). He argues that the 'surge of pro-Nazi tendencies during the pre-Hitler period could not better be confirmed than by the increase and specific evolution of the mountain films' (Kracauer 1970: 257). How can these aesthetic features now be linked to a tradition of representations of the Arctic and of Greenland? And does *SOS Eisberg* tell us anything about Greenland at all? I argue that what links all these elements – the *Bergfilm* genre, proto-fascist aesthetics, representations of the Arctic – is that they are all connected in one or other way with the concept of the sublime formulated by philosophers since the eighteenth century: they all operate with figurations of an overwhelming and inexpressible aesthetic experience in the face of natural (and, later, cultural/technical) spectacles. I trace the formulation and relevance of concepts of the sublime in the socio-cultural, political and medial context of *SOS Eisberg*. I argue that the conquering of Greenlandic icebergs is presented as the ultimate quest of expedition films and film expeditions alike; that it represents both the peak and, simultaneously, the collapse of the German *Bergfilm*.

What is more, the *SOS Eisberg* film expedition and the resulting film comply with imperialist representations of blank spots on the map – of which the Arctic, with its imagined infinite whiteness, might be the most literal one. Both the expedition members and the film make use of cartography and scientific techniques to survey and describe the Arctic landscape and geology. In contrast to Fanck's account of the expedition, which contains lengthy passages devoted to encounters with members of the indigenous population, the Inuit only appear in decorative mass scenes during the film's finale. This mode of representing the Inuit is consistent with what cultural anthropologist Ann Fienup-Riordan has termed 'Eskimo Orientalism' (1995). The main concern of *SOS Eisberg*, however, is not to convey a realistic or documentary image of life in Greenland, in contrast to the popular and dominant genres of filmmaking about Greenland of the first decades of the twentieth century: expedition films, travelogues or the so-called culture film in Denmark with its impetus of popular education. *SOS Eisberg* does not show the ethnographic interest of Flaherty's *Nanook of the North* (1922) or Rasmussen's *Palos Brudefærd* (*The Wedding of Palo*, 1934), nor an interest in presenting the 'modern, protected, colonial Greenland' (Nørrested 2012: 22) as it was the vogue in Danish Greenland film since *Den store Grønlandsfilm* (*The Great Greenland Film*, 1922) or *Inuit* (1938–40). One could claim that its main characters are not even people – the members of the expedition team – but the eponymous icebergs. Despite Fanck's preference for original footage of natural phenomena, the icebergs' main function in *SOS Eisberg* is a symbolic and aesthetic one. Thus, the first major feature film about Greenland, in Fanck's words, tells us little about Greenland and much about the preoccupations of the Nazi era: sports; alpinism; the disciplining of individual and collective bodies; the experience and aesthetics of the sublime.

THE *SOS EISBERG* FILM EXPEDITION

The 1920s and early 1930s had seen a vogue for adventure films shot in faraway and – seen from the perspective of American and European metropolitan centres – exotic locations. Given their success, *SOS Eisberg* was commissioned by the founder and president of Universal Pictures' Carl Laemmle, a Jewish-German immigrant. Laemmle had already distributed Fanck's earlier films in the US. Shortly after the release of *SOS Eisberg*, he was denied entry to Germany. In his autobiography, Fanck savours the memory of his luxurious trip to Hollywood (paid for by Universal), where the deal was made (Fanck 1973: 250–4). In his book about the film expedition, Fanck credits Laemmle for his 'rare courage in taking risks and genuine idealism' regarding the undertaking (Fanck 1933: 7). According to Fanck, Laemmle had 'thrown all caution to the wind' in commissioning what was considered to be the most daring of motion picture expeditions to date. Universal claimed they had taken out the largest insurance policy ever secured for a film shoot (Fanck 1933: 7). After having made the necessary diplomatic arrangements with the Danish colonial administration, director Fanck and his cast and crew of thirty-eight left Hamburg in May 1932 on a chartered whaling vessel. Aboard was Rasmussen, who would act as an adviser. The expedition was equipped with large tents, two motorboats, technical and scientific equipment, two biplanes and an additional stunt plane, *Die Motte* ('The Moth'). *Die Motte* belonged to World War I pilot and hero Ernst Udet, who plays himself in *SOS Eisberg*. It would later be sacrificed in a scene depicting a plane crash. Moreover, the film expedition brought enough (luxury) food and drink supplies with them to last a year, as well as three polar bears, a gift from Hagenbeck's Zoo in Hamburg. According to Fanck, this was necessary because polar bears were near to extinct on Greenland's West Coast (Fanck 1973: 263–5). According to Fanck, zoo director Hagenbeck was enthusiastic about the idea of finally having good pictures of 'polar bears in their natural habitat'. The film expedition then made huge efforts to build a 'natural enclosure' to house the zoo's polar bears while on location in Greenland. Denmark supplied sleighs and dogs. The film expedition faced many dangerous moments during the following months: crashes, collapsing icebergs, severe storms, and the near capsize of boats. Some of these events are actually incorporated into the film, such as a scene where mountaineers and actors Hans Ertl and David Zogg climb a tumbling iceberg (Fanck 1973: 276–8). Three films were cut out of the six months' worth of footage: the German-language version *SOS Eisberg*, the English-version *SOS Iceberg* which premiered in New York City in September 1933, and a comedy with the title *Nordpol Ahoi!* (Andrew Marton, Germany/US, 1934). The English version of the film is much shorter than the German one and has additional scenes and a new ending that Fanck boycotted. These were written by new scriptwriter and director Tay Garnett, who was flown in from Hollywood. *Nordpol Ahoi!* was a parody of *SOS Eisberg* and remains lost. The rest of the footage – spectacular images of the polar landscape was destroyed, to Fanck's profound distress.

Arnold Fanck and the '*Bergfilm*'

Fanck was born in 1889 in Frankenthal/Pfalz. He worked as a skiing instructor and wrote a dissertation in geology before founding the company *Berg-und Sportfilm GmbH* in Freiburg im Breisgau in southwestern Germany in 1920. In the years to follow, he directed documentary and feature films with self-explanatory titles such as *Das Wunder des Schneeschuhs* (*The Miracle of the Snow Shoe*, 1920), *Im Kampf mit dem Berge* (*The Battle with the Mountain*, 1921), *Die weiße Hölle vom Piz Palü* (*The White Hell of Pitz Palu*, 1929) or *Stürme über dem Mont Blanc* (*Storms Above Mont Blanc*, 1930). Fanck worked with mountaineers such as Luis Trenker (1892–1990), who became a very popular *Bergfilm* actor and director, and dancer, actress and film director Leni Riefenstahl (1902–2003). Preceding her leading role in *SOS Eisberg*, Riefenstahl had acted in several of Fanck's films and in 1932 directed her debut film, also a mountain film, *Das blaue Licht* (*The Blue Light*). Fanck, Trenker and Riefenstahl formed the core of a scene of mountain, sports and adventure filmmakers preoccupied with visualising an existential and often spiritual relationship between man and nature in dramatic mountain landscapes. Fanck recruited his photographers from the ranks of winter sportsmen, and worked closely with scientists. Some of them, like glaciologist and geologist Ernst Sorge, who had previously taken part in Alfred Wegener's Greenland expeditions, accompanied the *SOS Eisberg* film expedition.

Fanck's films thus stand out in terms of authenticity and credibility: all those involved – above all the actors – were supposed to undergo the same stresses and strains as the characters. This principle of authenticity is why Fanck did not want to cast Riefenstahl as a pilot in *SOS Eisberg*: there was no female character in the script originally, as 'no woman had ever been on an Arctic expedition' (Fanck 1973: 253). Riefenstahl had learned to ski and become an accomplished mountaineer during the filming of Fanck's *The Holy Mountain* (*Der heilige Berg*, 1926), their first collaboration. But she was not a pilot and in his autobiography, written some forty years later, Fanck expressed unhappiness with the 'inauthentic' result of her participation in *SOS Eisberg*. She was cast, he says, only on the insistence of the Americans. They had declared a film without a female character impossible and had wanted Riefenstahl because of her popularity following the release of *The White Hell of Pitz Palu* (Fanck 1973: 253). As is generally known, Trenker and above all Riefenstahl became deeply involved with the Nazi regime – a brief reference to her films *Triumph of the Will* (*Triumph des Willens*, about the 1934 NSDAP congress in Nuremburg, released in 1935) and *Olympia* (about the 1936 Olympic Games in Berlin, released in 1938) must suffice in the context of this chapter.

Fanck and his mountain films never figured prominently in the Third Reich. In his autobiography, Fanck claims to have convinced propaganda minister Joseph Goebbels of his being a radical 'Alleingänger' – a solo-walker in the alpine sense – with a general scepticism towards associations of any kind and a natural reluctance to subscribe to any ideology (Fanck 1973: 315–17). Christian Rapp and others argue, however, that Fanck's type of *Bergfilm*, with its focus on aesthetic appeal rather than story, never convincingly made the transition to the talking-movie era and had therefore already passed its peak of popularity, relevance and economic success when the National Socialists came to power (Rapp 1997: 9).

In common with all of Fanck's previous mountain films, *SOS Eisberg* has no documentary impetus and no ethnographic interest in the Greenlandic Inuit (in contrast to them taking up much space in Fanck's accounts of the expedition). According to cultural critic and curator Christian Rapp in *Höhenrausch*, it is characteristic for the *Bergfilm* to conceptualise landscape as symbolic rather than real (Rapp 1997: 9). The mountain landscape figures as a space that is decoupled from social interaction in the cities or even in the valley. It is imagined as a space detached from time and civilisation. Nature is never just the setting for a story, but the central topic for narration and visualisation (Rapp 1997: 8f). As Rapp puts it, the mountain film was the first and only feature film genre that abolished interpersonal dialogue as its fundamental technique, replacing the human partner with one of stone and ice (Rapp 1997: 16). The characters can be said to play the same role as the camera: they bring nature and its dangers to life, getting nature to talk instead of themselves. The characters in a *Bergfilm* never leave the alpine setting: the mountains are where they appear, act and vanish (Rapp 1997: 16).

GREENLANDIC ICEBERGS AND THE '*BERGFILM*'

In which sense can *SOS Eisberg* be said to radicalise Fanck's mountain films? Above all, this is due to the setting. As film historian Rainer Rother puts it in an article on *SOS Eisberg*: Greenland is, for the first time, turned into a location (Rother 2001: 148). According to Rother, Fanck's films operated with a logic of surpassing, of 'first ascents' ('Erstbesteigungen'), of 'filmic firsts' ('filmische Erstleistungen') – just like the scene based around extreme skiing, mountaineering and alpine exploration that he himself came from and depicted

Figure 10.1   Photograph by Richard Angst from the *SOS Eisberg* film expedition. The original caption in Arnold Fanck's book: 'Sepp Rist, the first man ever to stand on the peak of a really high iceberg' (1933: 117).

in his filmmaking (Rother 2001: 145f). We find formulations of this logic of novelties and superlatives in all accounts of the *SOS Eisberg* film expedition. The above-mentioned Hans Ertl and David Zogg, for example, are credited by Fanck in his autobiography for 'certainly being the first human beings on a tumbling iceberg', thus achieving a 'peculiar "alpine" record' (Fanck 1973: 278). In a combination of alpine and colonial discourse, Fanck describes a 'difficult climbing tour through icy Greenlandic rocks that no man had ever set foot on before' (Fanck 1973: 297).

SOS Eisberg mimics, in terms of both its story and production, a hazardous expedition to the Arctic. The simple story itself is reduced even further, with a simultaneous intensification of what Rother terms 'Schauwerte': visual value and appeal (Rother 2001: 151). The Hungarian-American film editor Andrew Marton, a member of the American film crew, told film director and critic John Gallagher in retrospect: 'Although the photographic background material that they shot was magnificent, it just didn't cut together. The footage was unsurpassed photographically, but it didn't make any sense' (Gallagher 2005). The narration steps back in favour of the image. The icebergs, functioning as the film's actual main characters, provide all the dynamics and action – climaxing in images of tumbling and calving icebergs, more dynamic than any mountain can ever be – while the human characters are doomed to merely persevere or perish. Dramatic climax makes way for the permanent danger of death, hopelessness, constant maximum physical endurance, and an accumulation of spectacular images – unprecedented in both quality and quantity. Fanck was convinced, according to Rother, that nowhere could ice be shot in more overwhelming images than in Greenland (Rother 2001: 151).

The visual appeal of the mountain scenery is not an anthropological constant, as Christian Rapp notes, but a result of cultural and media practices since the eighteenth century (Rapp 1997: 23). He locates the emergence of the notion that alpine peaks and glaciers are worth seeing and experiencing within the nature mysticism of Jean-Jacques Rousseau (1712–78) and, above all, in the concepts of the sublime formulated since the Irish enlightenment philosopher and politician Edmund Burke (1729–97). Psycho- and sociohygienic powers were linked to the mountain; mere fright and terror were transcended – first in theory, then by the ever-growing winter sports and mountaineering scenes – into an experience of awe and of exquisite aesthetic and physical pleasure. According to Rapp, one can trace in painting, literature and tourism a discourse of how, in the course of the nineteenth century, the border of what was perceived as beautiful scenery climbed further up the mountains, and how the more chaotic and wilder high mountain zones became worthy of visual and textual representation, became *picturesque* (Rapp 1997: 71f). So there is, in mountain landscapes, not only a tree line, but also a historically variable line of the aesthetic experience of the beautiful and the sublime.

SOS EISBERG AND THE SUBLIME

In his account of the *SOS Eisberg* film expedition, Fanck gushes about the images he and his crew were able to film in Greenland: the sounds of infinite vastness, the eternal blazing sun, collapsing and crashing icebergs, calving glaciers, deafening noise and complete silence, unbearable cold, lethal danger and ultimate challenges. It is as if he was ticking off the list of sublimation-inducing natural phenomena formulated by, among others, Edmund Burke, Friedrich Schiller and Immanuel Kant. Perhaps the most vivid example of this is Burke's description of the features constituting the aesthetic experience of the sublime: the feelings of awe or astonishment in the face of spectacular natural phenomena. According to Burke, what overwhelms the soul and mind and leads to a suspension of reason is the experience of power, suddenness, vastness, infinity, difficulty, magnificence, vacuity and solitude, of either obscurity or overpowering light and excessive loudness (Burke [1757] 1998: 101–27; 159–66). The Universal Pictures PR office obviously had the list at hand, too, when advertising *SOS Eisberg*:

> The Impossible Comes to the Screen! See the rescuing airplane piloted by a beautiful girl crash in flames against an iceberg! See the crashing masses of white death – crumbling worlds of ice menacing man and beast alike! See the terrific hand-to-claw battle between a man and a Polar Bear – the

man the loser! See the airplane piloted by Major Ernst Udet perform unbelievable feats among the ice crags! See a lone woman trapped on a melting and crumbling iceberg with five desperate men! See the birth of an iceberg – a mountain of ice exploded into the sea – mothered by a gigantic glacier! Icebound! Blizzard-Lashed! Facing Unknown Terrors! Facing Death itself – Not Once, but a Thousand Times – All to bring you this picture! The Screen's Supreme Adventure! (cited in Gallagher 2005)

The tale of *SOS Eisberg* – the plot as well as the images, supplemented by the accounts of the film's shooting by Fanck, Riefenstahl, Sorge and Udet – is a tale of the sublime. This could be seen as a futile undertaking, as the aesthetic experience of an image or text can never compensate for a 'real' experience, meaning that representations of the sublime are virtually impossible. But if there is a formula for the sublime, this is what the *Bergfilm* generally and *SOS Eisberg* specifically aim at achieving or conveying: a human being's encounter with majestic mountains, dangerous weather conditions and an uncontrollable landscape that seems to be hostile to life and reminds human beings of their smallness. In *SOS Eisberg*, the expedition encounters the droning noise of calving glaciers, the glaring splendour of vast ice landscapes in the infinite sunlight of polar summer, and uncontrollable waters. We are supposed to re-enact, as we see the film, the characters' feeling of solitude and exposure, of horror and awe.

The '*Bergfilm*' and Fascist Aesthetics

It is in the combination of what Kracauer describes as the 'mountain enthusiasm' of the pre-Hitler era (Kracauer 1970: 112) and concepts of the sublime that one finds the confluence of the *Bergfilm* and fascist aesthetics. According to Kracauer, the mountain climbers of the 1920s and 30s were 'devotees performing the rites of a cult', and Fanck was among those 'spreading the gospel of proud peaks and perilous ascents' (Kracauer 1970: 110f). By 'combining precipices and passions, inaccessible steeps and insoluble human conflicts', by presenting a heroic idealism in the face of the laws of nature and perilous danger, Fanck's mountain films lent themselves to fulfil the 'craving for a spiritual shelter' that Kracauer sees at stake in the culture of the Weimar Republic (Kracauer 1970: 110, 107). In other words, it is their figurations of encounters of man and nature in the mode of the sublime that make Fanck's mountain films, despite their apolitical intentions, an obvious example of pre-National Socialist aesthetics and ideology. Christian Rapp describes in *Höhenrausch* the German alpine movement's (*Alpinismus*) ideological evolution, promoting ideas of escapism, anti-rationalism, anti-modernism, anti-intellectualism and primitivism (Rapp 1997: 22–70). They could initially have been conveyed in the form of potentially healing psychic and physical encounters between man and nature, but gained political relevance and force with the *Gleichschaltung* of the German Alpine Association in the context of the *Machtergreifung* of 1933 and the introduction of an Aryan paragraph, which had already occurred in 1924. Notions about the psychohygienic aspects of alpine sports could easily be, and were, translated into other ideas: the concept of ethnic cleansing; a semantics of exploration and conquest; a struggle for *Lebensraum*; individual summit photographs into collective (or *Führer*-) victory poses.

Susan Sontag has prominently explored a connection between film, the sublime and National Socialist aesthetics in her 1975 essay on Riefenstahl, 'Fascinating Fascism', in which she draws heavily on Kracauer's findings. The essay was written on the occasion of Riefenstahl's then most recent publication, *The Last of the Nuba* (1974) and against the background of a tendency at the time to rehabilitate Riefenstahl by weighing her artistic merits and her powers of aesthetic innovation against her political entanglements. Sontag cautions against a separation of the two and points at the profound intertwinedness of aesthetics and ideology in all phases of Riefenstahl's work as an actor, film director and photographer. It all starts with the *Bergfilm*, with Riefenstahl travelling all the way to the Alps to get into contact with Arnold Fanck after having seen his *The Mountain of Destiny* (*Der Berg des Schichsals*, 1924). Her career kicked off with *The Holy Mountain*, directed by Fanck two years later, the first of a series of six joint *Bergfilme* that Sontag describes as 'Fanck's pop-Wagnerian vehicles for Riefenstahl'. Though they were 'no doubt thought of as apolitical when they were made', Sontag nevertheless concurs with Kracauer's evaluation that 'these films now seem in retrospect . . . to be an anthology of proto-Nazi sentiments' (Sontag 1975).

Sontag continues: 'The mountain climbing in Fanck's pictures was a visually irresistible metaphor of unlimited aspiration toward the high mystic goal, both beautiful and terrifying . . . heavily dressed people strain upward to prove themselves in the purity of the cold; vitality is identified with physical ordeal' (Sontag 1975). Most of the dangers faced by the film expedition's participants and the characters of *SOS Eisberg*, by the fictitious and factual expeditions alike, are self-created and not necessarily a feature of the Greenlandic landscape and climate: a swimming contest against a polar bear; the climbing of an iceberg which might collapse at any moment; Riefenstahl's Hella Lorenz flying from Berlin to northwestern Greenland in an open plane, with a polar fox jacket and undulated hair, swimming amongst icebergs in the polar sea. These risky, irrational and even implausible actions fall in line with some of the features of fascist – or to be correct, in this case, proto-fascist – aesthetics listed by Sontag: 'Fascist art glorifies surrender; it exalts mindlessness; it glamorizes death'. Furthermore, we come upon monumentality and a 'rendering of movement in grandiose and rigid patterns' – the ascents of icebergs, Ernst Udet's flying display, circling the peak of one iceberg after another – and the choreography of kayaks and oars in the grand finale. At the expense of common sense and plausibility, at least from today's perspective we can also trace the 'fetishism of courage, the repudiation of the intellect' that Sontag sees as a common denominator of fascist art. The expedition topos adapted by *SOS Eisberg* implies, however, an ambivalence between the rational and the irrational, between belief in progress and technological development on the one hand and nature mysticism on the other (cf. Müller 2011; Kreimeier 2005), with a tendency towards the latter. The hero and saviour is, after all, a pilot, and the survivors are rescued after a successful SOS call transmitted via international radio. The characters do not act for the sake of knowledge, but for the sake of the struggle itself. Fulfilment lies in danger and pain, medialised and aestheticised in a process described by Germanist Ralf Schnell as the 'codification of terror' (Schnell 2000), a sublime version of bliss.

As an unsurprising result of these reflections about the transfer of a German *Bergfilm* to a Greenlandic iceberg, one can register that *SOS Eisberg* also follows established patterns of imperialist conquest and exploration in the name of science, with the Arctic represented as a blank area on a map of Europe, ripe for exploration by eager, adventurous potential heroes; a hostile, vast, deserted landscape, inhabited by an exotic and primitive people. Moreover, the film's German version reflects the specific socio-cultural context of the end of the Weimar Republic, prefiguring what was to come and would be believed and supported in the years to follow.

GREENLAND AND SUBLIME ICEBERGS TODAY

But what does all this say about Greenland? Does the sublime iceberg have any relevance at all to Greenlandic self-images, or is it just a prominent symbol of the Arctic elsewhere, its meaning fluctuating between images of a threatening nature and that of a nature threatened? I would like to conclude with a scene from the Greenlandic film *Nuummioq* (2009), which provides a witty commentary on this issue. The main character Malik (Lars Rosing) is confronted with his good-for-nothing cousin Mikael's business idea: Mikael (Angunnguaq Larsen) plans to sell the pure ice of the Greenlandic icecap to the world. For his first commercial, he envisions an elderly man in the Bahamas, having a drink against the background of a Caribbean sunset (which is staged in Michael's room with photo wallpaper and expensive palm trees from a garden centre in Nuuk). In a dreamlike scene, the elderly man imagines himself back in his native Greenland when he was young, firing his rifle at a floating iceberg from a boat in the fjord, collecting and crushing the bits and pieces of ice that have fallen into the sea, just to put it into his whisky. He leans back in the boat, takes a sip, sighs happily and smiles. Reluctantly, Malik agrees to play the role and the two cousins set off in a boat on a mission

Figure 10.2   Malik and Michael on their quest for an iceberg in *Nuummioq*.

to find a suitable iceberg. But because it is summer in Nuuk, they cruise the fjords for quite some time (Michael falls asleep) before they finally find a rather minuscule iceberg.

This iceberg is neither majestic nor sublime; it is neither spectacular, nor an exquisite threat, nor a ubiquitous feature of the landscape, nor does it work as a symbol of anything beyond its practical value. At the most, it is a marker of individual or collective memory and identity. It just accidentally floats by on a calm and ordinary summer afternoon; it is there to be sold; it is a commodity. To Malik's objection that no one in Greenland will buy overpriced ice, and that it is already available at the supermarket, Michael counters that he, needless to say, is focusing on the international instead of the domestic market. His reply, as well as the image of the tiny iceberg, is a simple but accurate summary of the Greenlandic ice landscape, as seen from the outside and the inside. It can simultaneously be interpreted as a meta-comment on the asymmetrical relationship between a tradition of international Greenland films and a young up-and-coming Greenlandic film industry that arguably started with *Nuummioq*. It can even be seen as a comment on an ongoing debate about national sovereignty, about the sovereignty of representation, and of natural resources in Greenland and the Arctic. Greenland's ice? 'If we export it, it'll be luxury goods!'

Thanks to my students Leonie Kreutzer and Johann Schork for the inspirational discussions about SOS Eisberg and the sublime.

BIBLIOGRAPHY

Burke, E. [1757] (1998), *A Philosophical Enquiry into the Origin of our Ideas of the Sublime and Beautiful and Other Pre-Revolutionary Writings*, London: Penguin Classics.
Fanck, A. (1933), *SOS Eisberg: mit Dr. Fanck und Ernst Udet in Grönland. Die Grönland-Expedition des Universal-Films SOS Eisberg*, Munich: Bruckmann.

Fanck, A. (1973), *Er führte Regie mit Gletschern, Stürmen und Lawinen. Ein Filmpionier erzählt*, Munich: Nymphenburger Verlagshandlung.

Fienup-Riordan, A. (1995), *Freeze Frame: Alaska Eskimos in the Movies*, Seattle: University of Washington Press.

Gallagher, J. (2005), 'S.O.S. Iceberg', *National Board of Review*, December 2005, http://www.nbrmp.org/features/SOSICEBERG.cfm.

Giesen, R. (n.d.), 'Der Bergfilm der 20er und 30er Jahre', http://www.medienobservationen.lmu.de/artikel/kino/kino_pdf/giesen_bergfilm.pdf.

Kneiper, J. (1992), 'Alpträume in Weiß', in *Revisited. Der Fall Dr. Fanck. Die Entdeckung der Natur im deutschen Bergfilm. Film und Kritik* 1, 53–70.

Kracauer, S. (1970) [1947], *From Caligari to Hitler. The Psychological History of German Film*, New York: Princeton University Press.

Kreimeier, K. (2005), 'Naturmagie und Technik-Faszination. Arnold Fancks Berg- und Sportfilmwerkstatt', in A. Ehmann, J. Goergen, K. Kreimeier (eds), *Geschichte des dokumentarischen Films in Deutschland*, vol. 2: *Weimarer Republik (1918–1933)*, Stuttgart: Reclam, 474–92.

Müller, D. (2011a), 'Eiskalte Grenzgänge. Alfred Wegeners Grönlandexpedition im Kulturfilm von 1936', *Filmblatt* 45, 17–33.

Müller, D. (2011b), 'Zwischen Forschung, Unterricht und Populärkultur. Filmisches Wissen und Orte früher Filmkultur', in O. Fahle, V. Hediger, G. Sommer (eds), *Orte filmischen Wissens. Filmkultur und Filmvermittlung im Zeitalter digitaler Netzwerke*, Marburg: Schüren, 309–30.

Nørrested, C. (2012), *Blandt eskimoer, eventyrere, kolonisatorer og etnografer – Grønlandsfilm/Amongst Eskimos, Adventurers, Colonisers and Ethnographers – Greenland on Film*, Copenhagen: Forlaget North.

Rapp, C. (1997), *Höhenrausch: Der deutsche Bergfilm*, Vienna: Sonderzahl.

Riefenstahl, L. (1933), *Kampf in Schnee und Eis*, Leipzig: Hesse und Becker.

Rother, R. (2001), 'Wilde Landschaft, heroische Figuren. Arnold Fancks SOS Eisberg – ein Film-Expeditions-Film', in E. Wottrich (ed.), *Deutsche Universal. Transatlantische Verleih- und Produktionsstrategien eines Hollywood-Studios in den 20er und 30er Jahren*, Munich: edition text+kritik, 144–61.

Schnell, R. (2000), 'Der Nationalsozialismus und das Erhabene', in R. Grimminger (ed.), *Kunst–Macht–Gewalt. Der ästhetische Ort der Aggressivität*, Munich: Wilhelm Fink Verlag, 142–56.

Schöning, J. (2009), 'Drei Männer im Schnee. Knud Rasmussen und Alfred Wegener in Arnold Fancks SOS Eisberg', in J. Schöning (ed.), *Die arktische Leinwand. Grönland im Film. Von Knud Rasmussen bis Fräulein Smilla*, Lübeck: Verlag Schmidt-Römhild, 52–67.

Sontag, S. (1975), 'Fascinating fascism', *The New York Review of Books*, 6 February, http://www.nybooks.com/articles/archives/1975/feb/06/fascinating-fascism/.

Sorge, E. (1933), *Mit Flugzeug, Faltboot und Filmkamera in den Fjorden Grönlands. Bericht über die Universal-Dr. Fanck-Grönlandexpedition*, Berlin: Drei Masken.

Sperschneider, W. (2009), '100 Jahre Grönland im Film. Eine Filmgeschichte', in J. Schöning (ed.), *Die arktische Leinwand. Grönland im Film. Von Knud Rasmussen bis Fräulein Smilla*, Lübeck: Verlag Schmidt-Römhild, 22–37.

Udet, E. (1935), *Mein Fliegerleben*, Berlin: Ullstein.

11. THE THREAT OF THE THAW: THE COLD WAR ON THE SCREEN

Anna Westerståhl Stenport

Erected in 1961, the Berlin Wall is an artifact of the geopolitical tensions that marked the period of 1947–89. Initially constructed of bricks and barbed wire, and subsequently by large forbidding concrete slabs, the wall symbolised the ideological and political differences between communism and capitalism, the Warsaw Pact and NATO, and the USSR and the USA. Like other associated terms – such as the East and West blocs, or the Iron Curtain, or the Cold War – the wall helpfully bridged two conceptual realms: the material and the imaginary. It became an expedient way to conceptualise a prolonged conflict that by the early 1960s seemed eerily abstract and all-encompassing: sterile and frigid yet always on the verge of dynamic escalation and ensuing mass destruction. Though wars in Korea, Vietnam and Afghanistan had pitched the two powers against each other in destructive interactions that wreaked long-term havoc on small nations, the mainstream Western cultural imaginary of the Cold War was largely detached from embodied practices or localised combat. The Cold War was everywhere and simultaneously nowhere.

The space race escalated from the mid-1950s onward and extended outward from Earth itself. Culminating in the early 1980s, with Reagan's Strategic Defense Initiative (SDI) or 'Star Wars' programme (in a nod toward the significance of the cinematic imagination for shaping the Cold War), the Cold War's airborne military operations defied national boundaries, just as it did when it was waged underwater, in deadly nuclear submarines circling the earth, unseen by the public though charted on radar screens. Visualisations of such threats figured prominently in Cold War cinema, with situation rooms filled with blinking screens charting airborne progress or thwarted oceanic attacks a staple of the mise-en-scène (Shaw and Youngblood 2010; Palmer 2011; Shaw 2007). Films made in, about or alluding to the Arctic region and its distinctive environments and geopolitical tensions offer important perspectives for visualising a Cold War cultural imaginary. The Arctic through its climate – its coldness – and its distinctive environment – ice – can be understood as an emblem for the Cold War. This is evident in a range of films from the period, spanning European co-productions to Mosfilm and Hollywood, and, in the case of American TV, military documentary broadcasts. To unpack this set of issues, I draw on what for an Arctic Cold War imaginary can best be described as two mutually constitutive and interrelated conceptual categories: the environmental and the geopolitical.

ENVIRONMENTS AND GEOPOLITICS OF ICE

The Arctic can be situated within a continuum of environments central to the Cold War imaginary, from seafloor to outer space. The North Pole and the Arctic Ocean, with its permeable cover of ice, and associated extreme environments, from the Greenland icecap to the remote northern Siberian coastline or the Canadian archipelago along the Northwest Passage occupy a liminal space in the ecological and geographical spatiality of earth. The area is little known, little visited, little visualised, and characterised by extremes of oppositional light patterns (forbiddingly dark in the winter; viscerally light in the summer; see for example Crowly 2011 on 'edge situations'). That, of course, also makes them ripe for cinematic imagination.

In the geopolitical realm, following World War II, the Arctic was subordinated to either side in the East-West conflict in specific ways. Within this conflict, as political scientist Jay Chaturvedi argues, Arctic space 'came to be dominated by a militarized geography' (Chaturvedi 2000: 446) and 'to be perceived and treated throughout the Cold War as an inanimate, passive chessboard on which geostrategic moves and countermoves were made with very little reference to ecological considerations' (Chaturvedi 2000: 454). The Arctic Ocean was the most militarised sea in the world. The ideas of the Arctic as empty, open to conquest and visualised as an object governed by preset rules of logic – like a chess game – through which one opponent could gain supremacy over the other, came to dominate the imaginary. Cold War interests in the Arctic maintain the East/West ideological and military power balance, with the empty space used as an equilibrium, and as a projection screen on which small countries disappear, as do all environmental considerations. The so-called empty, abstract 'End of the World' territory becomes a primary stabiliser of geopolitical tension; the perceptual/imagined blankness is invested with significant power precisely because of its apparent vacuity. In addition, the Arctic became an abstract battleground for missile warfare and its concomitant defence system, the Distant Early Warning Line. From the late 1950s the DEWL's radar stations cut a ribbon slightly above the Arctic Circle from Eastern Greenland to Alaska. This line reflects that the shortest route for air strikes between the USA and the USSR went directly over the North Pole.

The Arctic Ocean thus became a key stabiliser in its present absence in the opposition between East and West. But the geopolitical Arctic also contains several smaller nation states – Denmark and Greenland, Iceland, Norway, Sweden and Finland – whose relative lack of political clout reflect their relative diminutive geographical size. These states were precariously positioned in between the two superpowers. In this context, specifics of particular places became subordinated to their relation to either entity in the East-West conflict. Arctic small nations were trapped and 'forc[ed] . . . to accept US perceptions' of their reality (Chaturvedi 2000: 447). '[T]hey could not escape the side-effects of a conflict in which the two imperial systems were bent upon establishing hegemonies within their respective areas'; an additional side-effect is that smaller nations thereby came to subdue indigenous cultures (the Sámi in Northern Scandinavia and the Inuit in Greenland) and arguably annexed their lands in a geopolitical race for domination (Chaturvedi 2000: 447–8). This aspect of an Arctic-located Cold War conflict is markedly absent in Nordic film history, with a few striking exceptions discussed below.

The Cold War and the roles that the Arctic played in it looked very different depending on which nation represented them. This tension between the environmental and the geopolitical plays a part in many of the Cold War films from the region, and becomes one of the ways in which the different Arctic imaginaries are engaged with and mobilised.

CINEMATIC ALLEGORY AND PROPAGANDA OF COLDNESS

In 1950s American feature film and broadcast documentaries, two different mechanisms are at play in regards to Arctic environments: the first allegorical, the second propagandistic. While generally understood as opposites, these two rhetorical strategies conjoin in Arctic Cold War representations. Allegory means conveying an idea or principle through characters, figurations or events in representational form, and by which a semi-hidden meaning (often political) can be discerned. Propaganda, instead, operates on explicitness, by which a doctrine is openly propagated, often systematically, in ways that reflect the political interests of those who advocate for a particular standpoint. In the Arctic, the allegorical and propagandistic are both related to ice, and especially to the manipulation of ice in the service of supposed scientific interests.

One of the first allegorical enemy invasion films of the 1950s, Christian Nyby and Howard Hawks' *The Thing from Another World* (USA, 1951), sees the literal thawing of an organic being, which, while frozen, could be easily posited as the enemy impersonated. Once this object – functioning as an allegorical construct – is thawed out, it assumes a life form, and boundaries between good and evil begin similarly to metamorphise. Based on a 1938 novella originally set in Antarctica (*Who Goes There*, by John W. Campbell), the relocation of the action to the Arctic is significant, since it allows for an unequivocal allegorical reading to a much higher extent than an Antarctic setting would have done in the 1950s (Glasberg 2012: 65). While geopolitically significant, Antarctica was off the radar. But in the early Cold War, the Arctic and polar regions were conceived as frontlines against the Soviet enemy by the US military. The region emerges in *The Thing* as a 'paranoid, spongy-bordered space of horror' (Glasberg 2012: 65), and where, in the words of one of the characters in the opening of the film, 'Russians . . . are crawling around like flies'. The thawed Thing respects no boundaries, symbolically invading the United States, in the region where in the 1950s the country saw itself as most vulnerable to attack, and which it had designated as a priority strategic area (Martin-Nielsen 2012). The Thing is presented as seeking to usurp scientific, military and media order, partly akin to a Frankensteinian monster meeting its demise on the polar ice at the end of Mary Shelley's novel. Furthermore, it challenges both explorer and scientific invincibility myths, while also embodying threatening internationalism, wreaking havoc on the early US policy of Cold War containment and defence in the process (Glasberg 2012: 65).

A frozen environment – literally, ice – is thus in *The Thing* an allegory for the rigid geopolitical opposition between East and West, and also for the threats that a thaw – literal as well as figurative – could pose. In this and other allegorical alien-invasion-in-frozen-landscapes films, environmental science and Cold War politics coalesce. This is also the case in the Swedish-American 1959 B-movie *Rymndinvasion i Lappland* (*Terror in the Midnight Sun*, Virgil Vogel). This cult classic – one of few science fiction films ever made in Swedish film history – features an American geologist and his girlfriend who travel north to investigate a supposed meteorite impact. Once there, they are attacked by a hairy monster whose spaceship has crashed into the icy landscape. Scandinavian film history is remarkably devoid of Cold War and spy thrillers, with *Rymndinvasion i Lappland* the most obvious allegorical film in this respect. The scarcity of Cold War representation in Scandinavian cinema in the 1960s and 1970s is striking, given the tenuous position of these small nation-states located right between two superpowers. Scandinavian countries handled this precarious situation in different ways: Norway was a NATO member, Sweden adopted neutrality, and Finland was situated precariously adjacent to the USSR. While there certainly are film-historical reasons for this paucity of thrillers and science fiction films engaging with Cold War politics, their absence perhaps reflects disavowed recognition of the pressure felt between East and West. Nordic film history, moreover, had previously disregarded the Arctic or polar regions as the set for little but ethnographically inflected melodramas and anthropological documentaries.

However, Denmark, and especially Greenland, offers a very different perspective on Cold War figurations of the Nordic region. Northernmost Greenland, in fact, became the location of some of the most propagandistic Cold War moving-images rof the late 1950s and early 1960s, in which environmental depiction and geopolitics coalesce. As recent research in the field of environmental and geographical history shows, the Cold War was not fought solely between Moscow and Washington, but also in strategic peripheral locations. The Greenland polar coast and interior ice sheet was such a 'privileged' space (see for example Martin-Nielsen 2012). With the construction of the US Thule Air Base at the top of the island,[1] Greenland came to stand for an increasing militarisation and politicisation of the Arctic, concomitant with indigenous cultures' disruption (a few Danish films engage with this history; see MacKenzie and Stenport 2013 for a brief introduction). Thule Air Base became not only a cog in a global military-industrial complex but also figured as an imaginary space. This is especially evident in a sequence of quite remarkable documentaries set in northernmost Greenland aired on American TV through the Army Pictorial Services' *The Big Picture* series, the most widely distributed documentary programme on television at the time (Kinney 2013). *The Big Picture* became a staple of postwar American television that steeped a generation of Americans in the militarised geopolitical ideology of the Cold War. In addition, popular documentary shorts about Thule, such as Walt Disney's Oscar-winning *Men Against the Arctic* (Winston Hibler, 1955), popularised the Arctic and polar regions as outposts of American sovereignty.

Men Against The Arctic tells the story of two Coast Guard icebreakers seeking to chart a course through the pack ice from the US base at Thule, in northwestern Greenland, up to Camp Alert on the northernmost tip of Canada. Images include animated cartographies that introduce Thule as 'the end of the earth' and as strategically important for the development of polar science, especially meteorology and (military) construction materials. The film posits the base as a 'modern miracle . . . a mammoth enterprise', where $300 million has been invested in the service of US national interests. The narrative, much like *The Big Picture* episodes set in the Arctic,[2] is quite literally of 'men against the Arctic', meaning that the environment, location and climate are as much the enemy as the Soviets, against which the many military installations in Greenland were supposed to protect. With the construction of Camp Century, a base built under Greenland's interior ice sheet north-east of Thule and powered by a mobile nuclear reactor during the first years of the 1960s, the aim was to provide a secret launch site for nuclear missiles: Project Ice Worm (Grant 2010; Petersen 2008).

The propagandistic interest of these films crystallise around the promotion of US presence in the Arctic and Polar regions for scientific reasons, with Cold War defence and mobilisation implied to audiences, but left unstated. The 'enemy' is nebulously configured as equivocal with ice and cold, thus presenting a verbal and visual conflation between the environment and larger geopolitical discourses mobilised in the films. In *Men Against the Arctic*, the scientific mission of the Thule-based scientists is stated as being explicitly to understand Arctic storms, or 'whiteouts', which are a 'peculiar meteorological state in which the light from the sky and the light reflected from the surface of the snow are of the same degree of brightness, so that all contours are blotted out' and provide extreme navigation and observation challenges in polar environments (Borge Fristrup, cited in Martin-Nielsen 2012: 73). The whiteouts – erasing difference, obscuring direction and preventing clarity – are of course apt metaphors for the threat of actual combat in the Arctic between East and West.

Some of these productions also explicitly engage the rhetoric of confinement integral to Cold War conceptualisations, especially evident in *Men Against the Arctic* and *The Big Picture's City Under the Ice: Camp Century* (1961). With the persistent threat of nuclear war, Earth itself is construed as increasingly vulnerable. It can provide only limited ways of escape – the burgeoning space race, with space stations posited also as providing habitation outside the atmosphere, plays into this context and as a direct response to a fear of confinement. Confinement is mobilised as a trope in *Men Against the Arctic* and *City Under the Ice*. Sea ice relentlessly envelops the icebreakers in *Men Against the Arctic* on their way north to Camp Alert, itself cut off from the world when not passable by sea. Tons of ice and snow are blasted through in *City under the Ice* to construct living quarters, lab facilities and an excavated space to host an active nuclear reactor under a constantly changing Greenlandic snow cover. Moving sea ice, icebergs threatening to destroy ships and cut off transportation routes, and the Greenlandic ice sheet's internal movement engage metaphors of confinement as well as destabilisation. Ice and snow, like an East-West stalemate, may be perceived as rigid, cold and stable, while simultaneously emerging as dangerously dynamic. Indeed, Camp Century closed in 1966 after it became fully evident that though the Greenland Icecap may appear solid, hard and immobile, the visco-elastic aspects of snow and ice make any structure change shape.

MEN ON THIN ICE: EXPEDITION POLITICS

While not explicitly addressed in many Arctic Cold War films, the explorer and expedition tropes that have governed Arctic visual representation for hundreds of years are nevertheless implicit in a majority of them; the 1950s public service/propaganda/documentaries about northern Greenland discussed above are a case in point. Of particular relevance is the figuration of a white masculine explorer or group of expeditioners, confronting a harsh and near-lethal environment, in service of nation, honour, science or resource extraction (Bloom 1993; Hill 2008). At the end of the 1960s, two prestige and large-budget feature films, one by the major Hollywood studio MGM and the other by Sovfilm, engaged with the masculine explorer figuration in ways that pulled into relief both perceptions of the environmental particularities of Arctic sea ice and its geopolitical significance.

The Red Tent (*Krasnaia Palatka*, Mikhail Kalatozov, Mosfilm/Vides Cinematografic, 1969) tells the story of Italian officer Umberto Nobile's 1928 Mussolini-sponsored attempt to reach the North Pole by airship. The film is an Italian-Soviet English-language co-production with an international cast (among them Bond actor Sean Connery playing Norwegian explorer Roald Amundsen who perished during the historical rescue operation). *The Red Tent* is one of the better known of a number of international USSR-initiated co-productions pursued in order to export Soviet filmmaking abroad and to gain production subventions by partnering with Western producers. With Leonid Brezhnev in power from 1964, state control over cinematic production had in fact increased, while, at the same time, film imports from around the world (including from the USA) remained high through the late 1960s, as a way to gain revenue from cinema exhibition in a time of increasing television viewing (Shaw and Youngblood 2010: 51). Specifics of the Soviet film industry thus illustrate the often porous and dynamic nature of Cold War geostrategic interaction: the 'changes Soviet and American Cold War cinema underwent in the early 1960s [show that this] was a period during which the two cinemas converged in terms of offering a forum for Cold War dissent to a greater degree than at any other point of the conflict' (Shaw and Youngblood 2010: 127).

The film's title refers to the canvas structure erected on the ice by the survivors of the airship crash, painted red for rescue visibility. When mobilised in the film's title, it also signals a 'red' Soviet ideological investment. The expedition's lead Officer Nobile is portrayed as having deserted his crew on the ice in order to fly back on his own in the one plane that eventually makes it to the Arctic, ostensibly to summon a larger air rescue at Spitsbergen. The Western attempts to find the survivors on the ice come to naught, and they are eventually located by a rural Soviet amateur short-wave radio operator, who manages to connect their coordinates to the upper echelons of Soviet bureaucracy so that a large icebreaker can set out to rescue them. Survivors returned to Italy, and the film is framed by flashbacks in which Nobile is shown as traumatically reliving his decision to abandon the group, conveyed in conversations with Amundsen, members of his crew, and a woman who lost her love in the expedition.

The Cold War geopolitical implications of the film are multiple. First, the particularities of making this co-production and setting it near the North Pole

Figure 11.1 As a Soviet icebreaker breaks through to rescue the stranded men, the polar sea ice is figured as a porous, dynamic and impermanent border between East and West (*The Red Tent*, 1969).

indicate the potential of the Arctic, and especially the expansive sheet of ice, to serve as an empty canvas on which to reimagine politics and nationalism. Late 1960s Italian cinema re-addressed fascism in multiple films, as in the case of Bernardo Bertolucci's *The Conformist* (*Il Conformista*, Italy, 1970). *The Red Tent* effectively opens up a means to rethink both the World War II opposition between Italy and the USSR, in addition to criticising the loss of lives and trauma incurred by a race to the North Pole in the service of nationalism, spurred on by media interests. The space race is the implied counterpart, with a Soviet loss of that race with the American Moon-landing in 1968. The Arctic Ocean's sea ice becomes a way to stage these interests on Earth. The film's scenes of a majestic Soviet icebreaker forging its way through the ice sheet to save a derailed Italian expedition (no matter that the expedition was commissioned in the name of fascist nationalism) conveys a trope common in Soviet Cold War cinema. This trope entails an ideological investment on the part of the USSR as being portrayed internationally as a beacon of world peace and progress, by which the Soviet military will come to the rescue even of its sworn enemies. The North Polar sea ice, as it is conveyed in *The Red Tent*, is thereby simultaneously a geographical and geopolitical reference point. While symbolically a chessboard in Chaturvedi's conception, in which figures landed on the ice are desperately moving to get rescued, the film also has numerous implications for the wartime opposition between communism and fascism. At the same time, and so effectively portrayed in wide-screen as the icebreaker crunches it up, the Polar sea ice is a porous, dynamic, and partially impermanent border area between East and West. While mostly neglected in film histories, *The Red Tent* articulates a number of the tensions and implications of how we perceive the Arctic region during the Cold War.

Spy thriller submarine film *Ice Station Zebra* (John Sturges, USA, 1968) re-engages similar environmental and geopolitical tropes of the North Polar ice sheet nearly simultaneously with *The Red Tent*, but to different effects. While the final scene of the film features a teletyper conveying to the world media that the British civilian polar weather observation station eponymous with the film title – and by extension a good chunk of the Northern hemisphere – has been saved from nuclear destruction by cooperation between the US and the USSR, the drama leading up to this announcement effectively pitches West versus East as a battle not only of good versus evil, but also of different masculinities. The all-male cast recalls the polar expedition trope. The hardship they endure in snowstorms and their struggle to discern who is on which side of the political conflict echo many polar narratives that mobilise tropes of being lost or stuck in the ice pack, and subject to unpredictable ice and climate conditions. In this and many previous narratives, being lost in the ice also carries the risk of losing oneself and the supposed mission. In this film, however, the Western powers (the USA and the UK) are figured unequivocally as collaborative, with the good intentions of humankind in mind, while the East is brutally single-minded in the short-term pursuit of information about missile sites. The frozen Arctic Ocean serves as a blank page in which different geopolitical standpoints can be imagined but not, in fact, effected.

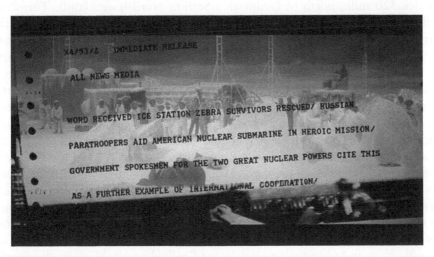

Figure 11.2   Only on the polar sea ice does Cold War collaboration seem possible, as conveyed by the teletyper superimposition in the final scene of *Ice Station Zebra* (1968).

Dull and jingoistic, MGM's *Ice Station Zebra* is a product of the rapidly decaying Hollywood studio system at the end of the 1960s. It was released in 70mm Cinerama and conveys the expanse of the polar landscape, while allowing for the wide-screen depiction of the cramped submarine quarters. Aesthetically and ideologically, the film is a throwback to an earlier era, situated right on the cusp of New Hollywood. One of the last films of director John Sturges and (gay icon) actor Rock Hudson's last hit, the camaraderie among the American military is nevertheless latently, but not explicitly, homoerotic. Filmmaker John Greyson notoriously intercut the film with gay pornography in his interventionist video *Moscow Does Not Believe in Queers* (Canada, 1986; see Marks 2013) and similar found footage analysis is found in Mark Rappaport's *Rock Hudson's Home Movies* (USA, 1992). Examining the tension of homoeroticism is not possible either within traditional Arctic expedition narratives (though potential for homoeroticism is also latent in those) or the Cold War film. The latter depended on the assumption of polar opposites – East versus West – to appear as rigid as those defining the contemporary heterosexual matrix. The Polar ice sheet, as depicted in *The Red Tent*, may be one of the locations in which this tension could be imagined as part of a Cold War ideology: far away, unknown and notoriously interstitial in its geopolitical and environmental composition, keeping the East and West in a stable and locked geostrategic power position and simultaneously offering a permeable surface that ruptures concurrent imaginaries of stability.

Ice Station Zebra opens with a parachute dropping an unknown object onto the ice 320 miles north of Denmark's Station Nord (Greenland). The scene reflects contemporary espionage surveillance techniques: satellites orbiting the earth captured on film images that were subsequently ejected in capsules to remote locations where they would be secretly retrieved. Images of the earth captured from space thus land in the Arctic, effectively connecting the two environments of space and planet. The American nuclear submarine eventually blasts through the ice, ostensibly on a mission to save the civilian British weather station. Its real target is to prevent the film capsule from getting into the hands of the USSR. These images connect the dots between dominant Cold War environmental imaginaries: the submerged underwater world, the Arctic Ocean's ice sheet, and outer space. The film capsules also constitute a meta-cinematic comment on the centraliy of film and moving images in the Cold War ideological battle. The tension between scientific and military endeavours in the Arctic are also mobilised in the film. As the idea of and perceived need for actual combat in the Arctic region subsided in the early 1960s, scientific investigation and observation sites instead picked up the slack in the geopolitical game of chess. This development reflects the close connection between science and military goals and operations in the Arctic.

The underwhelming special effects of *Ice Station Zebra*, however, compare unfavourably with Stanley Kubrick's major space epic *2001: A Space Odyssey* released the same year. The supposed North Pole scenes, filmed exclusively in a studio, seemed camp to contemporareous moviegoers and, of course, ridiculously inept at conveying an Arctic environment. The obvious constructedness of the sets and the location substitution of the Arctic manage to reassert the special case status of the Arctic in a Cold War imaginary: it is both present (in its studio configuration) and absent (in the difficulty of actually filming there), thereby reasserting its centrality both to geopolitical tension between East and West, and the environmental imaginaries mobilised by the period films. These tropes never going out of style, the film is reportedly slated for a Warner Bros remake, to be written and directed by Christopher McQuarrie and featuring (gay icon) Tom Cruise, signalling renewed interest in Arctic imaginaries.

THE BLOCKBUSTER COLD WAR AND THE SMALL NATION-STATE

American Anti-Soviet propaganda took a different turn in the early 1980s Reagan years and became markedly more explicit, which is evident also in film production (Shaw and Youngblood 2010). While the Arctic had by then receded as a central location for American geostrategy, especially with Reagan's initiation of the Strategic Defense Initiative in 1983, the fourth installment of the long-running *Rocky* franchise (*Rocky IV*, Sylvester Stallone, USA, 1985), engages an Arctic climate and environment partially to challenge such prevailing Cold War geopolitical and environmental rhetoric. Pitched against a Siberian imaginary, posited by Hollywood as a cold, desolate, rigid Arctic-y landscape (though filmed in Wyoming and Vancouver), Rocky Balboa and his Soviet counterpart Ivan Drago (played by Swede Dolph Lundgren) fight a physical and ideological match that eventually suggests potential for reconciliation and rapprochement between the two superpowers and therefore a thawing of icy relations. Their final fight is staged in a large arena (built for the 1986 World Exposition in Vancouver). Its design echoes German architect Frei Otto's 3 sq km pneumatic biosphere from 1971 – complete with an atomic power station and artificial sun – planned for scientists working in Arctic environments (Crowley 2010: 55). A similar sense of abstraction of Arctic landscapes is evoked in the Soviet-produced *Incident at MAP-Grid 36–80* (*Sluchay v Kvadrate 36–80*, Mikhail Tumanishvili, USSR, 1982). In this aerospace thriller directly critical of the United States, fighter planes cross the North Atlantic region as if it were an abstract chessboard on which pieces are strategically advanced. Explicit Arctic or polar landscapes are absent, while connections between the USSR's superpower status and neighbouring small nations are implicitly mobilised, recalling Chaturvedi's notion of the abstract geopolitical and environmental imaginary of the Arctic during the Cold War.

In the only Scandinavian Cold War action thriller from this period, *Orion's Belt* (*Orions Belte,* Ola Solum and Tristan De Vere Cole, Norway, 1985), these tensions come to the forefront.

Orions Bälte is ostensibly a national allegory for Norway's precarious position as a NATO member with possession of Svalbard, a strategically located archipelago in the Arctic Ocean and governed by an international treaty that permits substantial Soviet (now Russian) settlement, including in the mining town Barentsburg. Depicting three hapless Norwegian sailors and small-time Longyearbyen crooks, the plot centres on the men travelling to Greenland to sell a bulldozer they will supposedly dump in the ocean to earn insurance money, and therefore engaging in double dipping. On their return, they run across secret Soviet military installations at one of the outlying Svalbard islands. Victims of ruthless helicopter Soviet airfire, with all but one Russian masked and anonymised, two of the men die after having shot down one helicopter, while the local authorities at Svalbard attempt to cover up the incident. The film is an explicit critique of Norway's supposed complacency in enforcing the neutral political status of Svalbard: as one survivor flees Svalbard to relay events to the Norwegian government in Oslo, he is eventually killed before the story goes public. Though in some ways a pedestrian thriller with recognisable plot turns borrowed from East and West Cold War films – and with what, in comparison to superpower budgets for special effects, is a diminutive set of aerial fight-and-flight scenes – the producers grasped that the film could provide a distinct, and distinctive, perspective on the Cold War conflict to market in an international context. Employing a UK scriptwriter to adapt Jon Michelet's eponymous 1977 novel, *Orion's Belt* was shot in both Norwegian and English (it features two credited directors, Solum for the Norwegian-language version and Cole for the English one). The film was distributed for cinema release in the USA and Europe, and as a TV drama internationally.

Thus a story of a small nation's strategic political cover-up, in the service of prolonging friendly relations with the Soviet Union, the events in the film are illustrative in the ways in which a combination of geopolitical and environmental discourses run through Arctic-set Cold War films. The community of Longyearbyen is, however, figured as a cultural dead-end, though home to a hardworking mining and fishing population, with the occasional American tourist looking for polar bears. The striking and distinctive landscape – mountains, glaciers, and clear open skies – is featured to great effect. This includes contrasting pristine and extensive vistas with on-screen images that testify to a long history at Svalbard of destructive environmental resource extraction, especially mining and whaling for blubber. Svalbard is thus an image for the remote Arctic, land little-known and visited, while simultaneously indexing precisely such kinds of 'remote' locations within geopolitical, economic, and ecological frameworks.

The threat of Soviet nuclear warheads stored on the island is implied, just as a similar threat of US-stocked war arsenals at Greenland is implied in depictions of that island. Situated right between the USSR and the USA, near the shortest fly-over polar route between the two capitals for aircraft and missiles, the Svalbard location thereby connects with the ways in which Arctic locations and imagery are used in Cold War cinema. Figurations of permeable, porous ice interact with hard-and-fast ideological rigidity. *Orion's Belt* was released the same year Mikhail Gorbachev introduced the policy of Glasnost with the explicit aim of aiding Perestroika (the economic reforms put into play in 1987, which effectively led to the end of the Cold War). The film reflects decades of Cold War imagery of the Arctic as a primary ideological, political and environmental battleground between the superpowers, and the one location on Earth in which those oppositions were presented most consistently in forms both symbolic and concrete. Ice, snow and the presence-absence evoked by the non-inhabited, confining, frozen yet permeable polar sea ice that kept the two superpowers in a perpetual stalemate drive the narrative. At the same time, such depictions of the Arctic region evoke the tensions of small nation-states caught in the middle of the conflict, and whose perspectives present distinctly different views from that of a monolithic Cold War engaged primarily between power centres in Moscow and Washington, DC. Svalbard, like the divided city of Berlin, the example that opened this chapter, shows the complexity with which the Arctic during the Cold War operated on both concrete and imaginary levels in service of political and ideological agendas. These agendas were well served by alternately emphasising the rigidity of cold, ice and snow, and its dynamic potential when thawing and shifting shapes. Furthermore, the Svalbard example demonstrates that locations around the world were indeed governed, and protected, by international treaties by which the Cold War can be understood as less rigidly constituted than assumed. In this way, the Arctic functions like NASA's 'Earthrise' photo that helped coin R. Buckminster Fuller's influential metaphor of the 'Spaceship Earth'. When viewed from the Moon in 1968, Earth seemed like a small and fragile planet, offset by the dusty, grey and forbidding surface of a desolate moon (Fuller 1969; see also Höhler 2009).

CONCLUSION: THE THREAT OF THE THAW

One of the key claims of this chapter is that the way in which we understand Arctic images of the Cold War must be rethought. Rethinking these images allows us to accomplish a number of things: not only do the images themselves seem more internally conflicted than one might assume at first glance, but the ideological reasons for their production come into a new focus. Using the blank screen of the Arctic as backdrop, we see the true cause of the fear that lies behind cinematic propaganda: the USA and the USSR were not afraid of invasion – it was, after all, a Cold War. Instead, what these films foreground is the fear that the utopias offered by each side of the Iron Curtain were to some degree compelling to the citizens on the other side. Arctic imagery became a backdrop for the collision of these two ideological worlds, allowing the imaginary space to function as a stage to disavow for one's own citizens the appeal of the other side. Like the concerns about global warming today, these films and the ideologies behind them lived in fear of the thaw, and what a change in the frozen, hermetically sealed ideology of the two worlds would mean for their inhabitants and the political worlds that the ideology of these films upheld.

NOTES

1. The United States had seventeen military installations in Greenland during World War II. The Thule Air Base was constructed in 1951 without prior consultation with the Danish government or its representatives in Greenland. The local Inuit population were abruptly removed from their village Uummannaq in 1953 and forced to move several hundred kilometres to a new settlement, Qaanaaq.
2. *The Big Picture* aired in half-hour episodes weekly on ABC network television from 1951 to 1964 and in syndication for several years on some local television stations after the ABC run ended. It was broadcast on 350 stations weekly, and even airs occasionally today on the Pentagon Channel as part of its *Battleground* series. Episodes covering Greenland, as identified by Kinney (2013), include: *Operation Blue Jay* (TV-227, 1952); *The Ice Cap* (TV-273, 1953); *Exercise Arctic Night* (TV-337, 1956); *Research and Development in the Arctic* (TV-366, 1957); *Operation Lead Dog* (TV-494, 1960); *City Under the Ice – The Story of Camp Century* (TV-514, 1961); *The U.S. Army and the Boy Scouts* (TV-520, 1961); and *The Top of the World* (TV-543, 1962). In 1965, an additional retrospective of all Army activities in Greenland was aired under the name *Icecap* (TV-664, 1965).

BIBLIOGRAPHY

Bloom, L. (1993), *Gender on Ice: American Ideologies of Polar Expeditions*, Minneapolis: University of Minnesota Press.

Chaturvedi, S. (2000), 'Arctic geopolitics then and now', in M. Nuttall and T. V. Callaghan (eds), *The Arctic: Environment, People, Policy*, Amsterdam: Harwood Academic Publishers, 441–58.

Crowley, D. (2011), 'Cold War landscapes: looking down on spaceship Earth', *Autoportret* 2 (34), 50–60.

Fuller, R. B. (1969), *Operating Manual for Spaceship Earth*, Carbondale: University of Southern Illinois Press.

Glasberg, E. (2012), *Antarctica as Cultural Critique: The Gendered Politics of Scientific Exploration and Climate Change*, New York: Palgrave Macmillan.

Grant, S. (2010), *Polar Imperative: A History of Arctic Sovereignty in North America*, Vancouver: Douglas McIntyre.

Hill, J. (2008), *White Horizon: The Arctic in The Nineteenth Century British Imagination*, Albany: SUNY Press.

Höhler, S. (2009), 'Spaceship Earth: envisioning human habitats in the Environmental Age', Habilitationsschrift, Technical University of Darmstadt.

Kinney, D. J. (2013), 'Selling Greenland: The *Big Picture* television series and the Army's bid for relevance during the early Cold War', *Centaurus* xxx: 1–14.

MacKenzie, S. and A. W. Stenport (2013), 'All that's frozen melts into air: Arctic cinemas at the end of the world', *Public: Art Culture Ideas* 48: 81–91.

Marks, L. U. (2013), '"Nice gun you got there": John Greyson's critique of masculinity', in B. Longfellow, S. MacKenzie and T. Waugh (eds), *The Perils of Pedagogy: The Works of John Greyson*, Montreal: McGill-Queen's University Press, 371–82.

Martin-Nielsen, J. (2012), 'The other Cold War: the United States and Greenland's ice sheet environment, 1948–1966', *Journal of Historical Geography*, 38: 69–80.

Palmer, B. (2011), 'Cold War thrillers', in *The Wiley-Blackwell History of American Film*, vol. III, 1946–1975, Oxford, UK: Wiley Blackwell, 243–66.

Petersen, N. (2008), 'The Iceman that never came: "Project Iceworm", the search for a NATO deterrent, and Denmark, 1960–1962', *Scandinavian Journal of History*, vol. 33:1, 75–98.

Shaw, T. (2007), *Hollywood's Cold War*, Edinburgh: Edinburgh University Press.

Shaw, T. and D. Youngblood (2010), *Cinematic Cold War: The American and Soviet Struggle for Hearts and Minds*, Lawrence, KS: University Press of Kansas.

12. HOLLYWOOD DOES ICELAND: AUTHENTICITY, GENERICITY AND THE PICTURESQUE

Björn Norðfjörð

PROLOGUE

We approach Iceland from above, glimpsing it through the clouds. Steam rises from the barren landscape, draped mostly in black and grey, if not altogether devoid of green. Perpendicular overhead shots form abstract patterns out of the landscape, and the introduction of ice prompts new colour combinations. As we travel over the land through smooth camera movements, lakes and rivers enhance the spectacle before we finally arrive at the powerful and majestic waterfall Dettifoss. One might be inclined to believe that one was watching a tourist promotion of Iceland – albeit an unusually expansive and breathtaking one. But as we travel upstream towards the waterfall from below – lo and behold, a spaceship hovers over it. And walking towards the cliff's edge is an alien in the form of a mythical creature about to give life to humanity.

Most viewers of Ridley Scott's *Prometheus* (2012) do not see Iceland in the film's prologue, but prehistoric Earth, a landscape signifying universality rather than a specific place. The film's opening exemplifies a particular quality of Icelandic landscape that allows it to stand in for other places, imaginary or real. Nonetheless, *Prometheus* has much in common with a long tradition of depicting Iceland as an alien and wild location. Steaming geysers, harrowing mountains and icy glaciers prevail over culture and habitat, as few travel to Iceland in search of buildings or other monuments. This otherworldliness helps explain the smooth transition of the Icelandic landscape to Hollywood's fan-

Figure 12.1   A spaceship carrying Prometheus hovers over Dettifoss waterfall in the north of Iceland.

tastical mise-en-scène, in not only *Prometheus* but numerous recent runaway productions (using offshore location filming for economic and/or scenic reasons).

Although the role of Iceland can vary considerably, it is typically limited to a specific part or scenes in the completed films, and most often stands in for other places. Its nature as a stand-in complicates assumptions of, for example, landscape theory and criticism, in which a picture (painted, photographed or filmed) is usually understood to be a representation of the particular model/ landscape painted or captured. Ecocriticism makes comparable assumptions regarding the relations of location or environment to their filmic representation, although environmental issues are certainly central to runaway productions. An analysis of runaway productions also calls for an awareness of the global factors at play (Miller et al. 2008), which is particularly salient as the globe's most powerful film industry meets a particularly small national cinema. In this regard, runaway production films shot in Iceland are fascinating examples of transnationalism. Iceland literally stands in for another place, or its image is created by a foreign national cinema, in both cases with global appeal in mind. Trying to be sensitive to a variety of factors, my approach shares much with geocriticism, which according to literary scholar Bertrand Westphal 'places *place* at the center of the debate' (Westphal 2011: 112). In doing so Westphal certainly does not erase 'the text', but puts it on an equal footing with place, where they influence one another in an interactive relationship. Accordingly, place must be studied through not only a plethora of texts so as to gain a multifocal view of the place in question, but also a variety of texts, including even 'tourist guides and the advertising rhetoric of travel brochures' (Westphal 2011: 121).

In this chapter, I begin by looking at Hollywood's new-found interest in Iceland for its runaway productions. What is it that draws Hollywood to Iceland? And has this interest influenced Iceland's image – on-screen or otherwise – which has long been associated with exotic natural imagery? After surveying the logistics and economics of these overseas productions, I address their aesthetics in terms of the Picturesque, where local specificity makes way for generic (Arctic) exoticism. In concluding, I turn briefly to locally produced cinema to ask how Icelandic cinema itself has been affected by this alien visitor.

BEHIND THE IMAGE

The meltdown of Iceland's financial infrastructure in 2008 was remarkable for a variety of reasons. Notably, it was one of the first times in history that Iceland became the centre of media attention for something other than its nature. But with the banks gone, along with their global ambitions, things were back on familiar ground only two years later as the eruption of the glacial volcano Eyjafjallajökull put Iceland in the headlines again, now for the greatest disruption of air travel in peacetime. Once again Iceland became the exotic place just beyond Europe, ruled by an unruly nature.

Both the economic collapse and the volcano eruption had a considerable impact upon filmmaking in Iceland. While the local film industry faced budget cuts in its state subsidiaries, the collapse of the Icelandic króna made Iceland a more competitive location for runaway productions (just as it helped increase tourism). Even more important was the Eyfjallajökull eruption which, according to film commissioner Einar Hansen Tómasson (2012), functioned as a great advertisement, *gratis*, for location shooting in Iceland. However, the increased interest in location shooting originates much earlier, as far back as 2001, when the government introduced the 'Film in Iceland' project for the particular purpose of attracting foreign film crews, not least by means of production cost reimbursement incentives. As Tómasson confirms, cost reimbursement is absolutely essential in securing foreign film productions, as many location managers are not even allowed to consider other options (Tómasson 2012). It is a highly competitive industry, with nation-state and municipal representatives spanning the globe, including Arctic neighbours both east and west of Iceland, trying to attract foreign film crews bringing currency, jobs, prestige and valuable tourism promotion. In addition to pitching their location and financial benefits directly to studio personnel, film commissioners and production companies specialising in overseas productions market their 'product' at the annual Association of Film Commissioners International (AFCI) convention in Los Angeles. In the promotional material distributed at such fairs, glossy landscape pictures leave little doubt about what is Iceland's greatest pull. An introductory text headlined 'Scenery you won't get elsewhere' confirms:

Black sands, imposing glaciers and snowcapped mountains, otherworldly lava fields, majestic waterfalls, lakes and lagoons with floating icebergs, the stark highland interior, tundra, moors patched with blue ponds, steam emitting red and yellow sulphur mountains, active and dormant volcanoes or scenes of serene beauty. In Iceland this spectrum of scenery is all within easy reach.

Iceland's stark landscape and amazing range of geological and natural phenomena stems from the active forces of nature still sculpting this geologically young island, sitting on the top of the North-Atlantic ridge where the continental shelves of the Americas and Europe are drifting apart. The land of contrasts, fire and ice, midnight sun, northern lights and lingering twilight welcomes you. (*Film in Iceland*: 2)

At first sight, this promotional text might not seem particularly illuminative, rehashing as it does many clichés about Iceland. It does, however, signpost important reasons for Iceland's popularity for overseas film productions. The text emphasises conventional Arctic nature tropes like glaciers, snow-capped mountains, floating icebergs and northern lights, but also extends further, reflecting the more varied uses of Icelandic landscape in recent films. Tómasson explains: 'First filmmakers were attracted by the ice. Most every-thing was shot by [the glacial lake] Jökulsárlón. But now the black sands have come in strong. This "volcano look" – "another planet look". And now they have realised the potential of the waterfalls, and other such opportuni-ties' (Tómasson 2012). In Iceland, these varied landscapes, the promotional material points out, are 'all within easy reach' and not far from the capital Reykjavík (*Film in Iceland*: 2).[1] The 'short' distance from Reykjavík to mainland Europe or the United States is equally emphasised in promotional material: 'From New York the flying distance to Iceland and San Francisco is about the same' (*Film in Iceland*: 10). In a roundabout way, this also defines Iceland as that exotic place that is not distant enough. Unlike, for example, the 'mysterious Orient', which in both the past and the present represents a fundamentally different world, Iceland, despite its Arctic exoticism, is still part and parcel of Europe. No doubt that is one reason why Iceland figures so rarely as a location in the narratives for which it provides the mise-en-scène. It may be practical to film there, but Iceland is much too close for Hollywood exoticism, unlike say Siberia or the Himalayas – both places that Iceland has stood in for.

The Hollywood Picturesque

Thus economic, logistical and environmental factors all help to clarify the increased interest in Iceland as a film location. However, they do not explain why Hollywood does not rely solely on computer-generated imagery (CGI) but instead goes to the trouble of visiting Iceland or other offshore locations. Nor do they tell us much about the aesthetics of the final product. The concept of the 'Picturesque' as described by Malcolm Andrews is helpful in this regard: 'Picturesque taste favours natural scenery for its untouched status, its remoteness from the world of art and artifice – it delights in the result of accident, the traces of agency and time and organic growth, it celebrates what is alien and wild and spontaneous' (Andrews 1999: 129). Though Andrews is analysing an earlier historical period and pictorial traditions, he describes the 'Picturesque' as a paradigm that is 'part of common experience'. Shooting on location offers such an authenticity, removed from the 'art and artifice' of CGI (although actual location footage is certainly often intermixed with CGI). As a matter of fact, filmmakers working in Iceland have frequently emphasised the authenticity gained from filming at some of the island's 'alien and wild' locations even for the most outlandish of scenes. The resulting imagery, however, can hardly be considered 'spontaneous'. Such film expeditions are carefully prepared with the result on the screen ultimately generic and familiar. Such scenery becomes, by means of the Picturesque, 'domesticated – it is accommodated within our daily experience both as an artistic experience and as a tourist amenity; it is aesthetically colonized. [. . .] The formula derived from Picturesque conventions reduces novelty and variety to secure conformity. The Picturesque makes different places seem like each other' (Andrews 1999: 129). In the same manner, the Hollywood imagery of Iceland traverses – almost schizophrenically – the authentic and the generic. The Hollywood Picturesque diminishes the specificity of Icelandic locations and other exotic sites so that 'different places seem like each other'. To do so, it paradoxically needs the authenticity of actual natural locations, with Arctic scenery and locations a case in point, as these can stand in for other 'icy' settings such as the Himalayas. One way artists can challenge the Picturesque's homogeneity, Andrews notes, is to 'search out more remote, pictorially uncharted, regions of the earth' (Andrews 1999: 129). From this perspective the runaway productions can be considered a response to the Picturesque, but this tension seems to me to be inherent to the concept. Through Hollywood's search and capture of the novel or the exotic and the actual, it engages in a process of 'aesthetic colonisation' that transforms diverse locales into a universal spectacle. Place becomes space, so to speak.[2]

These two qualities of authenticity and genericity (by which I mean familiarity and sameness as well as reliance on Hollywood genres) are in ample display in most of the Hollywood films, whether Iceland figures diegetically in the narrative or provides the mise-en-scène for other settings. Different locations end up looking identical while the same locations are also used repeatedly, as evidenced by the screen time awarded to the glacial lake Jökulsárlón. An early runaway production, *A View to a Kill* (John Glen, 1985), opens with a panoramic shot of the lake before finding James Bond (Roger Moore) upon a snowcapped mountain above it. Spotted by Soviet soldiers, he begins an exhilarating descent, swapping skis for a snowmobile, and even a makeshift snowboard, while fighting the soldiers. Having reached the lake, he shoots down a helicopter before entering one of the glacial islands – a British submarine in disguise. Through seamless intercutting with mountain scenes shot in Switzerland, the Icelandic footage helps create an exotic, adventurous and rather farfetched Siberian setting. This popular tourist destination also figures prominently in *Lara Croft: Tomb Raider* (Simon West, 2001) where Jökulsárlón again stands in for Siberia – an icy and adventurous mise-en-scène for the title character (Angelina Jolie) and her party as they head on dogsleds toward 'the ruined city' that shelters the secret of time itself. In *Batman Begins* (Christopher Doyle, 2005), a nearby glacier, Svínafellsjökull, stands in for the Himalayas where Bruce Wayne (Christian Bale) overcomes a childhood trauma and is taught to fight by the League of Shadows, including an extended sword practice scene on ice with Henri Ducard (Liam Neeson). The wide-open blue vistas make a powerful counterpoint to the claustrophobic and dark city of Gotham. Films like these not only erase the actual shooting location from the diegesis, but their Picturesque aesthetics turn them into spectacles devoid of local specificity.

From here it is only a small step to pure fantasy. In *Stardust* (Matthew Vaughn, 2007), Icelandic settings add atmospheric touches to the fantasy world of Stormhold. *Judge Dredd* (Danny Cannon, 1995) reverts to Iceland in laying out the 'poisoned scorched earth', known as the 'Cursed Earth', outside the futuristic cityscape of Mega City One, to which Dredd (Sylvester Stallone) and Chief Judge Fargo (Max von Sydow) are exiled. Iceland represents Earth in 2077 in *Oblivion* (Joseph Kosinski, 2012), ruined by earthquakes, tsunamis, nuclear war and an alien invasion, and decorated with the CGI of a few well-known American landmarks in ruins. As drone repairman Jack Harper, Tom Cruise plays one of the last people left on Earth, allowing for some spectacular Picturesque landscape scenes. The television show *Game of Thrones* makes extensive use of Icelandic landscape in depicting the icy world north of 'the Wall' (indeed, how could Iceland not play a role in an adaptation of a fantasy novel series titled *A Song of Ice and Fire*?). Fantasy is the logical end-result of the Hollywood Picturesque – a non-place.

Iceland has also on occasion provided a realistic setting, most notably for *Flags of Our Fathers* (Clint Eastwood, 2006), where the invasion of the black beaches of the volcanic island Iwo Jima was staged at Reykjarnes. In exceptional cases, it can even be mundane, as in the British television film *The Girl in the Café* (David Yates, 2005), in which Reykjavík provides a bleak and grey background for a G8 summit and the ultimate breakdown of a romantic intrigue between its two main protagonists. Bored in Reykjavík, Gina (Kelly Macdonald) tells Lawrence (Bill Nighy): 'Tomorrow I think I go further afield. Try to find some actual ice since we're in Iceland.' But if Gina does go, we never leave town with her. The film plays with the expectations of the audience, which has travelled with the characters to Iceland, but ultimately thwarts its desire for exciting natural scenery.

Hollywood, rarely in the business of thwarting audience desire, approaches Iceland quite differently on the rare occasions its protagonists do visit the island. Perhaps Iceland's turn was bound to come up at some point considering the insatiable demand for exotic locations in the James Bond franchise. But *Die Another Day* (Lee Tamahori, 2002) is also suggestive of the circumscribed qualities of Iceland's exoticism. Despite its outlandishness, it is too close to the British home of the series. Unlike North Korea and Cuba, the film's other exotic countries, Iceland appears only as mise-en-scène. No Icelandic is spoken and no single Icelandic character is found in the film. The land simply appears out of the blue as we fly low over an icy setting before finding James Bond (Pierce Brosnan) driving his Aston Martin in a wondrous winterscape towards a fanciful ice palace. The film's stereotypically depicted villain Tan-Sun Moon (Will Yun Lee) is Korean and disguised through futuristic plastic surgery as the English entrepreneur Gustav Graves (Toby Stephens). He keeps his latest gimmick 'Icarus', which not altogether unexpectedly turns out to be a terrible secret weapon in disguise, in this unidentified winterscape. After a brief build-up, one of the franchise's over-the-top action scenes follows. Bond and Zao (Rick Yune), the villain's right-hand man, chase after one another at high speed between icebergs on Jökulsárlón, before driving into the now melting ice palace. Notably its interiors are modelled on 'ice hotels' found in Lapland, suggesting how the setting is a composite of geographical locations that form an imaginary ice world. Thus Bond's penguin joke may not be out of place, though the secret agent could not be much further away from their natural habitat.

The crew of *Journey to the Center of the Earth* (Eric Brevig, 2008) also made the trek to Iceland, the main setting of Jules Verne's novel from 1864. The film represents an early example of the ongoing 3D craze in Hollywood, which typically pursues fantasy and artificiality. Scientist Trevor Anderson (Brendan Fraser) travels with his nephew Sean (Josh Hutcherson) from Boston to Iceland in search of his brother and fellow volcano researcher Max (Jean-Michel Paré) who disappeared there while researching the volcanic glacier Snæfellsjökull. Joined in Iceland by Hannah, played by Icelandic actress Aníta Briem, they begin their descent. Given that the location of Iceland makes

Figure 12.2　The most popular runaway location in Iceland, Jökulsárlón, provides the setting for a spectacular car chase in *Die Another Day*.

way for pure 3D fantasy, it is puzzling why the film crew decided to film there. Despite Trevor and Sean travelling with Icelandair and driving through the countryside, even having fun on the road by trying to pronounce a few unfamiliar Icelandic words, the film makes relatively little use of Icelandic locations. Even the mountain they climb appears to be an ordinary hill rather than the majestic Snæfellsjökull itself. The Icelandic section is also much shorter than that found in the original novel, or even in the classic Hollywood adaptation (Henry Levin, 1959). It is clear that the filmmakers had no interest in Iceland per se; the location functions only as a brief stopover before the extravaganza underground takes over – a lack of interest quite in tune with *Die Another Day*.

But whether appearing as Iceland itself or standing in for real or fictional places, the filmic results combine authenticity with genericity. Remarkably, none of the films discussed so far needed to have been filmed there at all, as even those set in Iceland use it as an interchangeable background – whether a realistic one as in *The Girl in the Café* or a fantastical one as in *Die Another Day*. They have absolutely nothing to say about Iceland as a place or locale; their authenticity is solely found in offering an 'authentic' generic setting.

One exception to this rule is found in Hal Hartley's *No Such Thing* (2001), an unconventional take on *Beauty and the Beast,* as American reporter Beatrice (Sarah Polley) goes to visit a monster (Robert John Burke) living at Heimsendir ('End of the World') in Iceland. The inclusion of such well-known film actresses as Helen Mirren and Julie Christie, in addition to Polley, is balanced by an extensive Icelandic cast representing both realistic local city people and fishermen as well as outlandish figures in the countryside. The film's urban mise-en-scène also has a strong local flavour, and the landscape scenes are mostly devoid of the Picturesque. Thus, the representation of Iceland in *No Such Things* is of Icelandic rather than Hollywood origin. But then it is also an Icelandic-US co-production, with Friðrik Þór Friðriksson's Icelandic Film Corporation playing a key role. Friðriksson's own film *Cold Fever* (1995) is arguably the ultimate Icelandic Arctic film, as Japanese visitor Hirata (Masatoshi Nagase) travels around a wondrous winter scape, including Jökulsárlón.

Explicit Arctic settings are, however, quite rare in Icelandic feature film production, and typically far removed from realism. Examples include the strange world of *Nói the Albino* (*Nói albínói*, Dagur Kári, 2003), characterised by an 'ice blue' colour palette (Norðfjörð, 2010). In locally produced films, there has long been a strong correlation between global designs and the Picturesque and its emphasis on exciting nature imagery. Thus films like *Cold Fever*, *Agnes* (Egill Eðvarðsson, 1995), *Cold Light* (*Kaldaljós*, Hilmar Oddsson, 2004) and, to a certain extent, *101 Reykjavík* (Baltasar Kormákur, 2000) make explicit use of Arctic landscape otherwise rarely seen in locally produced cinema. The other and even more limited source of Arctic imagery is found in films indebted to Hollywood genre cinema like the glacial-thrillers *Cold Trail* (*Köld slóð*, Björn Br. Björnsson, 2006) and *Frost* (Reynir Lyngdal, 2012). A striking 'realistic' exception is *The Deep* (*Djúpið*, Baltasar Kormákur, 2012), a factual account of a local fisherman (Ólafur Darri Ólafsson) who miraculously managed to swim ashore after his vessel and fellow crew went down six kilometres from land during high winter – with ice, snow and northern lights in ample display.

Nonetheless, the typical landscape of Icelandic cinema is much more likely to be green and brown than white and black, and, more importantly perhaps, to be inhabited, unlike the empty spaces so frequently found in the Hollywood runaway productions. The rarity of Arctic imagery in particular, and the Picturesque aesthetics more generally, in locally produced films suggests its origin to be primarily foreign – the outside looking in – although Icelanders have been only too happy to participate in producing that imagery for purposes of tourism and other types of marketing.[3]

Epilogue

Filmmaking in Iceland has been transformed by the increasing number of runaway productions, which reached new heights in 2012, including work on *Noah* (Darren Aronofsky, 2014), *Oblivion*, *The Secret Life of Walter Mitty* (Ben Stiller, 2013), also partly set in Iceland, and *Thor: The Dark World* (Alan Taylor, 2013). Addressing this unparalleled interest, a cover of the Sunday magazine of newspaper *Morgunblaðið* depicted under its main headline 'Land of Cinema' (*Bíólandið*) an image of Iceland made of photographs of many of the international film stars and directors who had recently been at work there. The cover exemplifies how Icelandic filmmaking (at least domestically) is increasingly defined by foreign productions – equalling now the number of local feature films made annually but far outweighing their economics – as this definition of Iceland as a 'Land of Cinema' does not even include local cinema. Notably, during the summer of 2012, film crews were for the most part unavailable for local productions, and if the overseas trend continues, domestic productions may increasingly be set in wintertime – perhaps making the local cinema more Arctic in appearance. However, there appears to be little or no antagonism between domestic film companies and those servicing overseas productions, as the Hollywood productions provide additional work at very competitive salaries, help increase professionalism in the industry and link local filmmakers to the outside world.

Nonetheless, such a state of affairs begets questions regarding the unequal status of national cinemas, access to creative manpower, facilities and nature/land. As economics go, this may be no different from Iceland selling its hydroelectric power to aluminium corporations with global reach, or efforts to increase tourism (explicitly selling scenery) for valuable foreign currency. However, as always with cinema there is a fundamental difference in that the product produced is itself a representation. And this representation is ultimately very different from local ones – indeed its locale has been emptied out. No longer a place, Iceland becomes Picturesque scenery.

Notes

1. Directors and other creative personnel who have worked in Iceland emphasise this variety in a similar manner. Simon West, director of *Lara Croft: Tomb Raider*, states in *Digging into Tomb Raider* (2001), a 'making-of' documentary on the DVD: '[Iceland] gives me a lot of variation on location. There's lakes with icebergs, different sorts of mountains, rolling hills. So I can get a lot of different environments'. And Emily Cheung, associate producer on *Oblivion*, observes in *Promise of a New World: The Making of Oblivion* (2013): 'As soon as you arrive here you understand quite easily why it is being shot for all these different sci-fi locations because there are just so many wonderful different geothermal spots everywhere. You are just driving down the road and you come across a beautiful waterfall, or a geyser or a hot spring and the colors are just amazing. It's like being in another world'.
2. Here I follow Yi-Fu Tuan's influential distinction in which place is a lived space (Tuan 1977) – the latter being more abstract and devoid of local specificity. Of course most of the Icelandic settings are not places where people actually live but these locations are meaningful to the local populations in a variety of ways that evaporate when they are transformed into 'abstract' spaces or scenery. Indeed, Tuan's concept of place is quite broad: 'When space feels thoroughly familiar to us, it has become place' (Tuan 1977: 73).
3. An overall comparative study of the representation of Iceland (Arctic and otherwise) in foreign and local films is called for, but must remain outside the scope of this chapter. Other relevant topics that I have had to leave untouched include uses made of Iceland in other types of cinema, including art cinema and documentary, and the representation of Icelanders in Hollywood and other foreign films. Regarding the former, I am particularly struck by Chris Marker's use of the volcano islands Vestmannaeyjar in *Sans soleil* (1983), and more recently how in *Faust* (2011)

Aleksandr Sokurov shaped Icelandic scenery, including lava, glaciers and geysers (referred to explicitly as 'spectacle'), into his distinct aesthetics. As regards the latter topic, the character of June Gudmundsdottir (Greta Scacchi) in *The Player* (Robert Altman, 1992) is a pertinent example as the colours of her artworks and atelier are solely limited to the Arctic blue/grey/white palette, giving a strong counterpoint to the film's California setting.

Bibliography

Andrews, M. (1999), *Landscape and Western Art*, Oxford: Oxford University Press.
Blöndal, P. (2012), 'Bíólandið', in *Morgunblaðið*, 25 November.
Film in Iceland (2012), Reykjavík: Promote Iceland.
Miller, T. N. Govil, J. McMurria, Ting Wang and Richard Maxwell (2008), *Global Hollywood*, 2nd edn, London: BFI Publishing.
Norðfjörð, B. (2010), *Dagur Kári's Nói the Albino*, Seattle: University of Washington Press.
Tómasson, E. H. (2012), interview by author, Reykjavík, 3 December.
Tuan, Y. F. (1977), *Space and Place: The Perspective of Experience*, Minneapolis: University of Minnesota Press.
Verne, J. [1864] (1998), *Journey to the Centre of the Earth*, trans. W. Butcher, Oxford: Oxford University Press.
Westphal, B. (2011), *Geocriticism: Real and Fictional Spaces*, trans. R. T. Tally Jr, New York: Palgrave Macmillan.

13. WHITE ON WHITE: TWENTY-FIRST-CENTURY NORWEGIAN HORROR FILMS NEGOTIATE MASCULINIST ARCTIC IMAGINARIES

Sabine Henlin-Strømme

One of the tenets of Norwegian nationalism is the mastering of snow and cold climates, encapsulated in the motto 'Norwegians are born with skis on their feet'. The national discourse of what Benedict Anderson calls an 'imagined community' originated in the nineteenth century, when, looking for the idea of a Norwegian essence, the Norwegian elite chose extreme nature to symbolise the young nation but also promoted a relationship of superiority to it. These assumptions persist: 'Mountains, snow and winter had so far been seen as obstacles to life and culture – thanks to national Romanticism in the arts, the fledgling tourist industry and organized winter sports, these obstacles were over time transformed into assets and claims of a specific "Norwegianness"' (Sørenssen 2012). In the early twentieth century, the near canonisation of the polar explorers Fridtjof Nansen and Roald Amundsen confirmed this dominant cultural and historical construction. The trope of whiteness – as in snow, ice and white men conquering remote regions in harsh conditions – furthermore generated particular assumptions of a masculinist Norwegian Arctic. I call this concept 'white nature'. Surviving and conquering a frozen or Arctic landscape was systematically associated with masculinity, which correlates with the Romantic ideology of hostile nature being made sublime in order to become a source of pleasure. Thus the negative aspects of nature were sublimated, and instead made positive and beautiful for a nationalist purpose. White nature continues to figure prominently in the Norwegian cultural imaginary. In recent horror films, white nature is not sublimated but horrific. Thus there is a productive tension between early

Norwegian 'white nature' metaphors and the recent cinematic horror Arctic imaginary.

The concept of 'white nature' and how it promotes dominant white masculinity resonates with Richard Dyer's study on whiteness (Dyer 1997). White Westerners have created a dominant image of the 'white' world, Dyer argues, and thus construct the image of the world to their image, mobilising the cinema as a significant vehicle for the transmission of this ideology. Focusing on representations of whiteness and its complex articulations of gender framed within historical and cultural conditions, this chapter extends Dyer's work to investigate how a dominant white discourse equates white nature with white masculinity. Yet unlike Dyer, I show that cinema (here the horror genre) is a counter-voice to rather than a vehicle for that dominant ideology. Specifically, I argue that in appropriating the horror genre, recent Norwegian horror films not only challenge a (Norwegian) national snow mythology of the Arctic but propose transnational and subversively gendered versions of an imaginary Arctic.

Feminist analyses of horror by Carol J. Clover and Barbara Creed have denounced the patriarchal identification structure of American horror film. In contrast, playful gestures towards gender, genre and nature representations in contemporary Norwegian white horror propose the subversion of a masculinist discourse, by which a 'masculinist' work purports 'to be exhaustive, [but] forgets about women's existence and concerns itself only with the position of men' (Michèle le Doeuff's term, discussed in Rose 1993). In contemporary Norwegian horror, white nature serves new purposes: it challenges masculinity, reinvestigates the World War II occupation/Nazi legacy and, perhaps most importantly, questions default assumptions of the Norwegian nation-state. The case studies in this chapter do exactly this: *Dead Snow* (*Død Snø*, Tommy Wirkola, 2009) and *Cold Prey* (*Fritt Vilt*, Roar Uthaug, 2006) displace the notion of a sublime Arctic to create a horrific one that defamiliarises Norwegian locations such as the majestic Jotunheimen National Park or the northern province of Finnmark, while challenging nationalist and gender assumptions.

THE CONQUERING: THE ARCTIC AS MASCULINE PROJECT

The actual Arctic geography in the polar region figured prominently in the origin of the Norwegian nation and with it came some of the earliest visualisation of that space. Indeed, this connection between mastering snow and masculinity was further reinforced from the late nineteenth century to the early twentieth century when Norway distinguished itself in the exploration of the Arctic and the Antarctic. The polar explorer came to embody the Norwegians' conquest of the cold landscape and snow. This is especially true for two national heroes: Nansen and Amundsen. They symbolised the fight against the forces of nature embodied in bravery and/or endurance in the name of the nation. Amundsen became world-famous for his race to the South Pole against his British competitor Robert Scott in 1911, while Nansen, athletic and fair-haired, by then functioned as the very embodiment of the Nordic masculine ideal: his daring Arctic explorations made him the quintessential Norwegian national snow hero. As Amundsen's team carried a camera to shoot some of the expeditions, for the first time, the Arctic became a sublime spectacle. His writing relating the harsh conditions of white nature that nearly took their lives correlated with his images – at times comedic, at times realistic – of the difficulties encountered: bridging horror and wild beauty. Indeed, images of human figures in wide-open spaces subliminally supplemented Amundsen's tales of near death in frozen nature. Men as small figures set against the greatness of white, icy nature are a motif to be seen again even in contemporary Norwegian horror films (where vast, open spaces are often opposed to the enclosed indoors).

White nature has remained essential for the Norwegian nation since the conquering of the Poles, even in a global context. This association with national figures such as Nansen and Amundsen, who became early 'media stars', functioned as a kind of advertisement, not only nationally within Norway but also internationally, putting Norway on the map of nations with power. Similarly, Norwegian horror films put Norway on the map of transnational films in the way these works reuse familiar concepts such as white nature and masculinity in their visual aesthetic. In a global context, cinematic representations transform those conceptions into a transnational Arctic imaginary.

A NEW GENRE IN NORWEGIAN CINEMA

Until the early 2000s, there were no horror films produced in Norway. This long period of genre repression has resulted in recent films that are rather formulaic while using quintessential Norwegian nature such as dark woods and white nature, all capable of symbolising the repressed. Colloquially known in Norwegian as *skrekkfilm* (horror films) or *grøsser* (thrillers), representative examples include films taking place in the woods – *Dark Woods* (*Villmark*, Pål Øie, 2003), *Hidden* (*Skjult*, Pål Øie, 2009), *Manhunt* (*Rovdyr*, Patrik Syversen, 2008), *Detour* (*Snarveien*, Sevrin Eskeland, 2009) and *Troll Hunter* (*Trolljegeren*, André Øvredal, 2010) – while others are set in a snowy mountainous environment: the *Cold Prey* trilogy: *Cold Prey I* (*Fritt Vilt I*, Roar Uthaug, 2006), *Cold Prey II* (*Fritt Vilt II*, Mats Stenberg, 2008), *Cold Prey III* (*Fritt Vilt III*, Mikkel Brænne Sandemose, 2010) and *Dead Snow* (*Død Snø*, Tommy Wirkola, 2009). The emergence of Norwegian horror films shows the adaptability of the genre in a cinematic culture where it had been missing entirely. A strong censorship regime prevented the making of horror films, and state subsidies for horror films were unthinkable. The new genre, by an emerging generation of filmmakers and targeted at a youth audience, has been popular and relatively acclaimed. *Dark Woods* drew over 145,000 at the box office in Norway and *Cold Prey I* and *II* had over 200,000 box-office hits there.

If changes in subsidies have influenced the emergence of this genre, I claim also that the films dealing with archetypal topics about the Norwegians' relationship to nature hit a nerve. Yet, as mentioned, that relationship to (white) nature has changed: in a world of global warming where nature runs amok and humans lose control, Norwegian horror also follows the trend of a global white horror. In recent years, we have seen the growth of the international horror genre whereby various countries' horror productions have gone global. Those films often mobilise a type of uncontrolled Arctic invading the planet: *2012: Ice Age* (Travis Fort, USA, 2011), *The Day after Tomorrow* (Roland Emmerich, USA, 2004) or *Ice Quake* (Paul Ziller, USA, 2010) to name a few. Such environmental catastrophe films often portray threatening global warming or sudden, unexpected, drastic climate change. Accordingly, the emergence of such white nature films has influenced the ways in which horror is viewed in Norway, making those transnational films available on Norwegian screens and encouraging domestic productions. The result in Norwegian cinema is a threatening Arctic imaginary that negotiates local and global forces and genres. In addition, this development of a robust genre of horror film reflects a double movement of established horror genre codes mobilised along three axes: the semantic (the various expected horror elements such as a group of teenagers, weapons, desolate basement, darkness, confinement, isolation and so on); the syntactic (how those elements are organised in the plot development); and the pragmatic (the fact that an audience recognises them as such) (Altman 1999). Therefore, recent films address a trend of internationalisation and willingness for Norwegian cinema to be on the map of transnational cinemas, in other words, to become more global while emulating Hollywood genre productions.

NEGOTIATING SUBLIME WHITE NATURE AND TRANSNATIONAL GENRE

Cold Prey is the first film in a trilogy that became very popular in Norway; upon its release, it was presented as a genre film. For our purpose here, the film offers an instance of white nature reminiscent of the Arctic's vast, open space. The location of the outdoors scenes (Jotunheimen National Park) is a fact only mentioned in the reviews but not a part of the film's plot. Instead, the local Norwegian snowy mountain is transformed into a generic place of horror unmarked locally and aiming to be transnational. This non-marked white nature is what I call an Arctic imaginary, which like a white screen becomes the site on which genre can be written and traditional national representations undermined. A pre-credit sequence associates the horror genre and the snowy mountain. Another introductory scene ominously creates a montage of news items about deaths in the mountain and creates white horror. Those Norwegians who supposedly excel on skis are now ironically under threat and the outcome is death. The film debunks a positive relationship to white nature as it sets up the premise of horror.

Examining gender representation and especially how young males interact with white nature shows us another way to understand that environment. In the opening sequence of *Cold Prey*, five young adults (two heterosexual couples and a single man) are driving to the mountains while engaging in a discussion about their sexuality. Right away we encounter a stereotypical horror trope: a sexualised group that moves from civilisation to wilderness. The radio announces the busy opening of the ski season, but the group chooses to go off track. The group's concern seems to be about belonging to the normal pre-defined sexual category of the heterosexual couple, except one key single male character: the ambiguous Morten. The scene ends with a few long shots of the car speeding through white non-national openness accompanied by the song 'Welcome to the Mountains'. That sequence introduces the characters as young, sexualised and 'normal' skiers: a national practice also well known internationally while it sets up the basis for the horror.

The mountains are initially showcased as an admirably sublime object of spectacle to conquer for extreme experience. They subsequently switch to becoming the stage of horror. The 'normal' couples are great snowboarders. Yet, Morten is doubly singled out: he is single and has hesitations about skiing. As they look up the slope with admiration, the film introduces the mountain as sublime: with a slight tilt up, one huge peak is unveiled from bottom to top. The sublime is further conveyed when the film depicts white nature with long shots and aerial views from on high as they start climbing to the top with their equipment. The five characters are minimised by the immensity of the white expanse and appear as mere ants on the crest of the mountainside. Is that an instance of nationalism like Amundsen in the polar Arctic? Unlikely, as the music gives us a few notes that sound ominous in terms of what is to come. As the group reach the top, another sweeping camera movement passes by them and a celebratory music theme swells up. On the top, they become spectators of the sublime, all together gaping at the spectacle. The music (strings and brass orchestra mixed with voices) swells up again to a sublime climax: three panoramic shots display the white mountain range to the horizon. That scene clearly juxtaposes the group with the greatness of the scenery for the experience it gives them. It indicates that the mountain is overwhelming and beautiful but also dangerous. For the viewers, the idea of danger has already been established and thus we expect an accident to happen.

The shift from spectacle to horror occurs soon after in a performance scene featuring off-track snowboarding. The music changes and turns into electric guitar rock before we see all five people jump on their snowboards: sliding up in the air and down the slopes repeatedly. As in an advertisement or a music video, extreme long shots make them look like small black dots in the snow. But the music stops abruptly when Morten jumps and falls. The fall ends with a close-up on his face distorted with pain. The leg is broken and the bone is visible, following traditional horror visual assumptions. After trying unsuccessfully to use their cell phones to call for help, the group find refuge in an abandoned hotel with their wounded friend. The rest of the film takes place in and near the hotel where they are all gradually attacked and killed by a mysterious killer – all except one woman, or it seems an echo of Carol Clover's 'Final Girl' here replaced by a 'Final Woman', a fully sexualised woman who survives and manages to unveil the killer at the end. In this strong opening, sexuality and white nature are definitely linked but make room for femininity and potential homosexuality. Transnational youth culture images of snowboarding, music video of dangerous sports on snow prevent any kind of nationalist understanding. This addresses a young transnational audience who are as fond of snowsports as horror films. With that kind of imagery the local place matters little; what we see is white nature as a playground for youth and horror – in other words, a transnational imaginary Arctic par excellence.

Consequently, the early scenes of Cold Prey only seemingly conform to a traditional way of presenting male national characters on skis. Indeed, here the mountains are sublime objects that become a horrific place. The male snow-boarders are presented as mastering the mountains just as much as the female characters do. But what about the single character, Morten, whose masculinity is questioned? Is he still a virgin? Is he homosexual? Why is he single? There is a clear contrast between Morten, the inexperienced skier, and the other four characters, bold, willing and skilled. Yet, despite his 'deviant' sexuality (only compared to the group), his inability to master the snow is what carries the plot of the movie forward into the horrific. Similarly, the plot device of a final sexual woman who manages to outlive all her comrades also deviates from the conventional masculine feats on snow (and from conventional horror in that she is not a virgin). Thus, the two characters embody specific ways in which Norwegian horror challenges typical genre representation of masculinity. They appear then as ways to engage with and challenge the traditional stereotypical solely masculinist relation to white nature. In a concern to follow the horror conventions closely, Cold Prey thus also challenges Dyer's whiteness and proposes alternatives to an exclusive masculinist view.

ARCTIC ZOMBIES: DEFAMILIARISATION AND GLOBALISATION

Tommy Wirkola's *Dead Snow* contrasts with *Cold Prey* in several remarkable ways (for more on Tommy Wirkola, see Chapter 7 of this volume). Though the action takes place on a snowy mountain, this is a splatter zombie comedy, yet both works are identifiable as horror films. Whereas *Cold Prey* takes place in a famous national park, *Dead Snow* is set in northern Norway above the Arctic Circle, which is used as a playground for entertainment and horror purposes. Yet both films, respectively, engage with white nature and relate it to issues of nationality, masculinity and a transnational Arctic imaginary.

As a hybrid film, *Dead Snow* combines the horror subgenre of the zombie movie with a very local war legend about northern Norway. In this film, the concepts of the sublime and reverence of masculinity are literally annihilated. Rather, the film engages in a parochial localism to evoke global horror entertainment featuring splatter, chainsaw, snow scooters and Nazi zombies in a hyperbolic portrayal of masculinity mutilated in snow. The Nazi zombie characters evoke Dyer's idea of extreme whiteness, a whiteness that has reached disembodiment and death, which for Dyer is the terror of an unreachable death (Dyer 1997: 233). But where *Dead Snow* departs from that notion is that the very exaggeration of death and killing fosters comedy rather than horror. Many of the comedic aspects spring from the reflexivity in terms of nationalism and genre.

Fully acknowledging the traditional Norwegian practice of the winter holiday and the reflexivity of the genre, the film's narrative offers familiar pleasures for contemporary Norwegians as well as horror fans and viewers. *Dead Snow* (like *Cold Prey*) opens with a chase scene where one of the characters is a victim. Then, expectedly, and again as in *Cold Prey*, a group of friends (no less than six medical students) are on their way to a mountain cabin in the snow during the Easter ski holiday. A helicopter long shot swirls around a mountaintop to reveal the same fjord as in the chase scene, bordered by a road on which two cars drive. This time the group is divided into cars: one for the men and the other for the women. In both cars, the topics of discussion revolve around sexuality or dangers in snow. As in numerous horror films, the group is innocently on its way to a holiday of (sexual) fun. In a reflexive gesture, the single character, also a film 'nerd', asks his friends how many horror movies start with a group going to a cabin. The film thus playfully produces humour from genre reflexivity as it also sets up the threats to come (as we all know that this will not end well). Here the film joins a recent strain of horror films, such as *The Scream* cycle, marked by reflexivity.

National white nature is treated with great irony in the film as the pre-credit sequence of *Dead Snow* illustrates, blending horror with a famous national

Figure 13.1 Horror as parody: masculinity and the great white Norwegian wilderness in *Dead Snow* (*Død Snø*, 2009).

music theme. A long shot presents a fjord at night. The music starts: immediately recognisable is the famous musical theme of Edvard Grieg 'In the Hall of the Mountain King'. A chased woman runs away and pants heavily as the music increases in intensity. She finally falls to the ground and is attacked and devoured by several zombies, screaming as the music reaches its climax. Unlike in *Cold Prey*, this opening directly sets the tone for the rest of the film: the music is key in bringing the idea of irony to the scene and introducing us to the hyperbolic style of the film.

The point of the film then resides in the very annihilation of the hypermasculinity on display. All the male characters are killed mercilessly in a style close to slapstick comedy. Hypermasculinity is literally cut to pieces, chopped up or squashed. The only young man who explicitly has sex is killed first and his skull ripped apart, his brain falling to the ground. Another one ends up severing his throat with a fishing line, before he is also ruthlessly killed. Martin, the medical student who was afraid of the sight of blood, proceeds to cut off his arm with a chainsaw after being bitten on the hand. In an ultimate symbolic castration, a zombie also bites his groin before he manages to push him away. The killing scenes are full of blood splatters, extreme grimaces that are so hyperbolic that they become grotesque and theatrical. Thus, white nature becomes here the stage of comedic horror for the debunking of nationalism and masculinity.

The group's sexual power is not related to snowsport prowess in any way since we never see the characters on skis (they do not appear to have any with them). Instead, *Dead Snow* presents the snow area as a playground that brings forth a stereotypical hypermasculinity. Indeed, upon arrival, the leader Vegard uncovers the latest version of a snow scooter in close-up and caresses the engine with pride. While he goes ahead to the cabin on his scooter, the others follow the tracks to the cabin. His masculinity is on display as he rides up and down the slopes on the scooter, in several medium shots in snow and glorious sunshine. Upon arrival at the cabin, instead of settling in, they all play with a tyre and the same scooter. Inside the cabin, their activities involve board games and beer. The following day, they race on sledges. *Dead Snow* then takes time to establish white nature and winter holiday as a time for amusement and fun: the games point to an urban youth culture in the mountains. Moreover, the film recurrently offers the viewer a postcard shot of the cabin. Except for Vegard's use of the snow scooter, the group seem to have no interest in feats on snow and they barely notice white nature. So we have moved far from a masculinist view of white nature. The resulting Arctic imaginary is one of leisure and pleasure added to the horrific pre-credit scene. Needless to say, *Dead Snow* is all the more formulaic as it follows the horror genre convention almost painstakingly.

In geographical terms, the film displays the tension between local place and transnational genre. The group's alienation from local nature and history is at the crux of *Dead Snow*. Their lack of interest and knowledge about the local history is confirmed during the first night at the cabin when a local man unexpectedly tells them a crucial story. A local legend from World War II says that during the war, Øksfjord was a strategic passage between England and Finland and thus of interest to the Nazis. The battalion of Nazis posted in Øksfjord was known to be especially cruel towards the local population. The locals decided to join forces to counter the evil Nazis; they surprised the 300 soldiers at night and killed several of them, but a handful managed to escape into the mountains. The locals lost track of the fleeing soldiers who were never found again. It is believed that they froze to death, leaving the place cursed with an evil force that should not be awakened. As medical students, the group laugh off the story. Thus the legend reinforces their alienation from their environment. After the legend has been told, *Dead Snow* indulges in the gradual killing of all the characters. As a result, the clash between the young uninformed (they could be American tourists) and the local carries a new meaning. White nature here is the result of two forces: the locality of the Finnmark area and the horror genre. It demonstrates that the genre is flexible and open to local modalities. Indeed, *Dead Snow* borrows from the Norwegian cultural context (the mountain cabin Easter holiday, the local war legend, various linguistic or cultural jokes about northern Norway) and (American) horror films, thus bringing forth again the tension at work in the film.

CONCLUSION

Norwegian horror films like *Cold Prey* and *Dead Snow* question not only the national snow mythology but also create a new kind of transnational Arctic. This new imaginary Arctic straddles conventional American horror while joining a global horror trend. Thus, the 'Norwegian' frozen North becomes a more conventional place of horror, delocalised and translatable internationally. This shift in the characterisation of frozen nature affects the way masculinity is presented. In *Cold Prey* and *Dead Snow*, the relationship between masculinity and snowy mountains principally helps to construct the horror genre. In both films, a young group come to a mountain in search of pleasure and to enjoy white nature as a playground. In *Cold Prey*, sublime white nature inevitably leads to horror. In *Dead Snow*, death and killing in the snow take hyperbolic and theatrical proportions. As a result, white nature does not carry any notion of masculine national conquest. Instead, masculinity is commonplace, debunked and castrated, with skiing barely a concern.

If cinema for Dyer is a vehicle to mobilise dominant ideologies about whiteness, I argue that contemporary Norwegian horror can be critical and both appropriate and challenge nationalism. This results in a questioning of conventional nationalistic discourses and mainstream white hegemony, which become replaced with transnational white nature. This strategy has a direct impact on the representation of the Arctic: Norwegian cinema takes what Norwegians know best – snow and challenging conditions – to comment on its own nationality and globalisation while fostering a new Arctic imaginary.

BIBLIOGRAPHY

Altman, R. (1999), *Film/Genre*, London: BFI Publishing.
Clover, J. C. (1993), *Men, Women and Chain Saws: Gender in Modern Horror Film*, Princeton: Princeton University Press.
Creed, B. (1986), 'Horror and the monstrous-feminine', *Screen* 27: 1, 44–71.
Dyer, R. (1997), *White*, London and New York: Routledge.
Gillian, R. (1993), *Feminism and Geography*, Cambridge: Polity Press.
Sørenssen, B. (2012), 'From playground to frozen hell – winter landscape and masculinity as a theme in some Norwegian films', in J. F. Hovden and K. Knapskog (eds), *Hunting High and Low*, Oslo: Scandinavian Academic Press, 247–65.

PART III

ETHNOGRAPHY AND THE DOCUMENTARY DILEMMA

PART III. ETHNOGRAPHY AND THE DOCUMENTARY DILEMMA

Scott MacKenzie and Anna Westerståhl Stenport

For some, the cinema offers a historical and ethnographic document that acts as a means for the preservation of culture. For others, documentary and ethnographic strategies add verisimilitude to melodramatic narratives of other cultures. Another approach to ethnography uses the cinema to capture a past already gone, for the preservation of this way of life for outsiders. In other renditions, documentary cinema is understood to mobilise a 'travelling gaze' that purports to be detached and observational, while ethnographic filmmaking has always been considered in tension with that of the conundrum of a visual anthropologist, namely of being both participant and observer. In the history of Arctic cinemas, ethnographic and documentary films from the 1920s and 1930s have had a privileged status, which this section of *Films on Ice* uncovers. Indeed, the claims to realism that so often dominate documentary cinema have not been the only mode of production. Anti-realist forms derived from Soviet montage, for example, have also been central for Arctic representation from the 1920s and continue to influence contemporary experimental and hybrid documentaries. The same can be said of the use of self-reflexive or metacinematic techniques in documentary and ethnographic filmmaking, which foreground the status of the image as a construction. In 'The Creative Treatment of Alterity: Nanook as the North', Scott MacKenzie examines the many reiterations of Flaherty's influential film to show how it has been recast in documentary films, feature-length fictional accounts, indigenous media, IMAX and experimental cinema, delineating its continual and conflicted role in the popular imagination. Ebbe Volquardsen examines one of Denmark's best-known ethnographic feature films, contemporaneous with Flaherty's, to highlight the contested geopolitical status of Greenland in the early 1930s. His chapter 'From Objects to Actors: Knud Rasmussen's Ethnographic Feature Film *The Wedding of Palo*' foregrounds both the venerable status of Knud Rasmussen as an explorer and ethnographer in Danish history and how the film continues to be both cherished and mocked as a thwarted historical document for the Greenlandic population. In 'Arctic Travelogues: Conquering the Soviet North', Oksana Sarkisova examines how the depiction of indigenous peoples in the Soviet Arctic changed in accordance with the ideological narrative of a communist state in the 1920s and the 1930s. Examining films both central to and outside the canon of Soviet film history, Sarkisova uncovers a little-known history of Arctic indigenous representation. In 'A Gentle Gaze on the Colony: Jette Bang's Documentary Filming in Greenland 1938–9', Anne Mette Jørgensen discusses one of few women documentary filmmakers of the Arctic. Examining Bang's extensive travels on the island to capture, on colour film, 'traditional' practices and customs, Jørgensen shows how this nimbly shot and cinematographically deliberate film was made both with the intent to preserve Greenlandic life and as a testament to Denmark's benevolent colonial rule of Greenland. Archivist Caroline Forcier Holloway, in her contribution 'Exercise Musk-Ox: The Challenges of Filming a Military Expedition in Canada's Arctic', examines the extreme difficulty filmmakers in the 1930s faced filming in the Arctic. Interviewing filmmakers from the era, Holloway uncovers how film practitioners discovered new ways of filming in the Arctic's extreme cold. In '"*The Tour*: A Film About Longyearbyen, Svalbard". An Interview with Eva la Cour', Johanne Haaber Ihle and Eva la Cour discuss how historical assumptions of visual anthropology, present in many earlier films of the Arctic, are both present in and challenged by a participant-observer rendition of contemporary nomadic life in the remote Norwegian archipelago. In this film, the nomads are taxi drivers, tourists, scientists and miners, whose stories are offset against a partially obscured dramatic Svalbard landscape, to challenge precisely the notion that the landscape and location bear intrinsic meaning separate from cultural and aesthetic traditions of representing it.

14. THE CREATIVE TREATMENT OF ALTERITY: NANOOK AS THE NORTH

Scott MacKenzie

This chapter considers Robert Flaherty's *Nanook of the North* (US, 1922) – probably the most famous Arctic film ever made – and the many, often fraught, reiterations of the film in the cinematic imaginary of the Arctic. Starting with Flaherty's film – typically understood to be, *pace* John Grierson, the first 'documentary' – the chapter examines the ways in which the stories of 'Nanook' (played by Inuit hunter Allakariallak) and Flaherty have been continuously rearticulated throughout cinema history, in works as diverse as realist ethnographic documentaries like *Nanook Revisited* (Claude Massot, France, 1990), narrative feature film retellings of Flaherty's filming in the Arctic such as *Kabloonak* (Claude Massot, Canada/France, 1994), experimental documentaries like Philip Hoffman and Sami van Ingen's *Sweep* (Canada, 1995), to the recent 3D IMAX film *To the Arctic* (Greg MacGillivray, US, 2012), and Inuit film and video retellings of the past, in part as a riposte to Flaherty, such as the *Netsilik* film series (made in conjunction with filmmakers from the National Film Board of Canada) and the *Nunavut* series (made by the Inuit group Isuma).

A key question that is often asked about *Nanook of the North* is: what is the status of Nanook? Is this a documentary portrayal, a fictional creation or some hybrid of the two? To answer this question, we need to reframe it with another one, implicit in all the critiques of *Nanook of the North* but seldom addressed, namely: what is the status of Flaherty? By this, I mean not what is his status as a filmmaker, but what is his status within the imaginary history of the film's production and the myths about *Nanook of the North* that descend from and circle around it? If one begins to understand the signification of 'Flaherty', one can also begin to unravel the contested and contestatory debates that underlie the film, the reiterations of its history, and the reappropriation of its images in other films.

A secondary question that arises is why have the images from *Nanook of the North* taken such a central role in the conceptualisation of the cinematic image of the Arctic, as if it were a space in time frozen in history. One reason is, of course, the oft-cited remoteness of the region. When there were few images produced in the Arctic, the ones that were widely circulated became invested with a central and over-determined meaning. A recent example of the ubiquity of Nanook is seen in *To the Arctic* which uses images from *Nanook of the North* as unproblematic inserts of Inuit life, mobilising them as a constellation of Arctic representation. Here, the images from Flaherty's film stand as transparent and unchallenged images of historical authenticity. The use of this historical black and white stock, framed inside the large IMAX screen, surrounded by sublime images of snowdrifts and ice flows, work in a similar way to snapshots documenting the past in an profoundly unmediated fashion.

NANOOK OF THE NORTH, OR, WHAT ARE WE TALKING ABOUT, REALLY?

Nanook of the North, filmed in Northern Quebec over the period of a year in 1920, was financed by the fur company Révillon Frères, one of the Hudson's Bay Company's key competitors in Canada. Released by the Pathé Exchange, the film quickly became a worldwide success, and the first instantiation of what came to be known as the documentary (Rotha, Road and Griffith 1952: 81–5; Barnouw 1974: 36–48). Flaherty's film contained numerous staged and re-staged scenes: having his Inuit stars engage in hunting practices no longer used (using spears, for instance, instead of guns), and at times propagating the myth of the Inuit as gentle savages (Ruby 1980). The blurring between the 'documentary' impetus of *Nanook of the North* and Flaherty's own life are also present: Nanook's 'wives' were not his own and were actually the women who Flaherty was involved with during his time in the Arctic, including 'Nyla' (actually Maggie Nujarluktuk), who later fathered Flaherty's son Josephie, whom Flaherty never acknowledged and was a not-so-well-kept family secret.

Flaherty re-staged the past with the intent of making a film that would be popular in the US and Europe precisely when codification of classical Hollywood narrative was taking shape. At best, this makes *Nanook* into hybrid cinema; at worst, not what it seemed to be at all: a narrative family melodrama using a harsh environment and exotic othering to heighten the melodramatic tension of the film, built around the questions of sustenance and survival. Not for nothing is the original subtitle of the film 'A Story of Life and Love In the Actual Arctic'. As ethnographic filmmaker Timothy Asch notes: 'Flaherty used Eskimos as actors playing in their roles and in that sense created a prototype for feature narrative films rather than documentary films' (Asch 1992: 196). If in 1920, Flaherty wished to document the practices of the Inuit before their culture, in his words, 'vanished' (a profound form of benevolent colonialism), any re-staged images come to stand in unproblematically for the past, even though they were a re-creation of the past at the time they were made. Re-creation, it should be noted, is not *a priori* a negative thing, and the process has been used by indigenous Inuit documentary and feature filmmaking, from the *Nunavut* video series to the use of older, out-of-use Inuit dialects in *Atanarjuat: The Fast Runner* (Zacharias Kunuk, Canada/Nunavut, 2001). Yet the kind of re-creation that Flaherty engaged in has left behind a frozen image of the Arctic in the popular imaginary.

While the history of ethnographic film is replete with reconstructions and re-creations, what Jacob Gruber first called 'salvage ethnography' (1970), where an imagined past thought to be disappearing or to have disappeared is re-created by the ethnographer, the intent of these works is often quite different from that of Flaherty (Heider 1975: 100–1). Works such as *The Moontrap* (*Pour la suite du monde*, Pierre Perrault and Michel Brault, Canada, 1962) use film as a catalyst for local inhabitants in Ile-aux-courdres to re-stage a half-forgotten means by which to catch a whale in the St Lawrence River, with far more self-reflexivity than one finds in Flaherty's film, including as it does, within the diegesis, the role played by the filmmakers in this process (MacKenzie 2004: 135–8). These works of 'salvage ethnography' speak to the ethnographic dilemma of capturing an image of a culture in a particular moment of (reconstructed) time, like a fly caught in amber, standing as both an ahistorical and profoundly historical document of the past. *Nanook of the North* is in many ways the progenitor of these works, despite subsequent ethnographic films' somewhat different aims.

Therefore, despite the profound gap between what the film 'tells' Southern viewers about the Arctic and the Inuit, and their lived experiences at the time, *Nanook of the North* has come to stand in for the Inuit way of life in the imaginations of generations of film spectators as an account of the 'real' Arctic. Flaherty himself, as Ruby notes (1980), had no interest in documenting the Arctic as it actually was; he was far more concerned with creating a film that captured for Southern viewers a 'native' way of life that he felt was quickly disappearing. The film, then, in his mind, was a document of the past already fading away through the encroachment of white modernity in the North; a testament for Southerners of a way of life that he even felt no longer existed.

Many documentary filmmakers, from activist and indigenous filmmakers to *cinéma vérité* practioners, have taken issue with Flaherty's approach. For example, activist documentary filmmaker Jill Godmilow addresses the ethical and colonial aspects of documentary filmmaking that are subsumed under the guise of objectivity, examining *Nanook of the North* in particular because of its status as the founding film of realist documentary cinema:

> When the white man who owns the trading post shows a record player to Nanook, Nanook puts the plastic disk in his mouth and bites, to find out what it is and where the music is coming from. This scene impresses on us that Nanook is 'uncivilized', technologically backward and undeveloped. How can we admire (and enjoy) Nanook now – we who are civilized? Flaherty dissolves the contradiction: we can love him as our primitive ancestor or forefather. Flaherty's film presents Nanook as a perfect early version of ourselves, particularly in his role as the father of a nuclear family. (Godmilow 2002: 5)

Godmilow concludes that *Nanook of the North* is an instantiation of supposedly benign imperialism dressed up as objective reality:

> This is the ideological underpinning of *imperialism,* and its younger sister, *colonialism*, and its baby sister, *underdevelopment*. And this, in large part, is the history of the documentary film . . . A dishonest relationship has been created in the cinema through a false transaction between Robert Flaherty and ourselves. (Godmilow 2002: 5)

Flaherty, therefore, sets out to portray the Inuit as both timeless and a throwback to our pre-modern past, engaging in a benevolent colonialism wrapped up in a nostalgia for a world that may never have existed exactly the way he imagines. And the action he scripts for Nanook to engage with the phonograph is telling: whereas the apocryphal first viewers of the cinema ducked when they thought a train was charging towards them, Nanook bites the phonographic disc, demonstrating a sensory disconnect between his experience and his response, also implying that all the Inuit care about is sustenance, a myth Flaherty propagated throughout his life.

NANOOK REVISITED: ETHNOGRAPHIC REALISM AND THE STATUS OF THE IMAGE

One of the first 'returns' to the primal documentary scene of *Nanook of the North* is Claude Massot's documentary *Nanook Revisited*. The film opens with the image of Massot and his film crew flying into Inukjuak (formerly known as Port Harrison), where Flaherty shot his film sixty-eight years earlier.

Flaherty had shown rushes of his film in 1920 to the inhabitants of Inukjuak; according to him, it was met with much laughter, but did involve indigenous participation. As Ruby notes: 'The Inuit performed in front of the camera, reviewed and criticized their performance, and were able to offer suggestions for additional scenes in the film! A way of making films which, when tried today, is thought to be "innovative and original." Moreover, Flaherty trained some Inuit to be technicians!' (1980: 450). Despite this participatory element, the rescreening of the film sixty-eight years after it was released, when the film crew arrives in Inukjuak, raises a different series of issues about the status of the film as a documentary, this particular audience's cultural past and the effects these images had upon them, and their own sense of self-understanding.

Returning to the scene of primordial documentaries to rescreen films is a recent development in ethnographic filmmaking. In a similar vein, *The Prisoners of Buñuel (De gevangenen van Buñuel*, Ramón Gieling, The Netherlands, 2000) documents the long-term effects of Buñuel's *Land Without Bread (Tierra Sin Pan*, Spain, 1933) on the Las Hurdes region of Spain. Like the inhabitants of Inukjuak, the people of Las Hurdes have issues with how they have been portrayed on screen. After a screening of the film in the public square, they react with a wide range of emotions. As Gary Crowdus notes: 'An open-air screening of *Land without Bread* in the town plaza stimulates a . . . spirited debate among local residents, many of whom had never seen the film, revealing how to a great extent the region's inhabitants remain captive to the its notorious reputation' (Crowdus 2000: 49). The same holds true for *Nanook Revisited.* The first half of the film documents the French film crew coming to the village and talking to locals about the film and its history. Some do not like the image of the Inuit portrayed (especially that of Nanook with the phonograph); others argue that despite its flaws, it remains the only document of their culture in the 1920s. The screening of the film is enhanced by an exhibition of Flaherty's photos found in the Révillon Frères archive, where aging locals find photos of themselves as children. The screening itself provokes both laughter and anger on the part of the audience. A key problem in both cases is that these ethnographic films reduce complex societies to one set of images, something both colonial and futile.

If the first half of *Nanook Revisited* addresses the local response to the images made by a white Southerner sixty-eight years earlier, the second half places the contemporary white Southerner at the centre of the narrative. The crew goes to Flaherty Island, named after the filmmaker, and spends most of its time filming in a local school. One of the teachers, Joe Johnson, becomes the on-screen narrator, describing and participating in seal hunts, demonstrating how to eat raw seal, and teaching local Inuit children about the practice. He becomes the conduit of knowledge to the viewers; the Inuit members of the community, who no doubt know far more about these practices and indeed taught them to him, are denied a voice in articulating the importance of these practices. Johnson becomes an on-screen Flaherty, rearticulating and reframing Inuit practices for the white Southern viewers. *Nanook Revisited*, then, is a confused and contradictory text: on the one hand it attempts to document the impact of Flaherty's film on local culture, and on the other it replicates in detail the act of the white outsider telling the story of the local Inukjuak population.

KABLOONAK AND THE 'GREAT MAN' OF HISTORY

In the early 1990s, Massot decided to make a docudrama about Flaherty's time in the Arctic while shooting *Nanook*. Filmed in the Siberian town of Provideniya, Russia, and the Canadian Northwest Territories, *Kabloonak* replicates some of the complexity of Flaherty's work: the film shows how much involvement the Inuit had in the production of the film, and the ways in which Flaherty dealt with – at times in an imperial manner – culture conflict. *Kabloonak* can also be seen as a contemporary allegory for the debates about postcolonialism prevalent in the 1990s. As Margaret Dubin notes: '*Kabloonak* is most outstanding for its attention to contemporary intellectual issues. Formally a historical documentary, the film successfully addresses the issues of authenticity, the ethics of ethnographic research, and various modes of exploitation, including colonialism and cultural appropriation' (1997: 70). Yet, the trope of 'filmmaking against all odds' (Dubin 1997: 71) dominates the film and, in the tradition of 'Great Man' historiography, reifies Flaherty: it is his pain and remorse that frames the film's narrative.

The 'Great Man' theory of history was a nineteenth-century concept espoused by, among others, Thomas Carlyle, who stated: 'Universal History, the history of what man has accomplished in this world, is at bottom the History of the Great Men who have worked here' (Carlyle [1840] 1993: 3). In a similar vein, Flaherty in *Kabloonak* can be seen as the embodiment of Hegel's 'world-historical' figure outlined in his *Philosophy of History* ([1840] 1974: 31–3). *Kabloonak* holds up this vision of Flaherty's role in and of history, and therefore the story is Flaherty's and his alone, as can be discerned by the film's framing device: *Kabloonak* begins with Flaherty (Charles Dance) sitting forlorn in a New York bar, drinking heavily, for reasons unknown. The film then flashbacks to his arrival in the Arctic in 1920. *Kabloonak*'s Flaherty shows both affection and respect for the Inuit in the film, but is not too concerned with portraying their lives as they actually are. The Inuit actors agree with Flaherty that the images needed for the film, or 'aggie' as they call it, come before their actual need to hunt. In this way, Allakariallak and others are active participants in the fictionalisation of their lives. Furthermore, many key moments from the Flaherty mythology are re-created in *Kabloonak*: the tug-of-war that is shot to represent pulling a seal out of the water, and the oversized, proscenium stage igloo that is built with only one side, in order for Flaherty to have enough light to film. *Kabloonak* retells the myth behind the making of the film, and demonstrates active involvement by the Inuit community. Nevertheless, it is Flaherty who is the 'hero' of the film, the visionary who succeeds at his goal. At the conclusion of his Arctic sojourn, Flaherty says goodbye to both Allakariallak and to Nyla. Nyla seems at ease with his departure, despite the fact she is pregnant with his child. Allakariallak, on the other hand, reacts angrily to Flaherty's departure, but in the end forgives him and demonstrates his homosocial love by kayaking after Flaherty's ship and waving goodbye. This melodramatic ending demonstrates that *Kabloonak*, while supposedly deconstructing the myths of *Nanook of the North*, is indeed actively engaging in building new ones about Flaherty, Allakariallak and the meeting of two cultures.

Kabloonak ends by returning to Flaherty in the bar, still drinking his bottle of bourbon. We then see a telegram on the table, telling him that Allakariallak is dead. He leaves the bar and walks down the street, past a cinema marquee advertising his film. This fades to the concluding titles that repeat yet another myth propagated by Flaherty: that Nanook died of starvation while on a hunt. As Robert J. Christopher notes:

> Throughout his life, Flaherty maintained that within two years after his departure Nanook had died of starvation while on an inland caribou hunting trip. The story must be apocryphal, since there is no evidence that Allakariallak died in such as way. Bob Stewart kept Flaherty informed about Allakariallak's health, and in a letter of 28 January 1923 he informed him, 'Attata is sick just now. In fact he has been in bed all fall and winter. He is just skin and bones and [I] expect him to die any day. I'm surprised he has survived so long'. (2005: 387)

Massot's repetition of this myth (for a second time: it also appears in *Nanook Revisited*) delineates how hard it is to separate – and how tempting it is not to separate – mythology from the real. *Kabloonak*, despite its gesture towards an analysis of cultural interchange and hegemony, in the end replicates the implicit 'true' story of *Nanook of the North*: that the true story that needs to be told is not that of Nanook/Allakariallak and his fellow Inuit, but of the 'Great Man' Flaherty and his triumphant technological achievement of making a film in such (for the Southerner) a brutal and unrelenting climate.

SALVAGE ETHNOGRAPHY AND SUBJECTIVE RECONSTRUCTION

The 'fly caught in amber' aspect of Flaherty's film has a long tradition in ethnography. *Nanook of the North* can be understood as an early instantiation of cinematic 'salvage ethnography', described by James Clifford in the following manner: 'Ethnography's disappearing object is, then, in a significant degree, a rhetorical construct legitimating a representational practice: "salvage" ethnography in its widest sense. The other is lost, in disintegrating time and space, but saved in the text. . . . It is assumed that the other society is weak and "needs" to be represented by an outsider (and that what matters in its life is its past, not present or future' (Clifford 1986: 112–13). One can see this ethos in the way in which Flaherty himself wrote about his goals:

> I am not going to make films about what the white man has made of primitive peoples . . . What I want to show is the former majesty and character of these people, while it is still possible – before the white man has destroyed not only their character, but the people as well. The urge that I had to make *Nanook* came from the way I felt about these people, my admiration for them: I wanted to tell others about them. (Cited in Ruby 1980: 450)

Flaherty, then, like contemporaneous ethnographers such as Bronisław Malinowski, wished to capture for posterity a world already gone, not for the posterity of the Inuit, but for the cultural history and edification of Southern whites.

It would be, of course, reductive to claim that all 'salvage ethnography' is pernicious. Indeed, 'salvage ethnography' has also taken place in conjunction with and within indigenous cultures, both as a means by which to preserve the past, and as a retort to the 'salvage ethnography' of outsiders. For instance, the National Film Board of Canada's *Netsilik* film series (1963–5, rel. 1967) reveals a different kind of restaging, where Inuit families practise for the camera the traditions of their ancestors, set in the filmic present of 1919. Yet these reconstructions are not as transparently 'Inuit' as one might initially think: along with the memories of the past drawn from the local community, the other key source for these re-stagings is Knud Rasmussen's journals of his visit there in 1923, and the films themselves are directed, or rather 'facilitated', by white Southerners (a source also used from the Inuit perspective to different ends in *The Journals of Knud Rasmussen* (Zacharias Kunuk, Canada/Nunavut/Denmark, 2006). As Karl G. Heider notes:

> The behavior in the Netsilik films is . . . a puzzle. We know that an ethnographic present of 1919 was recreated in the 1960s. It is easy to see how artifacts can be reconstructed from drawings. But how is a complex process like hunting or fishing or housebuilding reconstructed? How much came from the actors' memories, how much from their parents' memories, and how much from Rasmussen's writings? (1975: 57)

The twenty-one half-hour films grant some agency to the Inuit to represent the past in a way that resonates with their own understanding of their oral history outside of the one often placed upon them by outsider filmmakers from

Flaherty onward. Yet, these reconstructions still have Flaherty haunting them as an inter-text.

Other re-creations, made by Inuit videomakers, have reappropriated reconstruction as a political act, most notably in Isuma's *Nunavut* series. Michael Robert Evans notes that: 'Among Inuit videographers, however, the objections to both the Netsilik series and *Nanook* lie less with their accuracy and more with their authorship. In a fundamental sense, the work of Inuit videomakers . . . functions as a reaction to attempts by non-Inuit to define and position the Inuit culturally and historically' (Evans 2008: 142). These reconstructions, then, are not as much about achieving a greater authenticity than Flaherty or the *Netsilik* series; instead, these works speak to the need for peoples to have their own control in the telling of their stories, and the agency to frame these stories as they see fit. No film or video will ever tell a 'complete' story of a culture; the very idea is absurd. Indeed, the claim that one film or video could ever do so belittles the culture in question. The goal of these works of 'salvage ethnography' is not to present a 'complete' picture; instead, it is to present a partial, subjective one, albeit one finally told from an Inuit point of view.

SWEEP, ETHNOGRAPHIC SURREALISM AND PROCESS CINEMA

Sweep is . . . sweeping the road clean, trying to start over again, sweeping away Flaherty' – Philip Hoffman (Hoolboom 2001: 218)

If 'salvage ethnography' has dominated *Nanook of the North* and its various retellings, other ethnographic forms have also been put to use to understand Flaherty's film and its legacy. Perhaps the most effective return to the primordial documentary scene can be found in Philip Hoffman and Sami van Ingen's *Sweep* (Canada, 1995). Hoffman, a Canadian experimental filmmaker and van Ingen, a Finnish one, set off to Fort George, on the shores of James Bay, where Flaherty, van Ingen's great-grandfather, shot parts of *Nanook of the North*. Part experimental documentary, part road movie, *Sweep*, unlike many of the journeys back to Flaherty's stomping grounds, foregrounds both the inability to return to the scene in order to capture and understand it, and the legacy that these Northern journeys have nevertheless left on the region and on documentary cinematic imaginations. The ethnographic dilemma lies at the heart of *Sweep*, as does the profound tension between the awareness of the way in which documentary always falls short of capturing the real and the concomitant need to use the camera as a documentary tool nonetheless. The film exists at the heart of this tension, exploring the ethical issues that surround the very practice of documentary filmmaking and the need to find new, inclusive, partial and tentative ways to document the world. As Tom McSorley notes:

What is clear from *Sweep* is that memory, as a mode of constructing forms of individual and shared knowledge, cannot be adequately
expressed or preserved within the documentary ... Of course, what
Sweep also makes clear is that it cannot be adequately expressed or preserved *without* them, either. (2008: 37)

To this end, one can understand *Sweep* as an instantiation of what James
Clifford has called 'ethnographic surrealism':

An ethnographic surrealist practice ... attacks the familiar, provoking
the irruption of otherness – the unexpected. ... This process – a permanent ironic play of similarity and difference, the familiar and the strange,
the here and the elsewhere is ... characteristic of global modernity.
(Clifford 1988: 145–6)

Sweep opens with images of archival polar exploration films from the 1910s
and 1920s. Setting the stage for the journey North as it is typically represented,
Hoffman, in a voice-over, addresses his family history in the North, and that of
van Ingen's, whose great grandfather was Flaherty. The film uses still images,
fragments from explorer films, family photos, and the footage shot by Hoffman
and van Ingen to create a collage of the trip to the North, the family histories
and ties they both have to the area, foregrounding the fragmentary nature of
both memory and the cinema's ability to represent it. Much akin to *Sans soleil*
(Chris Marker, France, 1983), *Sweep* is a surrealist ethnography based on the
principle of collage, antithetical to the kind of realist documentary practice

Figure 14.1   Van Ingen and Hoffman in *Sweep*. Courtesy of Philip Hoffman.

found in Flaherty's film. The principle of collage is what guides the aesthetic of *Sweep*: bringing together different realities, as constructed through a variety of forms of cinematic and still image representation, to create a fragmentary text. *Sweep* is far more about radically challenging totalising views of the Arctic, especially those made by outsiders, than it is about creating a new, authoritative 'vision' of the region. Van Ingen and Hoffman question their ability to tell their own family stories, as filtered through memory and subjectivity, and in so doing put face to the lie that anyone can create a totalising text that transparently offers an account of the past, from the inside or out. *Sweep*, then, like *Sans soleil*, is about the incessant need to document while at the same time calling into question what these processes of documentation can offer the viewer as knowledge.

This fragmentary, collage structure allows for different realities to exist side-by-side with one not obliterating the other: meaning itself is contsructed through juxtaposition and not transparent representation: in *Sweep*'s most heartening scene, which concludes the film, van Ingen and Hoffman turn their cameras over to the locals, letting them film what they want and film images of themselves (they choose to film Hoffman and van Ingen eating, along with an outdoor shot that the filmmakers only discover when they process the film). Here, Hoffman and van Ingen succeed where many of the other filmmakers discussed previously fail: they disavow the need to document the local culture as they see it and instead give up their own agency in making images. While

Figure 14.2   Van Ingen and Hoffman filmed by local inhabitants, reversing the camera, in *Sweep*. Courtesy of Philip Hoffman.

Hoffman and van Ingen maintain the final cut of the film, they embrace the practice that Hoffman often calls 'process cinema', where the film itself is discovered in the process of the shooting.

Hoffman describes *Nanook of the North* in the following manner: 'It offered a particularly white view on native practices, and was made in a time when white meant "objective"' (Hoolboom 2001: 217). In Hoffman's telling, then, *Nanook of the North* is the primordial documentary version of what Clifford calls 'anthropological humanism'. To this end, the images of the polar explorer on film also play a prominent role in *Sweep*, as Hoffman notes: 'We used archival home movies showing white men's journeys to appropriate the north. Sami's great-grandfather was just the most famous person who went up there' (Hoolboom 2001: 217). *Sweep*, then, is a move away from Flaherty's hegemonic and totalising views of the Arctic and the Inuit, foregrounding not only the way in which local narratives are elided by the explorer film, but also the way in which these films dissolve difference under the guise of univeralised and transparent understanding. In contradistinction to the work of Flaherty and those that followed, Hoffman notes: 'Throughout the trip many of the native people we met asked us to film them . . . We always refused, saying we don't want to tell your story, this is up to you, and it always has been. So the film's critique of ethnographic filmmaking shows the failure of white culture to integrate, proposing a movement alongside instead of the usual pictures of control' (Hoolboom 2001: 217). *Sweep* instead points to the effect that Flaherty and others have left on this Arctic community by commenting on the way in which travellers always want to take and make their own images of the region, with locals acculturated to play a starring role in these outside imaginaries. *Sweep* instead engages in what Clifford calls 'ethnographic surrealism', offering a fragmentary picture of the North, foregrounding the traveller's journey as an undeniable part of the process, and the profoundly incomplete document of the North that these journeys inevitably create.

CONCLUSION

The many iterations of *Nanook of the North* are historiographic documents not only of the figure and figuration of 'Flaherty', but also of a specific and particular rendition of 'Life and Love in the Actual Arctic' (as the film was marketed), which have become emblematic of the ways in which documentary filmmaking has been conceived, interpreted, analysed and reconsidered during nearly a century of filmmaking (scenes from *Nanook* indeed appear in the final chapter of Jean-Luc Godard's *Histoire(s) du cinéma: Les signes parmi nous* (France, 1998)). *Nanook of the North* and the many subsequent echoes of it put into relief the contested and contestatory status not only of 'insider' and 'outsider' in Arctic imagemaking. For Hoffman and van Ingen, the way in which the past is understood from the outside is a key component of *Sweep*, and of Flaherty's own journey to the Arctic. Hoffman highlights that when he and van Ingen were making *Sweep*, 'a feature length, France-Canada-produced drama was released about Robert Flaherty, which reveals a love affair he had with a native woman. Everything was suddenly out in the open. Sami and his family already knew this, but no one dared to speak about it. They were keepers of the legend, the great genius, the family name' (Hoolboom 2001: 217). This film was *Kabloonak*. Similarly, a film of global reach like few other re-enactments of citations of the 'Flaherty' legend and the *Nanook* artifact, the recent *To the Arctic*, uses the historiographic document of a 1922 black and white film – completely ahistoricised – for contemporary audiences seeking entertainment and enlightenment by narrating climate change as a story of, *pace* Flaherty, 'Life and Love in the Actual Arctic', though in the latter instance as a polar bear family melodrama in which the threat to the majestic and photogenic superfauna is only implicitly about global warming, whereas the more palpable threat is from interspecies fighting. The invocation of the 'Flaherty' approach to documenting the Arctic in this recent film, by proxy, makes a similar gesture toward the Earth's northernmost indigenous populations. As that film proclaims, humans can 'adapt', but wildlife cannot.

BIBLIOGRAPHY

Asch, T. (1992), 'The ethics of ethnographic film-making', in P. I. Crawford and David Turton (eds), *Film as Ethnography*, Manchester: Manchester University Press, 196–204.
Barnouw, E. (1974), *Documentary: A History of Non-Fiction Film*, Oxford: Oxford University Press.
Carlyle, T. [1840] (1993), *On Heroes, Hero-Worship, and the Heroic in History*, Berkeley: University of California Press.
Christopher, R. J. (2005), *Robert and Frances Flaherty: A Documentary Life, 1883–1922*, Montreal and Kingston: McGill-Queen's University Press.
Clifford, J. (1986), 'On ethnographic allegory', in J. Clifford and G. E. Marcus (eds), *Writing Culture: The Poetics and Politics of Ethnography*, Berkeley: University of California Press, 98–121.
Clifford, J. (1988), *The Predicament of Culture: Twentieth-Century Ethnography, Literature, and Art*, Cambridge, MA: Harvard University Press.
Crowdus, G. (2000), 'The Montreal World Film Festival', *Cineaste* 26.1, 49.
Evans, M. R. (2008), *Isuma: Inuit Video Art*, Montreal and Kingston: McGill-Queen's University Press.
Dubin, M. (1997), '*Kabloonak*', *Visual Anthropology Review* 13.1, 70–1.
Godmilow, J. (2002), 'Kill the documentary as we know it', *Journal of Film and Video* 54.2/3, 3–10.
Gruber, J. (1970), 'Ethnographic salvage and the shaping of anthropology', *American Anthropologist* 72.6, 1289–99.
Hegel, G. W. F. [1840] (1974), *Hegel's Philosophy of History*, Ithaca: Cornell University Press.
Heider, K. G. (1975), *Ethnographic Film*, Austin: University of Texas Press.

Hoolboom, M. (2001), 'Duets: Hoffman in the '90s, an interview', in K. Sandlos and M. Hoolboom (eds), *Landscape with Shipwreck: First Person Cinema and the Films of Philip Hoffman*, Toronto: Images Film & Video Festival/Insomniac Press, 211–21.

MacKenzie, S. (2004), *Screening Québec: Québécois Moving Images, National Identity and the Public Sphere*, Manchester: Manchester University Press.

McSorley, T. (2008), 'Time *Sweep*ing space', in T. McSorley (ed.), *Rivers of Time: The Films of Philip Hoffman*, Ottawa: Canadian Film Institute, 36–8.

Rotha, P. S. Road and R. Griffith (1952), *Documentary Film*, London: Faber and Faber.

Ruby, J. (1980), 'A re-examination of the early career of Robert J. Flaherty', *Quarterly Review of Film Studies* 5.4, 431–57.

15. FROM OBJECTS TO ACTORS: KNUD RASMUSSEN'S ETHNOGRAPHIC FEATURE FILM *THE WEDDING OF PALO*

Ebbe Volquardsen

During the summer months of 1932 and 1933, the 7th Thule Expedition led an international team of researchers, under Knud Rasmussen's guidance, to Greenland's east coast. There, the team conducted cartographic work, as well as archaeological and geological investigations. In 1921, Denmark had declared the entirety of Greenland and its surrounding waters to be Danish territory, and had since that time been in open conflict with Norway. The Norwegians, independent since 1905, regarded Greenland as their historical property, and recognised only the colonies situated on the west coast as Danish territory. They were not willing to stop their long-time practice of whaling and seal-hunting in the waters off the sparsely populated east coast. Finally in 1931 and 1932, they occupied two uninhabited coastal strips north of the settlement of Scoresbysund (Ittoqqortoormiit), founded in 1924 for the purpose of marking Danish territory, and south of Ammasalik (Tasiilaq), where Gustav Holm and Vilhelm Gaarde had already encountered widespread Inuit settlements, previously unknown to the Danes, during the Umiak Expedition of 1883. When Denmark brought the case to the Permanent Court of International Justice in The Hague in the spring of 1933, Rasmussen was part of the Danish delegation. The verdict of 5 April was significantly in favour of Denmark, whose sovereignty over the entirety of Greenland had now been affirmed by the highest international legal body. Rasmussen could thus start the preparations for the second part of the 7th Thule Expedition, during which the ethnographic feature film *The Wedding of Palo* (*Palos brudefærd*, Denmark, 1934) was filmed. The expedition to the area around Ammassalik would be Rasmussen's last journey. Just before Christmas 1933, he died from pneumonia, and thus never had the chance to see the finished film, which premiered only a few months later at *Palads-Teater* in Copenhagen.

Contemporary recipients looked at *The Wedding of Palo* not only as an actual cinematic work of art, but also as a worthy monument to Rasmussen. By securing Danish polar anthropology a place at the top of this worldwide emerging discipline, Rasmussen had managed to become a major national hero during his lifetime. At the premiere party, none less than Denmark's Prime Minister Thorvald Stauning gave the opening speech (Stauning 1984), which not only paid tribute to the deceased Arctic explorer, but also emphasised the centuries-old ties that existed between the Greenlandic and the Danish people. Stauning's oration, as well as a supporting film dedicated to the remembrance of Rasmussen – especially in the light of the recently compounded legal dispute with Norway – thus turned the event into a symbolic act of land appropriation (cf. Eglinger and Heitmann 2010). In the supporting film, which was recorded during the filming of *The Wedding of Palo*, Rasmussen is shown among his expedition team and the inhabitants of the East Greenlandic settlement. Rasmussen, always a few steps ahead of his entourage and, when aboard the expedition ship, the only one standing amidst the sitting crew, appears not only as a virile polar hero, but also as a mediator and translator between the cultures, a position that he achieved through his Danish-Greenlandic descent. The heavy technical equipment, ships, a seaplane and the omnipresent *Dannebrog* (the Danish flag) emphasise colonial power Denmark's mastery of the sublime Arctic forces of nature, a property often attributed solely to the Greenlanders, who – according to Stauning – were living in harmony with the rough nature by which they were surrounded.

In the 1920s and 1930s, several films – primarily of documentary character – were shot in Greenland, often with German participation (Sperschneider 2003). However, *The Wedding of Palo*, on which expedition leader and scriptwriter Rasmussen worked together with German documentary filmmaker Friedrich Dalsheim, is by far the most popular and most watched Greenland film of the colonial period. Among Greenlanders today, it is regarded as an amusing classic, still frequently watched at school or at social gatherings with family and friends. Before he wrote the script for *The Wedding of Palo*, Rasmussen had been involved in several film productions, for example Eduard Schnedler-Sørensen's *Den Store Grønlandsfilm* (1921) and Leo Hansen's *Med hundeslæde gennem Alaska* (1926), documentaries that were shot on Rasmussen's expeditions (Jørgensen 2003). But it was with *The Wedding of Palo* that he broke new ground. Here, Rasmussen supplements the documentary genre with a simple plot. *The Wedding of Palo* is thus a hybrid, which can be clearly classified as neither a feature film nor a documentary film. This has led Ebbe

Iversen (1984) to speak of the film as a documentary disguised as a feature film. However, Iversen's hierarchy, according to which the documentary elements in *The Wedding of Palo* appear as more substantial relative to the history of the Greenland film than the certainly meagre plot, ignores the fact that *The Wedding of Palo* must today be seen as a watershed precisely because Rasmussen, for the first time ever, recruited Greenlandic amateur actors for the film. Whereas until then, Greenlanders in all films playing in the Danish colony had appeared as passive objects exposed to the exoticising ethnographical gaze (the few previous Greenland non-documentaries were all cast with European actors; see Körber, Chapter 10 in this volume), in *The Wedding of Palo*, Rasmussen enabled them for the first time to face the European film-viewing public as actors in the most literal sense of the word. Other interpretations of *The Wedding of Palo* have therefore detected a personal effort by Rasmussen to refute Robert Flaherty (Gant 2009), who with *Nanook of the North* (1922) had shot the first feature-length documentary about the life of the Inuit in Canadian Nunavut (Fienup-Riordan 1995). In an interview with the BBC, Flaherty had certified the suitability of the Inuit to depict the life of primitive people, but denied their ability to show inner feelings, which would be a pre-condition for the production of a good feature film – for instance about the romantic affairs of the Eskimos (Gant 2009). Rasmussen adopted an almost opposite stance. According to his evolutionary world-view, Greenlanders had basically the same capabilities as any other people. It was therefore the Europeans' task to guide them up the imagined hierarchy of cultures in their own right (Thisted 2006, 2009; Volquardsen 2011). Hence, when Rasmussen, of all topics, chooses an amorous love triangle as the theme for his film plot, this may well be interpreted as a dig at Flaherty and the contemporary filmic representation of the Inuit.

In order to familiarise the fifty East Greenlanders participating as actors or extras with the medium film, which until then had been com-pletely unknown to them, Rasmussen had brought from home a canvas and a copy of one of the comedy duo Fy and Bi's silent films (Denmark's export hit of the Silent Era), and he showed the film in Ammassalik. The choice of actors for *The Wedding of Palo* took place during a celebration to which Rasmussen had invited all the residents of the colony and the sur-rounding settlements (Gilberg 1984). Since the development of sound film was still in its infancy at the beginning of the 1930s, it was not possible for Dalsheim and his film crew to make any sound recordings while filming in Greenland. However, *The Wedding of Palo* is not a pure silent film. Although, as in silent films, the attention of the audience is primarily directed by the dramatic incidental music performed by the Royal Danish Orchestra, Greenlandic voices are heard throughout the entire film. Rasmussen's short script (Rasmussen 1984) even includes some dialogues. The sound recordings,

Figure 15.1   Still from *The Wedding of Palo* (1934), capturing the famous drum dance sequence.

including typical Greenlandic chanting heard at the beginning, were recorded subsequently by Greenlanders living in Copenhagen. This explains why the voices are not always in sync with the lip movements of amateur actors. However, most of the spontaneously recruited voice actors were West Greenlanders speaking dialects very different from East Greenlandic. Due to the mixture of dialects, the often incoherent text fragments and the apparently unsuccessful efforts of some of the speakers to imitate the East Greenlandic language, even speakers of Greenlandic have difficulty following the dialogues (Sperschneider 2003). However, the amusing pidgin-like language contributes to the ongoing popularity of *The Wedding of Palo* in Greenland. For Rasmussen, the subsequent audio recordings were merely a means to achieve the greatest possible ethnographic authenticity. It was not even his intention that European film audiences understand the dialogues. Had that been the case, it would have been relatively uncomplicated to provide the film with Danish, English or German subtitles, or with inter-titles, familiar to audiences from silent films.

Rasmussen's script is divided into four acts, in which one may detect exposition, complication, falling action and dénouement. It is thus astonishingly reminiscent of the classical theatre of Aristotelian tradition. First we meet beautiful Navarana, who is doing the housework for her aged father and three unmarried brothers. The action takes place at a summer camp at the turn of the century. Thus, the East Greenlandic actors, who by 1933 were all permanently settled and also baptised, perform in *The Wedding of Palo* the everyday lives of their parents' generation, which had lived before the cultural encounter with the Europeans. We soon learn that two young men, capable sealer Palo and polar bear hunter Samo, are competing to win Navarana's favour. When Samo accidentally falls into the fjord while fishing and is mocked by Palo and the others, he erupts in anger and turns on his rival. But the community demands that Palo and Samo settle their dispute in the traditional way: through a singing contest and drum dance, where the objective is to mock the opponent and win the sympathy of the audience. During the contest, which forms the second act, and thus the complication in Rasmussen's script, an almost-defeated Samo breaks the rules of the traditional ritual, pulls out a knife and seriously wounds his rival Palo. In the meantime, Navarana and her father and brothers, who do not want to lose their housekeeper to one of the brawlers, secretly leave the summer camp and begin construction of a winter house at another location. In the third act, Samo travels after them and settles in close proximity to his chosen one. At the same time, Palo, back in the summer camp, is cured by an *angakkok*, a pagan Greenlandic shaman, and, in the final act, puts out to rough seas in order to fetch his bride. Navarana embarks Palo's kayak without hesitation, but his opponent Samo is still unwilling to admit defeat. He follows the couple and once again tries to kill Palo with a lance. Finally, as Samo's kayak capsizes, the villain drowns in the troubled sea. Palo and Navarana paddle off into the sunset.

The oppositional representation of the two male protagonists as hero (Palo) and villain (Samo) is conspicuous. Against the backdrop of the dispute between Denmark and Norway, Anders Jørgensen (2003) has interpreted this setting as a political allegory. Friendly Palo stands for the benevolent Danish colonial power, whereas envious Samo, who does not adhere to the community's legal order, embodies Norway, which from a Danish point of view is seen as an aggressor. Such an interpretation may have its charm, but also appears abundantly abstract, especially in view of the fact *The Wedding of Palo* is not set in the present, but at a time before the colonial encounter in East Greenland.

Other reviews have emphasised the film's allegedly ethnographically genuine and cinematographically beautiful recordings, and may likewise have overlooked the fact that *The Wedding of Palo* is set in the past. In any case, one may ask oneself why Rasmussen set the plot of his film at a time before the end of the colonisation and Christianisation of East Greenland. After all, by giving the Greenlandic amateur actors cinematic self-representation, he is, technically speaking, pursuing an emancipatory project, which seems to be in line with his strong rejection of a civilisation-critical romanticising and exoticising of the 'unspoiled noble savages', a stance he expresses particularly fiercely in his writings in Greenlandic (Thisted 2006). However, given that we know Rasmussen's unfinished plans, *The Wedding of Palo* seems to fit well with his perspective on Danish colonisation and on the future of the Greenlandic nation. Today, we know that *The Wedding of Palo*, shot in East Greenland, the last part to be colonised, was intended to make up the first part of a film trilogy. The second and third part would take place in Thule and in one of the larger colonies on the west coast – possibly today's capital Godthåb (Nuuk) (Gilberg 1984; Gant 2009). One may envision a context in which the entire trilogy was meant to portray the overall positive impact of Danish colonisation on Greenlandic society. It was certainly far from being Rasmussen's intention to disparage the pre-colonial Inuit culture shown in *The Wedding of Palo* as primitive. Yet, his writings clearly suggest that he saw the future of Greenlandic society in the modernised hybrid culture of the colonies. According to him, the indigenous culture had to die. By hybridising Inuit and European culture, a third and better people would emerge (Thisted 2006). Seen in such a light, *The Wedding of Palo* no longer appears to be the piece of essentialist 'ethno-aesthetics' (Arke 2010) that one might take it for at first glance, but transforms dramatically into a film of a more radical and transgressive nature.

BIBLIOGRAPHY

Arke, P. [1995] (2010), *Ethno-Aesthetics/Etnoæstetik*, København: ark, Pia Arke Selskabet & Kuratorisk Aktion.
Eglinger, H. and A. Heitmann (2010), *Landnahme. Anfangserzählungen in der skandinavischen Literatur um 1900*, Paderborn: Wilhelm Fink.
Fienup-Riordan, A. (1995), *Freeze Frame: Alaska Eskimos in the Movies*, Seattle and London: University of Washington Press.
Gant, E. (2009), 'Gute und böse Eskimos. Knud Rasmussen und Palos Brautfahrt', in J. Schöning (ed.), *Die arktische Leinwand. Grönland im Film von Knud Rasmussen bis 'Fräulein Smilla'*, Lübeck: Schmidt-Römhild, 38–47.
Gilberg, R. (1984), 'Optagelse af filmen', *Tidsskriftet Grønland*, 4, 132–8.
Iversen, E. (1984), 'Filmens anmeldelse', *Tidsskriftet Grønland*, 4, 143–8.
Jørgensen, A. (2003), 'Primitiv film? Knud Rasmussens ekspeditionsfilm', *Kosmorama*, 232, 181–206.
Rasmussen, K. [1933] (1984), 'Palo's bryllupsfærd', *Tidsskriftet Grønland*, 4, 95–102.
Sperschneider, W. (2003), 'Landet bag isen. Grønland i 1920'ernes og 30'ernes kulturfilm', *Kosmorama*, 232, 113–24.
Stauning, T. [1934] (1984), 'Indledningstale til "Palo's bryllupsfærd"', *Tidsskriftet Grønland*, 4, 150.

Thisted, K. (2006), '"Over deres egen races lig." Om Knud Rasmussens syn på kultur-mødet og slægtskabet mellem grønlændere og danskere', *Tidsskriftet Antropologi*, 50, 131–47.
Thisted, K. (2009), 'Knud Rasmussen', in O. Høiris (ed.), *Grønland – en refleksiv udfordring*, Aarhus: Aarhus Universitetsforlag, 239–80.
Volquardsen, E. (2011), *Die Anfänge des grönländischen Romans. Nation, Identität und subalterne Artikulation in einer arktischen Kolonie*, Marburg: Tectum.

16. ARCTIC TRAVELOGUES: CONQUERING THE SOVIET NORTH

Oksana Sarkisova

Early Soviet policies towards the numerically small Northern and Far Eastern indigenous populations emerged from a nineteenth-century populist framework that saw cultural extinction as a major problem (Kuper 1988: 2–3). In the early 1920s, the Soviet press frequently presented the situation of the indigenous population of the North as 'worsening', 'becoming harder', and finally reaching a 'catastrophic' stage (cf. Ianovich 1923: 251–4; Slezkine 1994: 131–83). Soviet nationality policy, defined by Francine Hirsch as a 'state-sponsored evolutionism', grounded the Soviet 'civilizing mission' in the Marxist concept of development through historical stages (Hirsch 2005: 7). Within this framework, the indigenous peoples were seen both as underdeveloped societies to be modernised and as complex cultures worthy of extensive ethnographic research. Nineteenth-century romantic primitivism fused with positivism resulted in a peculiar view of indigenous populations as a 'combination of the contemptible and the admirable', in which 'the native might be rebuked for eating rotten fish, abusing his wife, and killing his elderly parents, but he absolutely had to be praised for his simplicity, generosity, and stoicism' (Slezkine 1994: 79).

Cinematography, as the Bolsheviks well knew, was a powerful tool for visualising diversity and demonstrating desired developments and achievements. In the Soviet context, the 'disappearing' minorities were supposed to benefit from the new regime, at least on screen. The landscape they inhabited was imagined as a complex composite: a territory rich in material resources and an underdeveloped land; a home to endangered peoples; a vulnerable frontier; and the futuristic venue for an anticipated economic miracle. This chapter outlines the evolution of the imagery of indigenous populations and the Arctic North in the Soviet cinema of the 1920–30s. By focusing on the films by Vladimir Erofeev and Vladimir Shneiderov, I trace the transformation of the visual language of representation of the Far North. This transitioned over the course of a few decades from being represented as an exotic borderland with a variety of cultures to a harsh but tameable frontier in which the image of the indigenous population becomes that of a body of diligent apprentices.

THE CONTACT ZONE: NATIONAL VARIETY BEYOND THE ARCTIC CIRCLE

In 1927, journalist and film critic Vladimir Erofeev (1898–1940), one of the founding fathers of the Association of Revolutionary Cinematography (ARK), teamed up with experienced editor Vera Popova (1892–1974) to make the montage film *Beyond the Arctic Circle* (*Za poliarnym krugom*, USSR, 1927). Erofeev and Popova used the pre-Revolutionary film stock of the Khanzhonkov studio, which was an inexpensive way to increase film output and satisfy the growing hunger for film in the context of New Economic Policy (NEP) economic rationalisation. Creating films about the remote parts of the Soviet Union fitted well into the announced policy of promoting educational and 'enlightening' films, advanced by political leaders and expected of the film management. Their work should be seen in the larger context of Soviet expedition films, which flourished in the second half of the 1920s, starting with Dziga Vertov's hotly debated *A Sixth Part of the World* (see Sarkisova 2007, and Shembel, Chapter 26 in this volume). In Vertov's film, the portrayal of the remote and passive Samoeds (present-day Nenets) showed the inhabitants of the Soviet North as recipients of benefits offered by the technologically advanced and culturally dynamic centre. It assembled and accentuated the discursive features that had been associated with the Russian North for the past two centuries and inscribed these within the hierarchical 'centre-periphery' discourse of Soviet modernity. Vertov's approach, however, was not the only way to represent the Northern spaces and peoples.

Erofeev and Popova challenged this implicit hierarchy and sought to create an engaging travelogue for the wider audience and to advance the genre of the travel film in Soviet cinema. The challenges the editors faced were numerous: they had to construct a coherent and ideologically intact narrative out of footage recorded without their involvement and filmed in a different historical context. For Erofeev it was a particularly timely opportunity to find arguments in favour of geographic and ethnographic *Kulturfilm*. Borrowed from the German film industry, the genre cut across the conceptual boundary between fiction and non-fiction, prioritising the educational function of cinema. Erofeev had observed first-hand the success of *Kulturfilms* in Germany in the early

1920s (Erofeev 1926; Schlegel 2002). He celebrated the expedition films for their ability to introduce educational material in a format attractive to the general audience, which made the genre financially sustainable and ideologically beneficial. Popova provided the inexperienced Erofeev with invaluable editorial knowhow. With the intention of making a profitable and 'cultured' film, the editors set to work.

The footage used in the film had been recorded by Fedor Bremer who was affiliated with the Khanzhonkov studio. An experienced photographer and cinematographer, Bremer had worked on a number of big-budget productions, including the historical drama *1812* (Russia, 1913) made to mark the anniversary of the war against Napoleon in Russia, as well as newsreels of events involving royalty (Batalin 2002; Baklin 2003). In 1913–14, he was sent by the studio to film the Bering Strait, the Far East and Kamchatka. Bremer travelled on the *Kolyma*, which crossed the Polar Circle and became trapped in the Arctic ice. The winter cost the expedition three lives, and the whole crew suffered from scurvy. Upon his return, Bremer published accounts of his travels in Khanzhonkov's film magazine *Pegas* in 1915 and 1916, and a few short films were edited from his footage. Among them was the one-reel *Life of the North* (*Zhizn' Severa*, Russia, 1914), showing the *Kolyma* and interaction between her crew and the indigenous circumpolar population. The bulk of the footage, however, had not been edited prior to Erofeev and Popova's undertaking.

Bremer's account in *Pegas* starts with a dramatic account of the ship's encounter with an iceberg. A subsequent scene presents a meeting with the Chukchi, one of Russia's northernmost indigenous populations, whose territory spans coastal areas and interior tundra. While nature was presented as hostile, powerful and overwhelming, the locals were described in a condescending manner as 'miniature, fragile, pitiful' (Bremer 1915: 66). Bremer's description of the ensuing exchange emphasised the civilisational gap between the crew and passengers on the one hand and the indigenous population on the other. The description of the physical appearance and material goods of the Chukchi further underscored the writer's contempt: '[their] eyes are not visible, in their place there are only narrow purulent slits [*gnoinye shelki*]', the trade objects were described as 'useless goods: broken walrus fangs, dirty and old seal skins, rather bad lemmings' (1915: 66). The trade thus turns into a condescending 'rewarding' of the locals with small portions of tobacco and tea. Bremer lumped together the Northern ethnicities as 'All these Yakuts, Yukagirs, Chukchi', contrasting them with the superior, civilised white race (1915: 71).

Although Bremer found the North 'repetitive' and 'monotonous', he took his assignment seriously, and diligently filmed and photographed throughout his long journey, assembling an extensive visual archive. His footage constituted a rich record of the activities of both the *Kolyma*'s crew and the indigenous population. Once the footage was edited into a feature travelogue with a single overarching narrative in a different ideological framework, what became of the original recording context and the attitude of the cameraman? How did the editors make sense of Bremer's material?

The footage – about 10,000 metres – offered numerous narrative options. The editors thus had to decide on the structuring principles for the film, and relied on the use of commentary, which was routinely employed by Soviet film-makers to formulate 'correct' ideological messages. *Beyond the Arctic Circle* is structured chronologically, using the *Kolyma*'s itinerary as the backbone of the narrative. The editors did not draw attention to their use of archaic 1913 footage, nor did they credit Bremer's camerawork. Downplaying the temporal gap, *Beyond the Arctic Circle* features continuous movement – from the opening scenes of hustle and bustle in the port of Vladivostok to the actual sea voyage, to the movement of people themselves, using the conventions of early cinematographic travelogues (Rony 1996; Griffiths 2002).

Soviet expedition films were aimed at an audience for whom films replaced travel. They also performed a function of territorial appropriation of the 'new motherland', commanding loyalty across distances and cultural variance. The travelogues, combining the legacy of pre-Revolutionary *Picturesque Russia* film series with early ethnographic conventions, both highlighted and accommodated the differences between 'us' and the 'others'. The 'ethnographic principle' underlining Soviet reforms and attitudes toward the peoples of the North also shaped early Soviet politics of visual representations of Northern minorities. When the 'national' viewpoint won out over 'economic rationality' in structuring the Soviet universe (Ssorin-Chaikov 2007: 282), the local cultures were taken to be the 'elementary units' of a new socialist social structure, putting 'Yakuts, Yukagirs, Chukchi' at the centre of attention for filmmakers and editors.

The travelogue to the North, to borrow Thomas Gunning's apt categorisation, features a double 'phantom ride', moving 'into landscape via technology' (Gunning 2010: 36–7). The aesthetic penetration of the space is accompanied by time-travel, with the audience experiencing a range of anachronistic visual conventions of landscape films from the 1910s. Bremer's camera is largely static, remaining at eye level and at a significant distance from the recorded objects. It pans slowly to the left and to the right, only rarely making use of the vertical axis, and avoids dramatic angles, enabling the viewer 'to enter a scene safely and to be charmed by its novelty or its awe-inspiring grandeur' (Hint and Sampson 2004: 5). *Beyond the Arctic Circle* generally avoids fast-paced cuts, firmly anchoring the viewer in space and equating his/her gaze with that of the camera. The film followed the example of German and American travel films, making extensive use of continuity editing, tracking shots and long panoramas (Ruoff 2006). As a 'phantom ride', the film follows the visual convention of 'viewer as passenger' (Gunning 2010: 53).

Appropriating Bremer's 'traveller's gaze', the editors construct the landscape as a cross-cultural space, invoking 'the spatial and temporal coexistence of subjects previously separated by geographic and historical disjunctures' and emphasising 'how subjects are constituted in and by their relations to each other . . . in terms of copresence, interaction, interlocking understandings and practices, often within radically asymmetrical relations of power' (Pratt 1992: 7). Erofeev and Popova apply Kuleshov's and Vertov's lessons of 'created geography' [*tvorimaia geografia*] (Widdis 2003: 64–6) not to estrange the material or create phantom places by splicing together spatially disparate sites, but to ascribe meaning to the space without alienating the viewer. While preserving the editing pace of the early travelogues, the director-editors ascribe new meanings to the landscape via the juxtaposition of sequences and inter-titles.

The film begins with the image of a map, featuring the Far East and Alaska, with the Pacific Ocean occupying the centre. As Tom Conley has argued, the map not only 'underlines what a film is and what it does, but it also opens a rift or brings into view a site where a critical and productively interpretive relation with the film can begin' (Conley 2007: 2). This emphasis on a region, rather than on the country as a whole, on the borderland rather than the centre, zooms in on the territory and avoids a hierarchical landscape. The interpretation of the Northern landscape thus starts with its localisation, fragmenting the general, zooming in on the particulars, approaching the details as a whole.

The inhabitants of the North are shown as being in constant interaction, via trade and intermarriage, with Europeans and Americans alike, including Cossacks tracing their roots back to the seventeenth-century expeditions of Semen Dezhnev, Alaskan gold-diggers, and the Eskimo. Representation of local cultures as products of centuries-long interaction correlated with the ethnographic research of the day, which was instrumental in formatting the optics of 'virtual tourism' across the Soviet Union (Hirsch 2005: 194–5). Early 1920s policies towards national minorities were driven by the 'ethnographic principle' (Ssorin-Chaikov 2007: 282), which posited a variety of coexisting understandings of the reality. The film does not contain references to political borders, portraying the North as an open and culturally plural space with ongoing cross-cultural interactions, exemplified by the Chukchi's contacts with the Eskimo and the North American traders.

Another important influence on Erofeev and Popova's work was Robert Flaherty's *Nanook of the North* (1922), which established a number of visual and conceptual conventions in representing the North and its inhabitants. *Beyond the Arctic Circle* used a similar structure, introducing activities around the home, family life, hunting and trade. Both films followed the tradition of showing technical curiosities as 'signs of ingenuity and advancement', seen as proof of 'a more homogeneous, civilized, and scientific empire' – an image eagerly shared by the Soviet regime (Werrett 2011: 396). Thematising the advancement of technological modernity, Erofeev and Popova include an episode presented as the Chukchi's first encounter with a movie camera. The inter-title introducing the 'first meeting with a cameraman' is followed by a long shot of women and children looking at the camera, returning its gaze with curiosity and attention. In the 1920s, the camera topped the long list of technological wonders brought along by travellers as signs of technical superiority. But rather than suggesting fascination or attraction, beyond the surface of curiosity lurks an unspoken fear, which becomes palpable as some of the women take the children back to the tent.

While *Nanook* creates the image of a timeless and unchanging world ruled by the primary instincts of survival by underplaying both the complexity of social structure and the encroachments of the modern world, Erofeev and Popova continuously emphasise permanent communication across ethnic, cultural or political borders, putting an emphasis on local, particular and geographically-determined activities. The apolitical inter-titles of *Beyond the Arctic Circle* stand in striking contrast with the ideologically doctrinaire films of the period. The rejection of a 'salvage ethnography' romanticising rhetoric viewing the indigenous population as 'pure' and 'untouched' by civilisation allows *Beyond the Arctic Circle* to emphasise the cohabitation of the Chukchi with European settlers and cases of intermarriage.

Another connotation of 'purity' had by the early 1920s been established in the representation of the North in connection with the snowy landscapes. The whiteness of the background both marks the space as the 'North' and at the same time removes the specific visual markers of the landscape, argues Marina Dahlquist (2000). The abundance of snow and ice crucially impacts the mobility of the travellers, becoming the main vehicle of the narrative's development. Snow thus has a variety of functions: it represents a source of danger, an ultimate challenge and a natural habitat. Snow, Dahlquist argues, helped create 'specific Nordic landscapes' in Swedish cinema, and also served as a metaphor for purity and perfection, described by Richard Dyer as 'the idea of the excellence of white people seen as a heritage from the Romantics' admiration for remote, cold and "pure" places, and the virtues that it brings such as clean air, a harsh climate and terrain, closeness to God, and "the presence of the whitest thing on earth, snow"' (Dahlquist 2000: 328).

Contrary to the pairing of 'whiteness' for men and snow, *Beyond the Arctic Circle* uses the relationship of humans with their habitat to redraw asymmetrical power relations. Erofeev and Popova on numerous occasions emphasise how the Chukchi routinely manage the elements, while the crew and ship's passengers are facing extreme and deadly difficulties. The ambiguity of the imagery of snow and death returns in the episode of the hunt, where

Figure 16.1   *Beyond the Arctic Circle* (1927). Courtesy of RGAKFD, The Russian State Documentary Film and Photo Archive.

the crew kill a polar bear on camera. Following the hunt, the bear's skin is demonstrated as a sign of domination and triumph, yet the death of the crew members inadvertently places animals and humans on the same plane, denying both a model of linear progress and 'salvage ethnography', which argues for the preservation of the 'weak' and 'disappearing' cultures. The scene of the hunt offers an interesting contrast to the episode when Nanook hunts a walrus. While Flaherty demonstrates an archaic cultural practice and the beauty of the indigenous body in nature, untouched by modern hunting practices, Erofeev and Popova interpret Bremer's footage as an ambiguous commentary on humanity's relationship with the hostile and dangerous environment.

Beyond the Arctic Circle remains an exceptional case of localised representation of the Far North in Soviet cinema. Paradoxically, it was the nature of the footage that allowed the filmmakers to avoid the required signs of Soviet-induced change. What the film does instead is to present a paradigmatic 'contact zone' – 'the space in which peoples geographically and historically separated come into contact with each other and establish ongoing relations, usually involving conditions of coercion, radical inequality, and intractable conflict' (Pratt 1992: 6). The specificity of the contact zone in *Beyond the Arctic Circle* is enhanced by the extreme conditions of the North. In this liminal environment, the adaptability and skills of all the protagonists are tested. At the same time, rather than impose the traditional rhetoric of 'backwardness' on the local inhabitants, Erofeev and Popova consistently foreground the cultural predispositions of the indigenous population towards successful adaptation, showing them as better equipped than the travellers and explorers to master the elements in their daily routine.

ARCTIC CONQUEST: FROM CONTACT ZONE TO ICY DESERT

Difficulties in organising expeditions postponed active cinematic exploration of the North until the 1930s, when new approaches to landscape construction were developed. Unfolding industrialisation was accompanied by an extensive media campaign that ensured growing attention on the Soviet Arctic as a new frontier of symbolic spatial politics in the 1930s (McCannon 1997; Slezkine 1994: 280). One of the elements of this campaign was the actively mediatised 1932 expedition of the *Sibiriakov* icebreaker in the Arctic Ocean. The *Sibiriakov* and later the *Cheliuskin* voyages were featured in a series of films widely distributed in the Soviet Union and abroad (McCannon 1997; McCannon 1998). In the 1930s, the perception of the Soviet northern landscape underwent a dramatic transformation. One of the masterminds and a central subject of the explorative campaign was Otto Shmidt, a polar explorer and scientist whose consecutive expeditions on board the *Sedov*, the *Sibiriakov* and, finally, the *Cheluiskin* are paradigmatic case studies of the conquest and remapping of the Soviet landscape. Paying special attention to the public image of his explorations, Shmidt used his broad network of cultural connections to invite reporters, artists and filmmakers to join his polar expeditions, in order to leave behind properly crafted accounts of these heroic undertakings (McCannon 1997: 353–4).

Shmidt's expedition on the icebreaker *Sibiriakov* was undertaken with the ambitious aim of completing in one season the voyage along the northern shores of Russia from Arkhangelsk to the Pacific Ocean. The mission was predetermined to be a success, and artists, painters and filmmakers were invited to join the expedition with orders to create engaging works of art publicising the achievements of the explorers. Made to showcase Soviet-bred bravery and mastery over the North, the adventure film was largely scripted prior to departure. It was to include both reportage and reenacted episodes with the crew and scholars on board.

Shmidt invited filmmaker Vladmir Shneiderov (1900–73) and cameraman Mark Troianovskii (1907–67) to join the expedition. Shneiderov had met Shmidt while filming the 1928 expedition to Pamir, which the then Deputy

People's Commissar of Statistics joined as an amateur alpinist (Alexanderov et al. 2001: 259). Like Erofeev, Shneiderov started his career by re-editing short travelogues from available found footage, and quickly made a name for himself after the success of his first travel film by air, *The Great Flight* (USSR, 1925), filmed in the USSR, Mongolia and China. While Shneiderov's first film was largely an improvised recording of the sites and scenes, his later films made in Japan, Pamir and Yemen shaped his views on expedition cinema before his Northern journey. Shneiderov stepped in on the side of controlled and organised filming and argued that 'expedition film should be prepared the same way as a fiction film shot in pavilion is prepared. It needs a detailed, well-developed script' (Shneiderov 1973: 34–5; Nechaeva 1964: 50).

Shneiderov's films use extensive dramatisation that fuses the expedition and adventure film genres. His ambition was 'not to make a chronicle-report of the expedition, not a film diary . . . but to try to build a narrative film, with the expedition team as the film's protagonist, fighting with the ice of the Arctic, with the obstacles, which unexpectedly appear in their path' (Shneiderov 1973: 34–5). The film was produced by Mezhrabpomfilm, which spotted its high ideological and commercial potential. *Two Oceans (Dva okeana*, Shneiderov, USSR, 1933) was released as a sound film in 1933, and centred on the dramatic cruise of the *Sibiriakov*. While the ship suffered serious damage along the way and could only partially complete its mission, the backbone of the film becomes the story of the successful mastering of the elements. The premise of completing in a single season a Northern navigation route is presented not only as economically rational, but as a step towards political and economic autarchy. The existential struggle with nature and the maximum exertion of human capacities provide the driving force of the narrative. *Two Oceans* represents a marriage of the romantic blueprint with the modernist conquest of nature, situated within the framework of nascent socialist realism.

A number of structural similarities between *Beyond the Arctic Circle* and *Two Oceans* highlight their conceptual differences. In both cases, the directors deal with a linear voyage on board an icebreaker, featuring a visual diary of sorts. But if the former shows a long and difficult winter on the ice, the latter concentrates on avoiding delay and overcoming the unfavourable conditions at any cost. The focus of the filming shifts accordingly: Bremer's quiet observation gives way to Shneiderov's subjective dramatic angles. The focus on a geographical periphery with its 'ethnographic' practices is replaced by an attack on and competition with nature. The use of maps further highlights differences in spatial constructs: while Erofeev and Popova outline a culturally mixed region, Shneiderov cuts across the empty space, with progress measured in kilometres. The precise timing of *Two Oceans* further accentuates the expedition's linear progression: exact dates and even scenes of entries being written in the ship's log intensify the narrative in contrast to the seasonally-driven existence of the crew and the local population in *Beyond the Arctic Circle*.

The dynamic, mobile camera and dramatic angles of Mark Troianovskii differ radically from Bremer's static panoramic shots. Already archaic in 1927, Bremer's filming keeps a 'safe distance' from the recorded sites, while Shneiderov's cameraman Troianovskii uses close-ups and dynamic angles to dramatise the narrative. Despite excessive re-enactment, in the first inter-title the filmmaker claims for his film the status of a document that caught 'life unaware'. *Two Oceans* dramatises natural vistas and places humans in competition with nature. The film calls for individual heroism and features the North as hostile and bare. Low-angle shots of the moving icebreaker depict the might of the iron giant. The film's central episode is the crew's effort to change a broken propeller in the water: a single concerted effort is needed to transport several tons of ballast to lift the stern of the ship by sinking its bow. This collective effort is led and inspired by the head of the expedition Otto Shmidt, presented as a romantic larger-than-life polar explorer.

Other episodes in the film present each day as a heroic struggle against the hostile environment. Typical of early sound films, the film combines a symphonic soundtrack with inter-titles. The choice of poet and writer Boris Lapin (1905–41) as author of the film commentary is paradigmatic. An adventurer-traveller-writer, known for his essays on the border areas of the Soviet Union from the Pacific Ocean to Central Asia and the Caucasus, Lapin travelled across the Far North publishing accounts that freely combined his actual experience with fictional details, and enhanced the footage with the pathos of the 'new master' (Ruder 1993, 1998).

Lapin, Troianovskii and Shneiderov worked hand in hand to create a piece that eliminates any possible hesitations or questions regarding ideological mastery over space. The camerawork and dynamic editing emphasise the dangers and heroicise the explorers. *Two Oceans* extensively uses the mounted camera's 'phantom ride', but its impact and meaning have changed since the early travelogues of the 1910s. Soviet films in the 1930s recorded the triumphal feats of icebreakers and airplanes mastering the elements. What remains similar to the early phantom rides is the emphasis on actively penetrating the landscape, which feeds a 'fantasy of total visual dominance' (Gunning 2010: 58, 54). The film was released nine months after the completion of the trip. It presented a synchronised and edited media version of the expedition that was to become the official interpretation of the event.

The image of the North in the film is no longer that of a 'cultural zone' but a liminal space, featuring ideal conditions for testing one's physical and spiritual strength. The rare stop at the Yakut port of Tiksi provided the only occasion for a cameo appearance by the indigenous population. The fast editing pace allows only a few brief general shots of reindeer and their riders as a visual 'shortcut' to the population that had been mastered along with nature. The film's closing episode reinforces the message of success with another map of the original itinerary and a shot of Otto Shmidt reading a telegram from the Soviet government congratulating the whole crew on the completed mission. The motto of the film, also reproduced in other medial contexts such as newspaper reports, photographic albums and posters, is Stalin's slogan 'There are no fortresses that the Bolsheviks would not be able to conquer'.

Shmidt again took care to mediatise the travel, inviting a film crew and a number of artists to document the success of the mission. However the ship, unfit for its purpose, proved to be a disaster: the *Cheliuskin* was caught in the ice and its crew and passengers had to abandon ship hastily, after which it sank in the Bering Sea. Contemplating the significance of the voyage of the *Cheliuskin*, writer Mikhail Prishvin perceptively noted that

> the destiny of the *Cheliuskin* . . . [is] intertwined with our ship of state: no one dared to voice the most important message of this whole "epic." . . . But this is how it should be: the state is made strong by its people and the trifling nature of the motif disappears in the significance of the demonstration: there is something to show. (Prishvin 2009: 425)

The *Cheliuskin* rescue mission turned into one of the largest and best-orchestrated campaigns of the 1930s, branded by some as an epitome of Stalinist cultural politics: 'Cheliuskinites are the parade', laconically remarked Prishvin, equating the effect of the expedition with the media campaign (Prishvin 2009: 426).

Films about polar exploration gradually turned the celebrations following the completion of the expedition into an organic part of the narrative. The self-congratulatory happy ending usually took the expedition to the symbolic centre of the country, completing the spatial hierarchy. Another example of this genre, *Heroes of the Arctic* (*Geroi Arktiki [Cheliuskin]*, Iakov Posel'skii, USSR, 1934), was released just nine days after the rescue of the ship's team and passengers. Cameraman Arkadii Shafran was repeatedly praised for the exceptional quality of his reportage. Despite a shortage of film stock, he nevertheless succeeded in filming the crucial moments of the expedition, including the sinking of the ship and the arrival of the first rescue planes, without using re-enactments. Yet even the portrayal of 'routine' life on the ice was intended to exemplify the exceptional bravery and willpower of the crew and passengers (Shafran 1934). Posel'skii ends the film with the team's cross-country journey 'to the heart of the motherland' and a final parade, showing the whole country united in feasting the rescued and the rescuers. A combination of tracking and aerial shots of moving trains and cheering crowds, merging into a single cross-country crowd with indistinguishable faces but recognisable emotions, works as a unifying element of the Soviet identity. The heroicising low-angle close-ups of the 'country's heroes' set exemplary role models. At the same time, the crew of the Chelyuskin, with the exception of Otto Shmidt and a few others, remain anonymous.

The self-celebratory 'conquest pattern' was repeated continually in later films on expeditions to the North Pole. These include *On the North Pole* (*Na Severnom polyuse*, I. Venzher and M. Troianovskii, USSR 1937); *We Conquered the North Pole!* (*Severnyi polius zavoevan nami!*, S. Gurov and V. Boikov, USSR 1937); and *Papanin's Team* (*Papanintsy*, S. B. Posel'skii and I. Venzher, USSR 1938). This pattern left an imprint on the later representations of the Arctic. The total aerial surveillance matched the complete domination of land and sea as 'the inhospitable periphery' (Widdis 2003: 150) was successfully conquered. In the later films, the explorers heroically overcame the inhospitable natural conditions, demonstrating the desired strength and staying power of the new heroes and heroines by turning 'the wild into the domestic' and building a uniform-looking Soviet modernity across the country. This representative mode erased the earlier opposition between the culturally diverse landscape and the mythological space of the larger-than-life Soviet achievements. The changing image of the North in Soviet non-fiction exemplifies a gradual transformation of the idea of the 'conquest' itself, connected to the disappearance of alternative representations of space, emptied of its inhabitants' cultural plurality.

BIBLIOGRAPHY

Alexanderov, D. A., Dmitriev, A. N., Kolepevich (2001), *Sovetsko-germanskie nauchnye sviazi vremeni Veimarskoi respubliki*, Saint-Petersburg: Nauka.

Baklin, N. (2003), 'Vospominania o dorevoliutsionnom periode v kinematografii', *Kinovedcheskie zapiski* 64, available at http://kinozapiski.ru/ru/article/sendvalues/132/ (accessed 24 June 2013).

Batalin, V. (2002), *Kino-khronika v Rossii, 1896–1916*, Moscow: Olma-Press.

Bremer, F. (1915), 'Opasnyi Reis (Zapiski operatora-turista)', *Pegas. Zhurnal iskusstv* 1 November: 63–72.

Conley, T. (2007), *Cartographic Cinema*, Minneapolis: University of Minnesota Press.

Dahlquist, M. (2000), 'Snow-white: the aesthetic and narrative use of snow in Swedish silent film', in J. Fullerton and J. Olsson (eds), *Nordic Explorations: Film Before 1930*, John Libbey Publishing, 236–48.

Dobrenko, E. and E. Naiman (eds) (2003), *The Landscape of Stalinism: The Art and Ideology of Soviet Space*, University of Washington Press.

Erofeev, V. (1926), *Kinoindustria Germanii*, Moscow: Kinopechat'.

Griffiths, A. (2002), *Wondrous Difference: Cinema, Anthropology, and Turn-of-the-Century Visual Culture*, New York: Columbia University Press.

Gunning, T. (2010), 'Landscape and the fantasy of moving pictures: early cinema's phantom rides', in G. Harper and J. Rayner (eds), *Cinema and Landscape*, Bristol: Intellect.

Hight, E. M. and Gary D. Sampson (2004), 'Introduction: photography, "race", and post-colonial theory', in E. M. Hight and G. D. Sampson (eds), *Colonialist Photography: Imag(in)ing Race and Place*, London: Routledge.

Hirsch, F. (2005), *Empire of Nations: Ethnographic Knowledge and the Making of the Soviet Union*, Ithaca: Cornell University Press.

Ianovich, D. (1923), 'Severnye tuzemtsy', *Zhizn' Natsional'nostei*, 1.

Kuper, A. (1988), *The Invention of Primitive Society: Transformation of an Illusion*, London: Routledge.

McCannon, J. (1997), 'Positive heroes at the Pole: celebrity status, socialist-realist ideals and the Soviet myth of the Arctic, 1932–39', *Russian Review*, vol. 56, no. 3 (Jul.): 346–65.

McCannon, J. (1998), *Red Arctic: Polar Exploration and the Myth of the North in the Soviet Union, 1932–1939*, New York: Oxford University Press.

Nechaeva, M. (1964), *Vladimir Shneiderov*, Moscow: Iskusstvo.

Pratt, M. L. (1992), *Imperial Eyes: Travel Writing and Transculturation*, London: Routledge.

Prishvin, M. (2009), *Dnevniki. 1932–35*, Saint-Petersburg: Rostok.

Rony, F. T. (1996), *The Third Eye: Race, Cinema, and Ethnographic Spectacle*, Durham, NC: Duke University Press.

Ruder, C. A. (1993), 'Boris Lapin: unlikely modernist', *Russian Literature*, 34/2 (1993): 207–18.

Ruder, C. A. (1998), *Making History for Stalin: Tthe Story of the Belomor Canal*, Gainesville: University Press of Florida.

Ruoff, J. (ed.) (2006), *Virtual Voyages: Cinema and Travel*, Durham: Duke University Press.

Sarkisova, O. (2007), 'Across one sixth of the world: Dziga Vertov, travel cinema, and Soviet patriotism', *October* 121: 19–40.

Shafran, A. (1934), 'Kak ia snimal' *Kino* 30, 28 June.

Shneiderov, V. (1973), *Moi kinoputeshestvia*, Moscow: Byuro propagandy sovetskogo kinoiskusstva.

Slezkine, Y. (1994), *Arctic Mirrors: Russia and the small peoples of the North*, Ithaca: Cornell University Press.

Ssorin-Chaikov, N. (2007), 'Representing "primitive communists": ethnographic and political authority in early Soviet Siberia', in J. Burbank, M. von Hagen and A. Remnev (eds), *Russian Empire: Space, People, Power, 1700–1930*, Bloomington: Indiana University Press.

Werrett, S. (2011), 'Technology on display: instruments and identities on Russian voyages of exploration', *The Russian Review* 70 (July): 380–96.

Widdis, E. (2003), *Visions of a New Land: Soviet Film from the Revolution to the Second World War*, New Haven: Yale University Press.

17. A GENTLE GAZE ON THE COLONY: JETTE BANG'S DOCUMENTARY FILMING IN GREENLAND 1938–9

Anne Mette Jørgensen

Among a memorable series of Arctic explorers, scientists and adventurers during the past centuries, few women stand out. One exception is Jette Bang (1914–64), who produced photographic and filmic documentation of Greenland from 1937 onwards. Her extraordinary number of high-quality photographs, now available in a vast digital archive, had a profound influence upon Danish and Greenlandic perceptions of life in Greenland during and after World War II. Her early films, in contrast, were widely neglected and have only recently been made available.[1] In particular the film material she recorded in 1938–9 in West Greenland demands further attention. Recorded on the cusp of World War II, which effectively cut off Greenland from Denmark for a half decade, the films function both as early ethnographic representations of people on the West Coast of Greenland and as valuable documents about Danish colonisation of the island.

Bang was only twenty-two years old when, in 1936, she set out on the first of several extended stays in Greenland, returning in 1938–9, 1945, 1956–8 and 1961–2. With her cameras she documented, as no one else did, Inuit life during decades of major societal change – from decentralised and mainly hunter-gatherer based ways of living to increased 'modernisation', industrialisation and urban life. She was extremely productive with both her photo and film cameras. Moreover, she was remarkable for combining an aesthetic sense of framing, an ethnographic curiosity and a human sensibility which made men and women of all ages allow her and her cameras into virtually every sphere of life. Trained in photography and backed by Copenhagen's trend-setting avant-garde photo gallery Jonals and Co. (Meyer 2000), which put at her service the newest state-of-the-art equipment available in the world, the young and determined Bang produced an extraordinary body of photographic and filmic work.

When Bang returned from her first journey to Greenland in 1936, she arranged a large exhibition at the Kunstindustrimuseet (Danish Design Museum) in Copenhagen – one of the first major exhibitions to present Greenland to a broader Danish public. She also published around 190 of her photographs in a photobook, *Grønland* ('Greenland', 1940), and allowed others (for example, Birket-Smith 1961) to distribute some of her 4,000–plus photographs from the journey. In 1937, she travelled for another two months to the East Coast to photograph and record her first film, *Den yderste ø* ('The Outermost Island'). The film disappeared a few years later (Haagen 2010: 201–2).

Only one year later, Bang saw a significant opportunity when the Grønlands Styrelse (Danish Agency for Greenlandic Affairs) was looking for someone to make a film that would document the allegedly successful modernisation processes of the Danish colonial administration in Greenland. The film was intended to promote Danish colonial politics at a screening at the International Polar Exhibition 1940 in Bergen, Norway, in competition with, among others, Russian, German and American films. Bang managed to convince the director of the Grønlands Styrelse that she should be the person to carry out their ambitious plans over a period of one and a half years.

<h3 align="center">INUIT AND ITS POLEMIC PREMIERE</h3>

Bang travelled around all of West Greenland with her cameras from August 1938 to September 1939, starting at Narsarsuaq in the South, continuing up along the West Coast, and ending at the northernmost inhabited village in Greenland, Neqe, sixty kilometres north of Thule. In its instructions to Bang, the Grønlands Styrelse made its requirements clear:

> The ideal would be if a film were produced that would show a Greenlandic family living by the original, primitive conditions of the past, and if from there you would proceed to see the descendants of this family, walking step by step up to the current highest standpoint . . . The intention must be to show the ascent from the most primitive folk-life up to the complex and culture-influenced conditions of today. (Quoted in Bang 1941: 9)[2]

Bang assented to the evolutionary point of view of the Grønlands Styrelse, according to which technological and socio-cultural advancement was inescapable and necessary in Greenland. However, she was clearly more fascinated by the traditional ways of living than by processes of modernisation. While editing, she and her co-editors chose the scenes for what became her film *Inuit* (Denmark, 1940) exclusively from footage that showed traditional aspects of Inuit life in 1938–9. The initial sequences of the film depict icebergs, a dog sledge, the construction of a snow house, women and men working, and a male drum dancer entertaining his fellows. Throughout the film, the main focus is on the impressively well adapted technologies that enabled people to survive in the harsh climate. The focus is on the men fishing for salmon, mussels, *angmassets* (small oily fish), and sharks, and their hunting of seal, eider duck and reindeer. The women in the film participate in slaughtering the animals, processing the different skins, conserving and preparing the meat, and sewing *kamiks* (soft boots) and clothes, thus making use of every part of the prey. Bang shows a summer camp in skin tents, with kayaks coming back from the hunt bringing home an abundance of food, as well as a journey in large boats to the winter settlement, where the group constructs a turf house for the dark and cold months ahead. Everybody, young and old, is shown participating, and a father teaches his son to paddle his own kayak and use his spear, throwing board and harpoon as soon as he is able to sit up. In this sense, the film explicitly portrays Inuit life as it had been before the impact of the Danes transformed it significantly in the mid-twentieth century. The Inuit are depicted, in line with Flaherty's *Nanook of the North*, as 'timeless primitives' (Fienup-Riordan 1995: 52), who peacefully spend all their time working for subsistence in harmonious symbiosis with surrounding nature. The viewers do not get to know the individual personalities of the group portrayed in *Inuit*,

Figure 17.1   Still from Jette Bang's *Inuit* (1940).

as they do the protagonist in *Nanook of the North*. Although the camera is often pointed towards the men, women and children of the group, the framing is most often full-body with only a few instances of close-ups, and faces appear secondary to hands shooting, processing, cutting and sewing, and handling children, dogs, boats, skins, meat and tools. The impression is that the individual is not seen as such, but defined by his or her role in sustaining the heterodoxy of the collective. The admiration for the people and their natural environment turns this oeuvre into a kind of 'poetic ethnography', a genre somehow in between art and anthropology.

Because of the war, the 1940 International Polar Year exhibition in Bergen was cancelled and the premiere of *Inuit* instead became a national event. Hosted by the Grønlandske Selskab (the Greenlandic Society in Copenhagen), it was attended by around 600 of Copenhagen's political, cultural and intellectual elite, including the Danish king and other members of the royal family and the prime minister. Bang's film received excited applause several times, and newspaper reviews praised her camerawork and the spectacular scenes of nature and animal and human life. Most of all, the reporters were excited about the images of Greenlandic children.[3] Alongside all the positive reactions, only one, that of the director of the Royal Greenlandic Trade Company who had sponsored the film, stated with disappointment that the film did not demonstrate the technological and cultural progress achieved by the Danish colonial administration (Johnsen 2003: 38). This disappointment was important. Although demand to see the film was high,[4] it was screened on only five occasions after the premiere and then vanished from the sight of any audience. Attempts were made to obtain a wider distribution of the film in Danish schools, but they were thwarted by the argument that only one original 16mm master of the film existed, and that it was too risky to send it for copying in times of war, to the only place where that could be done, the US. There is confusion as to what actually happened, but in any case the film went out of distribution for four decades.

EARLY ETHNOGRAPHIC DOCUMENTS

The Grønlands Styrelse did not get the film it had commissioned Bang to produce. Why it turned out that way is not obvious. A film committee, including the Eskimology professor William Thalbitzer, had written detailed instructions for Bang's assignment, specifying desired sequences such as 'transportation of patients, hospitals, the college of education, grouse flying in sunshine over the snow, mining, chanting of hymns' (Bang 1941: 9), and Bang actually recorded every single scene it had requested. One can only speculate as to what happened when she and Paul Hansen (Haagen 2010: 201) sat at the editor's bench and created the 76-minute *Inuit* from the total of four hours of footage, but a conscious choice must have been made to neglect the originally planned evolutionary structure. Instead they – or perhaps somebody else – edited twelve additional shorter black and white documentaries, totalling 110 minutes, from the material. These recounted a history of Greenland successfully undergoing a process of modernisation. The short films show new shops, such as a bakery, a grocery store and a gunsmith; motorised boats taking over from kayaks and umiaks; patients being treated in a hospital; different kinds of schools; Lutheran religious practices such as baptism, confirmation and communion; the telegraph and the radio station; the first printing office; the procedures of one of the two country councils; the slaughtering and processing of seals; the collection of eggs on birdcliffs; traditional hunting of walrus and polar bear in the Thule district; winter life inside a turf house; the experimental breeding and slaughtering of sheep, cows, hens and foxes; and scenes from the marble and cryolite quarries and the coalmine.

Watching these images today provides an atypical experience to other films from the Arctic. The focus on 'modern', 'inauthentic' and recently introduced elements, ranging from mining technologies and radios to grey foxes and vaccination syringes is one unusual aspect. The limited use of scenic images of nature is another. A third striking difference is the respectful, curious and descriptive camera style, giving the viewer access to very different spheres of life. As an ethnographic documentation of the pre-war period in the history of Greenland, these films, and Bang's methodology and style, are unparalleled.

Watching Bang's films it is immediately noticeable that she was highly skilled at relating to the people she filmed. She participated as much as possible in the everyday activities of the numerous people she visited, stayed for a long time with people, talked and played, cooked and ate, travelled and worked with them. She largely behaved as an ethnographic participant–observer, and the final films sustain the illusion of actions taking place as they would even had the camera not been there. In reality, however, she intervened significantly to optimise recordings, provoked intended actions in front of the camera by mise-en-scène, and directed people to 'act themselves', to dress up for the occasion, or rearrange their environment (see Bang 1941: 25, 38–9). Despite this, her films were conceived as documentaries, and her cinematographic strategy proved successful. She wrote about her method in her diary:

> As a humble polar explorer it was to my advantage that I could travel around alone without too much hullabaloo, whereas other expeditions are hampered by large crews and conspicuous equipment [. . .] and my only chance of capturing the genuine Greenland was being able to move around unnoticed and slide naturally into the daily routines of people. During my two earlier visits to Greenland I had to a certain degree experienced how this method of behaving as a quiet and harmless person put

me in touch with all kinds of people without them having to offer me too much attention. (Bang 1940: 95)

In addition, being a woman probably gave her privileged access in many instances. She also successfully teamed up with Hannibal Fencker, an official based locally, who had grown up in Greenland and spoke the language, and who assisted her with practical matters, often staging and directing people during the film recordings (Bang 1941: 13).

Bang's crew was small, and although she used a noisy generator, a large and heavy battery, numerous specially constructed 24-volt lamps and several Bell and Howell cameras, she had less equipment than most other productions in the Arctic. Bang made use of films and cameras of a quality superior to what had hitherto been used in Greenland. She was offered the new Kodachrome reversal film (a process whereby a positive image is developed on the original stock) and she was impressed by the quality of this colour film 'which hitherto have been difficult, but had in 1938–9 improved to the extent that it could be used under almost the same conditions as black-and-white film' (Bang 1941: 184–5). She was the first person to use this film in Arctic conditions, where it was extremely advantageous to be able to shoot sharp images even when lighting was sparse. Luckily, the cold climate preserves celluloid film very well, and the films were not spoilt by having to be stored for months, awaiting transportation along the coast and then by ship to Denmark. The advertising company, Jonals and Co., for whom Bang worked when in Copenhagen, taught her to use the film correctly. Upon receiving her exposed films, the company would immediately develop them and analyse the quality. By telegraph they would instruct her to adjust exposures and other settings, and thus make full use of this newly invented film.

Bang did not do much herself to promote the shorter black and white 'modernisation' films. Possibly modernisation processes and industrialisation did not have the same appeal to a cinema audience as original Inuit life. Perhaps a genuine ambition existed to combine these films and *Inuit* once the war allowed access to the necessary facilities. One may speculate as to what actually happened to the twelve films but apparently they ended up on the shelves in the Grønlands Styrelse. In 1966, they were handed over to the National Museum. In my position as a visual anthropologist for the museum, I found them and realised their obvious value as ethnographic and historical documents of the dominant agendas in the relationship between Greenland and Denmark at that particular period in time: namely, a technological optimism, an ambition to transform Greenlanders' everyday lives so that they could become as close as possible to those of the Danes, and high expectations of the benefits of exploiting the natural resources of the vast country. The war put an abrupt end to these activities, because all contact between Greenland and

Denmark was cut off. After the war, relations between the two countries had to be negotiated anew and, although Greenland remained a Danish colony, the desire for independence now entered the political agenda. Modernisation efforts took new form and, in the 1950s, would be on a much greater scale than before the war. Probably these new agendas made Jette Bang's films look obsolete.

'JUMPING FROM THE STONE AGE INTO THE PRESENT'

If *Inuit* did not reach large audiences, Bang's photographs certainly did. In the selection of photographs for the photobook *Grønland* (Bang 1940), as well as the foreword, Bang and Director Oldendow of the Grønlands Styrelse stressed the transitional features of contemporary Greenland. In Bang's words, the book depicted 'the Greenlanders who by the guidance and rule of the Danes are jumping from the Stone Age into the Present. May they, by virtue of their Indigeneity, pass safely into Civilization' (Bang 1940: foreword). Oldendow stated that whereas the Danish colonisation of Greenland had in earlier times been ignorant about the qualities of Inuit life, times had now changed. Since the middle of the nineteenth century, the attitude of the Danish administrators had become respectful and they now included the Greenlanders in decision-making. While poverty and social challenges still existed, he admitted, the colonial administration had been highly successful in its ambitious actions '*for* and *with* the Greenlanders [. . .] We have learned from the deeds of white men towards native people elsewhere on the globe which has not always been flattering' (Oldendow in Bang 1940: 13). In other words, the Danish colonial administration was successful because it was humane and benevolent, and as such an exception to colonial repression elsewhere (Petterson 2012: 30). With this book, the Grønlands Styrelse probably received the propaganda for Denmark's allegedly solicitous and successful modernisation of Greenland that they had wanted. It was widely distributed to embassies and official organisations (Johnsen 2003: 81).

Due to the intense public interest in Bang's photographs, the photobook *Grønland* sold out even before its official publication date. She toured the country and lectured on her photographs and journeys in Greenland; in 1941, she published her diaries from the 1938–9 journey (Bang 1941). Danish and Swedish newspapers were impressed by this strong, pretty and unusually brave young woman, her photographic skills and her self-sufficiency under what appeared to them to be strange conditions. In 1944, five of her photographs were selected for exhibition in numerous Danish public schools. After the war, her photographs were exhibited in Paris, London, Tokyo and New York, and published in national magazines; in 1955, one appeared in the *National Geographic Magazine* (Johnsen 2003: 78). The photographs were familiar to

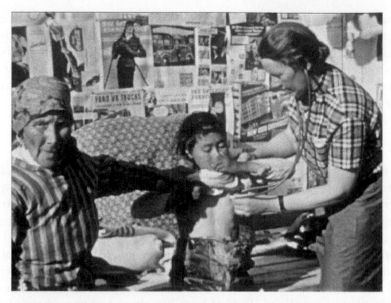

Figure 17.2   One of Bang's many thousands of photographs taken during multiple trips to Greenland, digitised and publicly available through the Arctic Institute in Copenhagen.

many people in Greenland, as in Denmark, but a formal exhibition of her work was not mounted in Denmark until 2006.

A GENTLE COLONIAL GAZE

Given the legitimising support of the Danish prime minister and the royal family, and the significantly greater authority ascribed to the photographic image in general in the middle of the last century, Bang's early images must have been perceived in Denmark and Greenland as rather authoritative testimonies to life in Greenland. Reading through contemporary newspaper clippings about her and her films, books and public presentations, she appears to have been a popular public figure and a prominent disseminator of images of the faraway colony, Greenland. The general public, and the press, agreed that Denmark's colonial engagement was legitimate and of a common good for Denmark as well as for Greenland. The narrative of Denmark's gentle colonial administration of Greenland was central to national self-perception, and Bang's images came to serve as an advertisement for this particularly Danish version of colonialism. She would later take a more critical stance towards Denmark's role in Greenland, for instance in her 1961 photobook *Grønland igen* ('Greenland again'). 'Ethnographic film began as a phenomenon of colonialism, and has flourished in periods of political change' writes De

Brigard (1995: 31), and Bang became one of the most prominent disseminators of images of life in the colony of Greenland through later decisive decades of political change in the postwar period. In 1952, Greenland changed its status from colony to Danish county. Bang continued her journeys to Greenland in 1945, 1956–8 and 1961–2, still meticulously documenting the changing life conditions of people there. These journeys resulted in the films *Ad lange veje* ('On Long Roads', 1952), *Et nyt Grønland* ('A New Greenland', 1954), *Trommedans på Østgrønland* ('Drumdance in East Greenland', 1964) and *En sommerboplads i Østgrønland* ('A Summer Camp in East Greenland', 1969).[5] Bang now increasingly shared the documentary filmmaking scene with others, most notably the productive and popular director Jørgen Roos.

Jette Bang died in 1964, at the age of fifty. Twenty years later, curator and archaeologist Helge Larsen released *Inuit* ([1940] 1984) in a new version for TV broadcast and education, and added a narrative voice-over to it. The narration here seemed to confirm the nostalgic point of view of the Grønlands Styrelse and Jette Bang in 1938–9 that Greenland necessarily, though sadly, had to change and become a modern society. The narration concluded: 'It was at the eleventh hour when Jette Bang's film salvaged for the world parts of a culture which had for four to five thousand years been the sole ruler in the Arctic area from the Bering Strait to East Greenland' (in *Inuit*).

NOTES

1. The main part of Bang's photographs, around 12,000, are accessible online on www. arktiskebilleder.dk, providing Greenlanders and others access to an incredibly rich documentation of past times in almost every inhabited space along the Greenlandic coast. Her films are available for research in the ethnographic collections of the National Museum in Copenhagen and at the film archives of the Danish Film Institute.
2. All translations from the Danish are my own.
3. 'Vor danske Arvelod i Grønland', *Socialdemokraten*, 18 October 1940; 'Danmark maa bevare Grønland for vores kommende Slægter', *Kristeligt Dagblad*, 18 October 1940; 'Den smukke Grønlandsfilm, der bør ses af alle', *Nationaltidende*, 18 October 1940; 'Tredje nationale Storfilm', *BT*, 18 October 1940.
4. 'Faar hele Landet Grønlandsfilmen at se?', *Aftenbladet*, 22 October 1940; "Rift om Grønlandsfilmen', *Vejle Amts Folkeblad*, 22 October 1940.
5. All these films are accessible at the database of the Danish Film Institute/Filmarkivet: http://www.dfi.dk/FaktaOmFilm.aspx.

BIBLIOGRAPHY

Bang, J. (1940), *Grønland*, Det Grønlandske Selskab, Copenhagen: Steen Hasselbalchs Forlag.
Bang, J. (1941), *30.000 km i sneglefart*, Copenhagen: Steen Hasselbalchs Forlag.
Bang, J. (1961), *Grønland igen*, Copenhagen: Spectator.
Birket-Smith, K. [1927] (1961): *Eskimoerne*, Copenhagen: Rhodos.

De Brigard, E. (1995), 'The history of ethnographic film', in P. Hockings (ed.), *Principles of Visual Anthropology*, The Hague, Paris: Mouton Publishers, 13–44.

Fienup-Riordan, A. (1995), *Freeze Frames: Alaska Eskimos in the Movies*, Seattle: University of Washington Press.

Gruber, J. W. (1970), 'Ethnographic salvage and the shaping of anthropology', in *American Anthropologist, New Series* 172 (6): 1289–99.

Haagen, B. (2010), 'Den – ikke – forsvundne film. "Filmen "Inuit"', in *Tidsskriftet Grønland* 3/2010, 190–203.

Illeris, N. (2000), *Glimt af Grønland. Jette Bangs fotografier som danske repræsentationer af 1930'ernes Grønland i historisk kontekst*, MA thesis from the Institute for History and Society, Roskilde University.

Johnsen, L. (2003), *Jette Bang i billeder og ord 1940–1961. Fotografiet som broskaber*. MA thesis from Eskimology and Arctic Studies, Department of Crosscultural and Regional Studies, University of Copenhagen.

Meyer, M. K. K. (2000), *Fra sortekunst til sagfotografi. Jonals Co. og det moderne fotografis gennembrud i Danmark*, Holte: Gl. Holtegaard.

Petterson, C. (2012), 'Colonialism, racism and exceptionalism', in Kristín Loftsdóttir and Lars Jensen (eds), *Whiteness and Postcolonialism in the Nordic Region. Exceptionalism, Migrant Others and National Identities*, Surrey: Ashgate, 29–41.

Rasmussen, K. [1932] (2011), *Den store slæderejse*, Viborg: Broe

Sperschneider, W. (1998), *Eskimos im Film. Zu Verstehen und Darstellen des ethnographisch Anderen im Film am Beispiel der Inuit Grönlands*, Ph.d-afhandling, Institute for Ehnography and Social Anthropology, Aarhus University.

Sperschneider, W. (2003), 'Landet bag isen. Grønland i 1920ernes og 30'ernes kulturfilm', in *'Film fra Nord' Kosmorama. Tidsskrift for filmkunst og filmkultur*, nr 232, vinter 2003, Det Danske Filminstitut/Museum & Cinematek, 113–24.

Thisted, K. (ed.) (2002), *Grønlandske fortællere. Nulevende fortællekunst i Grønland*, København: Aschehoug.

18. EXERCISE MUSK-OX: THE CHALLENGES OF FILMING A MILITARY EXPEDITION IN CANADA'S ARCTIC

Caroline Forcier Holloway

Canada's Arctic has always attracted explorers to its vast expanses to stake claims or to study its natural resources and its people. Motion picture film has played an important role in documenting those who have ventured to frozen lands to explore Northern regions. In films shot by either amateur or professional filmmakers, the common theme is often one of survival. This paper explores the journey of members of the British-Canadian Arctic Expedition (1936–40), and Exercise Musk-Ox (1946), who under very challenging conditions braved the elements, along with their motion picture cameras, just as many explorers who came before and after them.

The British-Canadian Arctic Expedition was sponsored by the University of Cambridge, England, to survey parts of Canada's Eastern Arctic (the coasts of Foxe Basin, Northern Baffin Island). Surveyor Tom Manning, geographer Patrick Baird, archaeologist Graham Rowley and others participated in the expedition. Relying heavily on the knowledge imparted by the Inuit inhabitants ensured their survival in the Arctic. Living off the land and adapting to the climate was a part of daily life.

The use of technology in the Arctic winter cold proved particularly challenging. In the National Film Board (NFB) production, *Along Uncharted Shores* (David Bairstow, Canada, 1964), the three surviving members of the British-Canadian Arctic Expedition share their experience and recount having to 'warm up the radio and batteries over a seal oil lamp before you could get a time signal, and get a proper astronomical fix for control of the survey'. Often, they encountered cold and blustery snowy conditions, limiting their ability to record activities on motion picture film. Technical difficulties included condensation forming on the camera lens, and parts that would not properly function in freezing temperatures. Frequent opening of the camera to change 100-foot rolls of film exposed their fingers to frostbite. In Patrick Baird's expedition diary, he laments about the climate and the challenges of handling 16mm film reels while shooting a rare walrus hunt: 'Now came the trouble of getting him (walrus) out. Alas my one film (fool!) was finished . . . A very successful day but I wish I had taken spare films tho' changing will be difficult in this cold weather' (Baird n.d.).

British-Canadian Arctic Expedition members were called to serve overseas during World War II. After the war, Manning, Baird and Rowley would once again reunite, this time serving with Exercise Musk-Ox, one of the largest non-tactical exercises to be held in Canada's Arctic. Its purpose was to study movement and maintenance of troops under cold weather conditions from February to May 1946. To do this, they had a moving force of forty-eight men travelling in twelve Canadian-built Bombardier snowmobiles or 'Penguins', originally designed for the invasion of Norway.

Figure 18.1 Snowmobile or 'Penguin' travelling on the Arctic tundra, as part of Exercise Musk-Ox. George Metcalf Collection, Canadian War Museum.

Musk-Ox had grown out of the Canadian government's concern about an enemy invasion of North America, via the north, and Canada's unpreparedness to respond. The Canadian Army and the Canadian Air Force were not set up to deal with Arctic conditions, either with equipment or clothing, winterised communications, or suitable landing strips. The Royal Canadian Air Force played a key role in flying their Dakotas, Norsemen and Hadrian Gliders to supply the moving force with drops of provisions and equipment. The moving force travelled from Churchill, Manitoba, north to Eskimo Point, Fort Prince of Wales, Baker Lake, Perry River, Cambridge Bay, Coppermine, and then southwest down to Dismal Lake, Port Radium, Fort Norman, Norman Wells, Fort Simpson, Lyard River, Fort Nelson, Fort St John, Peace River, Grande-Prairie and finally, Edmonton, Alberta, covering a distance of 2,900 miles.

Manning, Baird and Rowley were highly sought-after given their previous experience and familiarity with the Arctic terrain and conditions, and their fluency in Inuktitut. Patrick Baird was made commander of the moving force, and Graham Rowley was in command of a smaller party of eleven men, who pushed ahead to clear a landing strip on the ice, and establish a signal post. The force included an army component, as well as Canadian, British and American observers and scientists who were experts on equipment, navigation, Arctic clothing, magnetism and meteorology. Tom Manning, former British-Canadian Arctic Expedition member, served as a British observer, as did Lieutenant Colonel Andrew Croft, who had considerable experience in northern climate conditions as the lead of a three-man dog team that crossed Greenland's icecap in 1934 (Baird 1978: 27). Croft brought along his 16mm motion picture camera, submitting a 45-minute UK Kodachrome film record of his observations of the exercise for study by the British Army. Although Croft was not an official photographer, his 16mm amateur footage complemented in many respects Sergeant Roger Racine's 35mm professional film record of the trek.

Before official winter exercises took place, rigorous cold weather trials of equipment and clothing were carried out by the Canadian Army, Navy and Air Force in 1943 and 1944. *Cold Weather Trial: Clothing and Equipment* (Canada, 1944) is a 47-minute film record made by the Department of National Defence (DND), and sponsored by the Canadian Armed Services and the Royal Canadian Air Force (RCAF), under the direction of the Canadian Chiefs of Staff Sub-Committee on Protective Equipment with the cooperation of the Armed Services of Great Britain and the United States and of the National Research Council of Canada. Motion picture photographers from the No. 7 Photographic Wing of the Royal Canadian Air Force Photographic Section, the Royal Canadian Navy, and the Experimental Section of the A-33 Canadian Armoured Corps were out in full force to capture the events. In addition, the

No. 7 Photographic Wing also produced a 25-minute film record, *Fighting Cold* (Canada, 1945), based on similar reconnaissance team tests that took place during the same years, to find the material best suited to service in the Arctic. In both films, some personnel wore experimental clothing, undergarments, foot-gear, headgear and handgear, and others wore standard issued outfits. Scientists and observers compared both for effectiveness and durability. Sleeping bags, tents and skis were also tested. Scientifically prepared questionnaires and field data were reviewed, and a cold weather trials report with findings and recommendations was submitted. This would be a key directive in the preparation of the pre-Musk-Ox military exercises, including Exercise Eskimo (January–February 1945), Exercise Polar Bear (February–March 1945), and Exercise Lemming (March–April 1945).

Exercise Eskimo was held in north-central Saskatchewan to study dry cold performance. Varied snow tractors were put to the test, as well as a vast array of other equipment such as beard clippers, goggles and assorted tents (Halliday 1945: 30). Exercise Polar Bear, held in northern British Columbia, was similar in nature to Exercise Eskimo, but tested men and material under wet cold conditions. Exercise Polar Bear dealt with more complex terrain and demanding climate conditions in the mountains. A small Royal Canadian Air Force detachment supported the force. Establishing and using landing strips in open country was particularly challenging, as were high-level drops. Hay bales and oats were part of these drops, as this exercise made full use of pack animals to get through rough terrain and deep snow. For both Eskimo and Polar Bear, fictitious and highly improbable battle scenarios set the scene for the men.

Exercise Lemming was the smallest of the series of exercises aimed at testing snow vehicles in Arctic conditions, on sea ice and barren land covering a round trip from Churchill, Manitoba to Padlei, Northwest Territories, and back. Lieutenant-Colonel Patrick Baird was at the helm, having participated as an observer in Polar Bear, only to be pulled from it to attend Eskimo, and then be asked to draw up a plan for Lemming (Halliday 1945: 36). In particular, Exercise Lemming was demanding in terms of endurance for a small special force of parachutists living in sub-Arctic conditions. Sergeant Roger Racine, a nineteen year old who was loaned by the Canadian army to the National Film Board, took part in the Lemming training in preparation for Exercise Musk-Ox. Equipped with a 35mm Eyemo movie camera and Plus X-film stock (Canadian Department of National Defence 1945: 21), he had the added duties of documenting the force's activities.

Roger Racine was born in Ottawa in 1924. By the age of ten, he knew that he wanted to make movies. He worked at the National Film Board from 1942 to 1948 shooting propaganda films for the *World in Action* and *Canada Carries On* newsreel series, and other notable productions from the latter series including *It's Fun to Sing* (Roger Blais, Canada, 1948). Under the tutelage of directors Jean-Yves Bigras, Paul Gury and Richard Jarvis, as well as Director of Photography Jean Bachelet, Racine soon blossomed into the role of Director of Photography. He is heralded as being one of French-Canada's first sound feature film Directors of Photography, for such important films as *Le curé de village* (Paul Gury, Canada, 1949), *Les lumières de ma ville* (Jean-Yves Bigras, Canada, 1950), *Forbidden Journey* (Richard J. Jarvis and Cecil Maiden, Canada, 1950), and *La petite Aurore, l'enfant martyre* (Bigras, Canada, 1952) (Caron 2010). With the advent of television, he became a director at Société Radio-Canada, in 1952, and a decade later, he founded the production company Cinéfilms, in Montréal. In 2008, he was awarded a lifetime achievement award with the Canadian Society of Cinematographers.

The demands of military production were the driving force behind the National Film Board's participation in Musk-Ox and other exercises. Its exponential growth in the early 1940s can be attributed to the wartime production of varied documentaries and significant war propaganda series including *Canada Carries On*. One of the National Film Board's goals was to highlight Canadian achievements relating to the war, and military operations on the home front. The Canadian Army worked with the National Film Board to produce several military winter training films during and after the war years, including *Field Training in Winter* (1942), *Arctic Ops: Exercise Lemming* (1945), *Exercise Polar Bear* (1945), *Exercise Eskimo* (1945), and *Exercise Musk-Ox* (1946).

In September 1944, John Grierson, Government Film Commissioner, and Colonel J. T. Wilson, Director of Operational Research, met to discuss motion picture coverage for army winter manoeuvres from 1944 to 1945. They discussed the objectives of Exercise Eskimo and Exercise Polar Bear, whereby the National Film Board would provide a cameraman and/or an assistant and director, experienced in winter warfare, and the Canadian Army would pay for the film, processing for the completed film, and extra equipment (National Film Board of Canada 1944). The reality was that the National Film Board made every effort to find civilian cameramen for the exercises but their camera staff had been greatly depleted to supply overseas film units. This is where the transfer of army personnel was recommended for the job. The experience of documenting Eskimo and Polar Bear by motion picture camera would prove very trying, regardless of the climate. The Department of National Defence was aiming for a training product that met its specifications, portraying how a soldier should dress, live, travel and fight in varied cold climate conditions. In retrospect, the partnership between the Canadian Army and the National Film Board to produce training films would require a fair amount of planning and preparedness. Unfortunately, lack of time and planning meant that in filming

Musk-Ox, they would have to forego such considerations as a director or an assistant for young Roger Racine, who would have to tackle the assignment alone.

Adapting and conditioning the filming equipment proved challenging for National Film Board cameramen and technicians. In preparation for the exercises, they contacted the Eastman Kodak Company in Rochester, New York, to learn about winterising or 'Arcticising' motion picture filming equipment. The National Film Board was provided with a *Report on the Preparation and Operation of Cameras: Tropic and Arctic Conditions*, which addressed equipment preparation, camera adjustment, and lubrication and care of equipment in the Arctic. Kodak also stated that they had been 'supplying the (US) Armed Forces for the past three or four years wherein their picture-making activities range from minus 70 degrees to minus 40 degrees. Where lubrication is required, there are fish oils and sperm oils available which can be used onto minus 70 degrees' (Eastman Kodak 1945).

Just as members of the British-Canadian Arctic Expedition experienced hardships with manoeuvring camera equipment in the cold, Roger Racine had his own set of challenges. Without a doubt, weather conditions and cold climate were the greatest impediments he encountered, forcing him to be creative and innovative in order to adapt. The National Film Board had winterised his camera but out in the field, he discovered that the oil was too thick and was jamming the camera's mechanism. At one of the stopovers during the expedition, Racine ran into a hunter who told him about coal oil and kerosene, which he used for his hunting equipment as it did not thicken like other oils. Racine used medical syringes to insert the kerosene into the camera parts. At the time, this process was a godsend, although admittedly, after the expedition, the camera's moving parts fell apart due to the volatile nature of the oil.

The Department of National Defence's failure to recognise the particular needs of the cameramen was an added challenge. Out of necessity, the National Film Board hired Joe Gibson, a former United States Army military cameraman, to provide a workshop on shooting film in Arctic climate conditions. The sharing of his expertise proved useful in practical and mental preparedness. As was recommended by Kodak, silk gloves were essential for camera and film manipulation, so that fingers would not freeze to the camera. The National Film Board ensured that Racine was equipped with a pair of silk gloves, woollen mittens with a trigger finger, and large leather mitts with a canvas back and trigger finger. Because Racine was forced to work alone, he carried a bag of four or five reels of spare film stock. On average, he shot ten reels of 100-foot rolls a day, depending on the activity at hand. A tripod was provided but was never used, as Racine explains, 'At 70 degrees below zero, you don't have time to set up a tripod. You just shoot!' (Racine 2013).

Although most of the force had received intensive training on igloo building and cold climate survival, additional challenges ensued. An average day's travel totalled approximately 60 miles, and short daylight hours necessitated pitching camp at dark. The daily routine of travelling, setting up accommodations and eating were labour-intensive, leaving limited time to shoot film. The wind was a force in itself, especially when blizzards formed without warning. At times, velocity was measured at 50 miles per hour, and personnel had to dig out from a blowing snowstorm. Racine recounts the reality of his routine and mishaps:

> Daily, one must either build a snow house or put up a tent no matter if the meteorologist says the temperature is enough to kill a horse; but of course we aren't horses and we will survive, but the amount of time left for this actual camera work is but a few minutes daily, e.g. when we are not moving. So, one morning after drinking your morning coffee, you leave your tent to take out your equipment and discover the most unbelievable sight offered to the eyes of the human animal, and after rushing to the compartment of your snowmobile and take out the old camera you discover that the snow after blowing all night has infiltrated itself in the lens. (Racine 1947)

With his camera, Racine documented stops and encampments, living conditions, scenery, wildlife, events, daily activities and Northern inhabitants encountered along the way. The moving force halted at Cambridge Bay for seven days where Racine documented the men billeting on board the docked Royal Canadian Mounted Police patrol and supply vessel St Roch (in 1940–2 she became the first vessel to complete a voyage through the Northwest Passage in a west to east direction), activities of the Royal Canadian Mounted Police wireless office and happenings at the Hudson's Bay Company post. In Coppermine, he captured a human side to the trek when the force was met by Inuit who were curious about the snowmobile caravan. Many were invited on board to take a closer look. Upon arrival at Dismal Lake, Racine was keen to capture the first trees that the crew had encountered since Churchill. Here, scientists conducted snow tests to record thickness, depth, hardness and crystal formation, and other scientists studied the performance of oils, lubricants, rubber, anti-freeze, fuel and metal, which would be useful findings for the Canadian Army and private industries. Footage also included the arrival of mail, the difficulties of wireless reception, snowmobile motor replacement with flown-in parts, the Eldorado uranium and radium mine in Port Radium, the 225-mile crossing of Great Bear Lake, the most northerly of freshwater lakes in North America, accomplished in three days, and a large caribou migration. On the southerly descent, Racine's camera observed the first signs of spring, including night travelling given that snow conditions during daytime were too soft for travel.

Spring floods meant improvising to build bridges and rafts to float the snow-mobiles across the Mackenzie and Lyard rivers. Racine is particularly grateful that Croft documented the Mackenzie River crossing with his camera, given that he was running low on film stock. Also, they could not have shot the film without the use of flares to properly illuminate and document this notable feat. Dust storms were common as they travelled south on the Alcan Highway, causing severe mechanical snowmobile failure, forcing them to resort to riding the last 407 miles by rail to Edmonton. The men of Musk-Ox were greeted by crowds lining the streets of Grande Prairie, Alberta, as snowmobiles paraded through the town. Celebrations ensued in Edmonton, at a dinner hosted in their honour by the mayor of Edmonton. Racine's completed film reels were shipped back to various bases in specially designed canvas bags, and then transported back to the National Film Board in Ottawa, for processing.

The press and newsreel companies played an important role in stimulating national and international interest in Canada's 'Northland', with newspaper headlines such as 'Harvard scientists leave city on way to test Musk-Ox troops', 'Foreign groups observe Muskox', and 'Expects Muskox to clear up many secrets of Arctic'. Newsreel cameramen from Associated Screen News and Fox Movietone News journeyed to both the starting (Churchill) and finishing (Edmonton) points of Exercise Musk-Ox, to ensure full coverage, for dissemination in theatres, of this newsworthy event with newsreels such as Fox Movietone's *Operation Musk-Ox Starts at Churchill, Manitoba* (USA, 1946).

Overall, Exercise Musk-Ox was successful in that the force accomplished its goal of completing the long-distance trek, and doing so in the predicted eighty-one days. A post-expedition report compiled from notes submitted by personnel and observers, including Racine and Croft, provided observations on winter travel and new uses for aircraft, the need for improved clothing, equipment and rations. Recommendations included furthering the pioneering of Arctic resources, providing that men be properly trained and equipped to live and travel in safety. The possibility existed for some of the equipment used during Musk-Ox to be adapted for civilian needs. Racine's footage would be considered the official Canadian Army motion picture record for Exercise Musk-Ox. Despite countless challenges, his work paid off in shooting *Exercise Musk-Ox* (1946), a black and white, 58-minute documentary, directed by Douglas Wilkinson and narrated by Robert Anderson.

Even with wartime restraints, the National Film Board met much success in distributing its *Canada Carries On* series to nearly 700 theatres across Canada. By going to the movies, Canadians would be entertained by a feature, and also take pride in their contributions to the war effort, by watching a short propaganda film. The National Film Board produced an abbreviated

11-minute version of *Exercise Musk-Ox*, as part of the very successful *Canada Carries On* series, entitled *White Safari*, directed by Hugh Wallace, produced by Sydney Newman, and released in theatres in 1946.

In most Musk-Ox diaries and writings, little is written about Roger Racine, the young man behind the camera, but like most cameramen, he mostly preferred to let the camera do the talking. Baird praises Racine, as he recounts in one of his personal accounts, 'One of the hardest workers was our photographer, Sergeant Roger Racine, who often started on a leading machine, and after leaping off to run his movie camera, would have to scramble on to another vehicle for perhaps much of the rest of the day. Roger had been with me on Lemming. He draws the toughest assignments' (Baird 1978: 28–9). A *Montreal Gazette* review praises Racine as having done:

> an outstanding photographic job on Musk-Ox, with hardly a foot of the 45,000 that wasn't excellent from all standpoints. Whittling this tremendous footage down to the one-reel (1000 feet) size was no soft job. The result is the absolute cream of the (footage) turned in by Racine, a realistic record of the 3000-mile trek. So bitterly do the blizzards blow and so ice-draped, chilled and shivery do the men appear in the film that audiences will, it is claimed, be able to imagine frost rings on the theatre screen. (Anon., *Montreal Gazette* 1946)

After the sun had set on this truly incredible Arctic journey, Racine shared a different perspective of his observations relating to the natural beauty that greeted him through the lens of his camera:

> The Arctic is all at once the most desolate and yet about the most photogenic country I've been in. But, most of all, the great surprise that awaits the man who survives the climate is a paradise of colour. The few hours offered to the lens, is an invitation to the one who wants to picture the north with all its fantastic effects and peculiarities. In order to do this, one must be ready at a moment's notice, to shoot whatever presents itself to the camera, whether it be a snowmobile rolling across the snow, or a burning horizon piercing the moving surface of the snow covered barrens. (Racine 1947)

BIBLIOGRAPHY

Anon. (1946), 'Musk-Ox film record problem for N.F.B.', *Montreal Gazette*, 20 July.
Baird, P. (n.d.), Patrick Douglas Baird fonds, Diary of Patrick Douglas Baird, Library and Archives Canada, 28 October 1938, file 1–1.
Baird, P. (1978) 'Musk-Ox retold', *North/Nord*, September/October, 27.

Canadian Department of National Defence (1945), 'Exercise Lemming, CAORG Report No. 25', Ottawa: Department of National Defence, 21.

Caron, M. (2010), *Roger Racine: directeur photo*, Montreal: Le programme cinéma de l'école des médias de l'UQAM.

Eastman Kodak (1945), *Report of the Preparation and Operation of Cameras*, Rochester: Eastman Kodak Company, 1–2.

Halliday, H. A. (1945) 'Recapturing the North. Exercises "Eskimo," "Polar Bear" and "Lemming"', *Canadian Military History* 6.2: 30–6.

National Film Board of Canada (1944), Exercise Eskimo documentation file, minutes of a meeting held 9 September 1944 between Mr J. Grierson. Commissioner National Film Board of Canada and Colonel J. T. Wilson, Director of Operational Research, NDHQ, held as National Film Board.

Racine, R. (1947) 'Documentation of Exercise Musk-Ox', in Exercise Musk-Ox production file, National Film Board of Canada.

Racine, R. (2013) Telephone interview with Roger Racine, Montréal, Québec, 5 March.

19. *THE TOUR:* A FILM ABOUT LONGYEARBYEN, SVALBARD. AN INTERVIEW WITH EVA LA COUR

Johanne Haaber Ihle

Q. What is The Tour?

The Tour is a video montage produced as part of a thesis on Media and Visual Anthropology at the Freie Universität in Berlin, based on fieldwork in Longyearbyen on Svalbard in 2011 – a Norwegian archipelago in the High Arctic. Here I focused on a set of research questions around the relationship between lived and projected realities on Svalbard, which I sought to explore among a group of taxi drivers and by working as a taxi driver myself.

Retrospectively I would say that I was exploring, on the one hand, the notion of the guided tour as an institution for authorised perspectives on 'the ideal' and, on the other hand, the figure of the guide as an individual with personal motives, anticipations and value judgments relative to the place. The guided tour of Longyearbyen was interesting to me as Svalbard in many ways functions as representative for the Arctic, particularly visually. However, in crucial respects Svalbard challenges traditional ideas and perceptions of anthropology within regional Arctic studies, as the archipelago does not have a native population. Rather, the social environment on Svalbard has always been characterised by a great sense of temporality, as settlers of many different nationalities have come to work at the islands for a limited period of time: as whalers, explorers, scientists and miners, but also as service workers in the growing tourism industry, or merely as visitors and adventurers. This means that a high turnover of people has taken place continuously. Being there as an anthropologist, oneself becomes part of a shifting community within and across Svalbard, contributing to undermine the idea of a coherent and permanent community within certain geographical parameters. Today, residents stay at Svalbard for an average period of only four years.

Only a few people have lived in Longyearbyen, the main settlement of the islands, for most of their life. It is more common to leave the islands after a limited period of time and then, eventually, come back up again for another period of time. While Longyearbyen has around 2,000 inhabitants, many more people may have a feeling of belonging to the place.

The diverse composition of Svalbard society also has its historical reasons. When the Svalbard Treaty came into being and Norway gained, in 1925, the sovereignty of the archipelago, all the signing parties ensured their rights to continue activities and ownership of territories already claimed. Interestingly, the treaty continues to exceed Norwegian national law today and contributes to a feeling of being in a state of exception, where extremely different life stories account for a hyperconstructed society, of which any simple explanation and representation collapses.

It has become much easier and cheaper to get to Svalbard and to live there (if you find a job; if not, it is expensive). Moreover, during the past twenty-five years, the local communities have undergone a transformation. What used to be a company town relying on material extraction (coal-mining) has become differentiated and liberalised markets relying also on the production of knowl-

Figure 19.1   Eva la Cour's *The Tour* (2012).

edge and experiences – on science and tourism, that is. And with tourism comes an urgent need to reinvent an Arctic identity drawing on beautiful images of the past and contemporary discourses of the Far North, in order to generate cultural affection and economic investments. In my film, this particularly comes across as anticipations for the brand *Arctic-Tapas*, patented worldwide by one of the taxi drivers. In this regard, finally, development in Longyearbyen has been highly influenced by changes within international (post-Cold War) politics as well as by the global focus on climatic change, and by new information technologies that circulate and spread images of the Arctic 'out of context' and into the swirl of permanent deterritorialisation.

Q. Why did you choose to address this subject through film?
Drawing on classical methods within the field of ethnographic filmmaking – most importantly the observational style of filming – I chose to shoot most of my film through the windshield of a taxi mimicking the screen of a cinema and presenting the actual environment from the delimited space of the taxi. In a taxi, an Australian tourist is on a guided tour through the landscape. However, apart from this long single shot inside the taxi, the photographing style of the film is handheld, incorporating my own presence. Thus I address the problem of the location of the self within an image culture, while I suggest that the actual guided taxi tour, as much as the audiovisual montage of the film, structures a journey through a complex configuration of past events, physical buildings and particular objects, people and information.

This said, I wanted to make a film reflecting the particularities characterising Longyearbyen through an attempt to formally reflect these points: to appear immediate, to emphasise temporality and to juxtapose contradictions. For example, the interrupting and abrupt black frames throughout the film indicate the immediate collapse of representation and the incoherency and temporality of the place – that each visit to Longyearbyen is its own fractured encounter. The fact that these black spots are always present when my Russian protagonist is speaking can furthermore be regarded as an attempt to comment on the wide variety of life and life stories in Longyearbyen, which does not fit the stereotypical ideas and representations of life on Svalbard. In the film my three protagonists – a Danish, Norwegian and Russian taxi driver – articulate three very different motives and expectations of being in Longyearbyen.

Many films made on Svalbard are spectacular in a way which becomes ironically normative. Stereotypical and romantic ideas of 'the Arctic', labelled as the extreme, transgressive and sublime, are often expressed without much reflection on how such labels themselves are changing their cultural meaning gradually as the Arctic becomes more reachable and less risky and isolated. The opportunity to make a film was thus also an opportunity for me to somehow reflect on the conventional filmic portrayals of Svalbard.

Q. How is your film positioned between the fields of contemporary art and visual anthropology?

I think ethnographic films produced during a long-term fieldwork and in conjunction with a text have the potential to offer insights into social environments that go beyond mainstream representations. Such films often circulate in other contexts than, say, Hollywood movies, commercials or political campaigns, as they often address issues primarily interesting to scholars of cultural studies. Their aim is not to reach out to a big and diverse target audience or to generate economic yield, which means one is allowed to, e.g., incorporate social theory in the visual work without thorough explanation. But this also limits your audience. Moreover, I find that the discipline we denominate as 'ethnographic filmmaking' is dominated by rigid ideas of what makes film valuable to social science.

However, drawing on my training as a visual artist, I do find it relevant to make distinctions between a film's different qualities. For example, I believe artistic practices have a lot to offer epistemological inquiries within anthropology, but this potential is not what qualifies the outcome of such practices as art. Likewise the other way around: while anthropology gives birth to ideas and experiments to be explored artistically, I believe it is the task of anthropology to stay open to artistic works, methodologies and strategies relevant to anthropology. But let me be clear, this does not prevent works from entailing both 'anthropological' and 'artistic' qualities!

In the case of *The Tour*, the style of editing, for example – associative and in a montage style – has been commented as an experimental strategy drawing on my background as a visual artist. However, my primary ambition in this regard was to contribute to a broader debate about visual representations of the Arctic and the purposes of such. Fortunately, art and anthropology departments at universities tend to work closer together now than before, which means a new style of experimental filmmaking in anthropological contexts is taking shape.

Q. In what contexts have you screened your film and what were the reactions to it?

The Tour has been screened in ethnographic settings, but it has also been screened in contexts where most ethnographic films do not usually circulate, for example at established art galleries and independent film festivals. Thus, although originally part of a written thesis, my film has been reviewed in its own right in such settings. But there are layers of information in the film which are not accessible without an introduction to the complexities of Svalbard's history and politics, without 'thick descriptions' (of personal life stories and working conditions or of my personal relations with my protagonists, the cold temperatures during filming, changes of light – not to mention the process of post-production). The inclusion of such background information about the production is regarded as crucial in an anthropological context, but in a film product they can be left out. At regular ethnographic festivals, the choices and structure of the film have therefore been questioned sometimes. For example, the fact that you do not get a proper introduction to my protagonists and see their faces, has been debated. More surprisingly, I was once asked whether the black frames I mentioned earlier were only included because I had too little visual material! It has been easier for audiences interested in experimental cinema and visual anthropology to read and accept the style of the film as an independent work.

It has been crucial for me to try to understand relations between perceptions of my film and environments of its presentation – to regard the circulation of *The Tour* as an exploration of contexts and to avoid uncritical assumptions about 'neutral settings'. In the age of digital media production and file sharing, contexts of presentation include emerging venues and specialised sections at established film festivals, but also classrooms across disciplines and the private screens of a dispersed audience.

Obviously all this relates quite directly to my interest in the mediation of Svalbard. Not as a matter of the real Arctic, but as a matter of a reality of Arctic images circulating as and generating works of imaginations that ascribe cultural value to Svalbard as a tourist destination. (This term is borrowed from Appadurai who uses it to describe the influence of particularly media and migration on modern globalised reality). This might be the case of any place out of reach. However, the demographic constellation, geographical conditions and political constructions particular to Svalbard, as mentioned earlier, make the archipelago a great example (or image) of the Arctic as a space widely open for projections.

Q. But are all geographical areas not subject to oral and visual discourses creating stereotypical ideas of culture and spaces? And do such ideas not always reflect and serve various contexts and purposes? For example, how do you see a difference between the Western representations of Arctic regions and the representations of the Middle East criticised by Said in Orientalism?

Different scholars have used and translated Said's notion of Orientalism to what has been called 'Arctiisme'. Kirsten Thisted has, for example, shown how Greenland, particularly in a Danish context, historically (but still to some extent) has functioned as a fixation of that which both fascinated and disgusted official Denmark: mystery, artistic naivety and survivability in the harsh Arctic nature.

Now, in the case of Svalbard, historians and archaeologists are still discussing its discovery – by Russian Pomors? the Icelandic Vikings? or the Dutch navigator William Barentz? – but, compared to other regions in the Arctic,

259

'history' on Svalbard can be regarded as almost non-existing. At a conference, speaking to a group of physicists in 2009, Jim Oveland said, 'I guess this morning I am speaking for the polar bears'. What he referred to was the fact that 'the authentic voice' is not a man's or a woman's voice, and it is possible to argue that the polar bear is a substitute for 'the Other' since the Other is not present, but the idea of polar bears is. Semiotics play a key role in the processes of mediation. The cold, the white, the landscape formations, the bears, and so on, are gateways for self-projection of Arctic identities.

That said, *The Tour* emphasises how Longyearbyen on Svalbard is far from a blank page, but rather a constant montaging of stories. The taxi guided tour mixes in with numerous and constant (interrelational and institutional) encounters in Longyearbyen. That collapses the idea of a 'pure image' or representation. Rather, such encounters expose how mediation and experience are interdependent and simultaneous processes.

PART IV

MYTHS AND MODES OF EXPLORATION

PART IV. MYTHS AND MODES OF EXPLORATION

Scott MacKenzie and Anna Westerståhl Stenport

Cinema quickly became an extension of late nineteenth- and early twentieth-century exploration. These films captivated audiences around the world with images of a remote and largely unknown region and its indigenous populations. These films also documented the grandiose and perilous journeys of the explorers themselves. Filming was made more difficult by the limitations of technology in the extreme cold; the ability to document was often thwarted by brittle film and frozen cameras. Some explorer films were mostly about the expedition itself, where the returning explorer would often try to support new expeditions by showing films about his journeys on lecture tours. Others were about conquering the Arctic through the introduction of technologies that compressed space and time, such as the aeroplane or the railway. The final section of *Films on Ice* presents a historical trajectory from the very earliest filmmaking shot in the Arctic to contemporary digital media ruminating on the past, and it unearths a plethora of films that have been left out of the film historical canon. In the chapter 'The Changing Polar Films: Silent Films from Arctic Exploration 1900–30', Jan Anders Diesen discusses not only the first known examples of film shot in the polar region, but also elucidates the role polar expedition films played as cinema was becoming a broad attraction globally. Analysing footage from archives around the world, Diesen contextualises how mass media and technological developments for capturing and relaying to the world feats of exploration, often in the service of nationalism or personal gain, have come to shape the perception of the Arctic region to this day. Marina Dahlquist demonstrates in 'The Attractions of the North: Early Film Expeditions to the Exotic

Snowscape', how a large number of *actualités* – short non-fiction films from the early history of cinema – set in the Arctic are built around the exotisation and Othering of the Sámi. In 'Frozen in Motion: Ethnographic Representation in Donald B. MacMillan's Arctic Films', Rebecca Genauer examines how the explorer and prolific Arctic filmmaker MacMillan, who went on Robert Peary's 1908–9 expedition, disavowed narrative and generic conventions of ethnographic representation, which allowed his films to break from the supposed verisimilitude characteristic of contemporary explorer films. In '"My Heart Beat for the Wilderness": Isobel Wylie Hutchison, Jenny Gilbertson, Margaret Tait and Other Twentieth-Century Scottish Women Filmmakers', Sarah Neely explores the works of three Scottish women filmmakers who made films in the Arctic. These women are part of a largely unwritten history of the cinema: it was rare enough in the 1930s to be directing films; to have them go to the Arctic on expeditions is mostly unheard of. The trope of Arctic exploration has been used for political purposes all over the world, and the Soviet Union was no exception, as Lyubov Bugaeva argues in 'Here will be a Garden-City': Soviet Man on an Arctic Construction Site'. Bugaeva examines how Stalinist doctrines in Soviet cinema of the 1930s were reconfigured in films about Arctic expeditions by later generations of filmmakers in the 1970s. In 'Transcending the Sublime: Arctic Creolisation in the Works of Isaac Julien and John Akomfrah', Helga Hlaðgerður Lúthersdóttir analyses the aesthetic strategies and political impetus of contemporary film artists who challenge the notion of an Arctic explorer as a heroic white male, striding forth on his own to conquer the white sublime. This analysis allows her to foreground a complementary historical and cinematic record, which is explicit about the significance of identity politics and colonial legacies in the North, rather than reifying established representational norms. Our concluding chapter, 'DJ Spooky and Dziga Vertov: Experimental Cinema Meets Digital Art in Exploring the Polar Regions', by Daria Shembel, examines the montage-based filmmaking practice of Soviet director Dziga Vertov. Shembel puts this practice in productive tension with the recent work of DJ Spooky, and explores how Vertov's proto-digitality techniques greatly inspired contemporary multimedia artist Spooky in his Antarctic and Arctic projects.

20. THE CHANGING POLAR FILMS: SILENT FILMS FROM ARCTIC EXPLORATION 1900–30

Jan Anders Diesen

The Heroic Era of polar exploration – roughly from the 1890s to the death of Sir Ernest Shackleton in the early 1920s – produced many fascinating stories about remarkable men. The races to the Poles are richly described in hundreds of books, but this era also coincided with the development of film technology and the rise of commercial cinema. Many polar explorers saw potential in using this new technology as a research tool, and their sponsors saw the huge entertainment value of such recordings. As a result, a range of films from the polar expeditions of this era was created. Aside from some of the feature-length titles from Antarctica, such as Herbert Ponting's *Great White Silence* (UK, 1924) and Frank Hurley's *South* (UK, 1919), the polar films as a sub-genre have received little attention compared with the written accounts. The as-yet-unwritten story of these films is a rewarding one, with much to tell us not only about the extraordinary achievements of the first polar explorers and their pioneering cameramen, but also about the development of filmmaking and the cinema, and even the tastes of audiences and the fortunes of empires and nation-states.

With the advent of the aeroplane, the airship and the telegraph, the Mechanical Era of polar exploration had arrived. The Norwegian explorer Roald Amundsen played a major role in the development of this era; he claimed his use of aeroplanes was as important to the progress of polar exploration as his countryman Fridtjof Nansen's use of skis and dog sledges had been in the Heroic Era. Also during this period, the documentary film became a popular genre as a result of films such as *Nanook of the North* (Robert Flaherty, USA,

1922), *Grass* (Merian C. Cooper and Ernest B. Schoedsack, USA, 1925) and Osa and Martin Johnson's many safari documentaries. Newsreels also became popular, and many film companies around the world competed to get the best news items for their weekly news reviews. There were many such films from the Arctic in this period. The following examples illustrate how the explorers' motives for bringing a film camera changed, and also how polar expeditions became media events when distributed through the cinemas, and as constitutive features of early twentieth-century press and news media culture. Through a few examples, we will see how the explorers' motives for bringing a film camera changed, and also how polar expeditions became media events even in the cinemas.

DOCUMENTING EVENTS AND PLACES

The races for the Poles were costly, and many explorers needed financial support. The first well-equipped North Pole expedition in the twentieth century was the Baldwin-Ziegler Expedition of 1901–2. In an attempt to reach the North Pole, three ships sailed from the US to Franz Josef Land. The expedition comprised forty-two men equipped with 35 Siberian ponies, 400 dogs, air balloons, scientific equipment and tons of food. The leader of the expedition was Evelyn Briggs Baldwin, but the man who made the expedition possible was the American baking powder millionaire William Ziegler.

Ziegler claimed that: 'there was no problem, from baking soda to polar exploration, which could not be solved by American capital' (Capelotti 2008: 55). He was very rich, but he wanted to be famous as well, and he thought he could become so by tying his name to the first expedition to reach the North Pole. However, the expedition did not reach its goal and Baldwin had to be rescued from the coastal islands. The scientific gains of the expedition did not make Ziegler any happier. In an interview he said:

> All I want is to reach the North Pole. I don't care how much money it costs. If I can plant the Stars and Stripes there, I'll be the happiest man in the United States. I'm not after scientific research, although I know we will get as much as anyone. It doesn't matter if one expedition has failed. I'll send another. It won't be a lot of cigarette smoking dudes this time ... I sent Baldwin to discover the North Pole, not to eat pie or smoke cigarettes. The bone and sinew of a nation is not in its pie eaters or its cigarette smokers. (*Kansas City Star*, 1902; cited in Capelotti 2008: 67)

The following year Ziegler equipped a new expedition: the Ziegler Polar Expedition (AKA the Fiala-Ziegler Expedition) (1903–5). The leader was Anthony Fiala, who had been second in command and official photographer on the first expedition. The second Ziegler expedition was no more success-ful than the first, but Fiala did escape the anger of the fame-seeking million-aire: William Ziegler died before the expedition's return. Fiala did achieve one important success: he was the first person to bring moving images back from the Arctic. Ziegler wanted visual proof from the North Pole and hired a professional photographer as an important member of the expedition. The expedition's achievements were described in *National Geographic Magazine*: 'The Expedition, Mr Baldwin states, has yielded valuable results from a scien-tific point of view, especially in the direction of meteorology. The collection of photographs and kinematographs brought home is quite unique' (*National Geographic Magazine* 1902). These unique photographs and segments of film footage were not good enough for Ziegler, and they were not published. A obituary written in *National Geographic Magazine* in 1905 explains why Ziegler did not show these unique film takes to the public: 'Ziegler felt so badly about the failure of the expedition that he refused to give the pictures to the public until he should have something more to announce' (*National Geographic Magazine* 1905).

Fiala's film footage, as the first ever moving footage of the Arctic, is important, but just as important is the fact that he shared his knowledge on how he managed to secure those moving images from the polar regions. He wrote about the subject in articles and in a book for Kodak. His *National Geographic Magazine* article 'Polar Photography' is one of the first printed records to describe the specifics of shooting still and moving images in Arctic environments, and how the climate impacts both image composition and exposure.

> Part of the outfit comprised a bioscope, a form of moving-picture camera, with which I hoped to secure views of men, dogs, and ponies moving over the ice-fields, the advance of the *America* through the ice, and, if possible, a bear fight. Of all my photographic apparatus, the bioscope gave me the most trouble, particularly in the low temperature of spring and early autumn. The long celluloid film upon which the numerous little negatives were made (twenty to a second) became very brittle under the influence of the extreme cold, and would fly to pieces when the mechanism of the instrument was started, and pieces of celluloid would clog the gear wheels and jam between moving parts. After many failures, I hit upon the plan of warming the machine and wrapping it up in hot blankets just before taking a picture. The heating and wrapping was done in the hut at camp. I was thus enabled to secure some valuable films; a few of them reached a length of 300 feet. But always, as soon as the instrument became cold, the films broke like fragile glass. It was impossible to warm the bioscope on the trail, so I was limited to views near the ship and in the vicinity of camp.

We shot a number of bears for food. A bear fighting for his life, surrounded by a biting, snarling pack of dogs, would have been a splendid subject for a moving camera; but I was never so fortunate as to have camera and fight at the same time.

The pictures which show the ponies and dogs hauling their loaded sledges over the ice bring back in vivid reality the cold, white fields and the struggling men and animals fighting their way over the frozen wastes.

The explorer with a camera has gone over very nearly all the earth and has brought back as part of his record views of life and land in the far-off parts of the earth.

There is still land to be conquered; and it is good to know that when these unknown places are found and the flags of discovery are planted, that with the help of the sun and modern chemistry, we will all be able to view with the explorer what had once been forbidden and mysterious territory. (Fiala 1907: sec. 141f)

Fiala encountered the same problems that explorers in Antarctica had met earlier, and he solved them in his own way. For many years explorers had struggled to make film camera work in the cold climat, and Fiala's more famous colleague from England, Herbert Ponting, also wrote about his experiences. His book, *The Great White South*, contains abundant advice to fellow photographers working in polar regions: 'perhaps a few of the troubles I learned to avoid may be of interest' (Ponting 1923: 169). The most important advice was to remove all oil from the moveable parts of the camera. Fiala's and Ponting's accounts show that not only was polar photography difficult, but the technical limitations impacted the representation of polar and Arctic landscapes which to most audiences were already alien, unknown and different.

To 'thread' a film into a kinematograph camera, in low temperature, was an unpleasant job, for it was necessary to use bare fingers whilst doing so. Often when my fingers touched metal they became frostbitten. Such a frostbite feels exactly like a burn. Once, thoughtlessly, I held a camera screw for a moment in my mouth. It froze instantly to my lips, and took the skin off when I removed it. (Ponting 1923: 171)

Though Fiala's film was not screened in cinemas in the US, he did occasionally show some of the footage during his American lecture tours. It was, however, released some years later in England by the Charles Urban Trading

Company, under the title *A Dash to the North Pole* in 1909. The company's catalogue gives us an impression of Fiala's pioneering work:

A DASH FOR THE NORTH POLE

Showing the Hardships and Activity of the Members of the Ziegler Polar Expedition, under command of Anthony Fiala.

Instead of the usual monotony and lifelessness portrayed in other Polar Subjects, the entire length of this film brims with the greatest activity, occasioned by the momentous work achieved by a crew of 40 men and over 35 ponies and 450 dogs. (Urban 1912)

The catalogue adds to the synopsis with descriptions of eighteen scenes from the film: there are scenes from the voyage from Norway to Franz Josef Land and from the preparation for the dash for the Pole. Fiala's footage of men, dogs and horses close to the ships harbouring on Franz Josef Land shows us some of the difficulties they had with stormy weather and misplaced ponies. The last two scenes show: (17) 'Shooting the last Pony to Feed the Dogs' and (18) 'The Final Dash for the Pole. Laborious hauling of Sledges by Dogs and Selected Members of the Expedition, and many episodes never before Kinematographed'.[1]

ACTUALITÉS

Polar expeditions were media events, and newspapers around the world followed their progress. Around the turn of the century, the growing film industry was producing increasing numbers of actualities – short films of newsworthy events – and polar expeditions were sought-after subject-matter. Between 1894 and 1909, the American journalist Walter Wellman organised and led five expeditions in search of the North Pole (Capelotti 1999). The role of journalists was changing: they were not limited to recording events, but could also initiate them. Wellman's most ambitious attempt to make news was in 1906, when he constructed a base camp for his airship on Danskøya (Danes Island) at Svalbard, planning to fly over the Pole. *The Chicago Record–Herald*'s wealthy owner, Victor Lawson, sponsored Wellman's trip knowing that such material sold newspapers.

The expedition was a media event long before Wellman left for the Northern reaches with his airship. His plans were first announced in the American newspapers, and the European publications were not far behind. In Norway, Wellman was already front-page material when he moved north to establish his base on Danes Island in Svalbard. Many newspapers agreed that this was a great media event: 'Correspondent Walter Wellman's assignment to build an airship, proceed to the North Pole and report by wireless is the biggest one yet. It even outdoes Mr Bennett's memorable order to Mr Stanley to go to Africa and find Livingston (*Boston Herald*, 3 January 1906, quoted in Capelotti 1999: 119). In addition to attracting journalists and tourists and filling the newspapers with material on the Arctic, Wellman managed to awaken the interest of the infant film business. Two British film companies tried to get onboard the airship to make a film of the event. The Warwick Trading Company won the contract to follow Wellman:

> By courtesy of Walter Wellman, Esq. of The Wellman Record–Herald Polar Expedition, accommodation has been made to allow one of our operators to accompany the expedition, to what we hope will be their destination, the North Pole. As many of our readers are aware, the participators in this scheme are hopeful of carrying out their project by means of a gigantic Air Ship, in conjunction with Motor Sleighs, etc. The building of the air house and gas works, the putting together of the air ship, the trials, the departure, and, we hope, their successful return, should make one of the most unique series of animated pictures ever yet 'Bioscoped'. (*Cinematography and Bioscope Magazine* 1906)

The Warwick Trading Company's ambitious film project was never completed: Wellman did not make an attempt on the Pole in 1906. He did make an attempt the next summer, and also in 1909, but without any great success: he and his airship barely left the base.

Although Warwick failed to produce a film of the event, one does exist. Warwick's rival, the Urban Trading Company, had sent one of its photographers north on a tourist ship. On 30 May 1907, while the newspapers were filled with articles about Wellman's new attempt, an advertisement appeared in *The Kinematograph and Lantern Weekly* describing the newly released film *The Wellman Polar Expedition*:

> The departure from England on May 25th, of Mr Wellman, on his second attempt to reach the North Pole by Airship, having aroused special and general interest, we beg to remind Exhibitors and the Trade that the Urban Series furnishes absolutely the only animated picture record of the first attempt, in July of last year, and that it will prove all the more interesting and valuable on that account.

> A Unique and Beautifully Photographed Subject.

> Subject introduced: – In the Arctic Regions: Hunting Party leaving for the Coast. Panoramas of Bergen, Spitzbergen and the Fiords. – Life in a Lapland Village. – Return from the Hunt. – The Steamer aground on a

rock. – Visit to Danes Island. – Arrival at Mr Wellman's Headquarters. – Landing of the Scientific Party. – Panorama of the Camp. – Group of Lap Guides. – Mr Wellman leaving Danes Island etc., etc. (*Kinematograph and Lantern Weekly* 1907)

The footage of real events and places presented in the actualities was popular in cinema programmes. However, the audience grew to desire more structured films, and the polar explorers began to create documentaries and newsreels.

Travelogues and Ethnographic Film

George Hubert Wilkins started his career as a projectionist in a travelling cinema in South Australia. Even as a teenager, he understood that the camera could be his ticket to the world:

> Camera operators were racing one another to be the first with the pictures of coronations, wars and social struggles, and by 1912 their films were being updated in cinemas twice a week. Young Wilkins, with his enthusiasm and impressive abilities, was just the type for such a job, and the Gaumont man offered him work in London as soon as he could get there. (Nasht 2005: 18)

Wilkins made travelogues, actualities and news films, from 1908 onward, as a photographer for the Gaumont Company. He travelled the world filming pre-World War I military manoeuvres, battle scenes from the Balkan War, and the cocoa industry in Trinidad (Jenness 2004: 4).

In 1913, Wilkins was asked to be the photographer on an Arctic expedition led by the Canadian explorer Vilhjalmur Stefansson. Stefansson organised and directed the *Canadian Arctic Expedition* 1913–16, the purpose of which was to explore the northern part of Canada for the government. He had, on an earlier expedition in 1910, met Inuit groups who had never before encountered Europeans. Stefansson tasked Wilkins with securing footage of this group and their way of life. Wilkins travelled north in the spring of 1915 to meet them. In his diary, he describes the meeting and writes notes on the scenes he captures: 'the women at the camp as they mended boots, cleaning a seal skin, repaired an arrow, and later brought the caribou meat back from the hunting grounds' (quoted in Jenness 2004: 229).

> During the day, Wilkins wandered about the village seeking interesting scenes to photograph. The weather continued to be unfavourable, but he still managed to obtain several satisfactory pictures. He also obtained motion pictures of the Eskimos going about their normal daily activities and a number of close-up photographs (he called them 'figure studies'

of men, women, and children. One of these was of an intense young Coppermine River Eskimo, Anivrunna, seated by a tent singing and drumming, a picture that has been reproduced many times since. (Jenness 2004: 236)

Wilkins's film footage of these isolated Inuit is among the earliest ethnological films ever taken – many years before Flaherty would make his famous picture *Nanook of the North*. Wilkins filmed hunting and fishing scenes, and camping life. Unfortunately, he had problems with his camera while he was filming the Inuits hunting seals:

> During the next few days, Wilkins repaired his motion-picture camera and photographed some of the Eskimos seal hunting on the ice with their dogs. The dogs sniffed for the seals' breathing holes, which were generally snow covered. Once a hole was found, the Eskimos cleared the snow away, enlarged the central hole to about three inches in diameter, and set a floating indicator in the hole. The hunter then stood back, spear in hand, poised ready to strike. He would maintain this position for minutes or hours. When the seal poked its nose through the surface to breathe, it bumped the indicator, thereby alerting the hunter, who immediately plunged his spear into the hole, sometimes striking the seal in the head, sometimes in the neck or shoulder. To his great annoyance, Wilkins' motion-picture camera jammed after he had taken only a few feet, and he was unable to obtain the footage he wanted. (Jenness 2004: 329)

George Hubert Wilkins managed to secure about 9,000 feet of film footage during the years he spent with Stefansson, between 1913 and 1916,[2] a valuable scientific document of the lives of indigenous peoples in the Arctic.

PUBLIC LECTURES AND LECTURE FILMS

Many of the polar explorers devoted considerable time to lecturing about their expeditions. These appearances could be lucrative: Fridtjof Nansen earned as much per lecture when he toured the United States after his North Pole expedition in 1893–6, as he earned a year as a professor at the University of Oslo.[3] Roald Amundsen began conducting lectures after traversing the Northwest Passage in 1906. Later, after his success at the South Pole and several expeditions to the North, he spent much of the time between expeditions lecturing. Most of Amundsen's lecture activities took place abroad: the Norwegian market was not big enough for the polar explorer.

Lectures were popular entertainment for upper-class citizens in the metropolises of the world. Even though a few lecturers did well alone on stage, the lecture genre developed into what the Americans termed 'the Picture talks': illustrated lectures. The lecturers brought glass plates with hand-painted tableaus and hand-coloured photographs. The pictures were projected onto a screen, as slides, some even to musical accompaniment. In order to fill the lecture halls, the lecturers had to resort to various multimedia measures. A few professional 'showmen' toured with multimedia shows including slides, film, music and sound effects.

Amundsen did not want to be such a 'showman', even though he depended more and more upon his film footage. At the same time, he saw that documentary films from air expeditions, without a lecturer, were becoming popular in the cinemas. Consequently, he took professional film photographers on his attempted journeys to the North Pole. This resulted in four popular documentary films, created between 1923 and 1926.

DOCUMENTARIES

In his book *My Life As a Polar Explorer*, Amundsen writes of his interest in aircraft. He mentions how he had thought about the opportunities that aircraft opened up even before his South Pole conquests, and that he bought his first aircraft before World War I. In 1922, after the first part of the *Maud* expedition was concluded, he threw himself passionately into his aircraft project. He viewed himself as the great polar pioneer in this field:

> In this book, I have previously explained the importance of Nansen's revolutionary new methods – how his use of the light sleds and dog teams had shown all those who came after him the secret of his long and rapid pushes towards the poles. For my part, I would claim to have discovered a similar improvement by using the aircraft as a means in the service of polar exploration. (Amundsen 1927: 97)

Amundsen wanted to fly from continent to continent, from Point Barrow in Alaska to Svalbard, over the North Pole. This flight attempt forms the main theme of the documentary entitled *With Roald Amundsen's North Pole Expedition to the First Winter Quarter* (Reidar Lund, 1923). The film shows how the aircraft was transported north to Alaska on board the *Maud*, the preparations for the flight attempt, the breakdown of the aircraft, and wintering, in addition to beautiful shots of animals and nature and some footage of the lives of the local Inuit people.

The film *Roald Amundsen – Lincoln Ellsworth's Polar Flight 1925* (Paul Berge/Oskar Omdal, 1925) centres on the daring expedition that almost ended in disaster at a latitude of 87 degrees 44 minutes north. It presents both the preparations and the triumphant return to Oslo. The film entitled *With*

Figure 20.1   The airship *Norge* being towed into the hangar at Ny-Ålesund, Svalbard.

Maud across the Arctic Ocean (Odd Dahl, 1926) follows the voyage of the *Maud* from Point Barrow through the Northeast Passage, while *The Airship Norge's Flight Across the Arctic Ocean* (Paul Berge/Emil Horgen, 1926) shows Amundsen's long-awaited conquest of the North Pole. These films filled the cinemas while Amundsen himself toured lecture halls around the world with his stills and lecture films.

The conquest of the North Pole by planes was also a race: other explorer-pilots were competing to be the first. The American Richard Byrd claimed to have been the first a few days before Amundsen's airship passed the Pole on its crossing of the Arctic Ocean. Byrd had newsreel photographers following the expedition, and he secured footage from the actual flight. The film *America's Polar Triumph* (Pathé, 1926) tells Byrd's story. In contrast to Amundsen's documentary films, the American counterpart is a film made to prove the conquest and to portray a heroic explorer.

PROPAGANDA FILMS

Umberto Nobile, the captain of Amundsen's airship, felt that he had received too little of the glory from the *Norge* expedition in 1926. He used every occasion after his return to garner praise and give interviews about his own role in the expedition:

> It is so strange, I do not understand. All Ellsworth did was to give money for the flight. It was I, Nobile, who designed the Norge; it was I, Nobile, who commanded it; it was I, Nobile, who was responsible for its success. Without me the flight would have been impossible! . . . Lincoln Ellsworth was just a passenger. . . . He was a nice passenger, but that was all. (General Nobile in the *Pittsburgh* newspaper, quoted in *Time Magazine* 1926)

The *New York Times* attempts to place the expedition in a more correct perspective in an article that begins: 'There should be glory enough for all the members of the Amundsen-Ellsworth-Nobile expedition'. In order to fly across the Arctic Ocean, Amundsen, Ellsworth and Nobile needed each other. Still, the article concludes that 'In the history of Arctic exploration, the Norwegian captain will always be recorded as the very first person to lead an expedition across the North Pole' (quoted in Amundsen 1927: 204).

However, Nobile did not feel he had been given enough credit, so he decided to organise a new polar journey. He received the help of Italy's dictator Benito Mussolini, who wanted to mark Italy on every map, including the Arctic one. Nobile built a new airship in 1924: the *Italia*. Mussolini wanted to make a film that would be useful as fascist propaganda: a film to confirm once and for all that it was Nobile and the Italians who had mastered airship navigation. Nobile was to repeat the feat alone in order to prove that Amundsen and his assistants had simply been passengers on the first voyage to the North Pole.

The expedition ended in catastrophe. The *Italia* crashed in the pack ice during the return trip from the North Pole, and the film never became the fascist propaganda vehicle it was planned to be. However, this event did open the way for the Soviet filmmakers to produce a propaganda film. The Soviet film *Heroic Deed Among the Ice* (Georgi and Sergei Vasilyev, USSR, 1928) showed some of the rescue work performed in the search for the *Italia*. The film caused an outcry even before its premiere, as Mussolini censored some images of the Italian crew members the Soviets had recovered from the pack ice. *Heroic Deed Among the Ice* (1928) was assembled by Georgi and Sergei Vasilyev from the footage shot on the expedition as a compilation film in the tradition of Soviet montage.

In *Kino: A History of the Russian and Soviet Film* (Leyda 1960), the film is described as typical of the Soviet montage. The filmmakers of Sovkino glorified the unselfish men on board the icebreaker, and in modern film literature *Heroic Deed Among the Ice* is mentioned as important for that reason.

> Icebreaker Krassin was significant because it initiated a new trend in Soviet filmmaking. Between 1928 and 1933 Soviet filmmakers paid less attention to historical subject and more to the developing Soviet society. Many of their films, including Icebreaker Krassin, were documentaries that glorified Soviet achievements while claiming objectivity. (Murrey 1990: s. 138)

Nobile's desire for a heroic narrative featuring elements of fascist propaganda ended in tragedy and a Soviet documentary featuring elements of communist propaganda. The influential power of film had been clearly highlighted in the Far North.

NEWSREELS

The *Italia* accident became a media sensation, and Svalbard's Ny-Ålesund was overrun by journalists and film reporters in the aftermath of the event:

> The fiercely competing film photographers did everything they could to secure passage on boats heading north. One wanted to rent an icebreaker, another film photographer who was evidently fond of his creature comforts asked whether there were scheduled boat departures to the North Cape from the north-eastern region. (Arnesen and Lundborg 1928: 84)

There were German, Italian, Soviet and American film photographers present at Svalbard to report from the accident. One of them was John Dored, a Paramount photographer. In his memoirs he describes how he travelled from Paramount's European head office in Paris to Svalbard. He found accommodation at the hospital in a room he had to share with two other film photographers: Hearst News and Pathé News had already moved in. The two other photographers informed Dored that the battle for the news was tough; the Italians on board the *Città di Milano*, who were responsible for the search, were not letting anyone close:

> 'It's impossible to get near him', complained the Hearst man, 'there's a guard by the gang plank, and he gets physical if anyone tries to go aboard without permission'. 'There are two Italian film teams here now, and they are trying to maintain a kind of film monopoly on everything that's going on – the entire situation looks hopeless for us', said the other. (Dored 1955: 155)

Dored writes enthusiastically about how they fought for the news: everything was fair game. He describes how he sneaked away from his competitors and bluffed his way on board the rescue vessel *Braganza*, and how, after a long period of fruitless searching, the message came in that the *Italia* had been located. Dored is a little imprecise in his report about what actually happened, but he shot his footage and relates:

> We arrived in time to see the Swedish aircraft take off and return with one Italian after another. This was quality film material, and when General Nobile agreed to let me into the cabin, where I recorded some scenes of the very sick leader of the ill-fated expedition, I was more than satisfied with *my* bounty. I wondered what my two colleagues had achieved in the meantime. (Dored 1955: 160)

Dored concludes his report on Nobile with a description of his own return journey to Paris, transporting his film. Exclusiveness could be costly: 'Opportune transport from Svalbard to Harstad, rented fast boat to Narvik, train to Stockholm and rented private aircraft to Paris, which arrived in time to make it possible to screen the film that same evening' (Dored 1955: 161).

Dored's descriptions of the camera reporters at work convey the importance of obtaining exclusive images. Dored managed to get footage from Svalbard to screening in American cinemas in thirteen days and five hours – 'A Clean Scoop', according to *American Cinematographer* article from 1928. The battle for the news had become tougher – particularly the fight between the many newsreel agencies to be the first to screen film footage from media events at their cinemas.

CONCLUSION

The above examples demonstrate how the polar explorers used the new technology of the film camera to document their expeditions toward the Poles. These examples also illustrate how their motives differed: some explorers needed the camera as a scientific tool, some simply wanted to document aspects of their journeys, and others wanted to supply proof of their achievements or pictures of their own heroism.

Between 1900 and 1930, through the efforts of expedition and newsreel photographers, such films evolved from barely managed fragments to fully resolved features, from a simple cinema of attractions to narrative films telling exciting stories.

I could have chosen to use this material to tell a more complete film history about a limited field: a technological film history on camera and film equipment in the polar regions, an economic film history on the importance of films in the financing of polar explorations, or a social film history on who made the polar films and why, and on who saw the films, how and why. The limited body of films from expeditions going North (and South) can serve as good examples for many different studies in film history.

I am grateful to a number of colleagues and archivists in the work with this article: Tony Fletcher, Neil Fulton, Øivind Hanche, Harald Dag Jølle, Luke McKernen and Anna Westerståhl Stenport.

NOTES

1. The film from Urban Trading Company had a length of 1,000 feet. The British Film Archive still holds fragments of the film.
2. Only 3,000 feet has survived in the National Archives of Canada.
3. In a letter from Nansen to his wife Eva from Boston, 5 November 1897 (National Library, Oslo), he writes that his payment for the Boston lecture was $1,800 (7,000 NKR); as a professor in Oslo he made 4,500 NKR a year (Jølle 2011: s. 260).

BIBLIOGRAPHY

Advertisement for Urban Production's Film (1907), *The Kinematograph and Lantern Weekly*, May, 34.

Amundsen, R. (1927), *Mitt liv som polarforsker*, Oslo: Gyldendal.

Arnesen, O. and E. Lundborg (1928), *'Italia': Tragedien på nært hold*, Oslo: Gyldendal.

Capelotti, P. J. (1999), *By Airship to the North Pole*, New Brunswick, NJ: Rutgers University Press.

Capelotti, P. J. (2008), 'A 'radically new method': balloon buoy communications of the Baldwin-Ziegler Polar Expedition, Franz Josef Land, June 1902', *Polar Research*, 27.

Charles Urban Co. (1912), Film catalogues for Charles Urban Trading Company at National Median Museum, Bradford, ref. no. URB 10–13A.

Dored, E. (1955), *For meg er jorden rund: John Dored forteller*, Oslo: Aschehoug.

Fiala, A. (1907), 'Polar photography', *National Geographic Magazine*, February, 140–42.

Fiala, A. (1909), *Kodak at the North Pole*, Rochester: Eastman Kodak Co.

Jenness, S. E. (2004), *The Making of an Explorer*, Montreal: McGill-Queen's University Press.

Jølle, H.D. (2011), *Nansen. Oppdageren*, Oslo: Gyldendal.

Leyda, J. (1960), *Kino: A History of Russian and Soviet Film*, London: George Allen & Unwin.

Murrey, B. (1990), *Film and the German Left in the Weimar Republic*, Austin: University of Texas Press.

Nansen, Fritjof (1897), Letter to Eva Nansen, National Library, Oslo, Norway, Letter collection 48.

Nasht, S. (2005), *The Last Explorer*, New York: Arcade Publishing.

'Nobile V. Ellsworth' (1926), *Time*, vol. VIII, no. 5.

'Obituary: Mr William Ziegler' (1905), *National Geographic Magazine*, May, 355.

Ponting, H. G. (1923), *The Great White South*, London: Duckworth & Co.

'The Baldwin-Ziegler Arctic Expedition' (1902), *National Geographic Magazine*, vol. 13, 358.

'With the Wellman Polar Expedition' (1906), *Cinematography and Bioscope Magazine*, May, 33.

21. THE ATTRACTIONS OF THE NORTH: EARLY FILM EXPEDITIONS TO THE EXOTIC SNOWSCAPE

Marina Dahlquist

Since the emergence of moving pictures, putting the exotic (in all its diversity) on display has been a recurrent feature of film exhibition. Educating audiences about faraway places and customs, and the attraction of experiencing localities and regional customs via moving pictures were prime reasons for the medium's immediate impact. This is clear to a reviewer of the 1914 feature film *Högfjällets dotter* (*Daughter of the Peaks*, Sweden) about a young Sámi woman in Northern Sweden, directed by Victor Sjöström: 'Notwithstanding the multitude of misgivings the enemies of cinema might level against the very existence of film theatres, they cannot deny the importance of films for disseminating knowledge about different regions around world' (*Svenska Dagbladet* 1914).[1]

Before the global spread of domestic film production, the depiction of many regions and minority populations in the world was dependent on French, British and American companies. This is the case also in Northernmost Europe, where international but also Swedish film companies made travelogues from the North into a small, but quite discernible genre of early filmmaking that often mixed fiction and non-fiction storytelling.

'Actualités' featuring local and distant scenes were prominent in the very first film programmes offered by the Lumière brothers in 1896. Such representations would dominate their catalogue until the company abandoned film production in 1905 (see Aubert and Seguin 1996). When 'le cinématographe' was introduced in a new country – which occurred in rapid succession after the famous screening at the Grand Café in Paris in December 1895 – Lumière cameramen arrived with the equipment (a camera and projector in one) to supervise the film exhibition. In addition, they captured new scenes locally. These scenes would be included in the local programme and later added to the overall Lumière repertoire. In terms of exhibition, the company's world tours thus mixed local images with those from far-off countries. This was a successful production model and programming strategy, outlasting the Lumières (see Snickars 2001; Dahlquist 2005). Local vistas and scenery, and even familiar faces, offered a welcome contrast to films exploring fantasies about intangible foreign lands, peoples and cultural practices. On the other hand, such images of the local became 'exotic' when incorporated into Lumière's catalogues and distributed internationally as re-labelled titles. Film expeditions were also carried out by other established production companies such as Pathé Frères, as well as by adventurers, explorers and missionaries who cinematically portrayed a wide range of exotic 'Others' through ethnographic or colonising viewpoints (Rony 1996).

The Cinematographic 'Other'

When the film medium put 'unfamiliar' or indigenous peoples on display, it did so in an established context. Ethnographic exhibitions in museums or in temporary venues had showcased 'exotic' peoples for Occidental audiences since the first encounters between Europeans and the inhabitants of the Americas and Africa. During the nineteenth century, the phenomenon became increasingly prevalent as 'non-white' bodies were presented within a range of pre- and para-cinematic exhibition contexts, ranging from panoramas and photography exhibits to circuses and World Exhibitions. The mise-en-scène of Otherness was a strand of mass entertainment that quickly became integrated into early cinema, which, in Alison Griffiths's formulation, assumed a role as 'mediator between cultural differences' (2002). In a Swedish context, the Sámi were popular objects of exhibition around the time of the development of cinema as a mass medium. When the Stockholm open-air museum Skansen opened in 1891, Sámi had been hired for the exhibition with instructions to go about their daily life in front of curious visitors. At Skansen, the Sámi 'camp' was posited as a true-to-life environment, including reindeer to convey traditional aspects of Sámi culture. In Scandinavia around this time, the folk museum movement became an influential museological paradigm: it became what Mark Sandberg (2003) calls a 'living picture' medium. Traditional rural or indigenous culture was made available to modern urban spectators, especially impactful as Scandinavian geography with its remote northern regions had delayed contact between local culture forms and forces of modernity (see Sandberg 2003: 145–77).

Figure 21.1   A 1901 photograph from the collections of the Stockholm outdoor museum Skansen, which still maintains a Sámi exhibit. Photo: Nordiska Museet.

Interest in northernmost Sweden reflected modern society's fascination with the remote provinces, just as the extension of railway lines northward facilitated mining transportation and increased migration both north and south. What was then called Lapland became a symbol of a nation in its most original form, just as the Sámi could be construed as an unspoilt group living in harmony with harsh elements of nature. The reviewer of Sjöström's film *Högfjällets dotter* echoes these sentiments: 'You have heard about the fjeld's impressive beauty, about the grand view of a running reindeer herd, of the primitive in the Laplander cot, but despite that and numerous photographs you have not been able to get such a lifelike performance of all this beauty as the one that moving pictures can endow the images' (*Svenska Dagbladet* 1914).

EARLY FILM DEPICTIONS OF THE FAR NORTH. THE JOURNEYS OF PATHÉ FRÈRES

Arctic landscapes and its native peoples – Sámi and Inuit – were featured in numerous film titles made by Scandinavian and European producers during the early years of cinema, spanning a range of formats and forms of expression: fiction, actualities and, later, documentary. Pathé Frères, internationally the most important production and distribution company during the two first decades of film's history, produced titles depicting the Far North as early as 1897: *Une scène dans les régions glaciales le ballon d'Andrée* (*Andrée at the North Pole*) and a polar bear hunt in *Une chasse à l'ours blanc* (*Hunting White Bear*). In 1904, Sámi are portrayed during a journey along the Norwegian seashore to the North Cape in *De Christiana au Cap Nord* (*From Christiana to North Cape*). This film brings together several images of cinema of attraction, typical of the period. It begins by displaying boulevards in Christiana (now Oslo) and proceeds to open water; waterfalls at Stalheinfos; Sámi collecting dried codfish, herding reindeer and pursuing household chores; and finally presents the audience with a view of the midnight sun at North Cape.

The French film industry, dominated by Pathé Frères, had until 1910 spearheaded the industrialisation, growth and globalisation of the film market. To resume international success after declining earnings, Pathé began tailoring its productions to local markets by opening branches in a number of cities. Before establishing its Swedish branch in September 1910, Pathé Frères made at least one trip to Sweden, resulting in a number of films being shot in 1907 and 1908 (see Dahlquist 2005). Ethnographic films exploited the exoticism of the North as well as particulars of landscape, as exemplified by *En Suède* (*Sweden*, 1908), featuring large waterfalls and fishing scenes. The film aroused considerable attention in France. In *Exploitations de la glace en Suède* (*Ice Cutting in Sweden*, 1907), ice exported to France amongst other countries was shown, and winter sports were the topic of *Sports en Suède* (*Swedish Sports*, 1907). The tour included images from the north of Sweden to depict Sámi people in *Chez les Lapons* (*The Laplanders*, 1908). Pathé also made a film about the mines in Kiruna, *Les Mines de fer de Kiruna* ('The Iron Mines in Kiruna'), and Stockholm was featured in *Visite à Stockholm* (*Stockholm*), both titles from 1908. The films enjoyed international release through Pathé Frères' worldwide distribution network.

SWEDISH VIEWS ON THE NORTH THROUGH 'SWEDISH' EYES

Pathé's display of the exotic North was not that different to films produced in Sweden for a domestic audience. A romanticised image of the vast and barren landscape with its difficult conditions is prominent in these productions. Swedish production companies were located in the southern and middle part of the country, which could have influenced the style of depiction, while cinematic interest in the northern provinces coincided with promotional campaigns by the Swedish Tourist Agency (there were, for example, quite a few films featuring winter sports and mountain hiking). Robert Olsson shot *Lappbilder* ('Views of Sámi') in 1906 as part of the Swedish production company Svensk Kinematograf's national film series Svenska bilder ('Swedish Views'). These depict domestic issues featuring Swedish nature, industry and trade. The film was produced during three weeks of extreme hardship in the Lapland wilderness. Similar films include Anders Skogh's *Norrlandsbilder* ('Views of Norrland') and Svenska biografteatern's *Bestigning af Åreskutan* ('Ascending the Mountains at Åre'), both made in 1908. Threats posed by the Northern climate were mobilised as narrative components in films from the very early years throughout the 1920s, whether or not shot on location. Pathé's 1901 studio production *Le Mauvais riche* (*A Bad Rich Man*) features poor children seeking shelter from the cold, and in the dramatic picture *Au pays des glaces* (*In the Polar Regions*, 1905) a group of explorers become fatally stuck in polar pack-ice. Characters struggling against brutally cold landscapes and unforgiving environments would, in Swedish feature productions from the 1910s and 1920s, be related to perceptions of a hardy national character (see Dahlquist 1999). Films featuring explorer and expedition themes were still in vogue during the mid-1910s, made by producers such as Sveafilm, Svenska Biografteatern and Nordisk film. In 1914, AB Svenska Films Companiet advertised its exclusive right for the lease of *Kapten Kleinschmidts Nordpolsexpedition* (*Captain F. E. Kleinschmidt's Arctic Hunt*, Arctic Film Co., 1914), which depicts aspects of Inuit life such as trading and bartering practices. Pathé's programmes included *Från den norska Spetsbergsexpeditionen 1914 serie 1* ('From the Norwegian Expedition to Spitsbergen 1914, series 1', 1914), as well as *Med Stockholms nya isbrytare på provtur* ('A Trial Trip on Stockholm's New Ice-breaker', 1915).

FILMING THE SÁMI ON SITE IN EARLY CINEMA

Sjöström's *Högfjällets dotter* mixes non-fiction images of the Sámi with a fictional frame, conveyed through an outsider's perspective. At least three additional Swedish films depicted Lapland and the Sámi in 1915: Sveafilm advertised *I Lappland* ('In Lapland'); Svenska Biografteatern produced *På lapplandsfärd med d:r G. Hallströms etnografiska expedition* ('A Lapland Journey with Dr Hellström's Ethnographic Expedition'), featuring the archaeologist Gustaf Hallström; and Pathé shot another film about the Sámi during nine weeks from April to June in 1915 when Oscar A. Olsson documented a Sámi family's migration as they moved their reindeer from Soppero (in Northern Sweden) to Sätermoen in Norway. The production of this non-fiction film *Med svenska lappar på vårflyttning* ('With Swedish Laplanders on their Spring Migration') was received in the press as something of a feat as Olsson had lived and travelled with the Sámi for an extended period of time, sharing their everyday life and their adventurous journey.

Focusing on the Sámi reindeer herder Nils Henriksson and his family, Olsson's camera captured the preparations before the journey – catching the reindeer, taking down the cot, packing the family's possessions – and the migration across the mountains. The hardships of the journey, including snowstorms and difficult terrain, are vividly depicted, but the film also features everyday life and customs. The film premiered in Stockholm and Göteborg on 15 November 1915. *Med svenska lappar på vårflyttning* was advertised as unusual and highly interesting, and the trade paper *Filmbladet* published a two-page article about it (*Filmbladet* 1915). The film also featured well-known journalist and author Ester Blenda Nordström (with the pen name 'Bansai'), who played a part in the film as a temporary teacher in a nomad school. This role reflects her six-month stay with the Sámi community in 1915, detailed in a number of articles in the daily paper *Svenska Dagbladet* and book *Tent Folk of the Far North* (1916; see Stål 2008: 104–15). The book opens with a vivid description of a spring snowstorm, and though Nordström's depiction of the Sámi begins through the eyes of a visitor and describes their Otherness, her perspective gradually changes. Nordström's stint turned her into a very committed promoter of Sámi culture and customs and a champion of their rights in relation to Swedish law. In addition to the original film copy, another four prints were released during 1915. Subsequent non-fiction film expeditions capturing and exoticising the Sámi and their lives would include *I fjällfolkets land* ('In the Land of the Fjelds', AB Svensk filmindustri, 1923), the first film in a series about the young Sámi girl Inka Länta.

What an authentic film of indigenous people would look like is not self-evident. The ethnographic 'inventories' or staged scenes are problematic to say the least, which has been analysed in depth especially in regard to Robert Flaherty's *Nanook of the North* (USA, 1922). Films about the Sámi could either be produced by non-Sámi, which was the case during the timeframe outlined in this chapter, or by the Sámi themselves. However, films and television programmes produced by Sámi were virtually non-existent prior to the 1970s. The depiction of their culture and living conditions are, deliberately or not, presented from outsider perspectives for most of the twentieth century. Nevertheless, the fascination with the extreme conditions of the Arctic and its inhabitants lives on, in Sweden and elsewhere, with nature as well as fiction films juxtaposing the modern world and a notion of the Far North as one of the last wildernesses on Earth.

NOTE

1. Translation by the author.

BIBLIOGRAPHY

Aubert, M. and J. C. Seguin (1996), *La Production Cinématographique des Frères Lumière*, Paris: Bibliothèque du Film.
Dahlquist, M. (1999) 'Snow-White: The aesthetic and narrative use of snow in Swedish silent film,' in J. Fullerton and J. Olsson (eds), *Nordic Explorations: Film Before 1930*, Sydney: John Libby.

Dahlquist, M. (2005), 'Global versus local: the case of Pathé', *Film History* 17, 1.
Filmbladet (1915), no. 13, 15 July, 168–9.
Griffiths, A. (2002), *Wondrous Difference: Cinema, Anthropology, and Turn-of-the-Century Visual Culture*, New York: Columbia University Press.
L'Illustration (1908), no. 3425, 17 October.
Jernudd, Å. (1999), *Oscar Olsson's African films (1921/22): Examples of Touristic Edutainment*, Örebro: Örebro universitet.
Nordström, E. B. (1916), *Kåtornas folk*, Stockholm: Wahlström & Widstrand.
Rony, F. T. (1996), *The Third Eye: Race, Cinema and Ethnographic Spectacle*, Durham, NC: Duke University Press.
Sandberg, M. B. (2003), *Living Pictures, Missing Persons: Mannequins, Museums, and Modernity* (Princeton, NJ: Princeton University Press.
Snickars, P. (2001), *Svensk film and visuell masskultur 1900*, Stockholm: Aura förlag.
Stål, M. (2008), 'Möten med "Kåtornas folk": Ester Blenda Nordström och same-frågorna 1914–1918', in W. Hebbe and A. Lönnroth (eds), *Empati och engagemang: en kvinnolinje i svensk journalistik*, Enhörna: Tusculum.
Stockholmstidningen (1915), Advertisement, 15 November: 3.
Svenska Dagbladet (1914), Advertisement, 18 November.
Svenska Dagbladet (1915), Advertisement, 15 November: 10.

22. FROZEN IN MOTION: ETHNOGRAPHIC REPRESENTATION IN DONALD B. MACMILLAN'S ARCTIC FILMS

Rebecca Genauer

During the course of his nearly fifty-year career, Donald Baxter MacMillan undertook over thirty trips to the Canadian Arctic and Greenland, becoming a respected expert on Arctic exploration, natural history and culture. The American's career began auspiciously with his participation in Robert Peary's successful 1908–9 polar expedition, and continued to evolve, eventually encompassing a wide range of interests beyond geographic exploration. From the mid-1910s onward, MacMillan supported the work of university-affiliated researchers who accompanied the former on his expeditions. MacMillan, himself a teacher and scholar, contributed to the zoological, geological, ethnographic and technological research of others not only by transporting researchers to the Arctic, but also by conducting research, collecting artifacts, developing an Inughuit dictionary and extensively filming and photographing the region. Between trips to the Arctic, MacMillan's primary source of income was as a lecturer on Arctic subjects. It was this role, as an educator, that dominated MacMillan's last decade of Arctic travel, which was largely devoted to making teaching trips north with high school- and college-aged boys.

Though his experiences in the Arctic were varied, motion picture and still photography was, consistently and from the beginning, an integral part of MacMillan's trips north. Like all members of Robert Peary's 1908–9 polar expedition, MacMillan was expected to take photographs documenting the expedition and was contractually obliged to sign over the rights to his photos to Peary, who later used the images in his publications and popular illustrated lectures (LeMoine, Kaplan and Witty 2008: xli; David 2000: 75). MacMillan learned a tremendous amount from Peary, not the least of which was the value of photographic documentation. Indeed, though he seems rarely to have reflected on it, MacMillan became a prolific documenter of the Arctic; over the course of his long career as an explorer and researcher he took tens of thousands of still photographs and exposed nearly 100,000 feet of motion picture footage, including some of the earliest surviving Arctic footage (LeMoine et al. 2008: xxiv). MacMillan edited and re-edited his filmed material for use in his own lectures, as well as for distribution in the form of educational short subjects. Four of MacMillan's edited single-reel films – *Hunting Musk-Ox with the Polar Eskimo* (date unknown), *Travelling with the Eskimos of the Far North* (1930), *Eskimo Life in South Greenland* (filmed during a 1926 expedition), and *Under the Northern Lights* (circa 1928) – survive.[1] The first three of these films are the most thematically unified and the richest in terms of ethnographic content. *Hunting Musk-Ox* and *Travelling with the Eskimos* each feature arduous sledge trips, hunting and mundane activities, while *Eskimo Life* documents the work and leisure activities of Inuit living in the colonial fishing town of Holsteinsborg (now Sisimiut), Greenland. This material, in addition to the papers of MacMillan and his wife, Miriam Look MacMillan, forms the basis for this chapter.

At the height of MacMillan's activities as an Arctic lecturer in the 1920s and 1930s, public fascination with Arctic peoples centred on the myth of the smiling Inuit, endearingly clad in fur, whose courage and strength enabled him to survive in an unforgiving environment (Huhndorf 2000: 134). As an early Arctic filmmaker and successful lecturer, MacMillan offers a useful case study for an examination of how non-fiction film was harnessed to educate audiences about the Arctic, as well as how it could be used to simultaneously perpetuate and challenge prevailing notions about the North and its inhabitants. This chapter will briefly consider some of the historical pressures that shaped MacMillan's films, and will subsequently examine how three elements of the films' form – their linguistic content, visual organisation and narration – articulated the complex, sometimes inconsistent, vision of the Arctic that MacMillan offered to his audiences. In particular, I focus on the ways in which MacMillan both reinforced and challenged standard images through his choice of words and images, and the ways in which his denial of narrative continuity liberated his films from generic demands and illusionist tendencies while simultaneously putting his films at risk of connoting a perpetual present tense.

Two Factors of Film Form: Intention and Practicality

Before engaging in a stylistic analysis of MacMillan's films, it is important to consider briefly MacMillan's aims, unarticulated though they often were, as well as the circumstances under which his films were exhibited and produced.

As the rest of this chapter shall explore, each of these factors – MacMillan's ideological stance, his mode of exhibition and his mode of production – affected the films' form and their status as ethnographic representations.

While MacMillan was not immune to prevailing attitudes about indigenous cultures, his interest in scientific objectivity and his history of respectful collaboration with the Inuit compelled him to strive to represent the Inuit honestly and in a manner unaffected by prejudice and convention. MacMillan actively sought to situate his films in the discourse of sobriety described by Nichols in his discussion of documentary films (Nichols 1991: 3–4). For MacMillan, this meant differentiating his films from others depicting exotic locals and, because he understood that the form of his films was contingent upon the contexts in which they were exhibited, controlling the circumstances of their exhibition. MacMillan was adamant that generic demands not dictate the content or form of his films. As I shall discuss, MacMillan selected images that often flouted standard depictions of the Inuit, and he took pains to avoid the demands of conventional narrative. MacMillan's films were chiefly shown with his own lecture accompaniment in venues that were dedicated to education and uplift. Throughout the autumn and winter months of the 1920s, MacMillan lectured with his films daily (and often twice daily) at schools, churches, lodges and recreational organisations,[2] and he also used his films in his own anthropology classes at Bowdoin College.[3] In these exhibition contexts, the films served a subsidiary role in relation to MacMillan's lecture, and could function without integrated narration. MacMillan's resistance to imposed fictional narratives prompted his opposition to the distribution of his films outside the lecture circuits. Such was MacMillan's opposition to the constraints of generic representation that when the profitability of his lectures sharply plummeted during the Depression,[4] and he was forced to seek Columbia's commercial distribution for his films, his one caveat was that he was 'very much against changing any . . . subjects to conform to any fictitious story as other adventure films'.[5] When MacMillan did, as in 1921 and 1929, agree to produce a series of films for commercial distribution, he invariably retained the right to submit final approval of the films.[6]

MacMillan's interest in defying standardised images and narrative structures was not the only factor shaping his films. Often, matters of expedience aligned with MacMillan's aims. MacMillan's method of shooting, which was opportunistic rather than planned, accorded with MacMillan's prioritisation of interesting, discrete images over images subordinate to an integrated narrative. MacMillan shot footage as compelling images and events presented themselves and as time and weather permitted. An unpublished manuscript about his 1913–17 Crocker Land Expedition reveals MacMillan's receptiveness to ideal subjects and conditions for filming. He was quick to take advantage of striking, spectacular events, which he sometimes filmed in spite of poor lighting conditions and inadequate camera operation. He was so impressed by the sight of Inuit travelling up a glacier face into which they had cut steps, for instance, that he filmed the event even though his fascination distracted him so he 'could hardly pay proper attention to the camera'.[7] On other occasions, if the weather was conducive to filming, MacMillan filmed whatever routine activities were occurring. This method of collection resulted in an accumulation of discrete images whose specific use in a film was not preconceived.

MacMillan's often spontaneous method of filming also afforded a great deal of freedom in editing, an important benefit for a film lecturer. Given the inherently weak syntactic relations between images in his film footage, MacMillan was easily able to reuse footage between lectures without altering or distorting the meaning of the repurposed images. He also could replace or omit sequences if, for example, film became damaged during projection.[8] The ease of substitution and omission would doubtless have been valuable to a lecturer with a gruelling schedule and a single copy of his film.

DEFINING THE INUIT IN FAMILIAR AND UNFAMILIAR TERMS: LANGUAGE, VISUAL ORGANISATION, NARRATION

Language

I have alluded to some of the ways in which MacMillan's intentions were progressive. And yet, MacMillan did not elude the ingrained racism of his times or the limitations of his own cultural purview. The language he used in his lectures in many ways aligned with the manner in which Arctic peoples historically have been represented. MacMillan's verbal descriptions reiterated the contemporary, popular image of the primitive innocent, emphasised virtues common to the Inuit and explorer, and envisioned the Inuit as a yardstick against which the explorer could measure his own civility on the one hand, and his primal fortitude on the other. In this sense, like so many other representations of the Arctic, MacMillan's films reflected the Arctic through the distorting lens of the familiar and served to define the Westerner as much as (or more than) they did the Inuit.

The conventional linguistic tropes MacMillan employed in his lectures relied on dominant imaginings of Northern peoples. Lecture scripts reveal how MacMillan's language reproduced the popular image of the Inuit as a lovable, simple and upright being who by virtue of his physical strength lives a contented existence in the harshest natural environment. MacMillan described the prototypical Inuit as:

> a burly man, sturdy with a good pair of shoulders. His face is broad and stolid, his keen brown eyes gleaming and twinkling under a great mane

of black hair. The skin is dark and browned with the air sun and frost. His face always smiling, often shines, because of the grease smeared over the face ... He is strong and can stand a lot of strenuous work, while hunting and traveling.[9]

In accordance with the conventional representation of the Inuit as the rugged innocent, MacMillan's description reduces the Inuit to a catalogue of traits that he closely associates with the Inuit's natural surroundings. Simultaneously, and also conventionally, MacMillan evokes a vision of the Inuit as a primitive savage. His use of the word 'mane' is derogatory, if not in intention then in its beastly implication. Indeed, with its emphasis on physical build and stamina, the description bears a conspicuous and disconcerting similarity to a description (from a different lecture) of sledge dogs as:

hardy animals, each weighing from 85 to 100 pounds, greatly resembling the white wolf, and very intelligent. Note the erect ears, broad chests, heavy warm coats, husky tails and sturdy legs of this fine team, every dog alert and waiting for their supper at the end of the day's travel.[10]

MacMillan's language does not challenge established modes of representation. On the contrary, in a fairly typical manner, MacMillan's reproduction of familiar images and his evocation of animal imagery define the Inuit in terms of their idealised relationship to Westerners. Where MacMillan's language describes the Inuit as childlike and beastly, the Westerner is implied to be sophisticated and civilised.

The relationship between Inuit and Westerner is not, however, characterised only by difference, but also by strategically identified similarities. MacMillan elaborates on the relationship between Inuit and Westerner by highlighting the Inuit's embodiment of virtues and values that we esteem. As Fienup-Riordan has shown, this, too, has been a standard way of representing Arctic people since the age of the Arctic explorer in the nineteenth century, and has functioned chiefly to establish a mirror of the explorer, whose vitality, endurance and ingenuity allow him to conquer a malevolent natural world (Fienup-Riordan 1990: 16). MacMillan defines the explorer in these terms in one of his lectures, stating that the explorer was 'the man who experiences unbounded pleasure in pitting his physical body and his mental powers against the hostile forces of nature such as violent winds, pelting rains, cold sleet, drifting snow, tropical fevers, starvation, and death, and winning out'.[11]

Visual organisation

Though, as has been noted, MacMillan's language often marks the Inuit as an object of difference, he does articulate a comparison of Inuit and explorer

Figure 22.1   Frontal staging of women in MacMillan's *Eskimo Life in South Greenland*. Courtesy of The Peary-MacMillan Arctic Museum, Bowdoin College.

at the visual level in his films – specifically in sequences that foreground the physical strength and endurance of both Inuit and explorer. Admittedly, some images – such as a panning medium shot that presents a row of women for the audience's scrutiny in *Eskimo Life* and several shots of a child, a woman carrying an infant in her anorak, and a man entering the low door of an igloo – do make a spectacle of physical difference and culturally specific skills. In the first example, the frontal staging of the women and the slow rate of the pan right invite the audience's comparison of faces as sites of difference. In the last example, the repetition of the action of entering and exiting the igloo, the elision of intervening material via a jump cut, and the figures' direct looks at the camera all contribute to the demonstrative quality of the action and, subsequently, its value as spectacle.

In spite of these images that foreground difference, prominent sections of MacMillan's films visually collapse the distinction between explorer and Inuit in order to call attention to their common traits of strength and endurance. Protracted extreme long shots depicting sledge travel challenge the viewer to distinguish expedition members from Inuit. Though Fatimah Tobing Rony has argued that the use of long shot scales in ethnographic films emphasises the distance and difference between spectator and performer (Rony 1996: 95), in the context of MacMillan's films, which feature not just the Inuit but also crew members, extreme long shot scales perform an opposite function: obscuring our perception of difference, and stressing common behaviours and strengths. The extreme long shot scale reduces visual information that might cue the viewer's differentiation of human figures while simultaneously emphasising the magnitude of the explorer and Inuit's fortitude. Against the white expanse of the ice fields, the figures' travel seems inherently heroic.

As I have shown, MacMillan did rely on the convention of representing the Inuit as a projection of Western ideals. However, he also evidenced an opposition to standard tropes and images. This is particularly indicated in MacMillan's refusal to romanticise the primitive. Through the visual organisation and structure of his films, MacMillan actively defied the ethnographic tendency to depict indigenous cultures as either preserved relics of an ancient past or as tragically and essentially altered through contact with Western culture.

Instead, MacMillan's films are striking for their portrayal of the Inuit as culturally unique and yet highly adaptable. Frequently, MacMillan shows the Inuit incorporating Western technologies and customs into their own traditions. In the process, he paints Western culture neither as a salvation to struggling primitives, nor as a threat to a culture on the brink of extinction. A sequence in *Travelling with the Eskimos*, in which a broken sledge runner is repaired, illustrates MacMillan's admiration of the Inuit's ability to repurpose Western technology in a way that does not endanger indigenous cultural specificity. After the sledge runner breaks, an inter-title affirms that 'the Eskimos will soon have it fixed'.

The next shot shows an Inuit man aiming a rifle at the sledge and shooting, before an inter-title explains that '*Our* 22 rifle will make the holes' (emphasis added). Finally, the Inuit split a sealskin lashing which they use, along with an axe, to fashion a tourniquet to hold the sledge runner together. The sequence, in which the Inuit make novel use of both Western and indigenous technology to repair their own mode of transportation, demonstrates not competition between the modern and primitive, but resourcefulness, cultural accommodation and mutual benefit. The Inuit's ingenuity transforms the rifle into a convenient and unconventional tool for repair, while MacMillan, conversely, benefits from the indigenous means of travel represented by the sledge. *Hunting Musk-Ox* includes a similarly honest and appreciative look at how Inuit culture has been influenced by contact with Western technology, and the rifle in particular. MacMillan alludes to what was considered an essential element of Inuit representation by including a seal hunt in the film. However, unlike many other Arctic representations, including *Nanook of the North*, MacMillan refuses to perpetuate the myth of outdated hunting techniques. Whereas Robert Flaherty famously showed Allakariallak (as Nanook) using his harpoon to hunt a seal that had already been killed by rifle, MacMillan shows an Inuit man aiming

Figure 22.2   An Inuit man uses a rifle to repair a sledge in MacMillan's *Travelling with the Eskimos of the Far North*. Courtesy of The Peary-MacMillan Arctic Museum, Bowdoin College.

a rifle behind a white screen, which he uses to disguise himself as he creeps toward the seal. Moreover, MacMillan's voice-over focuses on the method of approaching the seal without it being aware, rather than on the use of the rifle, which, in fact, he does not comment on but presents as a matter of fact.

As a final example, *Eskimo Life* also typifies MacMillan's resistance to either romanticising or elegising the primitive. The film offers a sustained look at work and leisure in a colonial town, and unsentimentally reveals many of the ways in which the local Inuit culture reflects a long-term interaction with the Danes. An early sequence in the film depicts the Inuit fishing in their kayaks. MacMillan immediately shows, however, that this traditional mode of fishing exists alongside a modern cannery where Inuit men and women work. Thus, the Inuit's small-scale fishing is not inherently imperiled by Western industry. On the contrary, through his objective, descriptive inter-titles (including statements such as 'The girls make the cans', and 'The cans are sealed'), MacMillan suggests that there is nothing incongruous in the image of an Inuit woman wearing decidedly non-Western clothing – albeit made of imported Danish beads – and operating machinery. MacMillan's lack of commentary, as well as his insistence on showing both the traditional and modern within a single frame, defies the tendency of romantic ethnographies either to erase all signs of interaction with Western culture or to suggest that the integrity of an indigenous culture is tragically jeopardised by interaction. In depicting the Inuit's interactions with Western culture in Holsteinsborg, MacMillan shows that, rather than Inuit culture being defined by its primitiveness or isolation, it may be understood as dynamic and accommodating.

Narration

If MacMillan begins to articulate a progressive view of the Inuit through his choice of images, his enlightened stance is further bolstered at the level of his films' narration, and, specifically, through their failure to satisfy many of the basic demands of narrative continuity. MacMillan's films insistently impede the development of continuity by denying clear temporal or causal relations, limiting the establishment of characters, and blocking the development of suspense. The absence of narrative continuity, in turn, has important implications for the films' status as progressive ethnographic representation.

Like many ethnographic films, MacMillan's are structured around loosely related vignettes rather than a tight chain of causally linked events and unambiguous temporal relations (Heider 2006: 77–8). While MacMillan's films do contain sequences, they are syntagmatically weak, as they are structured episodically and have stronger thematic rather than causal or temporal connections. The material in *Eskimo Life in South Greenland* represents the activities of a typical day without articulating any specific temporal or causal relationships. The film depicts transportation to work, labour at the cannery, and men and women's leisure activities, but does not suggest that the individual sequences necessarily occur on the same day. *Hunting with the Musk-Ox* and *Travelling with the Eskimos* also are both organised in an associative manner rather than causally. The films imply the narrative of a sledge journey by including sequences depicting sledging, hunting and routine activities like mending mittens and drying boots – all events that would plausibly occur on any sledge journey. Though there are occasional references to the passing of time, such as inter-titles stating 'at the end of the day', such specific references are sparse, and the films do not give a clear sense of how much time has elapsed or how much geographical distance has been covered. The film is similar, in this regard, to *Nanook of the North*, whose episodic structure, connoting both the passage of two days and of a year, is similarly non-specific.

If the episodic structure of MacMillan's films is fairly typical of ethnographic films, where MacMillan's films deviate from others like *Nanook of the North* is in their emphatic denial of other signifiers of narrative continuity. This is most evident in MacMillan's conscious resistance to developing on-screen characters. MacMillan rarely identifies, either by name or description, the individuals depicted on screen. This, in conjunction with the preponderance of long and extreme long shots, makes it difficult to recognise individuals or even ascertain whether we are seeing the same people from shot to shot or sequence to sequence. In the absence of characters to unify and provide motivation for actions, the capacity of MacMillan's films to perform basic functions of narrative, such as articulating goals or developing suspense, is greatly diminished. The lack of on-screen characters with whom we might align necessarily curtails the depth and range of narration. Consequently, when we are able to deduce goals, they remain relatively diffuse and non-specific, unattached to individual characters. Similarly, when suspense is generated, it is activated only on a local level rather than sustained across a film. In *Travelling with the Eskimo*, for example, we understand that MacMillan and his crew are travelling with Inuit, but, without access to any individual characters, precisely what the aim of their travel is remains obscure. Hence, when a long take shows the Inuit struggling to pull their sledges up a steep ice face into which they have cut steps, though the audience is cued to anticipate their eventual success, the suspense that is cued is contained only within the moment. Without clearly established long-term goals or a narrative trajectory to stall or complicate, the sequence cannot elicit in the audience any sense of concern about whether the travellers will reach their destination.

The implications of MacMillan's narrative discontinuity are diverse and contradictory. On the one hand, MacMillan's minimisation of signs of narrative coherence released his films from the tyranny of narrative and opened them up to other forms of interpretation. On the other hand, depending on the context in which the films were exhibited, the blockage of narrative threatened to arrest the image and suggest a perpetual, and problematic, present.

Without pressure to organise his films according to the overriding demands of story, MacMillan not only evaded the force of generic demands, but succeeded in challenging the absorptive quality of narrative, which so often serves to conceal the constructedness of the image and the film text. In forsaking narrative, MacMillan could emphasise the problem of illusionism by injecting his films with moments of reflexivity. These moments foreground the process of filming and remind the audience of the relationship between the camera and pro-filmic event. This is subtly evident in *Hunting Musk-Ox* when we see an Inuit man wait for an off-screen cue before beginning to feed his dogs. Here, the relationship between the pro-filmic event and camera is preserved rather than cut out or disguised by the flow of narrative. More flagrant instances of reflexivity were supplied by MacMillan's verbal commentary rather than inhering in the image. At one point in *Hunting Musk-Ox*, for example, MacMillan explains that an abrupt stop in the picture is the result of a musk-ox charging past him in dangerously close proximity. Moments such as these, which lay bare the ways in which the film image is constructed, alert the audience that their vision of the Arctic is mediated and the result of past encounters.

While the reflexive element of MacMillan's narration provides opportunities for MacMillan to challenge generic demands and assumptions about an image's naturalness, the discontinuity of his film narratives also has potentially damaging effects on the films' status as ethnographic representation. Specifically, MacMillan's investment in the image as a descriptive, paradigmatic unit rather than as a syntagmatic one necessarily jams the propulsive system of narrative. Because individual images do not take part in a forward narrative drive, but are instead episodic, and because MacMillan's films tend not to generate suspense on any more than a local level, they have the capacity – if not the tendency – to stall, to privilege the moment over change or temporal progression.

What this potential to stall means for MacMillan's films is that they risk depicting the Inuit as static – frozen, as it were, in motion. To the extent that all films can be said, in a Bazinian sense, to embalm a duration of time (Bazin 2005: 9–16), MacMillan's are not unique in this regard. However, the lack of specificity inherent in MacMillan's films – a lack created through the denial of narrative signifiers already discussed – poses additional problems for this jamming of forward motion. Stripped of narrative specificity, the images in MacMillan's films have the possibility of functioning as generic and timeless signifiers. Actions that lack narrative motivation can slip into the mythic domain, which 'tries to seize the moment and make it perpetual' (Nichols 1991: 254). The resultant ethnographic representation fixes its subject in the past, stripping it of its historic specificity, and relegating it to the status of symbol. To illustrate with an example that has already been referenced, the family who exit and then re-enter an igloo through its low door in *Travelling with the Eskimo* achieve a timeless status through the lack of specific motivation attached to their actions. There is no imposed narrative motivation for the action, nor do MacMillan's inter-titles provide any specific historical explanation (the inter-titles simply state that the door is low and that the Inuit and pass through it easily). The descriptive quality of the image prevails, with the consequence that the image becomes unanchored from any specific referent; instead it serves as an enduring, immutable sign of individual people and a culture, which are, in fact, transient and mutable.

The rhetorical stance of MacMillan's films – and, specifically, whether his films encouraged an understanding of Inuit culture as stagnant and abstract or vital and specific – depended on the extent to which the images could be rescued from the mythic domain. In practice, MacMillan's lectures accomplished this by restoring historical specificity to the images. The restoration of specificity via narration is evident in a comparison of two identical shots of sledge travel in two films – one released with voice-over narration akin to MacMillan's live lecture, and the other released with inter-titles. In *Travelling with the Eskimos*, which was distributed with inter-titles, the shot of sledging is introduced with an inter-title explaining that, having been cut off from further progress by open water, the group was forced to travel over land. The shot functions in a relatively non-specific manner, as it primarily serves to illustrate sledge travel over land. As such, the image of sledge travel achieves a degree of timelessness; it can illustrate any instance of sledge travel at any time. When the same shot appears in *Hunting Musk-Ox*, however, MacMillan's voice-over narration fixes the image in a particular historical moment. MacMillan explains that one of the on-screen teams of dogs is straying from the other teams because it is his team, and they are running towards MacMillan, whom they see behind the camera. Beyond inflecting the shot with a reflexive quality, MacMillan's voice-over in *Hunting Musk-Ox* assigns the shot specific historic reference. Rather than representing 'sledging' in an abstract, purely descriptive manner, the shot accompanied by voice-over represents a very particular moment in history, on film. MacMillan's explanation of the image, which is far more precise and detailed than is offered in any inter-title, recovers the image from a mythic domain, and in so doing is a more sound ethnographic depiction.

It has become routine to point out that the indexical image does not guarantee truth. The image of Arctic peoples that Donald MacMillan disseminated to audiences is no exception. It is an image shaped not only by MacMillan's interests and intentions, but also by the conditions of film production and exhibition, and by the pre-existing conventions governing indigenous – and particularly Arctic – representations. MacMillan aimed not to allow familiar images and narrational strategies to dictate the content and form of his films. Though his success in this regard was not complete and MacMillan did at times reinforce entrenched racism, his films are neither conquests nor elegies of a noble savage. Instead, they offer an admirable balance of respect for indigenous traditions and acknowledgement that Inuit culture is neither stagnant and isolated nor tragically vulnerable. MacMillan accomplished this not only through the content of his films, but through the organisation of material, which at once increased the possibilities for progressive interpretation, while simultaneously making the films more reliant on the live lecture exhibition format.

Just as the image of the North that MacMillan presented to his audiences was contingent upon a variety of external factors, so does it remain today. MacMillan's voice no longer accompanies the screening of his footage, but the legacy of his career as an explorer, filmmaker and educator continues. While some of MacMillan's filmed material is inevitably lost, much of it remains in unedited form at the Peary-MacMillan Arctic Museum at Bowdoin College in Maine, where it continues to find new use. Re-edited by anthropologists and museum curators for use in exhibits, the films still evidence their scope and versatility and serve both as historical documents and as testimony of MacMillan's concerns as a filmmaker and anthropologist.

Notes

1. *Hunting Musk-Ox with the Polar Eskimo* exists in a silent version, as well as a version with MacMillan's voice-over narration. *Travelling with the Eskimos of the Far North* and *Eskimo Life in South Greenland* each have intertitles, while *Under the Northern Lights* does not.
2. 'Lecture Memoranda', box 5, folders 1 and 2, Donald Baxter MacMillan Collection, George J. Mitchell Department of Special Collections & Archives, Bowdoin College Library, Brunswick, Maine (hereafter cited as Donald Baxter MacMillan Collection).
3. Correspondence between Donald MacMillan and John Haeseler, 1932, box 3, folder 22, Miriam MacMillan Collection, George J. Mitchell Department of Special Collections & Archives, Bowdoin College Library, Brunswick, Maine (hereafter cited as Miriam MacMillan Collection).
4. 'Lecture Schedules', box 5, folders 1–5, Donald Baxter MacMillan Collection.
5. Letter from H. E. Young to Hal Hode, 14 April 1937, box 13, folder 28, Miriam MacMillan Collection.
6. Contract between Commonwealth Cinema Corporation and Donald MacMillan, 21 January 1921, box 2, folder 13, Miriam MacMillan Collection. Advertisement from Atlantic Motion Picture Service Company, c. 1929, box 13, folder 28, Miriam MacMillan Collection.
7. Donald MacMillan, 'My Moving-picture Sledge Trip' manuscript, box 17, folder 12, Miriam MacMillan Collection.
8. Lecture engagement memorandum, 3 April 1925, box 5, folder 1, Donald Baxter MacMillan Collection.
9. Lecture typescript, box 14, folder 6, Miriam MacMillan Collection.
10. *Hunting Musk-Ox with the Polar Eskimo*, lecture typescript, box 4, folder 26, Donald Baxter MacMillan Collection.
11. 'Lecture for Bowdoin', box 14, folder 9, Miriam MacMillan Collection.

Bibliography

Bazin, A. (2005), *What is Cinema?*, trans. H. Gray, Berkeley: University of California Press.

David, R. G. (2000), *The Arctic in the British Imagination: 1818–1914*, Manchester: Manchester University Press.

Fienup-Riordan, A. (1990), *Eskimo Essays: Yup'ik Lives and How We See Them*, New Brunswick and London: Rutgers University Press.

Heider, K. G. (2006), *Ethnographic Film*, Austin: University of Texas Press.

Huhndorf, S. M. (2000), 'Nanook and his contemporaries: imagining Eskimos in American culture, 1897–1922', *Critical Inquiry*, 27:1, 122–48.

LeMoine, G. S. Kaplan and A. Witty (2008),'Introduction', in Donald B. MacMillan, *How Peary Reached the Pole*, McGill-Queen's University Press, 2–33.

McGhee, R. (2005), *The Last Imaginary Place: A Human History of the Arctic World*, Oxford: Oxford University Press.

Nichols, B. (1991), *Representing Reality*, Bloomington, IN: Indiana University Press.

Plantinga, C. (2005), 'What a documentary is, after all', *Journal of Aesthetics and Art Criticism*, 62: 2, 105–17.

Renov, M. (1986) 'Re-thinking documentary: toward a taxonomy of mediation', *Wide Angle*, 8: 3 and 4, 71–7.

Rony, F. T. (1996), *The Third Eye: Race, Cinema, and Ethnographic Spectacle*, Durham, NC: Duke University Press.

23. 'MY HEART BEAT FOR THE WILDERNESS': ISOBEL WYLIE HUTCHISON, JENNY GILBERTSON, MARGARET TAIT AND OTHER TWENTIETH-CENTURY SCOTTISH WOMEN FILMMAKERS

Sarah Neely

This chapter examines the work of two Scottish women filmmakers, Isobel Wylie Hutchison and Jenny Gilbertson, who like Scottish filmmaker and poet, Margaret Tait, were compelled to make films independently and on a small scale. Like Tait, they were drawn to the North (the Arctic in the case of Hutchison and Gilbertson) in their own search for extremes to, in the words of Tait's poem 'Storms', 'test their strength against' (Tait in Neely 2012: 39).

Isobel Wylie Hutchison (1889–1982), born in Edinburgh, travelled throughout Greenland and Alaska, collecting flowers and plant life for her work as a botanist, and recording her experiences through her writing and filmmaking. In addition to filmmaking she published both poetry and prose, much of it documenting her travels. She was also a regular contributor to *National Geographic* throughout the 1940s and 1950s. Jenny Gilbertson (1902–90), born in Glasgow, first trained as a teacher and journalist before moving to Shetland in the 1930s where she lived and worked for several decades. Later in life, after raising a family, she relocated to Northern Canada. She made several films in both Shetland and Canada. *A Crofter's Life in Shetland* (UK, 1931), her first film made in Shetland, was purchased by the GPO Film Unit. John Grierson, who was the director of the GPO Film Unit at the time, described the film as 'one of the best descriptions of life in the country anybody has yet made' (London Film Co-op 1994). In Canada, Gilbertson travelled to the High Arctic, documenting her journey through both written and filmed diaries. Two of her Arctic films were produced for CBC and the BBC.

The focus of this chapter is on the work of Gilbertson and Hutchison during their time in the Arctic; however, this will be considered alongside the work of Tait and within the general context of Scottish women filmmakers during the twentieth century. In particular, the chapter will examine their shared yearning for lone adventures, which all three were compelled to document and explore on paper and through the lens of a camera.

WOMEN TRAVELLERS IN TWENTIETH-CENTURY SCOTLAND

Although there is no direct personal connection between the three filmmakers, Hutchison, Gilbertson and Tait were all connected to a number of key women writers and filmmakers in Scotland in the twentieth century who could be described as pioneering for eschewing conventional married and family life in favour of the pursuit of their own unconventional ambitions. Often, the paths they followed were not ones that were open to women at the time and, in many cases, it was their affluent backgrounds that enabled them to pursue their interests and to develop their skills in the disciplines in which they were interested. These women could also be related to earlier notable figures such as Isabella Bird (1831–1904), an Englishwoman who left her family on the Isle of Mull in Scotland to explore the Rocky Mountains on her own. In 1892, Bird became the first woman to be inducted into the Royal Geographical Society. Writing on Bird in relation to other women travellers, Mona Domosh writes:

> Victorian women explorers could not escape the contexts in which they lived – contexts that were, in significant and well-documented ways, quite distinct from those of men. And those contexts shaped not only their outlook on personal matters and the structure of their social networks, but operated in very material ways, by limiting the resources and support networks available to women in their travels. (1991: 96)

Although Domosh is writing specifically on women in the Victorian Age, similarities could be drawn to later generations and, in particular, the two filmmakers referred to in this chapter, whose own explorations and practice as filmmakers in the Arctic were often self-funded and supported outside more conventional networks.

As Domosh describes in relation to the Victorian women travellers, they drew from their own expenses, were often middle-aged, or had 'fulfilled family "duties"', and were in search of 'places where they could live a type of life denied them at home' (1991: 97–8). For many of the women travellers, Domosh writes, 'their satisfaction was derived not in the external discovery of "new" geographies, but in the process of exploring, in experiencing a world in which they could participate in their own definition' (1991: 98). Similar to the 'Storms' Tait identifies as providing a means by which she is able to 'test [her] strength', for Hutchison and Gilbertson, the opportunity provided by Arctic exploration was not just tied to geographical discoveries, but personal ones too.

For many of the women explorers, across the Victorian Age and into the late twentieth century, writing and the expression of experience was an important part of the journey. They kept diaries and they wrote poetry, novels and short stories. Perhaps freedom from the restrictions of conventional domestic life, but also the exclusion from the 'professional' discourse of their chosen field, meant they were liberated by uncharted paths and were able to explore their own voices more freely. Certainly, the women focused on in this chapter worked across a number of different formats and forms. Hutchison wrote articles, poetry, non-fiction books, novels, made films and produced a number of watercolour sketches of the places she travelled to, many of which are included as illustrations in her various publications. Tait wrote across the same range of forms and made films too; she also was an accomplished artist and painter. Jenny Gilbertson made films, but she was also a trained journalist, and documented much of her journey in written diary form as well as on film.

Women Filmmakers in Twentieth-Century Scotland

The three filmmakers received varying degrees of support for their filmmaking activities. As mentioned previously, Jenny Gilbertson was supported and nurtured by John Grierson. After his enthusiasm for her film *A Crofter's Life in Shetland* (UK, 1931), she made five further films about Shetland, all of which Grierson purchased for the GPO Film Unit (McBain 1998). Isobel Wylie Hutchison's films were made as part of her work as a botanist and although she built a successful career employed by the Royal Botanic Gardens in Edinburgh and Kew to collect specimens on her travels throughout the Arctic, much of her work and travels were organised and funded largely by herself. Tait's existence on the periphery of the literary and artistic circles of twentieth-century Scotland was a reality throughout her working life. She was friendly with Hugh MacDiarmid, but was never an active member of the Rose Street scene. Her work was admired by John Grierson, but she rejected his advice for editing her work and refused to work on his terms. She opted instead to work on her own, or as MacDiarmid described in his article on her, she worked 'ploughing a lonely furrow' (1960: 416). All of the filmmakers in this chapter could also fit MacDiarmid's description of Tait. Gilbertson, like Tait, did collaborate with other filmmakers a couple of times during her career – first with Scottish filmmaker Elizabeth Balneaves on *People of Many Lands: Shetland* (UK, 1967). The two planned to film in Canada together until Balneaves became ill. Gilbertson also made *Prairie Winter* (Canada/UK, 1935) with the Canadian-born filmmaker Evelyn Spice, who was a significant figure in both British documentary production and the Canadian Film Board. Still, all three filmmakers largely worked independently. Jenny Gilbertson referred to her films as a 'one woman job' (Wade n.d.) and Tait was billed as a 'one-woman film-industry' (Calton Studios 1979).

Dominant approaches to filmmaking in Scotland in the early half of the twentieth century were epitomised by the documentary movement largely led by the Films of Scotland committee, of which Grierson was a founding member when it was formed in 1938 by the Secretary of State for Scotland and the Scottish Development Council. The committee held the express remit to encourage the production of films of 'national interest'. The committee's influence is seen in some of the films in their often self-conscious celebratory representations of industry and cultural life – for instance, Nettie McGavin's film *Holidaying in Harris* (UK, 1938), produced around the same time as the Empire Exhibition, a celebration of the empire and industry held in Glasgow's Bellahouston Park. McGavin's film, focusing on the outer Hebridean Isle of Harris, strikes an appropriate tone for the time. A 12-minute film, it is short but intensely focused on the herring industry and the production of Harris Tweed, both central to the island's economy. McGavin, a filmmaker often overshadowed by the her brother, Frank Marshall, one of Scotland's most celebrated amateur filmmakers, made many films during her travels throughout Africa and India (her family were tea importers).

As I have written in greater detail elsewhere (Neely 2008, 2009), women filmmakers in Scotland (and elsewhere too) have historically been brandished with the label of amateur filmmakers. The justification for the label can be tied to a number of reason such as a lack of formal training, or prohibition from training, exclusion from professional bodies or other markers of authenticity, or simply because their approach to whatever genre they were working in did not adhere to established forms and formats (rather than celebrate the work as avant-garde, it was labelled as amateur). Certainly this was evident across many areas of film production. For instance, women were not employed by the colonial film units. Women who were engaged in filmmaking activities usually did so alongside their husbands. Although there are significant collections of films made by women at the time, across the British Empire, they are largely outside formal filmmaking contexts and are generally classified as 'amateur'. Many, like Nettie Gavin's films, were made within the context of their travels (Sandon 2010: 328).

Isobel Wylie Hutchison's filmmaking activities were largely connected to her work as a botanist, a field in which she was also charged with being an amateur.

In one article in a Canadian newspaper, the *Daily Star*, Gordon Sinclair refers to Hutchision as a 'Scottish geranium and petunia hunter', emphasising that the expedition was paid for by herself (Gordon Sinclair 1934, cited in Kelcy 2001: 94). Mona Domosh, writing of the gendered divide between amateurs and professionals in the field of geography, explains that membership to the Royal Geographic Society was not opened up to women until 1915; up until that point, when the discipline was undergoing a period of professionalisation, and geography became 'rigorously defined', women who were denied access to formal training, but who were able to undertake fieldwork by drawing on their own resources, were removed from the newly defined label of 'geographer' (Domosh 1991: 96–7). The resulting reality for the women geographers, as is the case in other disciplines, including filmmaking, was that women who were committed to the pursuit of their chosen field of interest, without the support of the recognised professional bodies, no matter how developed their skills and abilities became, were always doomed to be the amateur, to be trivialised as the frivolous petunia hunter, and unlikely to be taken seriously. In reality, both Hutchison and Gilbertson made very significant contributions to their respective fields, including the history of Arctic filmmaking.

NORTHERN LIGHTS: WOMEN FILMMAKERS AND OTHER WAYS OF LOOKING

For all three women, there is a shared passion for the elemental, unknown qualities they associate with the North. This is evident in their films, but also in some of their writings and poetry. For example, in a passionate closing sentence of Hutchison's book, *North to the Rime-Ringed Sun, An Account of Her Journey through Alaska*, she writes: 'But I had heard the call of the wild on star-lit nights under the Northern Lights; I had slept in a snow-hut; I had broken a new trail at the foot of the splintered Endicotts, and my heart beat for the wilderness' (1937: 237).

Although Hutchison's films were made largely as part of her work as botanist, and a lot of her films focus on documenting plant life on a rather scientific level, her camera regularly shifts to other subjects, including the native people. Many of her films concentrate on the particular details of community life. For Hutchison, as well as Tait and Gilbertson, the inherent rhythms of the everyday were an important focus of their approach as filmmakers. It is also an approach that makes their work unique. Despite some of the films' ethnographic nature and often rather rigid documentary intentions, many of the films still seem to reveal slight deviations from dominant forms and styles of the time. Often, the way of looking presented in the films is different to that of other films focusing on the same or similar subjects.

Gilbertson's film *Jenny's Arctic Diary* (Canada, 1978), depicting her year living in the High Arctic, in Grise Fiord on Ellesmere Island, is remarkable for

Figure 23.1   Jenny Gilbertson in *Jenny's Arctic Diary*.

a film of its kind for looking at the domestic and the everyday and for noticing the detail. From her delight in the children playing on a frozen pond behind the school to her explicit dislike of seal hunting ('I don't like seeing seals killed. Hunting is a means of survival for Inuit'), Gilbertson, at the age of seventy-six, captures day-to-day life spanning thirteen months (1977–8) in the Inuit community in Grise Fiord. Gilbertson had been filming in the area for CBC throughout the 1970s. As with her other films, there is no large crew, only Gilbertson who is occasionally glimpsed in her parka with her camera in hand. She is on intimate terms with the community she is filming. They are friendly and refer to each other by first name. She is even poked fun at for showing concern for the seals and making reference to a British society for animal protection.

Over forty years after making her film following a year in the life of a crofting community in Shetland, there is a poignant resonance in the filmmaker's return of focus to filming a remote community living at the edge of the sea. In fact, Gilbertson frequently showed the films together (Taylor 1986: 15). The cyclical structure, in both films, following the course of a year, enables the inherent rhythms of the people and their environment to emerge. The filmmakers' year-long commitment to the communities they were filming meant they were far more engaged with their subjects on a personal level than many of the films that had been made in the Arctic, Shetland and Orkney. Many of these films collected material over very short and intermittent periods of time which meant that life was often performed in front of the camera instead of it being allowed to unfold more naturally in real time. Gilbertson's diary approach, in particular, seems to allow for the fullness of reality to emerge. Attention is given to the subtle changes in the seasons and the natural habitat, but also to the rich and varied culture within the community, encompassing both traditional and modern elements (for example, local traditions such as carving and hunting are depicted alongside accounts of the disco and local bands).

Fortunately, the achievements of Gilbertson and her more candid approach to filmmaking were recognised and supported, first by Grierson in the 1930s and then later by the BBC and CBC. Unfortunately, Tait's close observation and open approach to structure were often mistaken as amateurism. This was likely to be the case with Grierson's observations regarding Tait's film *Orquil Burn* (UK, 1955), a meandering portrait of a burn running past Tait's uncle's farm. It is a longer short film in comparison to Tait's other work and is structured around the camera's quest to follow the burn up to its source in the boggy Orkney hillside. Tait rejected Grierson's suggestions to edit the work, as she explained in an unpublished manuscript, *Personae*:

> All the poetry I have written up till now is folk-poetry or blood-poetry. It is the raw material of poetry in Paul Valery's sense. In the same way, 'Orquil Burn' is the raw material of a film rather than a film itself. But that doesn't mean that some busybody of a Grierson could take it and hash it about – edit it and make it into a tak-tak-tak natty little short film. It isn't that kind of raw material. It's not just footage. It is a made thing. It is a made thing, set like that on purpose. (1959: 63)

All three filmmakers privilege close observation and the ability to respond to the subject of what they are filming, rather than forcing it into any preconceived structure or ready-made form that Tait describes resisting in the extract above. For all three women, the multi-generity of their approach is evidence of their wholehearted embrace of new experiences and environments. They wrote, painted and filmed, exploring in full the expressive potential of various media for representing the world around them. Hutchison's films were made for illustrative purposes rather than any real artistic intentions (for example, serving to document the plant life she encountered). However, her similar concern with close observation, which is on the level of poetry that Tait describes, is also evident in her films. These are generally characterised by their steady succession of close-up static shots of plants and wildlife. For example, her film, *Flowers and Coffee Party at Umanak* (UK, 1935), as the title suggests, is split into two sections: one, focusing on the flowers and plant life in the surrounding area of Umanak, and the other on a coffee party hosted by the Governor of Greenland. The opening of the film features a sequence of captioned shots of local flora and fauna such as azaleas, bog cotton and the Arctic poppy, all in great detail and close-up befitting to the work of a botanist. Nevertheless, her attention to detail extends beyond her treatment of plants, suggesting that in a similar way to Tait, Hutchison's filming casts a poetic eye over the detail of everyday objects that are likely to go overlooked in other styles of documentary filmmaking whose aim is broader and all-encompassing. For instance, in Hutchison's *Salmon River Near Unalaska* (UK, 1935), the camera lingers on the salmon; you can see the pulsating qualities of the light on their skin; you can see their mouths opening and closing.

Hutchison's examination of the world around her was explored through her camera. Similar to Tait and Gilbertson, Hutchison lived for a considerable amount of time within the community she was filming. In Hutchison's case, this was in Uummannaq/Umanak, in Northwestern Greenland. Like Tait and Gilbertson's films, there is a deep connection with the environment that is registered in her films. Although the filmmakers rarely turn the camera on themselves to serve as subjects in the film, their films recognise that they are behind the camera. There is an intimacy with their subjects that is registered in the smiles exchanged with the camera. Both Hutchison and Gilbertson also take a less formal approach to filming in that little effort is made to conceal any kind of 'behind-the-scenes' work; the process of their journey and filming their journey is made explicit. In some cases, we get a rare glimpse of the filmmaker. For instance, in *Flowers and Coffee Party at Umanak,* this occurs with self-deprecating humour in a few shots of Hutchison in her botany attire, replete with a mosquito net hood. The caption appears: 'Mosquitos and flies torment the botanist'. Several of Gilbertson's films also include a shot or two of her filming with her camera. Many of them also involve her own voice-over account of events, presumably drawn from her written diaries, likewise foregrounding process. In *Jenny's Arctic Diary* (1978) and *Jenny's Dog Team Journey* (UK, 1977), Gilbertson describes her journey in great detail, often referring to her subjects by their first name. Even in a later film, the *Walrus Hunt* (Canada, 1987), which employs a male voice in a more formal narration, the address remains fairly personal; it is 'Tommy and Tommy's sons' that 'make up the crew'. In general, the tone of her address in the films which use her own voice-over is informal and peppered throughout with Gilbert's own subjectivities (for example, 'not that I cared'). Gilbertson's use of her first name in the title of both films is perhaps another signal of the level of directness and informality.

The apparatus of the camera is also acknowledged in Gilbertson's films. In *Jenny's Dog Team Journey,* a film depicting a 300-mile journey across the High Arctic by sled, when the filmmaker goes into an igloo to change a reel of film (because it is too cold to do it outside) and the igloo collapses on her, she throws the camera to one of the dog team crew so that he can film her crawling out. Even in her Shetland films, produced over forty years earlier, the process of filming was revealed rather than concealed. In *A Crofter's Life in Shetland* (UK, 1931), Gilbertson's titles explain the filmmaker's dilemma when faced with the remoteness of the clifftop location where the cormorant chicks she would like to film are nesting. And so, as the next title reads, 'one has to drop in on them rather unconventionally'. The subsequent shots then present Gilbertson scaling down the side of a cliff, precariously tethered to a man at the top of the cliff by a thin rope. The reward of the stunning close-ups of the cormorant chicks then follows, a truly astonishing feat for a filmmaker working with limited resources in the 1930s.

Much is to be commended in the methods developed by both Hutchison and Gilbertson in their filming in the Arctic – their independent way of working which allowed for a close engagement with the community in which they filmed and their responsive and open approach to filming the world of which they were a part. Yet, with both filmmakers, it is sometimes difficult, considering their commitment to capturing the rhythms of the everyday, to understand their lack of engagement with wider political and social issues faced by the communities they filmed. For instance, considering Gilbertson's open and direct approach described throughout this chapter, it is hard to grasp why Gilbertson chose not to acknowledge the troubled foundations of the Inuit community at Grisefiord. Only recent productions by Inuit writers and filmmakers such as *Martha of the North* (Marquise Lepage, Canada, 2009) and *Exile* (Zacharias Kunuk, Canada, 2008) have been able to give long and overdue attention to the plight of the Inuit people in their resettlement to the High Arctic in the 1950s, in which they were told they would be moving to a land of plenty when in reality the opposite was the case: there was no vegetation, it was very cold, and the conditions were generally inhospitable. In other ways, Gilbertson's film does not shy away from criticising the Canadian government. In a segment of the film that looks at the difficulties in maintaining a basic water supply in Grisefiord, she tells the story of government officials who had the idea to chain an iceberg to the shore, which then broke away: 'the Inuits laughed – no wonder they call us crazy whites'. Gilbertson's position is clearly one of an outsider, but it is the candid nature of her filmmaking, its open attitude to expressing the sometimes excluded nature of her point-of-view in relation to the community she is filming, that gives her films their 'clarity of observation and unique warmth' (London Filmmakers Co-op 1994). The work of all three filmmakers looked at in this chapter could be said to possess similar qualities.

In her book on European women in the Canadian North before World War II, Barbara E. Kelcy responds to potential allegations that looking at women explorers 'only valorizes their imperialist pursuits', by saying that the women 'were not heroines in any sense; rather they were heroic on a personal level, using the true meaning of the word'. She goes on to offer a number of illustrations of personal heroines, including Isobel Wylie Hutchison 'who could accept her situation, apparently dispense with the formalities, remain unconcerned about the proprieties, and write a book about her experiences' (Kelcy 2001: 177). For Hutchison, as with later filmmakers such as Tait and Gilbertson, the experiences they sought to explore through the lens of their cameras were intended to test their strength. This personal quest is what makes their method of filmmaking extraordinary, because the intention of their filmmaking is not just to document, but to explore their own personal connection to the world around them.

Bibliography

Blunt, A. and G. Rose (eds) (1994), *Writing Women and Space: Colonial and Postcolonial Geographies*, New York: The Guilford Press.

Boyd, J. (1974), 'Commentary: on some white women in the wilds of Northern North America', *Arctic*, 27: 3, 167–74.

Calton Studios (1979), Film Programme, 6 May, Margaret Tait collection, Orkney Archive, D97/25.

Domosh, M. (1991), 'Toward a feminist historiography of geography', *Transactions of the Institute of British Geographers*, New Series, 16: 1, 95–104.

Gilchrist, J. (2002), 'Action woman', *The Scotsman (Weekend)*, 9 February, 10–11.

Hoyle, G. (2001), *Flowers in the Snow: The Life of Isobel Wylie Hutchison*, Lincoln and London: University of Nebraska Press.

Hutchison, I. W. (1928), 'Walking tour across Iceland', April 1928.

Hutchison, I. W. (1937), *North to the Rime-Ringed Sun: An Alaskan Journey*, New York: Hillman-Curl Inc.

Kelcy, B. (2001), *Alone in Silence: European Women in the Canadian North Before World War II*, Montreal and Kingston: McGill-Queen's University Press.

London Filmmakers' Co-op (1994), 'Crofters on the Scottish Isles', programme notes from a screening at the London Film Co-op Cinema, 29 April 1994.

MacDiarmid, H. (1960), 'Intimate film making in Scotland: the work of Dr Margaret Tait', *Scottish Field*, October 1960, reprinted in A. Calder, G. Murray and A. Riach (eds) (1998), *The Raucle Tongue*, Manchester: Carcanet, 415–17.

Maddrell, A. (2010), *Complex Locations: Women's Geographical Work in the UK 1850–1970*, Oxford: Wiley-Blackwell.

McBain, J. (1998), 'The Rugged Island', *Journal of Film Preservation*, 57, December 1998, 39.

Neely, S. (2008) 'Stalking the image: Margaret Tait and intimate filmmaking practices', *Screen*, 49/2, Summer 2008, 216–21.

Neely, S. (2009), '"Ploughing a lonely furrow": Margaret Tait and "professional" filmmaking practices in 1950s Scotland', in I. Craven (ed.), *Movies on Home Ground: Explorations in Amateur Cinema*, Newcastle: Cambridge Scholars Press, 301–26.

Neely, S. (ed.) (2012), *Margaret Tait: Poems, Stories and Writings*, Manchester: Carcanet.

Neely, S. and A. Riach (2009), 'Demons in the machine: cinema and modernism in twentieth-century Scotland', in J. Murray, F. Farley and R. Stoneman (eds), *Scottish Cinema Now*, Newcastle: Cambridge Scholars Press.

Sandon, E. (2010), 'Women, empire, and British cinema history', *Framework: The Journal of Cinema and Media*, 51: 2, 324–33.

Shepherd, N. [1977] (2008), *The Living Mountain: A Celebration of the Cairngorm Mountains of Scotland*, Edinburgh: Canongate.

Sinclair, G. (1934), 'Wife-swapping now obsolete in the Arctic', *Daily Star*, Toronto, 24 February.

Tait, M. (1959), *Personae*, unpublished manuscript, Margaret Tait collection, Orkney Archive, D97/23.

Taylor, N. (1986), 'Film-maker at 83 still tempted at 83 for another trip to the Arctic', *The Citizen*, Ottawa, 12 February, 15.

The Herald (2006), 'Elizabeth Balneaves', obituary, 11 November.

Wade, A. (n.d.), 'Biography of Jenny Gilbertson', *Scottish Screen Archive,* http://ssa.nls.uk/biography.cfm?bid=10013 (accessed 22 June 2013).

Wade, A. (n.d.), 'Biography of Isobel Wylie Hutchison', *Scottish Screen Archive,* http://ssa.nls.uk/biography.cfm?bid=10018 (accessed 22 June 2013).

24. 'HERE WILL BE A GARDEN-CITY': SOVIET MAN ON AN ARCTIC CONSTRUCTION SITE

Lyubov Bugaeva

The Soviet Union in the 1970s was marked by colossal construction projects. Among them was the Baikal-Amur Mainline (BAM), 'the construction project of the century' in the words of then General Secretary of the Central Committee of the Communist Party of the Soviet Union, Leonid Brezhnev. Built largely in the permafrost area and intended to connect Eastern Siberia with the Russian Far East, this and many similar projects originated in the late 1920s and 1930s. Thus, BAM is part of the Great Northern Route, an uncompleted project of railroads intended to link the Barents Sea with the Strait of Tartary near Sakhalin Island, thus cutting through Eastern Russia. The idea of a second railroad in the Far East was restored in the 1970s in anticipation of new discoveries of natural resources in the Urals. Leonid Brezhnev raised the question of building BAM in March 1974. In April 1974, at the Congress of the All-Union Leninist Young Communist League, known as the Komsomol, BAM had already been declared an intensive (shock-work) Komsomol construction project and a team comprising 600 workers was transported to the site (Parfyonov 2010: 104).

The cinema of the 1970s follows the same logic as the history of great construction projects. Falling back on the history of the 1930s, it develops and transforms the ideas of the early Stalin period. It is no wonder that in search of inspiration, film directors of the 1970s turned to the period of the 1930s and bypassed the Stalin purges. They wanted to extract the pure essence of the great construction projects and plant it in the ground of the 'developed socialism' of the 1970s. Yet by then the enthusiasm for building a new life and a new world had already waned.

However, the 1970s attempted to borrow from the previous decades the romanticism of the pathfinders and explorers of uncharted territories, and this resulted in the emergence of a ramblers' subculture based on romanticising the life of geologists in harsh climatic conditions. The simple life of field geologists in the taiga and high lands, or in permafrost areas, was viewed as free and liberating in contrast to the unnatural and constrained life of people in the cities. To spend time in challenging climatic areas had become an expected common behaviour, especially for the intelligentsia. The products and commodities of urban existence, along with built-in social conventions, were entirely missing in the primitive life of ramblers. However, such absence was considered virtuous, as it coincided with the general assumption at that time of high ideals prevailing over the low materiality of ordinary life. Naturally, any hunt for commodities was seen as sinful. It had become fashionable among city intelligentsia, having returned to the city, to continue wearing a windproof jacket and sneakers. Lines from the backpackers' songs were widely used in communication and served as passwords when establishing new contacts; demonstrating familiarity with these songs was typically expected and even required. Cinematography in the 1960s reflected and supported such behavioural and conversational norms as well as the fashions and styles established by the subculture of ramblers; the best-known and most influential films contributing to the cult of pathfinders and ramblers were *Brief Encounters* (*Korotkie vstrechi*, Kira Muratova, Odessa Film Studio, 1967) and *Vertical* (Stanislav Govorukhin, Odessa Film Studio, 1967). The northern parts of Siberia, traditionally a place of imprisonment and exile and in that sense 'the other world', continued to be conceptualised as the other world in the 1960s and 1970s but in a different sense. By then they were seen as a space free from politics, bureaucracy and censorship, and as a domain where personal qualities and basic human values prevailed over social stereotypes, career expectations and hierarchical considerations (though none of this was true). One can say that by then the romantic spirit had left the cities and industrial plants and concentrated itself in the mountaintop areas, the Taiga and the Far North.

The logical move for film directors looking for ways to reproduce the enthusiasm of the 1930s was to combine a well-known construction theme that had lost its appeal with the still appealing, vital and timely theme of the exploration of little-known geographical regions. Naturally, the portrayal of construction was placed beyond the Arctic Circle – in the Taymyr Peninsula, in the Kara Sea; on Dikson Island, between the Kara Sea and the Laptev Sea; and the northern part of Krasnoyarsk Krai, in the basin of the Arctic Ocean. The mythology of discovery and conquest was transformed into the mythology of construction and conquest, but the conquest of nature and climate, rather than land. Shock-work construction projects became one of the characteristics of the period and established a certain perception of the Arctic: as a wasteland, or virgin land, which was to be changed into an oasis through the creative and constructive imagination of the Soviet man. Seeking to amend a breech in Soviet ideology in the period of what is called Brezhnev Stagnation, and to bring new life to a battered construction theme, a number of film directors chose the North as a film site; their efforts resulted in films that can be seen as examples of the dialectical tension between the Soviet ideology of the 1930s and the disillusionment of the 1970s.

SERGEI GERASIMOV, THE 1930S AND ARCTIC EXPLORATION

Among the films that develop the concept and create the image of a Soviet hero as a builder and engineer in the Arctic is the well-known Soviet establishment director Sergei Gerasimov's *The Love of Mankind* (*Lyubit' cheloveka*, Gorky Film Studio, 1972). *The Love of Mankind* is the middle film in a trilogy comprising *By the Lake* (*U Ozera*, Gorky Film Studio, 1970) and *Daughters and Mothers* (*Dochki-materi*, Gorky Film Studio, 1975). According to the prominent Soviet and Russian film historian Neya Zorkaya, the trilogy aspires to raise vital problems of contemporaneity but deals with them at a most superficial level: 'these films, long and cumbersome, shot in a realistic manner, with actors' whispering intonation, and with truthful and highly accurate details scattered throughout, are in fact propaganda works of Soviet pseudo realism' (Zorkaya 2006: 398). *Perestroika* brought a negative re-examination of the authority of Sergei Gerasimov, a recognised Soviet mainstream film director, screenwriter and actor, and the value of his films was seriously questioned. However, despite the re-evaluation and soul-searching that were characteristic of *perestroika* times, *The Love of Mankind* still stands out, for a number of reasons.

The themes of construction and the North were both familiar to Gerasimov. The son of political exiles to Siberia who later moved to the Ural region, Sergei Gerasimov (1906–85) lost his father at the age of three, when he died during a geological expedition. In his young years, Gerasimov was involved (with Leonid Trauberg and Grigori Kozintsev) with the Factory of the Eccentric Actor group, a school for young actors and a platform for bold artistic experiments, and he first appeared as a grotesque actor in Trauberg's and Kozintsev's films *The Overcoat* (1926), *The New Babylon* (1929), and *Alone* (1931). In the early part of his career, in the 1930s, aligning with the mainstream and arguably setting the stage for his later establishment films, Gerasimov made two films about the explorers and exploration of the new Northern lands: *The Seven Bold Ones* (*Semero smelykh*, Lenfilm, 1936) and the *City of Youth* (*Komsomolsk*, Lenfilm, 1938).

Figure 24.1 Pyotr Aleynikov as cook Moliboga; Nikolay Bogolyubov as Ilya Letnikov, the chief of the expedition; Tamara Makarova as doctor Zhenya; and Ivan Novoseltsev as pilot Bogun (Sergei Gerasimov, *The Seven Bold Ones*).

The Seven Bold Ones (screenplay by Sergei Gerasimov and Yuri German), the first sound film made by Gerasimov, demonstrated his strong interest in the life of certain young Soviet people who, from his point of view, represented the front line of the young generation; this interest in, and desire to catch, the atmosphere of the time continued throughout his entire life. A master with a background in experimental avant-garde cinematography, Gerasimov nevertheless deliberately chose a realistic style of filmmaking in order to comply clearly and convincingly with contemporary expectations. Mikhail Ermolaev (1905–91), a Soviet Arctic explorer and polar geologist, served as a prototype for one of the film's characters, the chief of the expedition. Ermolaev took part in twenty-one expeditions to the Far North, including the expedition of the icebreaker *Krasin* which rescued Umberto Nobile and his team in 1928 after the crash of the airship *Italia*, which was searching for the North Pole; he also participated in expeditions to Novaya Zemlya (Nova Zembla) in 1932–3. In order to reproduce the atmosphere of the polar expedition more convincingly, the film crew took part in expeditions to the

Barents Sea, climbed the icecap of Mount Elbrus, and mastered skiing in the Khibiny Massif of the Kola Peninsula in the Arctic Circle, bordered by the Barents and White Seas.

The film tells the story of the 'seven bold ones', members of an iconic Soviet geological expedition who answered a Soviet newspaper's call to explore virgin Arctic lands and were chosen out of 409 volunteers. The opening frames of Arctic summer with the waves breaking on the rocks and birds flying over the Barents Sea are quickly replaced by a more severe and unfriendly depiction of nature; on the 72nd parallel, winter lasts 275 days. Ten days of non-stormy weather are considered a remarkable gift, which is marred by a crash involving the aero sleds. In the film, almost all the technical devices, except the radio transmitter, are unreliable: aero sleds break, an aeroplane breaks down, skis escape from skiers. In contrast to technology and nature, only people are reliable. The characters battle with the unfavourable weather, save the life of a Chukchi wounded by a bear (the Chukchi are an indigenous people in Northern and Northeastern Russia), assist each other in difficult situations, and despite the difficulties, frost and failure of technology, they discover tin ore and therefore successfully fulfil their mission. The explorers do not just survive in the Arctic, they are permanently engaged in one search or another – for tin ore or for friends who are in trouble.

Filmed on the Kola Peninsula, *The Seven Bold Ones* corresponds to a quest for the legendary Ultima Thule, a no-man's land that is impossible or hard to reach and that has always attracted the human imagination. The number of the 'bold ones' – seven – is symbolic in Russian culture and alludes to fairy-tales where seven is a magic number that corresponds to a quantity of epic heroes and charmed objects. In the film, which is still considered a masterpiece and one of the best of Gerasimov's productions, cultural and mythological references are intertwined with Soviet propaganda. The Northern Arctic policies of the Soviet Union in the 1920s and in the early 1930s were multi-focal. The state was concerned with establishing Soviet power there, governing the 'small peoples of the North', and developing the North alongside the other territories of the Soviet Union (McCannon 1998: 21–3). This period saw several major expeditions to the North. These included the *Sibiriakov* voyage (1932) and the notoriously unsuccessful *Cheliuskin* voyage, which was nevertheless glorified by the press (1933–4). At this time, the 'Arctic myth' constitutive of Soviet ideology was fully coined. By now the Arctic was a blank space to be filled in, a battleground in the war with nature, an enemy to be conquered, a wild animal to be tamed, and a potential friend. The genuine heroism of polar explorers was exploited to impress ordinary Soviet people and to animate Stalinist totalitarian culture (McCannon 1998), and this is equally true for Gerasimov's film. As a result of the skilful manipulation of mythology and ideology, *The Seven*

Bold Ones, which is a romantic story of an adventurous journey and of conquering severe natural conditions, had a strong appeal for viewers and became a blockbuster in the Soviet Union in 1936.

The reception of the film in Marxist circles outside the Soviet Union was much more reserved. *The New Masses*, an American Marxist magazine published in 1926–48, describes *The Seven Bold Ones* as 'a minor Soviet film about the heroic adventures of an Arctic expedition . . . exciting in parts, but too slight in the conception to be of major importance' (Ellis 1936: 30). The enthusiasm for exploring the Arctic, combined with communist ideology, that was successfully exploited in the culture of the Soviet establishment seemed unfamiliar to American Marxists. Connected in American history and culture to the Klondike and Alaska Gold Rushes and Jack London's stories, the North theme did not excite American Marxists, who did not see the inspirational potential of the Arctic that was used by Soviet filmmakers. Besides, left-wing contributors to *The New Masses*, which chose radicalism over the conformity of mass culture, rightly noted Gerasimov's affiliation with the culture of the establishment and hence a shortage of radical and revolutionary character in the film.

BIRTH OF A CITY AND THE PASSION FOR CONSTRUCTION

While *The Seven Bold Ones* is the story of explorers working in the Arctic winter, Gerasimov's *City of Youth* tells the story of building the city of Komsomolsk-on-Amur, located on the Eastern part of the Baikal-Amur Mainline. Due to its remote location and harsh climate, it was equated with the Far North in terms of labour compensation in the Soviet regime. In the film, the creation of a new city is overshadowed by a sabotage theme and images of saboteurs who want to destroy the construction plans by starting a fire in a storeroom. Saboteurs and foreign agents populated Soviet films in the 1930s, and Gerasimov's *City of Youth* is no exception. The sabotage theme in the film, with its image of an enemy disguised as a Komsomol member, and his unmasking with the help of an ingenious young man, is rather poorly presented and destroys the general atmosphere of enthusiastic construction work. However, the romanticism of the construction of a new city by young people is appealing and evokes some of the ideas of the Russian avant-garde. Avant-garde artists such as Vladimir Tatlin, Kazimir Malevich, El Lissitzky and Vladimir Mayakovsky argued that the new social order requires new revolutionary art – architecture, painting, photography, poetry, prose – produced by young revolutionary-minded artists and combining artistic principles with ideology, which in turn will help to construct a new mentality and finally to build a 'new man'.

Though at the time, *City of Youth* received an extremely positive response in the Soviet press, the response from Marxists abroad was again restrained, and they blamed the director for his failure to capture and convincingly convey the excitement of labour, which is the most significant theme of the time. One US critic's verdict, expressed in *The New Masses*, was harsh:

> In a combination of documentary shots taken during stages of building and a plot enacted by professional actors, S. Gerasimov, the director, has failed to catch the epic of Komsomolsk. He has recorded the patient tenacity of the builders, their discouragements, the sexual adjustments, the plots of saboteurs, and Soviet triumph at the end, but the sense of magnificent achievement, the suspense of the work itself is missing. (Dugan 1938: 29–30).

Gerasimov in *City of Youth* in a sense balances the straightforwardness and saboteur-enemy banality of socialist realism on the one hand and authentic romantic passion on the other. The film is a kind of staged propagandistic documentary of the construction of Komsomolsk-on-Amur. It was partially filmed on site in Komsomolsk-on-Amur, and the background actors were local construction workers because the construction that had begun in 1932 was still in progress in 1937–8. A large proportion of the workers were young volunteers – Komsomol members; only after *perestroika* did it become widely known that the city was built with the use of political prisoners as well. The film has all the features of socialist realism, including devoted, progressive workers, guidance by the party, and the proclamation of the desirable as already existing. Thus, seventeen girls working at the construction site write a letter inviting other girls from all over the Soviet Union to join them; in their letter they declare the existence of well-equipped nurseries, a water sports centre, and a recreation park running down to the Amur River. The affirmation of the desirable looked to turn fantasy into present-day reality. At least the turning of fantasy to present-day reality is what the principal character Natasha (Tamara Makarova) and the other girls think is happening. And reality meets their expectations: a water sports centre is built, a park is being built, and the first 230 girls, eager to join the project and too impatient to wait for transportation, arrive in Komsomolsk on skis! The enthusiasm is unmistakably there. All the characters are young, energetic and industrious. The film shows volunteers building a sports centre, as well as tired and sleepy characters overcoming their sleepiness and valiantly going to work; it displays mutual friendships and support and the joy of accomplishment when the building of a river port is finished and the first ship is launched.

The depiction of the excitement of construction work is supported by the symbolism of seasons. The story begins in spring with volunteers arriving at the construction site; important accomplishments, including opening a sports centre and a year later launching a ship, take place in summer; a serious threat to the construction site occurs in winter, and all disasters (treachery, murder and fire) happen in the open, on the white snow. Gerasimov does not cultivate the theme of the North in the *City of Youth*, however; the threat to the construction project is created not by the weather or climate but by enemies. The authentic romantic passion for construction and creation is still present and does not require reinforcement with challenges posed by harsh and unfriendly nature.

The genesis function of such films as Gerasimov's *City of Youth* or Alexander Dovzhenko's *Aerograd* (Mosfilm and Ukrainfilm 1935), portraying the building of a city on the Pacific Ocean, is significant in 1930s Soviet ideology, as these films describe the birth of a city. These are stories of a heroic creative act, which is 'the beginning after the beginning' (Smirnov 2009: 181), as the October Revolution was already the absolute beginning of the new socialist world. Stories of the birth of a city are reminiscent of the act of creation of the state, and they support the idea of total renovation, thus signalling the triumph of communism. The nature of cinema itself supports the idea of reproduction, in Walter Benjamin's sense, which in this case is the reproduction of the act and passion of creation. The themes of beginning and of creation are themes that Soviet filmmakers in the 1970s would use in their Arctic construction films to recreate the enthusiasm of the 1930s.

ARCTIC CONSTRUCTION IN THE 1970S

The construction-themed films of the 1970s aspire to recreate and reincarnate the origin-of-the-state myth and the excitement of creation skilfully exploited in the 1930s, and without references to the actual historical context of the Stalin regime or its obsession with saboteurs and foreign spies. By the 1970s, the Arctic myth had become overshadowed by the space flights of the 1960s, and by the concerns of everyday life in the Soviet Union. However, it is still attractive for aesthetic and political reasons. This is due in part to the contribution made by the ramblers' subculture to the image of the Northern area as a wild and romantic place, in part to the popularity of several authors who were writing about the North, including a Chukchi writer Yuri Rytkheu (1947–2008), and in part to the cinematographic images of the North as a challenging place. Some of the most significant state ideological events of the 1970s are also related to the exploration of the North. For example, the first nuclear-powered icebreaker *Arktika* reached the North Pole in 1978, an event that was interpreted as proof of the all-powerfulness of a Soviet Union that could tame the Arctic Ocean. The first ski expedition sponsored by the newspaper *Komsomolskaya Pravda*, headed by Dmitry Shparo, reached the North Pole in 1979, leaving behind a container box with the symbol of the Baikal-Amur Mainline (Parfyonov 2010: 238). Telling the story of the expedition, Shparo shares his thoughts (or what were supposed to be his thoughts) when they reached the North Pole, equating the expedition to the Pole with the eternal human quest for the unknown:

> Here is the Pole. Many were aspiring to reach it and many sacrificed their lives for the North Pole dream. Perhaps people will arrive here after us. Thanks to us they will probably strive to reach the North Pole with even greater effort than they did before. Man will always strive to reach the stars, mountaintops, and the Poles. Today is our victory day. (Shparo and Shumilov 1987; my translation)

Soviet cinema tries to catch up with life. From the late 1950s to the late 1970s, it was generally characterised by the dominance of a natural or *cinéma-verité* style, as inspired by Dziga Vertov's *kino-glaz* ('film-eye') theory from the 1920s. Vertov promoted the camera as an instrument for documenting everyday life (Beumers 2009: 128–9). The 'passion for the real' (Alain Badiou) in the context of 1970s Soviet cinema is not limited to documentary cinema proper, but embraces a wide spectrum of genres. Originating in the early Soviet period, the desire to intervene in reality itself aspires not only to access historical reality through representation, but also to use it as a rhetorical device, as an instrument for the emotional manipulation of the spectator, and as a powerful tool for creating the illusion of what is supposed to be the reality but is absent. Gerasimov worked in a similar semi-documentary manner, as evidenced by many of his films, such as *Men and Beasts* (*Liudi i zveri*, Gorky Studio with DEFA, GDR 1962), *The Journalist* (*Zhurnalist*, Gorky Studio 1967), *By the Lake* (*U ozera*, Gorky Studio, 1969), and *The Love of Mankind* (Gorky Studio, 1972).

Figure 24.2   Anatoly Solonitsyn as Dmitry Kalmykov, demonstrating his project for the Arctic with a winter garden (Sergei Gerasimov, *The Love of Mankind*).

In *The Love of Mankind* Gerasimov applies various methods of addressing film as a document, including embedded documentary footage, authentic architectural projects, and other links to reality. The film tells the story of Dmitry Kalmykov (Anatoly Solonitsyn), a passionate architect in his mid-thirties, who during a short visit to Moscow meets Maria (Lyubov Virolainen), an interior designer, and brings her to Krasnoyarsk Krai near Norilsk (after Murmansk, the second-largest city inside the Arctic Circle), where he works at a construction site. The film is about the difficult process of building a close and harmonious relationship between the characters and about the difficult process of building the city, where achievements alternate with setbacks.

In the introductory section of the film, the participants in a symposium on architecture look at various projects of fountains, a library and a palace of culture intended for Soviet Central Asia, and watch an authentic documentary, embedded in the film, about Mexican architecture, which features David Alfaro Siqueiros. The connection between the warm climate and the architecture is not accidental: Gerasimov establishes through his character a direct link between climate and the progress of civilisation. The answer to the question 'Why did civilisation start in the Mediterranean Sea area?' is 'Because the 21 degrees Celsius temperature provides the necessary conditions for the advance of culture and civilisation'. The aspiration of the film's protagonists, the architect Kalmykov, his wife and his colleagues, is to create such conditions in the Far North. Yet providing comfortable living conditions for people does not mean turning them into regular consumers; the struggle for survival is seen as limiting creative activity, unnecessary and destructive, while creating comfortable living conditions releases creative potential.

According to Katerina Clark, snowy landscapes are typical of Russia; they symbolise the final triumph of the Russian Empire over Napoleon and serve as a mythological space of dramatic action. It was true for Gerasimov's *The Seven Bold Ones* and *The City of Youth*. In this vein, *The Love of Mankind* both refers to and challenges the images of the Arctic in the 1930s. Whereas in *The Seven Bold Ones* the winter explorers fight with an unfriendly nature and try to adjust to it, in *The Love of Mankind* the characters transform the environment; whereas in *The Seven Bold Ones* they explore the Arctic land and dream about building roads and inhabiting the land, in *The Love of Mankind* the land is already explored, and roads, houses and apartment complexes are being built. Whereas in *The City of Youth* the characters are executors of someone else's project and perform mainly hard physical work, in *The Love of Mankind* the characters are creators. Compared to the 1930s, the emphasis is transferred from *man versus nature* to *man and nature*, and from *man and work* to *man and creative work*.

ARCHITECTURE AND A GARDEN CITY: SERGEI GERASIMOV

In the Moscow episodes of the film, one becomes acquainted with a modern-day apartment building with around 400 apartments designed as a complex that includes a canteen on each floor, a gymnasium, a club, a movie theatre and a library. A typical apartment has two rooms and a kitchenette. The innovative complex, which is reminiscent of the commune houses from the time of the first five-year plan, is a House of the New Way of Life by architect Natan Osterman. Kalmykov admires the commune-style building, but his plans for the Arctic are different. Gerasimov puts in the character's mouth the ideas developed by the architect Alexander Shipkov and he heavily borrows facts from Shipkov's biography. Thus, Shipkov came to Norilsk together with his wife, also an architect, and was a chief architect of Norilsk in 1964–7. Norilsk, which is used as a setting in the film, served in the 1960s–1970s as a stage for the boldest architectural experiments. The first phase of developing the North in the 1930s is characterised by the desire to recreate familiar architectural forms, and it resulted in the creation of little versions of Leningrad or Moscow in the icy tundra. The phenomenon can be seen not as the assimilation of the Northern space but as a means of isolation. Every apartment is an isolated unit evoking nostalgic feelings for the world left behind. The idea developed by Shipkov during his years in Norilsk and by Kalmykov in the film is to oppose the integrity of living space to the infinity of the Arctic. An infinite and object-less area does not necessarily open space for imagination; it also induces a sense of loneliness and isolation.

In one of the film's episodes, Kalmykov presents a complex that comprises two houses connected through a winter garden. The project emphasises the idea that accommodation in the Arctic is neither a way to isolate oneself from nature nor a way to connect them; it is both. The complex for 1,000 inhabitants unites under one roof an apartment building, cafes, a library, a gymnasium, a movie theatre, service units and so on. The idea of a multi-purpose building reminds one of the House of the New Way of Life and of the commune houses from the 1930s, yet it is different. The complex is declared to be similar to a mitten (in which fingers are twisted together so they do not freeze) in order to combine a living space, a place of work and nature. The main attraction of the project is a winter garden. In the complex house planned for Norilsk, every inhabitant was supposed to have 9 square metres of living space and 6.5 square metres of winter garden. The garden was to be protected by a transparent cupola that would open in summer (Sheiko 1976: 90–4).

This is the conception of life Gerasimov develops in *The Love of Mankind*. A winter garden from Shipkov's project is, in the film, a garden, and Kalmykov insists on defending his ideas at the city and ministry levels. For Gerasimov a garden is much more than a real garden; it is a place where 'humanity will be renewed' (Dostoevsky). In *The Seven Bold Ones*, the chief explorer hopes that, in the future, gardens will grow in the Arctic; in *The City of Youth*, one of the first things to be built is a recreation park (a garden) running down to the Amur River. Whatever Gerasimov hints at in his earlier films has been materialised in *The Love of Mankind*, which is a film that revises the whole former conception of the North. The young architects struggle not for survival or fulfilment of great state plans but to create a comfortable and fulfilling life for Soviet people. They do not struggle with nature; they struggle with a bureaucracy that creates obstacles to the realisation of their projects. In the Arctic, people should not work together uncomfortably; rather, they should comfortably live together. *The Love of Mankind* unfolds in details an architectural plan of an apartment complex combining various activities and uniting people in the North. Gerasimov explores the conception of the North as 'the other world', where personal qualities prevail over social stereotypes and the romantic spirit prevails over the calculating mind that was formed in the Soviet culture in the 1960s and 1970s. Gerasimov, however, goes further. He creates an image of the North as a place of possibilities where socialist dreams come true. The Arctic is presented as a unique and proper place where Dostoevsky's dream of Regenerated Humanity takes its concrete shape. A clever film director, Gerasimov combines literary associations with a romantic spirit of exploration of the North and of the birth of a city – associations that date back to the 1930s.

Construction and a Garden City: Alexei Simonov

Sergei Gerasimov is not the only film director who addressed the Arctic and the construction themes with reference to the culture of the 1930s. *The Ordinary Arctic* (*Obyknovennaya Arktika*, Lenfilm 1974) is another example that addresses the period in the search for enthusiasm and excitement, and at the same time combines the themes of construction and the North. *The Ordinary Arctic* is the debut film of Alexei Simonov (b. 1939), the son of Soviet writer Konstantin Simonov (1915–79). Looking for a literary basis for his first film, Alexei Simonov took the advice of his father and chose the collection of stories *The Ordinary Arctic* (1939), written by the Soviet writer and Stalin prize laureate Boris Gorbatov (1908–54). Boris Gorbatov, who was a friend of Konstantin Simonov, worked in the Arctic in the 1930s as a journalist for the newspaper *Pravda*. The book reflects his impressions of life and people there. Several stories from the collection were chosen for the script, which was written jointly by Alexei and Konstantin Simonov. The title of the film and of the book, *The Ordinary Arctic*, suggests that the Arctic is not necessarily a unique place that requires extraordinary people and exceptional efforts in order to survive, but is somehow a normal place, like everywhere else.

However, readers' and viewers' expectations are denied, as both the book and the film present everyday life in the Arctic as heroic, though in an unusual way.

The script and the film diverge from the original literary source. Both the script and the film belong to the 1970s and reflect the dominant attitudes and tendencies of that period, while the book reflects those of the 1930s. The collection of stories with different characters in each is unified by the Arctic location and the approach to the theme of the North. The goal is to describe everyday life in the Arctic, which is romantic and heroic in its most trivial forms. Gorbatov's Arctic of the 1930s is a place where the characters are tested. It is also a place of self-actualisation that reveals the hidden potential of people. For people who work and settle in the Arctic, their own lives may seem usual, routine and unadventurous; however, seen from the outside, they are exceptional and heroic. Thus, 'The Spring Flood' tells the story of an old village man who every spring risks his life going to Dikson Island in order to deliver and pick up mail. He starts his trip as soon as the spring flood begins, an event that signals the beginning of the navigational period. In a hurry to deliver and get mail after a long winter interval, the old man endangers his life without realising how courageous he is.

The film too develops the theme of heroic lives in the Arctic, though the heroism theme in that case is connected with the theme of construction. The film is primarily about a great construction project in the Arctic and about how people are changed by taking part in it. The story of a voluntary postman risking his life is one of the subordinate strains of the film's multi-path narrative. The central intrigue is connected with the construction of the foundations for the future seaport at Cape Dalny on the Kamchatka Peninsula. The film consists of several interrelated and interwoven stories that are united not only by their Arctic location, but also by the figure of the newly appointed chief of the project (Oleg Dahl), a strict, military-style commander who is passionate about building the port. His goal is to leave behind him concrete results of the work carried out, to have something built. Following the logic of the film, one may say that constructing various objects is the principal meaning of human life. The idea of immortalising oneself through construction attracts and unites the poorly disciplined Arctic workers, who at first are suspicious of the new chief, antagonised by his austere behaviour and ascetic habits, and sceptical about their work in general and its possible results.

Drawing on the stories of discovery in the North and the construction theme of the 1930s, the cinema of the 1970s brings this theme to the forefront and combines it with the theme of discovery. Boris Gorbatov's stories in Alexei Simonov's film are adjusted to fit this conception. Konstantin Simonov travelled to the Arctic while writing the script with his son; in his introductory words to the film, he notes the great changes that had taken place in the Arctic since Gorbatov wrote his book. He talks about the Arctic as a construction site. This is what the film is about, but in this respect it differs from the book. The film tells the story of the origin of a port in the Arctic Ocean and people uniting in their passion for construction; the book tells the stories of people conquering the Arctic in their everyday activities and in their seemingly ordinary life. The garden theme, in the sense of Dostoevsky's Garden City, is present in the film but absent in the book. The doctor (Rolan Bykov), who came to the Arctic out of practical considerations to earn money to buy a house with a garden, has obviously changed his mind. He realises that the Arctic is what is supposed to be a garden in a symbolic sense, and he gives up his initial plans. In this light, the story of the doctor guiding a patient through labour and childbirth via radio transmitter becomes a story of the regeneration and renewal of humanity. And a canary brought to the polar station by the chief engineer, a detail absent from the book, symbolises the transition to the future Garden City in the Arctic.

CONCLUSION

While, in the 1930s, the North was seen as a dangerous and enigmatic space in which one must struggle to survive, explore and conquer, in the 1970s the intention is not merely to survive, but also to transform the Arctic space in order to bring it closer to the comfortable and favourable climatic conditions of ancient and modern civilisations. In the 1970s, the Arctic is no longer seen as a liminal zone in rites of passage in which the Arctic explorers find themselves. The harsh climate of the North, along with the challenges it poses, is not a test of the strength of will or courage of people engaged in a struggle with nature. Initiation into the higher order of strong characters is not implied in Gerasimov's or Simonov's conceptions of the North. Instead of being a place for self-actualisation in extreme situations, the North becomes a place for self-realisation and the realisation of creative ideas, especially in Gerasimov's films of the 1970s. The heroic struggle is of a different kind, and is associated with creative activity and building the cities of the future.

BIBLIOGRAPHY

Beumers, B. (2009), *A History of Russian Cinema*, Oxford; New York, NY: Berg.
Clark, K. (2009), 'Imperskoe vozvyshennoe v sovetskoi kulture vtoroi poloviny 1930 godov', *Novoe literaturnoe obozrenie*, no. 95, 58–80.
Dostoevsky, F. (1994), *A Writer's Diary*, trans. K. Lantz, with an introduction by G. S. Morson, vol. 1: 1873–1876, Northwestern University Press, 590–1.
Dugan, J. (1938), 'Movies', *The New Masses*, 20 September, 29–31.
Ellis, P. (1936), 'Current films', *The New Masses*, 30 June, 30.
McCannon, J. (1998), *Red Arctic: Polar Exploration and the Myth of the North in the Soviet Union, 1932–1939*, New York, NY; Oxford: Oxford University Press.
Parfyonov, L. (2010), *Namedni. Nasha era. 1971–1980*, Moscow: KoLibri.

Sheiko, R. (1976), 'Dom v Zapolyarie', *Yunost*, no. 7, 90–4.
Shparo, D. I. and A. V. Shumilov (1987), *K polyusu*, Moscow: Molodaya Gvardia.
Smirnov, I. (2009), *Videoriad. Istoricheskaya semantika kino*, St Petersburg: Petropolis.
Zorkaya, N. (2006), *Istoria sovetskogo kino*, St Peterburg: Aleteia; St Petersburg University Press.

25. TRANSCENDING THE SUBLIME: ARCTIC CREOLISATION IN THE WORKS OF ISAAC JULIEN AND JOHN AKOMFRAH

Helga Hlaðgerður Lúthersdóttir

Through Western culture's long-distance love affair with its northernmost regions, the Arctic simulacrum has become synonymous with vastness, whiteness, tranquillity and, especially, the sublime: the ultimate awe-inspiring no-man's land. The connection between the Arctic and the sublime is a powerful and lasting one, even if increasingly questioned in the past decades. Today, connotations of spaces previously 'seen as literally and symbolically white' are no longer the 'site of a privileged white masculinity' as the myth of no-man's land is rapidly being creolised (Sandhu 2010; Bloom 2010: 31). Indigenous peoples now compete with neo-imperial interests in ownership of their homelands, objecting to the Anglophone concepts of 'wilderness' and 'landscape' dominating the discourse on the Nordic regions because such 'approaches erode the appreciation of distinctively Northern and Indigenous aspects of land and life' (Lehtinen 2012: 108). Indeed, the Arctic region itself is increasingly seen as needing protection rather than being regarded as the awe-inspiring challenge it once was.

While artists were instrumental in creating the simulacrum of the Arctic and maintaining its sublimity, they have been equally influential in changing our understanding of the region via a range of media, as can be seen, for example, from artistic involvement in David Buckland's massive Cape Farewell project; Magali Daniaux and Cédric Pigot's array of digital works; Nele Azevedo's travelling installations of her Army of Melting Men; or DJ Spooky's multidisciplinary project *Terra Nova: Sinfonia Antarctica*, discussed at length by Daria Shembel in Chapter 26 of this volume.

This chapter focuses on two London-based visual artists, the filmmaker John Akomfrah and the conceptual film artist Isaac Julien. Both artists explore and manipulate Arctic imagery through creolisation of the landscape, thus actively challenging Western nature ideology and (neo-)imperial claims of ownership albeit through different means and with different agenda. Akomfrah relies on the medium of film and the framework of the documentary which he then pushes to the extreme, leaving the audience to decipher meaning whichever way they can, while Julien actively rejects the rigid screen-viewer axis by screening his fragmentally narrated film installation on multiple panels, frequently accompanied by a selection of stills (Gröner 2006: 15).

Akomfrah's documentary *The Nine Muses* (UK, 2010) is a hybrid work, described by Nina Powers as 'a poetic film essay' as it 'shifts between archive clips of cold, dreary, snowy Britain in the 1960s to icy footage of Arctic tundra and choppy seas' (Power 2011: 59). Reworking his artistic documentary *Mnemosyne* (UK, 2010) in *The Nine Muses*, Akomfrah seeks to convey the experience of migrants arriving in postwar Britain by juxtaposing BBC's archival footage with extended scenes of new footage of Arctic landscapes, as well as recent British imagery. Rather than directly narrating his film, Akomfrah loosely connects the fragmentary footage with a wide array of literary references, from Homer's *Odyssey* to Shakespeare to Samuel Beckett, and a soundtrack of musical amalgamation ranging from popular songs and Indian compositions to classical European components.

Conversely, Julien's *True North* is a large scale audiovisual installation, the first instalment of Julien's gripping trilogy of film installations also including *Fantôme Afrique* (UK, 2005) and *WESTERN UNION: Small Boats* (UK, 2007), where Julien explores 'the impact of location – both cultural and physical – to resounding effect through a juxtaposition of opposing global regions' ('*WESTERN UNION*', 2007). Introduced as comprising 'reflective images of the sublime', the Arctic landscape is central to the installation (Merali 2004). The installation is loosely based on an account by Matthew Henson, a polar explorer and a member of the Robert Peary expedition, who arguably became the first person to reach the North Pole.

Shot on location in Iceland and Northern Sweden, the installation presents an Arctic region that both is (the locations are real) and is not (they are not the actual locations, nor is Iceland north of the Arctic Circle). Furthermore, as stressed by Veit Gröner, the 'simultaneous screening on three adjacent projection surfaces is fragmentation, preview/retrospect, and supplement in one', as is further emphasised by the fragmented, whispered narrative (Gröner 2006: 16). Neither available on DVDs nor distributed to cinemas, Julien's film installations may only be viewed by attending exhibitions of his work, where Julien artfully manipulates both the layout and colours of the exhibition space to invite the viewer to literally enter his aesthetic vision for a whole-body and mind experience. Through engulfing imagery and sound, Julien thus physically draws the viewer into dialogue with his creation, manipulating the viewer's senses and interpretations, presenting a fragmented story heavily laced with politics of race, gender, colonialism, imperialism and environmentalism.

Akomfrah's presentation of grey, unquiet seas and snowy windswept slopes already breaks away from the traditional depiction of the Arctic no-man's land since the ferry, the roads, the passing lorries and the various structures presented serve as a constant reference to human presence, yet these humans are entirely absent except for the repeated depiction of a solitary figure dressed in blue or yellow parka, turning its back to the camera. Nina Power sees this figure as 'representing perhaps the personal nature of travelling to another country, but also a more classical figure of the epic hero whose very mode of being is the journey' and labels the film's concern as being both 'personal and metaphysical' (Power 2011: 59). Read thus, the loneliness and isolation of the figure is exaggerated by an acute sense of apocalyptic abandonment conveyed by the lack of human accompaniment in this landscape that still clearly bears the mark of inhabitation. This sensation is heightened as the Alaskan winter is juxtaposed with the archival footage showing streets in Britain, snowswept, but filled with people battling the weather.

It is worth noting that unless one is familiar with the Alaskan landscape, one must read the credits at the end to realise the actual location of this footage, even if, as one reviewer noted, 'it's fairly obviously not anywhere in Britain' (Robson 2010). What is gained by this additional layer of disorientation? Robson ponders:

> Perhaps the idea was to heighten the sense of strangeness and disloca-
> tion, reminding the audience that, to the new arrivals, England seemed
> as strange and forbidding as this landscape does to us. But I can't help
> feeling that choosing somewhere like Snowdonia or the far north of
> Scotland would have produced the same effect and provided more of a
> cultural reference point for the audience. (Robson 2010)

More specifically, especially given the loaded connotation of Arctic imagery, would a directly relevant location not have provided more of a cultural reference point for the people actually depicted in the film, as well as their descendants? In spite of its artfulness, this is still a documentary intended to depict the subject's experience of emigrating to the UK, not Alaska. This break with the subject's perceived experience seems to favour the individual and suggest a depiction in line with the traditional notion of the Arctic as threatening and dangerous, the ultimate challenge that might never be overcome as implied by the lack of human interaction. Yet, it implies a challenge to be conquered by the parka-clad epic hero, a depiction dangerously close to reinstating the (neo-) imperialist Western notion of conquering and claiming 'new' lands, a notion reinforced by these lands being presented so devoid of human presence.

Incidentally, when Nina Power asks Akomfrah to speak 'about the relationship in *Nine Muses* between the images of frozen Scottish and Alaskan landscapes . . . and the archive footage of cities with traffic jams and crowds', inquiring how he moves from 'one world to the other', Akomfrah ignores the geographical component of the question. Referring to immigration 'folklore' of coldness and greyness, he describes the film as premised on 'mythology or apocrypha' of these two ideas while addressing the experience of the migrant: 'How you move from a place of certainty – your country, your town, your continent – into this other thing, which is not really either here nor there' (Power 2011: 62). But 'this other thing' is the UK, not Alaska, and to thus blatantly ignore the fact that Alaska is a place with an entirely different migration history of its own is highly problematic.

Julien's approach in *True North* could not be more different. Far from the grey bleakness of Akomfrah's Alaska, Julien's imagery of vast, frozen slopes and winter sun radiates shades of white, grey and teal, its play with light and shadow conveying the stillness, timelessness and deep tranquillity traditionally associated with the Arctic. The immediate effect is truly sublime.

Julien's vision is much more heavily mediated and technologised than is Akomfrah's, due to his compilation of stills and video installations, but also due to his signature use of multiple screens or, specifically, a triptych in the case of *True North*. Furthermore, Julien's installations tend to be accompanied by photographs taken with a professional-grade camera alongside the moving image of the installation. Thus, the photographs present moments frozen in time while the installation moves events forward and introduces human

Figure 25.1   Isaac Julien's *True North*.

presence along with multi-layered and fragmented narratives. The clearest of these, presented as a whispered voice-over, combined with the filmic effects of 'sound, spectacular shots, and rapid montage utilized in the three-screen installation emphasize the perils of a voyage to the North Pole with its historical drama of endurance and conquest' (Shaked 2005). Thus, a central narrative is introduced representing polar exploration that 'exceeds both purposeful activity and the instrumentality of the earlier colonial narrative of exploration, science, and discovery' (Bloom 2010: 35).

But there are other narratives in action as well, represented by the theme of the actual landscape displayed on the screen, i.e. the glaciers and mountains of Iceland and Northern Sweden, as well as vast plains of Arctic lands surrounding the North Pole. In conversations with Cheryl Kaplan, Julien emphasises the materiality of 'the land itself' while simultaneously stressing the importance of the location (Northern Sweden and Iceland) and the Arctic. When he reminds us that these 'are not empty landscapes, emptied of people or history or meaning', we cannot help but be reminded of Northern Sweden and Iceland as well as the Arctic, even if Julien continues to stress that it is 'looked upon as a space for possible colonization; the Inuit folks and culture were there', thus specifying the Arctic 'region' (Kaplan 2005). Similarly, Julien's references to the toughness and hardness of the landscape conflicting with its vulnerability end up reflecting on both the actual and the implied locations. Julien continues,

> I'm interested in the idea of a contaminated landscape. It's a white landscape linked to the sublime, but actually it's not a sublime, ideal landscape at all. It's 'raced,' it belongs to a culture, but in a post-colonial sense – it's the embodiment of ideals people have about themselves in relation to fixed notions of identity and national belonging as well as a European idea about landscape. I want to break this open. It's a radical positioning in terms of a black subject reclaiming a space and history that has been 'raced'. (Kaplan 2005)

It is true that Julien never directly addresses the politics of 'race' in Swedish or Icelandic landscape, but his ready acknowledgement of the shooting locations, the mesmerising beauty of the actual landscapes depicted (never compromised for the politics), the fragmented narrative, and the non-linear representation of the triptych invite the viewer to contribute to creolisation on a much deeper level than provided by Akomfrah's juxtaposition of the UK versus Alaska. In the words of Shaheen Merali:

> The installation offers a fascinating new visual reading of space and time and its relation to counter histories. Here, the sublime moment of cogni-

tion of the image is presented to the mind which, in turn, can only comprehend the absolute of magnitude which itself defies conceptualisation. The installation contests binaries which are present in many notations of the expedition and of adventure that clutter the history of discovery . . . (Merali 2013)

One of the most negative connotations of the Arctic sublime is one of the Arctic spaces 'seen as literally and symbolically white' (Sandhu 2010). Politics of race are a powerful counter-history in the works of Akomfrah, himself an immigrant from Ghana, and Julien, the English-born son of immigrants from St Lucia, and both artists actively creolise the notion of racial whiteness in Arctic imagery.

Akomfrah's use of archival film footage bears a direct witness to the immigrant's experience while simultaneously challenging the assertion that 'somehow the truth resides in the archives, unsullied, unmediated' because, 'the archive survives in a very complicated way for diasporic subjectivities' (Power 2011: 62). According to Akomfrah,

the archive is also the space of a certain fabulations and fictions. So there needs to be critical interrogation of the archive. One of the important ways of doing this is to remove the narrative voice. Once you remove the voice, nine times out of ten the images start to say something else . . . You need to extract the images and the narratives and the stories out of a certain performed chain. (Power 2011: 62)

The result is black and white montage of immigrants arriving, settling down, going about their lives, almost exclusively set against the backdrop of a dreary English winter. The audience are left to decipher meaning and provide their own narratives for the imagery.

But these stories have not only been extracted out of a performed chain, they have been reinserted into a new chain of images, a poetic ode to migration simultaneously conveying common immigrant folklore of cold and greyness. While the migratory component of the performed chain is duly noted, the racial component poses a number of questions. First of all, the footage depicts primarily immigrants from the Caribbean and Africa while, as Sheila Seacroft notes in her review, 'the rather desultory appearance of Indian subcontinent characters towards the end seemed an add-on' (Seacroft 2010). Problematically, this implies a certain sameness to all immigrant experience, while Indian experience and understanding of winter differs vastly from African or Caribbean experience. More problematic, however, is the juxtaposition with the Alaskan winter in this ode to migration and dislocation as Alaskan racial and migrational politics – here entirely ignored – differ immensely from the British experience.

The viewer may be unable to guess the race of Akomfrah's parka-clad figures, but nothing implies they are Native, indigenous or even migrating to Alaska. Rather each solitary figure conveys the air of non-belonging while Akomfrah's choice of poetry in place of narrative brings to mind Suzanne Robinson's contemplation on communications between the South and the North: 'When reading English poetry we are taught winter is a metaphor for death. There you have the gap in communication because in the north the word desolate is a crazy description for an abundant home and winter means life and good hunting' (Robinson 2012: 228). The Arctic has been stripped of its own identity and reduced to an empty backdrop, literally and figuratively, because, as Ari Aukusti Lehtinen reminds us: 'When a term such as "landscape" or "wilderness" is unilaterally applied to a peripheral region, the inevitable result is cultural compression and loss' (Lehtinen 2012: 118).

Whereas Akomfrah focuses on something specific – the experience of the black British immigrant – Julien pursues the universal. In his depiction of the polar explorer Matthew Henson and two of his Inuit assistants, Julien certainly addresses racial politics but, to him, it 'is universal, because in the end we are all humans'. Julien adds, 'It's very interesting how people read what is the universal, and they always read whiteness or the West as being the universal' (Kudláček 2007).

Yet, there is no lack of specifics in the case of Matthew Henson, an African American assistant to Robert Peary in Peary's polar explorations. Being charged with breaking the route for Peary, who himself travelled on a sled, Henson had orders to stop before reaching the pole so that Peary might overtake him and reach the pole first. Henson, however, overshot his mark and reached the pole 45 minutes ahead of Peary. Peary refused to congratulate him and, in spite of confirming the location to be the Pole, claimed the following day to have found the 'true' Pole at a different location. The two men along with their four Inuit helpers journeyed back in total silence to a hero's welcome claimed by Peary alone. Not the official story, it still existed in an interview with Henson, and provided 'a perfect alibi for making a piece of work about snow and ice' which Julien had long desired to make (Kernebone 2007).

As already noted, Julien did not shoot his film at the North Pole or even in the Arctic region. Even so, the landscape depicted indisputably becomes a part of the narrative, not only visually but literally as Julien explores 'the idea that modernity is made through violence' claiming that in *True North*, 'there's a violence of the landscape itself . . . very close to memory and suppression' (Kaplan 2005). Taking racial politics to the forefront, Julien refers to the bond between Henson and Peary as 'master/slave dialectic', and introduces the landscape as an active player in the racial drama, when he states: 'In *True North*, when we're talking about his identification with the Arctic landscape,

Matthew Henson says "my soul won't rest until it's mine." There's a twisting of the heroic' (Kaplan 2005).

Whether or not the Arctic should still be considered a 'site of a privileged white masculinity', the two artists discussed here represent gender very differently in their work (Bloom 2010: 31). While Akomfrah's archival footage depicts women, men and children alike, his Arctic footage is intermittently void of human presence or occupied with either of his two solitary figures. Although Jeff Robson describes these figures as 'so swathed in protective clothing that their race and gender remain unknown', I must confess to always having read their posture and movement as male (Robson 2010). Be that as it may, without a clear signal these figures can at best be read to comment on race in Arctic imagery while ignoring aspects of gender.

Julien, on the other hand, aims for 'meditation and a contemporization of questions that could be seen as historical' when he chooses to cast a younger black female protagonist, Vanessa Myrie, to retract Henson's steps and re-articulate his interview, 'using his memory to tell this other story that's not part of that official history' (Kaplan 2005). But Julien's protagonist does more than force the viewer to reflect on race and gender. In an interview with Martina Kudláček, Julien speaks to his practice of working with non-actors or 'models', as in 'characters taken from life', siting Robert Bresson as his inspiration. However, while Bresson limited each of his 'models' to appearing in only one film, never using the same 'actor' twice, Julien literally uses Vanessa Myrie as a leitmotiv (Bresson 1986; Totaro 2004). Myrie, a senior sales executive for the Prime Focus Group, appears in all films of the trilogy, wearing different versions of her signature white sheath, thus providing a tangible, visual and highly stylised connection between the three films. Furthermore, she also stars in Julien's film installation *Baltimore* (UK, 2003), where her black shearling coat bears a striking resemblance to the black coat she wears in *True North*. Julien essentially uses Myrie as 'a character who *builds* over the series of films' (Kudláček 2007).

No matter whether Akomfrah and Julien intended to comment on environmental politics, the Arctic has gained such attention in discussion of climate change that it has become impossible to depict Arctic imagery without being subjected to environmental readings. As Saffron O'Neill reminds us in her study of imagery of climate change: 'Images can transcend linguistic and geographical barriers', and they 'come to be seen as "speaking the truth", and are readily absorbed in an unmediated manner' (O'Neill 2013: 11). While it is difficult to imagine Akomfrah's Arctic ever warming up, his Alaskan imagery is loaded with environmental meaning, for the simple reason the footage originated in Akomfrah's making of his 2009 documentary, *Oil Spill: The Exxon Valdez Disaster*. In this documentary, Akomfrah visits the site of the oil spill which occurred in Prince William Sound, Alaska, twenty years earlier, when the oil tanker *Exxon Valdez* struck a reef and spilled up to 750,000 barrels of crude oil into the sea. Yet, as already discussed, there is no inclusion of the communities or indeed Alaska as an actual place in Akomfrah's *Nine Muses*, and the connections to the documentary are obscure.

Julien, on the other hand, has always been quick to comment on geopolitical aspects as they are brought up in interviews, even if he tends to direct them right back at his installations, such as when he reminds Fenella Kernebone that 'the ice is literally melting' and describes it as 'a fantastic metaphor where we deal with all the questions of culture difference and all the problems we have with that' (Kernebone 2007). Similarly, he connects the theme of 'the journey of no return' to visiting Iceland to 'see that the ice is melting', which he then connects to 'questions of difference, we're obsessed with them, we start wars because of them; this is done on a planet that has scarce resources' (Kaplan 2005).

Environmental politics may not at first glance look like they have much in common with politics of race or gender but, as O'Neill points out, images are 'normative statements portraying a particular way of seeing the world', rather than portraying an objective reality as such. Consequently, she states, 'the visualization of climate change is in itself political, as the repetition and normalization of particular visual frames (or their absence) manifests and enables (or withholds) power from particular groups or voices' (O'Neill 2013: 12). That is, exactly as does the visualisation of race and/or gender.

Akomfrah and Julien share a great talent for presenting breathtakingly beautiful images of the Arctic region. Juxtaposing this imagery with racial, gender, and/or environmental politics, they creolise the sublime and question the simulacrum of the Arctic, thus actively challenging Western nature ideology and (neo-) imperial claims of ownership, each in his own way. Yet, Akomfrah's limiting focus on race and failure to address the Arctic for its own worth stops him short of reaching the breadth of Julien's work, who presents the viewer with layer upon layer of meaning, each more complex than the next.

BIBLIOGRAPHY

Bloom, L. F. (2010), 'Politics and aesthetics in *True North* and *Gender on Ice*', *Journal of Contemporary African Art*, 26 Spring 2010, 30–7.

Bresson, R. [1975] (1986), *Notes on the Cinematographer*, translated from the French by J. Griffin, London: Quartet Encounters.

Gröner, V. and E. Bernasconi (eds) (2006), *Isaac Julien: True North – Fantôme Afrique*, Berlin: Hatje Cantz.

Gröner, V. (2006), 'The Poetic grows beyond the Factual', in V. Gröner and E. Bernasconi (eds), *Isaac Julien: True North – Fantôme Afrique*, Berlin: Hatje Cantz, 15–16.

Julien, I. (2007), 'WESTERN UNION: Small Boats', *Isaac Julien: Installations*: http://www.isaacjulien.com/installations/smallboats.

Kaplan, C. (2005), 'True North: A conversation between Isaac Julien and Cheryl Kaplan', *db artmag*, 26 2005, http://db-artmag.com/archiv/2005/e/2/1/320.html.

Kernebone, F. (2007), 'Transcript of an interview with Isaac Julien for ABC TV, 15/04/2007', *ABC Television*, Sidney, http://www.abc.net.au/tv/sundayarts/txt/s1898399.htm.

Kudláček, M. (2007), 'Isaac Julien', *BOMB*, 101 Fall 2007, http://bombsite.com/issues/101/articles/2954.

Lehtinen, A. A. (2012), 'Politics of decoupling: breaks between indigenous and imported senses of the Nordic North', *Journal of Cultural Geography*, 29: 1, 105–23.

Merali, S. (2004), 'True North', *Isaac Julien: Installations*: http://www.isaacjulien.com/installations/truenorth.

Merali, S. (2013), 'Press release for Isaac Julien's 2007 installation of *True North* at the Roslyn Oxley9 Gallery', Sidney, http://www.roslynoxley9.com.au/news/releases/2007/02/27/122/.

Nash, M. (2006), 'Expeditions: *True North* and *Fantôme Afrique*', in Veit Gröner and Eveline Bernasconi (eds), *Isaac Julien: True North – Fantôme Afrique*, Berlin: Hatje Cantz.

O'Neill, S. J. (2013), 'Image matters: climate change imagery in US, UK and Australian newspapers', *Geoforum*, 49, 10–19.

Power, N. (2011), 'Counter-media, migration, poetry: interview with John Akomfrah', *Film Quarterly*, Winter, 65, 2, 59.

Robinson, S. (2012), '"Take it from the top": Northern conceptions about identity in the Western Arctic and beyond', *Polar Record*, 48, 246, 222–9.

Robson, J. (2010), 'The Nine Muses (2010) film review', *Eye For Film*, http://www.eyeforfilm.co.uk/review/the-nine-muses-film-review-by-jeff-robson.

Sandhu, S. (2010), 'Songs of migration', *Sight and Sound*, 20: 2, 8.

Seacroft, S. (2010), '54th London Film Festival part 1: *The Nine Muses*; *The Mosquito Net*', *Flotation Suite*: http://www.floatationsuite.com/index.php?option=com_content&task=view&id=1934&Itemid=45.

Shaked, N. (2005), 'Third Pole: the stills of Isaac Julien's *True North*', *X-TRA Contemporary Art Quarterly*, Winter, 8: 2.

Totaro, D. (2004), '"Notes" on *Notes on the Cinematographer*', *Offscreen*, 2004, 8:4: http://www.horschamp.qc.ca/new_offscreen/notes_cinematographer.html.

26. DJ SPOOKY AND DZIGA VERTOV: EXPERIMENTAL CINEMA MEETS DIGITAL ART IN EXPLORING THE POLAR REGIONS

Daria Shembel

Paul D. Miller, also known as DJ Spooky That Subliminal Kid, is a multimedia artist, musician and writer who performed a *Kino-Glaz/Kino-Pravda* remix at the Tate Modern in London. *Kino-Glaz/Kino-Pravda* (which could be translated from Russian as 'The Cinema Eye/The Cinema Truth') is a remix based on a newsreel series, *The Cinema Truth (Kinopravda,* 23 issues, 1922–5), and a documentary film, *The Cinema Eye (Kinoglaz,* 1924), directed by the Soviet filmmaker Dziga Vertov.

A joyful reception of the *KinoGlaz/Kino-Pravda* remix across the globe would probably please Vertov, whose experiments in montage earned him the status of a pioneer of digital media. Although his films received an extremely hostile reception back in the 1930s, as soon as new media emerged and scholars began researching the continuity between traditional and digital art, Vertov was rediscovered and glorified as one of the most significant artists presaging future media and database culture. To list just a few examples, Vertov has been credited with the inception of surveillance photography, with the development of contemporary open-source and user-generated practices, with the invention of the 360-degree camera that is used in video games, and digital compositing. New media scholar Lev Manovich describes Vertov's work as 'the most important example of a database imagination in modern media art' (Manovich 2001: 239), while Paul D. Miller refers to Vertov as 'the first YouTube director', 'the Photoshop director', and 'the first collage multimedia director' (Miller 2012).

In 2007, Paul D. Miller launched a multimedia and multidisciplinary project dedicated to the investigation of polar culture. In 2008, he chartered a decommissioned Soviet military icebreaker, *Akademik Ioffe,* and went to Antarctica to work on the first part of his polar project. This became the multimedia symphony *Terra Nova: Sinfonia Antarctica.* Since 2008, it has been performed at galleries, theatres, universities and festivals around the world. A companion volume, *The Book of Ice,* was released in 2011. Miller is currently collecting materials for the second part of his polar series, *Arctic Rhythms: Ice Music.* He went to the North Pole in 2010, but says that this project is going to take some time to finish because 'a bigger population of the Arctic makes for a different project' (Hoffmann 2011: 279).

Terra Nova might be seen as a perfect example of new media and database culture, combining a mixture of music, archive footage, maps, timelines, visualisations and metadata. It pays homage to Vertov and, in particular, to his documentary *A Sixth Part of the World* (*Shestaia Chast' Sveta*, 1926). This film was in its time one of the most ambitious projects to feature the Soviet Arctic and the life of the Sámi community on the Arctic island Novaya Zemlya. Given that Miller regularly writes about Vertov's influence on his work and even offers creative reworkings of Vertov's *oeuvre*, this chapter traces the cinematic origins of contemporary digital media by examining the work of two artists, Dziga Vertov and Paul D. Miller, who offer cinematic portraits of the polar regions eighty years apart.

A SIXTH PART OF THE WORLD AS A 'CORPORATE' FILM

A Sixth Part of the World was what we call today a corporate film. It was commissioned by Gostorg, the Russian State Bureau of Foreign Trade. There are few modern corporations of comparable size. Gostorg was simply enormous: it had an absolute monopoly on all trade operations in the USSR and controlled all import and export transactions in every region of the country. As often happens with corporate clients, directors of Gostorg envisioned the corporation not just as a service provider, even a huge one, but as an essential world agent with a grand mission. Gostorg needed a grandiose film, and Vertov's ambitions were perfectly suited to the task.

By the time Vertov embarked on this project, he had already developed and implemented his major montage method, the cine-eye. Formulated for the first time in 'We: A Variant of a Manifesto' in 1919, it assumes two major procedures: shooting authentic factual material (life-facts) and organising that material into cinematic phrases (film-objects). Vertov was striving for maximum efficiency and the rationalisation of information. In one of his manifestos, Vertov states, 'Kino-eye plunges into the seeming chaos of life to find in life itself the response to an assigned theme. To find the resultant force amongst the million phenomena related to the given theme' (Vertov 1984: 88). The cine-eye reflected the new regime's need to deal with a tremendous increase in the flow of information and overall rationalised building of the new world. Vertov's objective was to document the essential symbols of the new regime (blocks of communication), reveal the process of their interaction, and create a precise and inspiring map of the new reality.

With this method at hand, Vertov could picture Gostorg as an entire universe full of stories that showed the 'routine of the extraordinary' and developed simultaneously in the most distant parts of the Soviet Union. He could show how those stories were connected with each other by guiding the viewers through Siberia, Central Asia, the North Pole, the Caucasus, and the capitalist West. By creating a complex network of peoples, goods, transportation means and places involved in the agency's daily operations, Vertov's film would reveal the grandeur of the Soviet trade industry, Gostorg's prominence and the impact of a new socialist world. This is how the project was greenlighted by the directors of Gostorg. What they did not know – and would not have signed off on – was how Vertov was going to implement this idea.

VERTOV'S PROTOCOL

To understand how such a film could be made in the computer era, we could envision a transmedia project that aggregates a number of stories and places them on the map. It also would be natural for a database project to present a story through a number of short fragments, organise them as a database, and implement a certain protocol that links and arranges these fragments. Such a database would allow for an increasingly large number of combinations (stories) using a relatively small number of initial elements (fragments). Finally, software uses a binary code (1s and 0s) to represent all the diverse elements within the story. Vertov's representation of the Arctic could be seen as masterfully arranged sequences of '1s' and '0s'. His *protocol* presupposed fragmenting reality into small elements and re-arranging them into a new entity. It also attempted to exhaustingly classify and order the things of the world. This kind of aesthetics involved the atomisation of the narrative into minimal structures, for example, the legs of a Sámi, a polar owl, a ship, pelts, dogs and so on. This way he could describe an endless multiplicity of both the achievements of the new regime and the natural objects of the 'sixth of the world'.

In a heated discussion of the film after its release, critics mentioned that in order to film a Sámi's feet and a snowy owl, it was not necessary to travel all the way to Novaya Zemly (Sokolov cited in Tsivian 2004). Indeed, the critical reception of the film was ferocious (for a representative selection of reviews and commentary, see Tsivian 2004: 184, 206, 207, 220, 230). Gostorg was not happy, either. This lead to Vertov's expulsion from the Sovkino (State

Committee for Cinematography) and marginalisation within the USSR film industry. But those shots of legs, a polar owl or a rocky patch of ground were important variables in Vertov's code. Writing his rudimentary protocol on celluloid, he had to compile his database manually. In order to make his 'computer' work, he had to travel around the world to collect those '1s' and '0s'.

Customers usually love it when a corporate film shows as many items as it possibly can. The director's script of *A Sixth Part*, which is kept in the Russian State Archive of Literature and Arts (RGALI), consists almost solely of lists of goods traded by Gostorg. Vertov had to picture them all. Below are the frames from the second reel of the film, in which Gostorg items are presented in a form of a detailed catalogue (inter-titles read, 'Buffalo / goats of Ulu-Uzen / camels from the steppes of Kirghizstan / the deer / the squirrel / the trapped polar fox / the marten / the brown bear / the sable tracked in the Far North / the Astrakhan / your oil / your cotton / and sheep / wool / your butter / fish / your flax / your tobacco'). This approach could potentially give him endless opportunities to generate stories. In *A Sixth Part,* Vertov anticipates the ability of a digital database to produce new data and data combinations using the same interface. The sequences below show how the same minimal montage units (the legs of a Sámi and spinning train wheels) can be combined with a variety of different shots within the film's interchangeable structure. In Sequence 1, the shot of a Sámi's legs is used in three different narratives:

Figure 26.1 Frame montage. Dziga Vertov, *A Sixth Part of the World* (1926).

Figure 26.2   Frame montage. Dziga Vertov, *A Sixth Part of the World* (1926).

(1) people from different parts of the country partook in 'overthrowing the power of Capital' (the inter-titles read, 'you in Siberian Taiga / you in Tundra / you have overthrown the power of Capital in October); (2) there are still obstacles on the way to socialism (inter-titles read, 'the Ships stuck in the ice / and someone departs into the distant icy unknown'); and (3) it is difficult to destroy the old ('the old departs slowly / like you who departs into the icy unknown').

In Sequence 2, the shot of the spinning train wheels is used in (1) a segment that shows how 'export goods are moved along all the roads of the Soviet land'; and (2) a segment narrating how Saami submit their pelts to Gostorg station (the inter-titles read 'To submit their pelts / to be exported to the lands of Capital').

While a traditionally organised narrative can lose some of its integrity by skipping particular elements or even whole sequences, one missing '1' or '0' in a computer code would make the whole programme crash. So Vertov went to Caucasus to shoot bunches of grapes and to Central Asia to shoot caracul, to the Baltic Sea to shoot an approaching ship, and to Novaya Zemlya to shoot legs standing on the ground – or so the footage implied. In fact, Vertov had never been to the majority of the places he showed us. Such an extensive shooting plan would have never been realised if Vertov had tried to film everything on his own. So the idea of what we now call 'user-generated content' was implemented. The second part of the script includes a list of shooting crews (*kinoks* or 'cine-eye men') and objects they are assigned to film.[1]

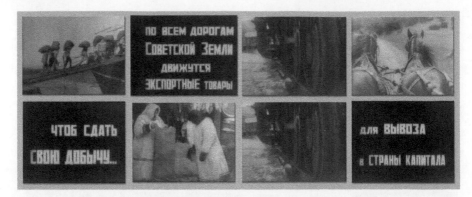

Figure 26.3　Frame montage. Dziga Vertov, *A Sixth Part of the World* (1926).

As a computer fragments data into bite-sized segments and then processes and re-assembles them, Vertov's *protocol* involved amassing large amounts of footage (they shot 26,000 metres of footage, out of which only 1,000 metres were used (Sokolov in Tsivian 2004: 235) and breaking it down into smaller montage units. Information intentionally omitted in individual shots was added later during the montage stage of the cine-eye method. Since Vertov trusted the camera to penetrate into reality, edit it and search it for the symbols of new life, he was committed to providing effective links between those fragments of reality and organising them into a synthesised and coherent whole during the post-production stage. Vertov's pre-electronic database never simply listed data. It employed rigid classificatory mechanisms to stratify and organise recorded 'life-facts' into 'film-truth'. Through a rigorously structured montage design that governs the structure of *A Sixth Part*, Vertov expands the narrative value of individual shots and delivers his ideological message. The ideological content of different sequences of *A Sixth Part* also partakes in the structure of interchangeability. It reflects on the massive and well-organised mechanism of incorporation of even the most 'exotic' and isolated peoples of the USSR into the communist project.

VERTOV'S ARCTIC

The film opens with a shot of a plane and an aerial view over the 'sixth of the world'. This translucent gaze of the cine-eye offering the viewers an enlarged and organised space from the top-down perspective immediately reveals some of Vertov's intentions. He posits cartography and the collection of data at the centre of his documentary, makes communication itself the subject of art, and points to the fact that, by bringing together the farthest possible sites of the 'sixth of the world', the cine-eye resolves the problem that the Soviet authorities experience with the dissemination of information across the country's vast geography. *A Sixth Part of the World* consists of six parts, echoing its title. The first part deals with the world outside the USSR – 'Capitalism' – and is based on contrasting images of European bourgeois entertaining themselves in cabarets and restaurants juxtaposed with shots of workers and 'slaves' in the colonies, intercut with heavy machinery, factories and industrial objects. The other five parts embrace the geography, resources and peoples inside the USSR, featuring diverse Soviet ethnic groups and their activities. They document vast territories of Soviet space – 'from Matochkin to Bukhara', 'from the Kremlin to the Chinese Border' – and present Soviet totems to the audience: 'your factories', 'your wool', 'your fish', 'your tobacco', and so on. The film also features various kinds of transportation means carrying goods around Soviet terrain, and portrays the complex network by which Gostorg supervises the export of Soviet manufactured goods to capitalist countries and their subsequent exchange for heavy machinery needed for the Soviet industry. The film's final part documents the country's immense leap forward from the backwardness of pre-revolutionary culture. The shots of Oriental dancing and occult rituals are followed by an elaborate sequence with an icebreaker, shot at a heroic high angle, and rhythmically intercut with the emblematic entities of Soviet export-import exchange: grain and heavy machinery. Thus, the film represents an impressive database of people and places ranging over the most distant areas of the USSR and beyond, cataloguing the rituals and everyday activities of its inhabitants, documenting Soviet totems, categorising various kinds of heavy machinery, factories and oil pumps, and listing various transportation means. From automised, fragmented pieces, Vertov creates a 'portrait' of the Soviet Arctic. Images of the Arctic and Sámi people are scattered throughout the film and, along with the shots of other isolated regions and exotic peoples, are incorporated within the narratives of integration into the new regime.

Vertov's intention was to minimise the centre and concentrate particularly on the most isolated and unexplored regions of the USSR. This commitment to show the 'periphery' coincided with Sovkino's attempts to bring together film and ethnography in order to provide general audiences with a broader and more educated view of the country's rich environments (*Report of the Committee on Culture and Cinema* 1925). This Sovkino *Report* states that cinema, with its ability to document reality, is a unique tool for providing a comprehensive and comprehensible corpus of ethnographic materials. It establishes guidelines for presenting the subject-matter and stresses that directors of ethnographic films should cover political, educational, scientific, aesthetic and agricultural considerations as they provide information on the major fields of ethnographic research: material values, social order, and the cultures of various ethnic groups. In *A Sixth Part* Vertov closely follows the guidelines, and particularly the recommendations to bolster the audience's knowledge of agriculture, animal husbandry, handicrafts and the natural resources of various regions of the USSR in order to inform the West about the possibilities of import from the country. Ironically, he was criticised particularly for dwelling on animal husbandry as if it were one of the major branches of the Soviet economy.[2]

The fifth part of the film features the longest sequence about the Arctic and shows the Arctic island Novaya Zemlya. It is thematically organised around a Gostorg freighter arriving at the Sámi village to bring supplies – produce, bolts of cloth, guns and other manufactured goods – and take away pelts and fur from them. The section starts with the inter-titles 'far away / beyond the Polar Circle / where the sun does not set for half a year / and for half a year lasts the night', intercut with the shots of the ocean and the shoreline emphasising the boundless extension of the surrounding space. After the opening panoramic shots of water, Vertov cuts to the Sámi sitting on the barren, icy shores of the ocean watching the arrival of a Gostorg ship. Already in the introductory sequence, spaces are not delineated but invade each other. Shots are rather juxtaposed than developed and are organised into a set of oppositions between, for example, the water and the land, light and dark, stasis and movement, and a person and a landscape.

When Vertov moves forward to depicting what the ship brings the Sámi and further to the interaction between them and the sailors from the freighter, the shots still do not unfold in a linear succession or follow cause-and-effect logic. In fact, Vertov further atomises the narrative space by singling out items from the list of supplies brought on the ship: the shots of dogs, flour, lumber and manufactured goods appear on the screen as if in the manner of a slideshow, with every shot preceded by an inter-title specifying what we are about to see.

The section depicting the interaction of the Sámi with the sailors is also conceived by means of isolated shots, mostly close-ups of people and objects,

Figure 26.4   Frame montage. Dziga Vertov, *A Sixth Part of the World* (1926).

while the syntactic connections between them are provided through inter-titles: 'Each year Gostorg ships come to their Novaya Zemlya / Samoyeds come to visit the sailors / they listen to sound records of "Lenin himself" / the next day the ship sails away / taking away the furs of animals / and now these furs are at the trade show in Leipzig'. An elliptical trajectory of his Arctic tale in *A Sixth Part* consists of multiple events and stories: the triumphant arrival of the Soviet freighter, the Soviets' encounter with the exotic other, the Sámi going on board the ship to interact with the sailors and listen to the recording of Lenin's speech, an exchange of goods, the establishment of polar laboratories on the island of Novaya Zemlya, and so on. Despite the colonial rhetoric of organising and educating primitive societies along party lines (including shots of Sámi reading a Soviet newspaper *Northerner* or listening to Lenin's speech) and the establishment of Soviet institutions on indigenous lands (a shot of reindeer treated in the Soviet polar lab), the film reports on Sámi's economic importance for the Soviet Union. The inter-titles read, 'The ship takes the pelts obtained by Samoyeds / to exchange for machines that build machines'. This in turn functions to create preconditions for the victory of socialism in the world.

This neocolonial duality of Sovietisation policy (equality among all nationalities combined with moral and political education and economic dependency) reverberates with the ambiguity of the cine-eye strategy. One of the most important objectives of the cine-eye was to liberate older forms of linear representation and establish a new kind of perception suitable for a 'new world'. Vertov insisted on filming 'unawares', which required shooting on location and portraying real people whose work routine was never inter-rupted. Moreover, the aesthetics of the cine-eye hinged on the presumption of the camera's limitless mobility and its capacity to infiltrate any point of the universe. His camera never watched from a fixed position: it was always within the action and in those places that were out of range for the human eye. While filming *A Sixth Part*, Vertov made his cameramen lie between the rails filming a train rushing above, tied them to a ship's ladder and swung it to the side, made them climb on top of buildings, had them lie in snowdrifts, and placed them on the backs of deer during the reindeer races.[3] One can see those extraordinary camera movements in the complex structure of Vertov's montage, which through its rhythmic linkage of the most distant possible points of the world transcends spatial and temporal boundaries and reinforces the superiority of cinematic vision. Vertov's fragmentation of reality is insepa-rably linked to his ubiquitous camera and the loss of a dominant point of view. In the utopian communist world created by Vertov's camera filming inside the things, the relations between the viewing subject and object are modified. The privileged, perceiving subject is liquidated in favour of universal varia-tion and interaction between moving signs and images. This is why Vertov often inscribes the viewers onto the screen: in the meta-cinematic ending of the second part of *A Sixth Part*, the spectators in a movie theatre are shown watching the beginning of the same reel that was just featured in the film. This utopian construct of 'the sixth of the world' with equality for all could be seen as Deleuzo-Guattarian rhizome, a heterogeneous space that establishes infinite connections linking 'any point to any other point' of the social world via the process of assemblage (Deleuze and Guattari 2005). The cine-eye offers an 'a-centred' vision that goes beyond the confines of the privileged human viewpoint and eliminates the distance between the human being and the rest of the world. Vertov's cine-eye seems to simultaneously erase and create new boundaries within and outside the Soviet space. The depiction of Sámi as owners of the 'sixth of the world' and their importance for the Soviet economy is definitely stressed in *A Sixth Part*, but the freedom epitomised by liberated vision has its reverse side: the rigidity of rhythmic stratification, which is a powerful ideological instrument that allows the film to modify and limit knowledge about a particular ethnic group or locale. As for the ethnographic heterogeneity of *A Sixth Part*, undoubtedly, numerous geographic locations and ethnic groups are featured, and local rituals and traditions are occasionally rendered. However, it is important to remember that there is just one protocol for all the nations.

Vertov's representation of the Arctic has often been compared with that of Robert Flaherty is in *Nanook of the North* (1922) (Sarkisova 2007; Hicks 2007). Flaherty's pioneering ethnographic film grew out of long expeditions to the Arctic and from true immersion in the local culture. Vertov, in contrast, dispatched his cameramen for short, targeted trips just to get enough footage for his bigger project (Hicks 2007: 49). The fact that, unlike Flaherty, Vertov did not even travel to the Arctic to do ethnographic research himself but instead sent his cameraman to Novaya Zemlya on a Gostorg ship perfectly illustrates Vertov's preference for a collectivist approach to authorship. He intended to pass on the skill and technical experience of the 'Council of Three' to the 'rising generation of new workers': kinok-observers, kinok-cameramen, kinok-editors, and so on (Vertov 1984: 75). He also dreamt of creating models of films that everyone could fill in with new content. Vertov repeatedly insisted on the utilitarian nature of his films, and called *A Sixth Part* (among other works) a 'film that begets films' (Vertov 1984: 122). In this sense, *A Sixth Part* is indeed a perfect 'DNA model', a database in which all parts are interchangeable and the contents of its catalogues can be easily replaced.

PAUL D. MILLER'S *TERRA NOVA: SINFONIA ANTARCTICA*

The way Miller creates the portrait of the continent in both his multimedia symphony and *The Book of Ice* is strongly reminiscent of Vertov's cine-eye method, by which the latter sought to overthrow the existing norms of linearity in order to create a revolutionary cinema. In an interview about his Antarctica project, Miller states, 'People like to have *narrative*, so I thought, let's give them something different' (Miller 2011b). And, indeed, what unfolds in front of the viewer during the *Terra Nova* performance has little to do with linear modes of representation. It is a fluid movement through and inter-penetration of a variety of media elements and digital processes. The work is shown as a large-scale data projection split between two monitors and is chan-nelled through a turntable with selection tools and an authored application on an iPad. Spectacular images of ice, glaciers and icebergs fill the screens and alternate with maps, information visualisations, statistical graphs on Antarctic climate change, pages from Miller's musical scores, propaganda art and footage from a Soviet Antarctic expedition. Miller creates a unique microcosm of the continent through a media landscape consisting of digital montages of diverse media elements that can be positioned and repositioned through the computer-based mechanism of his turntable.

In his interviews and books (for example, *Rhythm Science* (2004); *The Book of Ice* (2011)), Miller has consistently insisted on the cinematic origins of contemporary digital culture, particularly emphasising the fact that the collage aesthetics of digital media are deeply rooted in the avant-garde film montage techniques employed by such directors as Sergei Eisenstein, Dziga Vertov, Mikhail Kalatozov and Walter Ruttman. Miller suggests that his remix of Dziga Vertov was a 'first step along the path to understand how cinema of the 20th century set the tone for the info-aesthetics of the 21st century'. He also notes that his installations and film projects represent a direct reflection of a historical search for the roots of the Soviet dialectical montage and aim to show the connections between modernist film practices and contempo-rary digital art and sound composition (Miller 2009). And although Miller is thoroughly familiar with the work and ideas of many prominent figures of the Soviet avant-garde (he produced an installation based on remixes of Malevich's Constructivist prints and Alexander Rodchenko's film posters), he singles out Dziga Vertov in particular as a precursor of today's new media sensibility and even suggests that Vertov envisioned the principle of 'ambient awareness' that characterises twenty-first-century social networking. Miller actually claims that one of his reasons for going to Antarctica was to make the continent accessible to the general public, so that it would become 'mediated' similar to urban centres instead of being only accessible to scientists: 'I think that people need to hear Antarctica because it is at the edge of the world . . . New York is probably one of the most mediated places on earth. If I have a conversation at a café, someone will put it on a blog. If I walk down the street, someone will put photos of it on Flickr . . . Antarctica represents a place medi-ated by science' (Miller 2011a: 19).

Similar to Vertov's dialectical construal of reality expressed in a two-stage process of filming 'unawares' and subsequent 'decoding' by means of multiple reorganisations of footage, Miller posits, 'once something is recorded, it's basically a file waiting to be manipulated' (Miller 2011a: 18). While Vertov's 'decoding' represents a rigid system of rhythmic organisation of 'life-facts' into 'film-objects', Miller also points out that potentially malleable film or music compositions undergo a 'ruthless logic of selection that you have to go through to simply to create a sense of order' (Miller 2004: 81).

Miller and Vertov have much more in common than just their obsession with cuts. Vertov has been credited with pioneering so many areas of new media art that we can safely add to the list that he was one of the first DJs as well. When Vertov studied at the music academy in his native town of Byalistok, Poland, he experimented with the montage of stenographs. It was particularly those experiments with sampling that carried him to the Russian avant-garde scene when his family settled in Moscow after the outbreak of World War I. After resuming his higher education in Russia at the Petrograd Psychoneurological Institute, Vertov continued experimenting with the rhythmic montage of sound patterns, that time already under the influence of various Futurist groups that resided in Petrograd. He established a 'Laboratory of Sound' in his apartment. The purpose of the 'laboratory' (whose equipment consisted of one pathephone) was to record natural sounds, break them up into separate constituent elements, and reorganise the components into a new work (Feldman 1977: 11–14).

Moreover, Vertov was definitely one of the first active users and creators of an 'open-source' model upon which the remix aesthetics of DJ culture is predicated. The footage for *A Sixth Part* was taken from a variety of sources, including an upcoming film of the Soviet director Lebedev, *Through Europe*, for which Lebedev was not credited; Dubrovsky's *October in Everyday Life* (Sokolov in Tsivian 2004: 242); and German industrial films (Sarkisova 2007: 28). As he freely appropriated others' footage, he had always advocated the model of collective authorship and strived to create models of films that everyone could fill in with new content.

While Paul Miller's Arctic project is still under development, the artist claims that it is going to be even more ambitious than *Terra Nova*: 'my first Antarctic symphony project was an 'acoustic portrait' of Antarctica as a place that has no government . . . the *Arctic Rhythms* project will take that path and go further along' (Miller 2010). Miller has already begun conceptualising the impressions from his 2010 trip to the Arctic, and, as it appears from his blog *Arctic Notes*, the piece is intended as a complex blend of sound and image and will continue to explore relationships between elemental forces of nature of the polar regions, science, politics and info-aesthetics. The project might even feature choreographic elements that will contribute to the visual and acoustic portrait of the Arctic. In 2009, Miller collaborated with the choreography group *Ekko Collective aka The League of Imaginary Scientists*, and created a few electronic music compositions to accompany dancers' routines that reflected the slow motion/time lapse of a glacier (Miller 2010). Another major addition that will mark *Arctic Rhythms* is that the acoustic part of the piece, which will consist of several string quartet pieces and a symphony, will also feature segments of folk music of the indigenous Arctic population that Miller collected during his Arctic expedition (Miller 2013).

Drafting montage sequences for the *Arctic Rhythms*, Miller considers the inclusion of historic and scientific footage, molecular diagrams, archival charts showing the changes in Arctic ice-mass, weather patterns and his personal footage, as well as plans to feature various nations that participate in the Arctic Treaty System, and show historic texts projected from Emerson, Whitman and Thoreau (Miller 2010). The project promises to create an entire digital environment, in which video sequences, visualisations and taxonomies merged with the acoustics of the continent's natural sounds will bring together a profound understanding of historical, scientific and ethnographic values that shape the uniqueness of the North Pole region.

NOTE

1. RGALI – Russian State Archive of Literature and Art, f. 2081, op. 2, ed. khr. 397.

BIBLIOGRAPHY

Beskin, O. (1926), '"A Sixth Part of the World", Sovetskoe Kino, Nos 6–7, 1926', in Y. Tsivian (ed.) (2004), *Lines of Resistance: Dziga Vertov and the Twenties*, Gemona, Udine: Le Giornate del cinema muto, 204–6.
Borisov, D. (1927), '"A Sixth Part of the World" (A separate opinion)', *Kino*, 15 January, in Y. Tsivian (ed.) (2004), *Lines of Resistance: Dziga Vertov and the Twenties*, Gemona, Udine: Le Giornate del cinema muto, 217–18.
Deleuze, G. and F. Guattari (2005), *A Thousand Plateaus: Capitalism and Schizophrenia*, 11th edn, Minneapolis: University of Minnesota Press.
Feldman, S. (1977), *Evolution of Style in the Early Work of Dziga Vertov, with a New Appendix*, New York: Arno Press.
Hicks, J. (2007), *Dziga Vertov: Defining Documentary Film*, London; New York: I. B. Tauris.
Hoffman, J. (2011), 'Q & A: Climate-change DJ', *Nature*, 477.7364: 279.
Manovich, L. (2001), *The Language of New Media*, Cambridge, MA: MIT Press.
Miller, P. D. (2004), DJ Spooky That Subliminal Kid, *Rhythm Science*, Cambridge, MA: MIT Press.
Miller, P. D. (2009), *Kino-Glaz/Kino-Pravda: Remix. Artist Statement*, http://www.djspooky.com/articles/vertov.php.
Miller, P. D. (2010), *Arctic Notes*, http://djspooky.com/articles/cape_farewell_notes.php.
Miller, P. D. (2011a), *Book of Ice*, PowerHouse Books, Brooklyn, NY.
Miller, P. D. (2011b), Interview by Maria Popova, 26 July, http://www.brainpickings.org/index.php/2011/07/26/book-of-ice-dj-spooky/.

Miller, P. D. (2012), *Digital Epoch Voice*, Lecture, 25 June, http://digitaloctober.ru/en/events/knowledge_stream_lektsiya_pola_dj_spooky_millera_tsifrovoy_golos_epohi.
Miller, P. D. (2013), personal interview, 31 August.
Report of the Committee on Culture and Cinema for the Central Executive Committee of the USSR on the Production Planning of a Series of Scientific and Ethnographic Films (1925), vol. f. 2091, op. 1, ed. khr. 77. RGALI – Russian State Archive of Literature and Art.
Sarkisova, O. (2007), 'Across One Sixth of the World: Dziga Vertov, travel cinema, and Soviet patriotism', *OCTOBER*, Summer 2007, 19–40.
Shklovsky, V. (1927), 'On the fact that plot is a constructive principle, not one from daily life, in their present time', in Y. Tsivian (ed.) (2004), *Lines of Resistance: Dziga Vertov and the Twenties*, Gemona, Udine: Le Giornate del cinema muto, 266–9.
Sokolov, I. (1927), 'On the film 'A Sixth Part of the World'', Kino-Front, no. 2, in Yuri Tsivian (ed.) (2004), *Lines of Resistance: Dziga Vertov and the Twenties*, Gemona, Udine: Le Giornate del cinema muto, 233–9.
Sosnovsky, L. (1927), 'A Sixth Part of the World', *Rabochaia Gazeta*, 5 January, in Yuri Tsivian (ed.) (2004), *Lines of Resistance: Dziga Vertov and the Twenties*, Gemona, Udine: Le Giornate del cinema muto, 220–2.
Tsivian, Y. (2004), *Lines of Resistance: Dziga Vertov and the Twenties*, Gemona, Udine: Le Giornate del cinema muto.
Urazov, I. (1926), "A Sixth Part of the World", in Y. Tsivian (ed.) (2004), *Lines of Resistance: Dziga Vertov and the Twenties*, Gemona, Udine: Le Giornate del cinema muto, 184–187.
Vertov, D. (1984), *Kino-Eye: The Writings of Dziga Vertov*, ed. A. Michelson, Berkeley, CA: University of California Press.

NOTES ON THE CONTRIBUTORS

Marco Bohr is a photographer, academic and researcher in visual culture. He received his PhD from the University of Westminster in 2011 and was appointed Lecturer in Visual Communication at Loughborough University in 2012. Bohr has contributed to a number of edited volumes such as the book series *Directory of World Cinema* and *World Film Locations*. He has also contributed to the *Dandelion Journal*, the exhibition catalogue for *Modernity Stripped Bare* held at the University of Maryland, and the artist book *Kim Jong Il Looking at Things*, published by Jean Boîte Éditions. Bohr is on the editorial board for the forthcoming journal *East Asian Journal of Popular Culture*. In 2013 he was awarded a Fellowship by the Japan Foundation for his ongoing research on the photographic representation of post-Tsunami landscapes.

Marian Bredin is Associate Professor in the Department of Communication, Popular Culture and Film, at Brock University in Canada. She is a member of the Transmedia Research Network at Brock and teaches in the MA programme in Popular Culture. She recently co-edited *Canadian Television: Text and Context* (Wilfrid Laurier University Press, 2012) and *Indigenous Screen Cultures in Canada* (University of Manitoba Press, 2010).

Lyubov Bugaeva is Dr hab. in Philology and Associate Professor at St Petersburg State University, Russia. She is the founder of the Kinotext Group in St Petersburg. She is the author of *Literature and rite de passage* (St Petersburg, 2010), editor of four books in Russian, and co-editor of

Ent-Grenzen: Intellektuelle Emigration in der russischen Kultur des 20. Jahrhunderts (Frankfurt am Main, 2006). Her current interests are in film analysis, neurocinematics, and the theory of literature.

Marina Dahlquist is an Associate Professor of Cinema Studies at the Department of Media Studies at Stockholm University. She has published articles on cinema and civic education, health discourses and colonial structures. She is a recipient of a research grant from the Swedish Research Council (2011–13) for the project 'Cinema and Uplift: Health Discourses and Social Activism in the U.S. 1910–1930'. Recent publications include the edited volume: *Exporting Perilous Pauline: Pearl White and the Serial Film Craze* (University of Illinois Press, 2013). Primary research interests are historical reception, educational films, and issues of globalisation.

Jan Anders Diesen is Professor of Film History at Lillehammer University College, Norway. He is an expert on silent Norwegian films and on documentary films. For the past five years, he has been researching the silent films from the polar expeditions and has published books and articles on Roald Amundsen's films. To put these Norwegian films into an international context, he has for the past three years visited polar archives around the world to research other explorers' films from Borchgrevink, Fiala and Bruce to Amundsen, Nobile and Byrd. His book *The Irreplaceable Cinematographic Film: The Story of the Polar Explorer Films* will be published by The Fram Museum, Oslo in 2014.

Ann Fienup-Riordan is a cultural anthropologist and independent scholar who has lived and worked in Alaska since 1973. Her books include *Eskimo Essays* (1990), *Freeze Frame: Alaska Eskimos in the Movies* (1995), *The Living Tradition of Yup'ik Masks* (1996), and *Wise Words of the Yup'ik People: We Talk to You because We Love You* (2005). In 2000, she received the Alaska Federation of Natives President's Award for her work with Alaska Natives, and in 2001 the Governor's Award for Distinguished Humanist Educator. Since 2000, she has worked with the Calista Elders Council, the primary heritage organisation in southwest Alaska, documenting traditional knowledge. In 2012, she and co-author Alice Rearden received an American Book Award for their book *Qaluyaarmiuni Nunamtenek Qanemciput/Our Nelson Island Stories*.

Rebecca Genauer is a film studies PhD candidate at the University of Wisconsin, Madison. Her dissertation-in-progress examines narrative structure in early American feature films. As an undergraduate student she worked as a research assistant at the Peary-MacMillan Arctic Museum at Bowdoin College.

Sabine Henlin-Strømme received her PhD from the Department of Cinema and Comparative Literature at the University of Iowa in 2012. She has previously taught French and film classes at the University of Iowa, in Oslo and Bergen, Norway. Her areas of interest are US independent cinema, national cinemas with an emphasis on Norwegian cinema, and nature in film. She currently teaches French at the Bergen Community College.

Caroline Forcier Holloway is an Audio-Visual Archivist at Library and Archives Canada. She acquires moving image and sound recordings, and is responsible for major governmental portfolios including the National Film Board, and Department of National Defence, as well as oral history, amateur film, and Aboriginal and northern content. Forcier Holloway has conceptualised and developed film-related exhibits and produced promotional tools, taught and lectured on film preservation, home movies, sound recordings and oral history. She served on the executive of the Canadian Oral History Association, and the Archives Association of Ontario – Eastern Chapter.

Johanne Haaber Ihle holds a BA degree in Arabic from the University of Copenhagen and a MA degree in Visual Anthropology from the University of Manchester.

Gunnar Iversen is Professor of Film Studies in the Department of Art and Media Studies at the Norwegian University of Science and Technology. He has recently published books on the Norwegian documentary filmmaker Per Høst, the Norwegian *auteur* Arne Skouen, and is co-writing a book on film history and film historiography that will be published in 2014. His writings have appeared in *Early Popular Visual Culture*, *Film History*, *The Journal of Scandinavian Cinema*, and many Scandinavian-language journals.

Anne Mette Jørgensen has an MA in anthropology and is a PhD candidate at the Department of Cross-Cultural and Regional Studies, University of Copenhagen and the National Museum of Denmark. She was project manager (2005–13) at the National Museum of Denmark on projects about cultural heritage management and Denmark's colonial history with a focus on West Africa and Greenland, respectively. Her research interests are in memory and visuality; visual anthropology, archives and museums; natural resource management and colonial connections. She is currently undertaking a PhD project on Greenlandic Visual Memories in which, by introducing film in her fieldworks, she examines how visual memory is negotiated and revised.

Pietari Kääpä is a Lecturer in Media and Communications at the Department of Communications, Media and Culture, University of Stirling. His research investigates the concept of ecocritical media in a wide variety of frameworks, from debates on transnational cultural production to digital environmentalism. Kääpä has published widely on Nordic media, environmental film, audience studies and minority film production. He is the author of *Ecology and Contemporary Nordic Cinemas* (Continuum, 2014) and co-editor of *Transnational Ecocinemas* (Intellect, 2013).

Lill-Ann Körber, Dr phil., is an Assistant Professor at the Nordeuropa-Institut, Humboldt-Universität zu Berlin. She was co-art director of *Greenland Eyes International Film Festival* in Berlin 2012. Her research interests include the colonial history of Northern Europe; postcolonial theory; contemporary Greenlandic culture; imaginations of Greenland and the Arctic; entanglements of Scandinavia, Africa and the 'Black Atlantic' as reflected in literature and cultures of memory.

Eva la Cour holds a degree from the Jutland Art Academy in Denmark and from Media & Visual Anthropology at Freie Universität in Berlin. She has conducted fieldwork on Svalbard, with an interest in notions of temporality, guiding and mediations of the past. She has recently been a participant at the Sound-Image-Culture Program in Brussels for audiovisual research. Currently she is artist-in-residence at Global High-Schools in Denmark, teaching the course 'Mediating the Arctic'.

Helga Hlaðgerður Lúthersdóttir holds a PhD in Comparative Literature from University of Colorado, Boulder. She currently runs the Icelandic BA Programme at the Department of Scandinavian Studies, University College London, where she teaches courses in popular culture and Icelandic language. Her research interests include visual representations of the Nordic Region, especially within the framework of popular culture and social media, as well as all things Icelandic and popular.

Scott MacKenzie teaches film and media at Queen's University, where he is cross-appointed to the Graduate Program in Cultural Studies, and a Visiting Research Associate at the Danish Film Institute (2013–17). His books include: *Cinema and Nation* (with Mette Hjort, Routledge, 2000); *Purity and Provocation: Dogma '95* (with Mette Hjort, BFI, 2003); *Screening Québec: Québécois Moving Images, National Identity and the Public Sphere* (Manchester University Press, 2004); *The Perils of Pedagogy: The Works of John Greyson* (with Brenda Longfellow and Thomas Waugh, McGill-Queen's University Press, 2013); *Film Manifestoes and Global Cinema Cultures* (University of California Press, 2014); *The Cinema, too, Must be Destroyed: The Films of Guy Debord* (Manchester University Press, forthcoming); and

Critical Arctic Studies (with Lill-Ann Körber and Anna Westerståhl Stenport, forthcoming).

Monica Kim Mecsei is a PhD candidate in the Department of Art and Media Studies at the Norwegian University of Science and Technology. Her research explores relations of cultural identity, transnationality and visual culture in Sámi feature films, with a special focus on representations of Sáminess and how cinematic narratives contribute to the formation of notions of collective identity.

Sarah Neely is a Senior Lecturer in the School of Arts and Humanities at the University of Stirling, where she is a member of the Centre for Scottish Studies and the Centre for Gender and Feminist Studies. She is the editor of a new edition of *Margaret Tait: Poems, Stories and Writings* (Carcanet, 2012) and is currently completing a monograph on Tait's work as a filmmaker.

Björn Norðfjörð is an Associate Professor in Film Studies at the University of Iceland. He has published widely on Icelandic cinema in English, including a monograph on Dagur Kári's Nói *The Albino*, while in Icelandic he writes about Hollywood and world cinema. Recently, he has been focusing on the interrelations between Hollywood and Nordic cinema.

Russell A. Potter writes about the depiction of the Arctic the nineteenth and early twentieth centuries; his book *Arctic Spectacles: The Frozen North in Visual Culture, 1818–1875* was published in 2007 by the University of Washington Press. He teaches English and Media Studies at Rhode Island College.

Mark Sandberg is Professor of Film and Scandinavian Studies at the University of California-Berkeley. His research engages with late nineteenth-century visual culture and silent film as a medium. He has specific film specialities in American silent comedy, Scandinavian cinema history, in certain Scandinavian directors (Sjöström, Stiller, Dreyer, Bergman, von Trier), and in the contributions of visual culture (museology) and architectural theory to the paracinematic visual culture around the birth of cinema. He regularly teaches courses on film historiography, pre-cinema, silent film comedy, Scandinavian *auteurs*, and other topics in early and silent cinema. Current film-related research includes projects on the history and theory of location shooting and on the TV series *Mad Men*.

Oksana Sarkisova, PhD, is Associate Researcher at Central European University working on the issues of socialist cultural history, memory and representation, film history and amateur photography. She co-edited *Past for the Eyes: East European Representations of Communism in Cinema and Museums after*

1989 (Central European University Press, 2008) and has published extensively on Soviet cultural history and film, film industry, nationality politics, contemporary Russian and Eastern European cinema, and amateur photography. Since 2004 she is Program Director of Verzio International Human Rights Documentary Film Festival.

Daria Shembel earned her PhD in Slavic Studies and Film from the University of Southern California, Los Angeles. Since 2005 she has been teaching European Studies, New Media and Film at San Diego State University. Her primary academic interests lie in Soviet and European film theories and histories, new media/old media historiography, Russian Modernism with an emphasis on poetry and visual culture, global, European and Eastern European media. Her publications have appeared in *KinoKultura*; *Digital Icons: Studies in Russian, Eurasian and Central European New Media*; *Studies in Russian and Soviet Cinema*; *Blok: The International Journal of Stalinist and Post-Stalinist Culture*; and various book collections.

Anna Westerståhl Stenport (PhD, University of California, Berkeley) is Associate Professor of Scandinavian Studies and Media and Cinema Studies at the University of Illinois at Urbana-Champaign and a visiting research associate at the Danish Film Institute (2013–17). Her research and teaching focuses on Nordic and Arctic cinema, media and popular culture. Having published articles in *Cinema Journal, Convergence: The International Journal of Research into New Media Technologies*, and *The Journal of Scandinavian Cinema*, she is the author of *Nordic Film Classics: Director Lukas Moodysson and 'Show Me Love'* (University of Washington Press, 2012) and co-editor with Scott MacKenzie and Lill-Ann Körber of *Critical Arctic Studies* (2015). She has also written extensively on European literary and theatrical modernism and is the author of *Locating August Strindberg's Prose: Modernism, Transnationalism, Setting* (University of Toronto Press, 2010) and editor of *The International Strindberg: New Critical Essays* (Northwestern University Press, 2012).

Kirsten Thisted is an Associate Professor at Copenhagen University, Institute of Cross-Cultural and Regional Studies, Minority Studies Section. Her research areas include minority-majority relations, cultural and linguistic encounters, cultural translation and postcolonial relations. She has published several books and a large number of articles about Greenlandic oral traditions, modern Greenlandic literature and film, Arctic explorers and Scandinavia seen in a postcolonial perspective. She is currently leading the project 'Denmark and the New North Atlanti': http://tors.ku.dk/forskning/.

Ebbe Volquardsen is a Doctoral Fellow at Justus-Liebig-Universität Giessen (Germany). He obtained his Master's degree in Scandinavian Studies,

European Ethnology and Political Science from Humboldt-Universität zu Berlin with a thesis on nation, identity and subaltern articulation in the earliest Greenlandic novels. Volquardsen's scholarship focuses on the literary and cultural history of Denmark and its former colonies, Nordic exceptionalism, postcolonialism, globalisation theory and global history. He is editor-in-chief of *NORDEUROPAforum – Journal for the Study of Culture*.

INDEX